NETWORKS AND SYSTEMS

NETWORKS AND SYSTEMS

PETER H. O'N. ROE *University of Waterloo*

ADDISON-WESLEY PUBLISHING COMPANY

READING, MASSACHUSETTS · PALO ALTO · LONDON · DON MILLS, ONTARIO

TO MARY

who spent many lonely hours during the preparation of this book

PREFACE

This book is concerned with the analysis of physical systems which can be described by linear algebraic and differential equations. For many years it has been well known that the same mathematical structure results from the analysis of many different types of such systems. This knowledge encouraged the growth of methods which depend upon converting one kind of system to another by means of analogies. One of the drawbacks of this approach is that it becomes *necessary* to attain a thorough understanding of one type of system before one is prepared to acquire knowledge of another.

Recently, however, a trend has arisen toward the development of a unified discipline of system theory. This discipline does not proceed from the knowledge of any particular kind of system; instead it provides a general background which leads to the rapid assimilation of problems from many different areas on their own merits.

The discipline of system theory can, of course, draw upon the accumulated reserves of one or more of its branches; but in teaching or learning it, one need not necessarily give equal emphasis to all of the various kinds of physical systems which it encompasses. This fact is reflected in this text and in its title, *Networks and Systems*; both need a word of explanation.

For those convinced of the efficacy of the discipline of system theory, the subject of network analysis does not appear to be a separate entity which deserves special mention, let alone preferential treatment. Indeed the concepts of system theory are so independent of the specific physical systems to which they are applied, that in a comprehensive exposition one could very well draw upon examples from various types of physical systems simultaneously. The systems discipline as it has been developed and taught at Michigan State University by Professor Herman E. Koenig and his group has followed such a course with a considerable measure of success.

Nonetheless, it is not easy to follow this course within the existing framework of engineering curricula. University professors will readily agree that, even when acceptance for proposed curriculum changes is gradually forthcoming, it is no mean effort to realize these changes in a short time. Consequently, one is obliged to explore possibilities for the dissemination of the systems discipline within the existing framework.

This text was prepared by revising and amplifying a set of classroom notes for a system theory course which, at the University of Waterloo, replaces one of the conventional courses on network theory. As much flexibility as possible has been maintained in the manner of its presentation. In the first five chapters, it is addressed entirely to the electrical example, while in the sixth chapter the broader scope of linear system theory is introduced. In our classroom experience, this manner of presentation has been enthusiastically received. The student quickly grasps the fact that the very same concepts are applicable to many systems other than electrical ones, and that he can use identical methods of analysis.

Great pains have also been taken to make sure that the subject of electric network analysis is adequately covered; with the omission of Chapter 6, this text would be entirely suitable for use in undergraduate network theory classes. On the other hand, the material of Chapter 6 has been arranged in such a way that it can be read concurrently with the earlier chapters, if desired, in a general system-theory course.

In the first three chapters the basic concepts of network theory are discussed, and several methods of formulating suitable mathematical models of linear systems are introduced. The solution of network equations is presented in detail for step and sinusoidal driving functions, while the response to arbitrary periodic functions is discussed through the use of superposition and Fourier series. In Chapter 4 the analysis of large systems by treating subsystems as components is introduced. Many other topics, such as Thévenin's and Norton's theorems, two-port representations, and equivalent networks, are discussed here on the same basis.

Chapter 5 is concerned with time-domain techniques in the analysis of linear systems. Methods are introduced for the direct formulation of a "state-space" model whose state vector includes only measurable variables. Analytical, numerical, and analog techniques for the solution of state equations are presented.

Finally, in Chapter 6, the wider framework of system theory is introduced. Here we abandon the exclusive use of the electrical example, and indicate the direct applicability of all the concepts and methods of the previous chapters to mechanical, hydraulic, and mixed systems.

In an intermediate text such as this, considerations of clarity and precision often conflict, but I have endeavored to give precedence to the former. I have had no hesitation in introducing matrix notation and operational methods quite early, partly because I am convinced that they make for a clearer and more concise presentation of the organization of the subject. The mathematical background necessary for the understanding of this text, namely matrix algebra, Laplace transforms, and Fourier series, is contained in the appendixes. It is assumed that the student has a knowledge of elementary calculus and physics.

I have, perhaps, followed somewhat formal methods throughout the text; this formalism is necessary for complex problems and for understanding the logic of the methods. However, I have discussed some of the "shortcut" techniques which are usually taught in a conventional course on network theory. This not only establishes the tie between the techniques described here and more traditional methods, but also serves to make the student aware that it is not always necessary to invoke the more elaborate methods; simple problems can be solved by "direct from inspection" techniques.

It would be impossible for me to acknowledge all the contributions of those individuals who influenced the preparation of this text. However, I must express my heartfelt gratitude to Professor H. K. Kesavan of the Indian Institute of Technology, Kanpur, for his friendly advice, counsel, and guidance, which helped me through many difficult moments. Special mention should also be made of the encouragement given me by my students, and by Professor B. R. Myers of the University of Notre Dame. I am also indebted to Professor John Strohbehn of Dartmouth College and Mr. Barry Wills of the University of Waterloo for their careful reading and constructive criticisms of the text. Finally, I must thank Mrs. Gaye Matthews for her efforts in typing the complete manuscript.

Waterloo, Ontario   P.H.O'N.R.
May 1966

CONTENTS

Chapter 1

INTRODUCTION

In this book we shall discuss various kinds of *systems;* we must first, therefore, decide on the nature of systems in general, and indicate just which types will be studied. We should also have at least a glimpse into the overall methods which we shall use throughout the book. In the first chapter, then, our discussion is centered around the boundaries of the area which we shall study, the mathematical tools which we shall find necessary for the characterization of the components of the various systems, and the models which describe their interconnections.

1.1. PHYSICAL SYSTEMS

A *system* can be described as an orderly interconnection of parts into a meaningful whole. We can easily recognize three broad classifications of systems: *natural systems*, such as the solar system, whose operation is beyond man's control; *man-made systems*, such as aircraft flight control systems, which are devised and operated by men; and *hybrid systems*, such as artificial rain production systems, which are only partially controllable by mankind. In this book we shall be concerned only with man-made systems; indeed the systems which we shall consider constitute only a small, though important, class of these.

Systems, by their very definition, contain parts, or components. Therefore, in the analysis of a system, we must use information about all of the parts, and in addition, we must use our knowledge about the interactions and interconnections of the components. Only when both of these factors are taken into account can we expect to obtain useful information about the operation of the system or its response to given inputs.

What are the components of a system? The answer to this question depends entirely on the point of view of the individual in relation to the system with which he is concerned. For example, the designer of an automobile may choose to regard the motor, transmission, and differential as components of the overall system. On the other hand, the engineer concerned with the design of the transmission would regard the individual gears and shafts as components of the system under his control. Similarly, in a high-fidelity sound reproduction system, we may consider an electronic amplifier as a component, whereas in the design of the amplifier we would consider the individual transistors, capacitors, resistors, etc., to be the components. Since a given device may be considered either as a system in its own right, or as a component of a larger system, our method for analyzing systems must be capable of dealing with large subsystems as components. It would be disastrous, for example, if we were forced to examine such large-scale systems as satellite-tracking networks in terms of the individual resistances in the amplifiers!

1.2. LINEAR SYSTEMS

Systems can be divided into two kinds: *linear* and *nonlinear*. A linear system can be described by sets of linear equations. They may be algebraic, differential, integral, or partial differential equations, but the characteristic of linearity is such that the variables which appear, their derivatives, and their integrals only occur to the first power. For example,

$$M \frac{d^2x}{dt^2} + B \frac{dx}{dt} + Kx = 0 \qquad (1.1)$$

is a linear equation, while

$$Ax \frac{dx}{dt} + Bx = 0, \qquad (1.2)$$

$$A \left(\frac{d^2x}{dt^2}\right)^2 + B \left(\frac{dx}{dt}\right)^{1/2} + C \sin x = 0 \qquad (1.3)$$

are not. The first term in Eq. (1.2) and all three terms in Eq. (1.3) are nonlinear.

Usually the relations which describe the interconnections of the components of a system turn out to be linear algebraic equations; it is the set of characteristics of the components themselves which may be nonlinear. There are major difficulties inherent in the analysis of nonlinear systems; usually one finds that there is no mathematical technique available to complete the analysis. Because of this, we shall limit ourselves, for the most part, to linear systems in our discussion. However, one should not consider this as a major limitation, for, although almost every system is nonlinear to some extent, it is very frequently possible to obtain useful results by approximating nonlinear systems by suitable linear ones.

In addition to our restriction to the study of linear systems, in this book we shall limit ourselves to the discussion of systems which can be described by algebraic or ordinary differential equations. In other words, we shall not discuss systems with distributed parameters, which are characterized by partial differential equations; we shall therefore be concerned with linear lumped-parameter systems. Furthermore, it will normally be assumed that the parameters are constant; that is, they do not vary with time.

Linear lumped-parameter system theory, although it makes up only a fraction of the complete field of system theory, covers a very wide area. Such subjects as electric-network theory, electronics, electronic control, electromechanical systems, and many hydraulic, mechanical, and pneumatic systems come under its purview.

While it may be possible to introduce all these kinds of systems simultaneously, it is easier to learn about one type at a time. We shall therefore first treat electric networks; in Chapter 6 we shall indicate those changes which we must make in our methods when we encounter other systems.

1.3. ELECTRIC NETWORKS

Usually electric-network theory is concerned with systems containing components with only two terminals. Here, however, we shall not be so restrictive, and shall include other devices, such as vacuum tubes and transistors, which have more than two terminals. We therefore define an electric network as a physical system whose components have a finite number of terminals with respect to which it is fruitful to measure voltage and electric current.

The components of electric networks are interconnected only at their terminals, and as may be expected, we shall see that in many cases it is useful to regard subnetworks as being in themselves components of the given networks.

1.4. VOLTAGE AND CURRENT

The primary aim of all network analysis is to establish the behavior of the network with respect to its terminals. Specifically, we are interested in determining the voltages and currents associated with each terminal pair. For this purpose, it is sufficient to base our further development on the *operational* definitions of voltage and current. In the following, therefore, we shall regard voltage as a variable which is represented by a measurement taken with a standardized voltmeter. Similarly, we shall regard current as a variable which represents a measurement taken with a standard ammeter.

The above operational definitions of voltage and current may not be very appealing to those who wish to inquire into the true meanings of these phenomena. However, any such inquiry would eventually take us into the realms of philosophy, and we would like to avoid such questioning.

The mechanisms by which standard voltmeters and ammeters are effective in taking measurements will not be investigated here; we shall be concerned only with the way in which they are connected to the components of a system in order to give meaningful indications, and in the mathematical correlations between the measurements so obtained.

1.5. TWO-POINT ORIENTED MEASUREMENTS

There are many types of meters capable of measuring voltage and current; all of them have the property that the indication may be related to the real number system. For our purposes, it is useful to consider those instruments which indicate instantaneous values of the variables which are being measured. As examples, we may cite the oscillograph and the cathode-ray oscilloscope. The property of such instruments in which we are most interested is the fact that, if a voltage or current is a function of time, they will give us enough information to specify these functions completely. Furthermore, the observed functions depend on the way in which the meters are connected. Thus, if a voltmeter is connected between two terminals, and at some instant it indicates a particular positive number, a reversal of the terminals of the meter would cause it to indicate a negative number at that instant. The meter indication depends on the method of connection of the meter. A similar statement holds for current measurements.

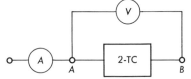

FIG. 1.1. Ammeter and voltmeter connections for a two-terminal component (2-TC).

Every measurement of voltage or current that we make is related to a pair of terminals on a component. Thus voltmeters must be connected between, or across, a pair of terminals of a component, and ammeters must be connected in series with the terminals in question. Figure 1.1 shows this method of connection for a two-terminal component. Since the meter indications reverse when the terminals of the meter are reversed, it is necessary to record which way the meters are connected before any meaning can be attached to the indications. A very simple method for doing this is to mark one terminal of each meter with a distinguishing symbol, called a *polarity mark;* almost without exception, meters are marked in a standard way, so that deflections in the same direction are obtained when different meters are connected in similar ways with respect to their polarity markings. As a result of these marks, which we shall show as a plus sign beside one of the terminals of the meters, it is possible to recognize four distinct methods in which the meters can be connected. These are illustrated in Fig. 1.2. It should be noted that we assume that the meters involved are ideal; that is, no current flows through the voltmeters, and no voltage is developed across the ammeters.

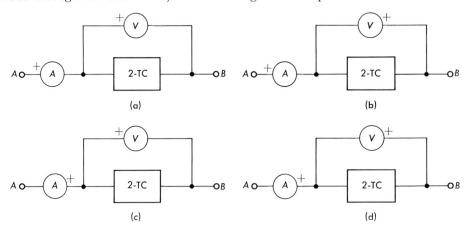

FIG. 1.2. The different possibilities for ammeter and voltmeter connections.

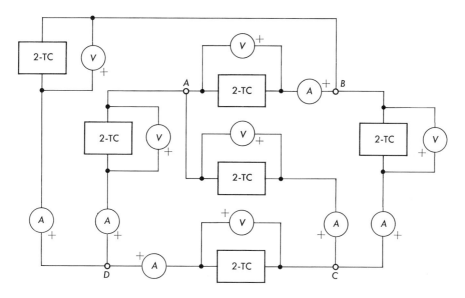

Fig. 1.3. A simple network, showing the voltmeter and ammeter locations.

We can always choose to make measurements by connecting our meters in any one of the four ways depicted in Fig. 1.2, but it is convenient to select one method of connection and use it consistently. In all of the following, therefore, we shall assume that voltage and current measurements are made with the meters connected as in Fig. 1.2(a) or (d). This choice is, of course, entirely arbitrary, although it enables us to obtain a single reference system for measurements of both voltage and current.

Since we shall always be dealing with the quantities that can be measured in an electric network, it is necessary to make a record of which way we have agreed to connect the various meters. To do this, we could use symbols such as those of Fig. 1.2, in every branch of the schematic diagram of the network. A glance at the simple network of Fig. 1.3, in which this has been done, should be sufficient to show that this procedure is tedious, and makes the resulting schematic diagram unnecessarily complicated. Therefore, we shall use a more simple method to indicate all the meter orientations. If a two-terminal component is connected between two terminals A, B in a given network, we shall indicate the meter orientations by a line segment between two corresponding points a, b. An arrowhead is placed on this line segment, *pointing away from a if the marked terminals of the meters are connected to point A*, or away from b if the marked terminals of the meters are connected to point B. This is illustrated in Fig 1.4, and the line segment,

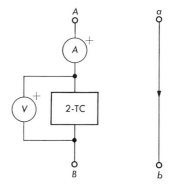

Fig. 1.4. The terminal graph of a two-terminal component.

together with its endpoints and arrowhead, is called the *terminal graph* of the two-terminal component. Associated with this terminal graph are its corresponding voltage and current variables, called the *terminal variables*.

To summarize this section, we note that measurements of voltage and current are always made with respect to a pair of terminals. In addition, the meter indications reverse when the meter connections are reversed. Together these properties define a *two-point oriented measurement;* thus voltage and current measurements are two-point oriented measurements. We have also seen that the orientations and location of a pair of measuring instruments may be conveniently recorded by the use of the terminal graph. We shall introduce the terminal graph for components with more than two terminals in a later section.

1.6. ORIENTED LINEAR GRAPHS

The terminal graph introduced in Section 1.5 is a somewhat trivial example of an oriented linear graph. Our study of electric networks will frequently require us to work with more complex graphs, so that it is appropriate that we should introduce here some of the terminology and simple properties connected with the subject. To mathematicians, linear graph theory is frequently regarded as a specialized branch of the field of point-set topology, so that all the relevant concepts may be defined very precisely and rigorously. We shall not, however, follow this course; it is indeed quite unnecessary for our purpose to do so, and we shall merely give descriptions of the various entities which we encounter.

Consider Fig. 1.5. This figure is obtained by uniting the endpoints of all the terminal graphs corresponding to the measurements indicated for the components of the schematic diagram of Fig. 1.3 in one-to-one correspondence with the interconnections of the components. The emphasis is on the pairs of measurements between the terminals and not on the components; it is quite possible to make a pair of measurements between terminals which do not have a component connecting them. Diagrams formed in this way are called *system graphs*, and are examples of *oriented linear graphs*. A common name for the system graph is *network graph;* we use the former name to emphasize the fact that these diagrams are useful in situations other than the analysis of electric networks, as we shall see in Chapter 6.

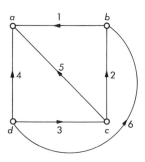

FIG. 1.5. A typical system graph.

An oriented linear graph is seen to be a collection of oriented line segments which intersect only at their endpoints. The line segments, together with their endpoints, are called *elements* or *edges*, and the endpoints are referred to as *vertices* or *nodes*. Note that we make a distinction between terminals and vertices. Terminals are points of interconnection of the components of a network and are always identified by capital letters. Vertices, on the other hand, refer to the graph and are identified by the corresponding lower-case letters.

We shall find it useful to refer to certain *subgraphs* of a given graph; these are merely subsets of the elements of the given graph. The *complement of a subgraph* is, as its name implies, that subgraph which remains when a subgraph is removed from the given graph. For example, in the graph of Fig. 1.5, elements 1, 2, and 5 form a subgraph whose complement consists of elements 3, 4, and 6. A graph is *connected* if it is possible to trace at least one *path* along its elements, passing through every vertex; if it is not connected, a graph is composed of connected *parts*. Each part of a graph is therefore a connected subgraph which has no vertex in common with its complement.

We refer to an element as being *incident on a vertex* if that vertex is an endpoint of the element. A *circuit* is a connected subgraph such that on every vertex there are incident exactly two elements. In other words, there are two distinct paths between every pair of vertices of a circuit. For example, elements 1, 2, 3, and 4 of the graph of Fig. 1.5 form a circuit.

A subgraph of particular interest is called a *forest*. For a graph with p parts, a forest is one which includes all the vertices of the graph, is connected within each part, and contains no circuit. A *coforest* is the complement of a forest. In general, there are many forests in any given graph. Consider the graph of Fig. 1.6, which has 11 vertices, 14 elements, and 3 parts. A typical forest, indicated by the heavier lines in the figure, is composed of elements 1, 2, 3, 9, 10, 11, 12, and 13. Of course, the reader can find many more. It may be observed that the number of elements in the forest is 8, which is just equal to the difference between the number of vertices and the number of parts. This fact is no accident. It can be proved that if there are v vertices and p parts in a given graph, the number of elements in any forest is just $v - p$. Hence, if there are e elements in the graph, the number of elements in the coforest is

$$e - (v - p), \qquad \text{or} \qquad e - v + p.$$

For convenience, we give the name *branch* to an element in a forest, and call its coforest elements *chords*. In the special case when the given graph is connected, the forest has only one part, and we call it a *tree;* the coforest is then referred to as the *cotree.*

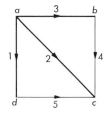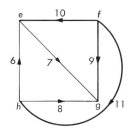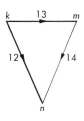

FIG. 1.6. A three-part graph.

1.7. THE INTERCONNECTION EQUATIONS FOR ELECTRIC NETWORKS

The system graph corresponding to a given network is an abstraction from the schematic diagram of a record of the way in which measurements of voltage and current are to be made. This, in conjunction with two fundamental postulates to be introduced in this section, may be regarded as a *mathematical model* of the interconnections and measurements in the given network. That is, the system graph provides a vital link between the physical system and the equations which describe it. We shall define these interconnection equations, or graph equations, in the following paragraphs, beginning with the vertex postulate.

Postulate 1. *The vertex postulate.* The *oriented sum* of the current measurements implied by the elements incident on a given vertex is zero at any instant of time.

We need now to explain the term "oriented sum." First note that there are two possible orientations of the elements incident on a given vertex; "toward" or "away from" that vertex. In order to form the oriented sum of the current measurements, we arbitrarily choose one of these as a "standard orientation" and multiply the measurement corresponding to each element which has this orientation by $+1$; those with opposite orientation are multiplied by -1. Thus the oriented sum is similar to an algebraic sum for quantities which have specified orientations.

The vertex postulate leads immediately to the set of equations

$$\sum_{k=1}^{e} c_{km} i_k(t) = 0, \qquad m = 1, 2, \ldots, v, \tag{1.4}$$

where

v = the number of vertices in the system graph,
e = the number of elements in the system graph,
c_{km} = 0 if element k is not incident on vertex m,
c_{km} = $+1$ if element k is incident on vertex m and has the standard orientation,
c_{km} = -1 otherwise.

It is worthy of note that the vertex postulate is simply a mathematical statement of Kirchhoff's current law. The difference lies in our viewpoint, in that we need not think in terms of something flowing in the wires of an electrical circuit; we merely postulate that the sum of the indications of a set of measuring instruments is zero.

Let us now turn to the second fundamental postulate.

Postulate 2. *The circuit postulate.* The oriented sum of the voltage measurements implied by the elements in a given circuit is zero at any instant of time.

To form the basis of an oriented sum here, we note that as we traverse a circuit, some of the orientations of the elements encountered will have the same sense as our direction of travel; the remainder will be oriented in the opposite direction. We choose one of these senses as our standard orientation.

We may now write a set of equations corresponding to the circuit postulate, as follows:

$$\sum_{k=1}^{e} b_{km}v_m(t) = 0, \qquad m = 1, 2, \ldots, c, \qquad (1.5)$$

where

c = the number of circuits in the system graph,
e = the number of elements in the system graph,
b_{km} = 0 if element k is not in circuit m,
b_{km} = $+1$ if element k is in circuit m and has the standard orientation,
b_{km} = -1 otherwise.

Just as the vertex postulate resembles Kirchhoff's current law, so the circuit postulate is similar to Kirchhoff's voltage law. Here again, from our point of view, we look at the postulate of the mathematical model rather than the statement about the corresponding physical phenomena.

EXAMPLE 1.1. The vertex equations for the system graph of Fig. 1.6 are

Vertex	Equation
a	$i_1 + i_2 + i_3 = 0$
b	$-i_3 + i_4 = 0$
c	$-i_2 - i_4 - i_5 = 0$
d	$-i_1 + i_5 = 0$
e	$-i_6 + i_7 - i_{10} = 0$
f	$i_9 + i_{10} + i_{11} = 0$
g	$-i_7 - i_8 - i_9 = 0$
h	$i_6 + i_8 - i_{11} = 0$
k	$i_{12} + i_{13} = 0$
m	$-i_{13} + i_{14} = 0$
n	$-i_{12} - i_{14} = 0$

$$(1.6)$$

and the circuit equations

Circuit	Equation
$abca$	$-v_2 + v_3 + v_4 = 0$
$abcda$	$-v_1 + v_3 + v_4 - v_5 = 0$
$acda$	$-v_1 + v_2 - v_5 = 0$
$efhe$	$v_6 - v_{10} + v_{11} = 0$
$efge$	$-v_7 + v_9 - v_{10} = 0$
$efghe$	$v_6 - v_8 + v_9 - v_{10} = 0$
$fghf$	$-v_8 + v_9 - v_{11} = 0$
$gheg$	$v_6 + v_7 - v_8 = 0$
$gefhg$	$-v_7 + v_8 - v_{10} + v_{11} = 0$
$egfhe$	$v_6 + v_7 - v_9 + v_{11} = 0$
$kmnk$	$-v_{12} + v_{13} + v_{14} = 0$

$$(1.7)$$

Little information is readily available from the vertex and circuit equations written in the form of Eqs. (1.6) and (1.7). By suitably choosing our standard orientations, however, we may write these equations in matrix form as

$$
\left[
\begin{array}{cccccccc:cccccc}
1 & 0 & 0 & 0 & 0 & 0 & 0 & 0 & 0 & -1 & 0 & 0 & 0 & 0 \\
0 & 1 & 0 & 0 & 0 & 0 & 0 & 0 & 1 & 1 & 0 & 0 & 0 & 0 \\
0 & 0 & 1 & 0 & 0 & 0 & 0 & 0 & -1 & 0 & 0 & 0 & 0 & 0 \\
0 & 0 & 0 & 1 & 0 & 0 & 0 & 0 & 0 & 0 & 0 & 1 & 1 & 0 \\
0 & 0 & 0 & 0 & 1 & 0 & 0 & 0 & 0 & 0 & 1 & -1 & 0 & 0 \\
0 & 0 & 0 & 0 & 0 & 1 & 0 & 0 & 0 & 0 & -1 & 0 & -1 & 0 \\
0 & 0 & 0 & 0 & 0 & 0 & 1 & 0 & 0 & 0 & 0 & 0 & 0 & 1 \\
0 & 0 & 0 & 0 & 0 & 0 & 0 & 1 & 0 & 0 & 0 & 0 & 0 & -1 \\ \hdashline
-1 & -1 & -1 & 0 & 0 & 0 & 0 & 0 & 0 & 0 & 0 & 0 & 0 & 0 \\
0 & 0 & 0 & -1 & -1 & -1 & 0 & 0 & 0 & 0 & 0 & 0 & 0 & 0 \\
0 & 0 & 0 & 0 & 0 & 0 & -1 & -1 & 0 & 0 & 0 & 0 & 0 & 0
\end{array}
\right]
\begin{bmatrix}
i_1 \\ i_2 \\ i_3 \\ i_9 \\ i_{10} \\ i_{11} \\ i_{12} \\ i_{13} \\ \hline i_4 \\ i_5 \\ i_6 \\ i_7 \\ i_8 \\ i_{14}
\end{bmatrix}
= 0,
\tag{1.8}
$$

$$
\left[
\begin{array}{cccccccc:cccccc}
0 & -1 & 1 & 0 & 0 & 0 & 0 & 0 & 1 & 0 & 0 & 0 & 0 & 0 \\
1 & -1 & 0 & 0 & 0 & 0 & 0 & 0 & 0 & 1 & 0 & 0 & 0 & 0 \\
0 & 0 & 0 & 0 & -1 & 1 & 0 & 0 & 0 & 0 & 1 & 0 & 0 & 0 \\
0 & 0 & 0 & -1 & 1 & 0 & 0 & 0 & 0 & 0 & 0 & 1 & 0 & 0 \\
0 & 0 & 0 & -1 & 0 & 1 & 0 & 0 & 0 & 0 & 0 & 0 & 1 & 0 \\
0 & 0 & 0 & 0 & 0 & 0 & -1 & 1 & 0 & 0 & 0 & 0 & 0 & 1 \\ \hdashline
-1 & 0 & 1 & 0 & 0 & 0 & 0 & 0 & 1 & -1 & 0 & 0 & 0 & 0 \\
0 & 0 & 0 & -1 & 1 & 0 & 0 & 0 & 0 & 0 & -1 & 0 & 1 & 0 \\
0 & 0 & 0 & 0 & 0 & 0 & 0 & 0 & 0 & 0 & 1 & 1 & -1 & 0 \\
0 & 0 & 0 & 0 & 1 & -1 & 0 & 0 & 0 & 0 & 0 & 1 & -1 & 0 \\
0 & 0 & 0 & 1 & 0 & -1 & 0 & 0 & 0 & 0 & -1 & -1 & 0 & 0
\end{array}
\right]
\begin{bmatrix}
v_1 \\ v_2 \\ v_3 \\ v_9 \\ v_{10} \\ v_{11} \\ v_{12} \\ v_{13} \\ \hline v_4 \\ v_5 \\ v_6 \\ v_7 \\ v_8 \\ v_{14}
\end{bmatrix}
= 0.
\tag{1.9}
$$

Because of the presence of the unit submatrices in (1.8) and (1.9), we observe that the first 8 equations of (1.8) are linearly independent, as are the first 6 of (1.9). Note also that the number of branches in any forest of the given graph is 8, while there are 6 chords. In the following sections, we shall show that *there are always as many independent circuit equations as there are chords, and as many independent vertex equations as there are branches in any given forest.*

1.8. CUT SETS

Suppose that we pick some forest of a given system graph. If we force all the current measurements corresponding to the *chords* to be zero, the vertex postulate immediately tells us that the branch current measurements will also be zero. This follows from the fact that there can be no circuits containing only branches. Thus the branch currents are dependent on the chord currents; it is possible to express all the branch currents uniquely in terms of the chord currents. Furthermore, if

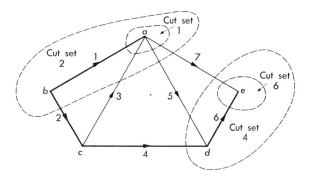

Fig. 1.7. A typical system graph, showing the cut sets.

one of the forest currents is also independent, it will be possible for it to have some nonzero value when all the chord currents are zero; on the other hand, if some of the chord currents are not independent, it will be possible to set all the currents to zero without opening all the circuits. Thus, we may state that the number of independent current measurements is $e - v + p$, which is the number of chords, and the number of independent vertex equations is $v - p$.

We have already pointed out that the branch currents may be expressed uniquely in terms of the chord currents. Thus we may write

$$[i_b(t)] = -[A][i_c(t)], \tag{1.10}$$

where the subscripts b and c refer to the branch and chord variables for our chosen forest. Note that these equations may be rearranged to have the same form as the vertex equations; that is, we may write each equation as a linear combination of currents, equated to zero. Thus (1.10) becomes

$$[U \quad A] \begin{bmatrix} i_b(t) \\ i_c(t) \end{bmatrix} = [0], \tag{1.11}$$

where U is a unit matrix.

In order to show how Eqs. (1.11) may be written from the system graph, we introduce the concept of a *segregate set*. Suppose that the vertices of a given graph are divided into two mutually exclusive sets A, B. Then those elements which have one vertex in A and the other in B form a *segregate set*. If a segregate set contains exactly one branch of a given forest, it is called a *cut set* with respect to that forest. The forest which we use to define our cut sets will be called the *formulation forest*. Consider Fig. 1.7. This figure shows a typical system graph, formulation tree, and the corresponding cut sets. The cut sets are conveniently defined by drawing closed lines through the graph such that each closed line cuts exactly one branch. This branch and all the chords cut by such a closed line form a cut set. Clearly, there are exactly as many cut sets as there are branches.

Let us write the vertex equations at vertices a, b. These are

(a) $-i_1(t) - i_3(t) + i_5(t) + i_7(t) = 0,$

(b) $i_1(t) + i_2(t) = 0,$

and their sum is

$$i_2(t) - i_3(t) + i_5(t) + i_7(t) = 0.$$

Now vertices a, b are those enclosed by the closed line used to find the elements of the cut set including branch 2, and the sum of the vertex equations at these vertices contains only the current variables corresponding to the cut-set elements. It is left to the reader to satisfy himself that this will always happen. Thus, we may write a set of "cut-set equations" which have the property that each branch current occurs in exactly one cut-set equation.

In a cut set there are elements with different orientations with respect to the two sets of vertices A, B. For definiteness, therefore, we shall define the *segregate orientations* of the cut-set elements. This is done by choosing as positive the orientation of the branch defining the cut set. If the orientation of any element of the cut set coincides with this orientation, it is positive; otherwise, it is negative. Using this segregate orientation, we may write the cut-set equations in the form

$$\sum_{k=1}^{e} a_{mk} i_k(t) = 0, \qquad m = 1, 2, \ldots, v - 1, \tag{1.12}$$

where

$a_{mk} = 0$ if element k is not in cut set m,

$a_{mk} = +1$ if element k is the defining branch of cut set m or if the orientation of element k coincides with the segregate orientation,

$a_{mk} = -1$ otherwise.

Since the branch currents always occur with a plus sign, we may always arrange to write the cut-set equations in the form of Eqs. (1.11). For the graph of Fig. 1.7, these become

$$\begin{bmatrix} 1 & 0 & 0 & 0 & 1 & -1 & -1 \\ 0 & 1 & 0 & 0 & -1 & 1 & 1 \\ 0 & 0 & 1 & 0 & 0 & 1 & 1 \\ 0 & 0 & 0 & 1 & 0 & 0 & 1 \end{bmatrix} \begin{bmatrix} i_1(t) \\ i_2(t) \\ i_4(t) \\ i_6(t) \\ i_3(t) \\ i_5(t) \\ i_7(t) \end{bmatrix} = \begin{bmatrix} 0 \\ 0 \\ 0 \\ 0 \end{bmatrix}, \tag{1.13}$$

while for that of Example 1.1 (Fig. 1.6), they consist of the first eight equations of (1.8) when we choose elements 1, 2, 3, 9, 10, 11, 12, 13 for our formulation forest.

1.9. FUNDAMENTAL CIRCUITS

By specifying that all the *branch* voltage measurements for our formulation forest are zero, we can use reasoning similar to that of the previous section to show that the *chord* voltages may be expressed uniquely in terms of the *branch* voltages. Furthermore, the number of independent voltage measurements is $v - p$, and the number of independent circuit equations is $e - v + p$. Because of this, we may therefore write

$$[v_c(t)] = -[B][v_b(t)], \qquad (1.14)$$

and these equations may be rewritten in the form

$$[B \quad U] \begin{bmatrix} v_b(t) \\ v_c(t) \end{bmatrix} = [0]. \qquad (1.15)$$

Note that Eqs. (1.15) have the same form as the circuit equations; we shall now show that they may be written as special cases of the circuit equations. We note that we can always choose a set of $e - v + p$ circuits in the given graph such that each circuit contains exactly *one chord* and some branches. We shall call these *fundamental circuits*. Clearly, there are as many fundamental circuits as there are chords. Let us suppose that we write the circuit equations for the fundamental circuits, taking the "standard orientation" or circuit orientation as that which agrees with the chord in any circuit. Then each chord voltage will occur in just one circuit equation and will have $+1$ as its coefficient. The resulting set of equations has exactly the form of (1.15), and since we have agreed that the relationship between the chord and branch voltages is unique, the fundamental circuit equations and (1.15) are identical.

EXAMPLE 1.2.   We write the fundamental circuit equations corresponding to the system graph and tree of Fig. 1.7. These are

$$\begin{bmatrix} -1 & 1 & 0 & 0 & 1 & 0 & 0 \\ 1 & -1 & -1 & 0 & 0 & 1 & 0 \\ 1 & -1 & -1 & -1 & 0 & 0 & 1 \end{bmatrix} \begin{bmatrix} v_1(t) \\ v_2(t) \\ v_4(t) \\ v_6(t) \\ v_3(t) \\ v_5(t) \\ v_7(t) \end{bmatrix} = \begin{bmatrix} 0 \\ 0 \\ 0 \end{bmatrix}. \qquad (1.16)$$

EXAMPLE 1.3.   If in Fig. 1.6 we pick elements 1, 2, 3, 9, 10, 11, 12, 13 for the formulation forest, the fundamental circuit equations are just the first six equations of (1.9).

1.10. THE RELATION BETWEEN THE COEFFICIENT MATRICES OF THE CIRCUIT AND CUT-SET EQUATIONS

Although it is not necessary to choose the same formulation forest and arrange the elements in the same order when we write sets of fundamental-circuit and cut-set equations, it is very convenient to do so. This is because the coefficient matrices $[A]$ of Eqs. (1.10) and $[B]$ of (1.14) can then be obtained one from the other by the relation

$$[A] = -[B]', \qquad (1.17)$$

or

$$[B] = -[A]', \qquad (1.18)$$

where the prime indicates the transpose of the matrix

EXAMPLE 1.4. For the system graph and tree of Fig. 1.7, and from Eqs. (1.13) and (1.16), we have

$$[A] = \begin{bmatrix} 1 & -1 & -1 \\ -1 & 1 & 1 \\ 0 & 1 & 1 \\ 0 & 0 & 1 \end{bmatrix}, \qquad [B] = \begin{bmatrix} -1 & 1 & 0 & 0 \\ 1 & -1 & -1 & 0 \\ 1 & -1 & -1 & -1 \end{bmatrix},$$

and

$$[A] = -[B]'.$$

EXAMPLE 1.5. For the system graph of Fig. 1.6, when we pick elements 1, 2, 3, 9, 10, 11, 12, 13 for the formulation forest, we have, from Eqs. (1.8) and (1.9),

$$[A] = \begin{bmatrix} 0 & -1 & 0 & 0 & 0 & 0 \\ 1 & 1 & 0 & 0 & 0 & 0 \\ -1 & 0 & 0 & 0 & 0 & 0 \\ 0 & 0 & 0 & 1 & 1 & 0 \\ 0 & 0 & 1 & -1 & 0 & 0 \\ 0 & 0 & -1 & 0 & -1 & 0 \\ 0 & 0 & 0 & 0 & 0 & 1 \\ 0 & 0 & 0 & 0 & 0 & -1 \end{bmatrix},$$

$$[B] = \begin{bmatrix} 0 & -1 & 1 & 0 & 0 & 0 & 0 & 0 \\ 1 & -1 & 0 & 0 & 0 & 0 & 0 & 0 \\ 0 & 0 & 0 & 0 & -1 & 1 & 0 & 0 \\ 0 & 0 & 0 & -1 & 1 & 0 & 0 & 0 \\ 0 & 0 & 0 & -1 & 0 & 1 & 0 & 0 \\ 0 & 0 & 0 & 0 & 0 & 0 & -1 & 1 \end{bmatrix},$$

and

$$[A] = [-B]'.$$

These examples serve as verifications of Eqs. (1.17) and (1.18), but they do not, of course, constitute a proof. We shall not give a proof here, but merely point out that this result allows us to write just one set of the equations from the graph; the other set is immediately obtained by using Eq. (1.17) or (1.18).

1.11. THE TERMINAL GRAPH FOR MULTITERMINAL COMPONENTS

In the previous sections we saw how voltage and current measurements for an electric system are interrelated. Although we referred our measurements to two-terminal components, we said nothing which can lead us to the conclusion that our results are limited only to this case. Thus voltage measurements sum to zero around any circuit, regardless of the number of terminals on the components of the system to which they refer. Let us consider the voltage and current measurements which may be made on the system of Fig. 1.8(a). This figure shows a five-terminal component connected to some voltage generators in a way which could be chosen if we wished to determine the characteristics of the component in the

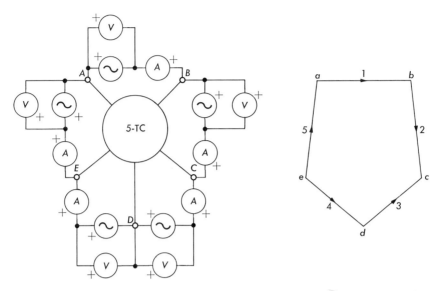

FIG. 1.8.   Measurements on a five-terminal component. (a) A system consisting of a five-terminal component and five voltage drivers, showing the locations of measuring instruments. (b) The graph corresponding to the measurements in (a).

laboratory. When we write the circuit equation for the graph of Fig. 1.8(b), which corresponds to the indicated measurements in Fig. 1.8(a), we obtain

$$v_5(t) = -v_1(t) - v_2(t) + v_3(t) + v_4(t), \qquad (1.19)$$

which says that $v_5(t)$ is completely determined when we know $v_1(t)$, $v_2(t)$, $v_3(t)$, $v_4(t)$. Furthermore the voltage measurement that would be obtained by inserting a meter between any other two terminals of the five-terminal component may also be obtained as a linear combination of these four voltages. Thus we need only measure the four voltages $v_1(t)$, $v_2(t)$, $v_3(t)$, $v_4(t)$ in order to determine the voltage between any pair of terminals. Moreover, we need not have picked the four measurements $v_1(t)$, $v_2(t)$, $v_3(t)$, $v_4(t)$; any set of four voltage measurements not excluding any terminal, and not including any circuits, would have been sufficient, as a little reflection will show.

Generalizing this result, we may therefore state that *for an n-terminal component, exactly* (n — 1) *voltage measurements, defined by a tree graph, are sufficient to determine the voltage between any pair of terminals.* Of course, we already know that for a two-terminal component, we measure only one voltage; and since this measurement in itself defines a tree graph, we may regard the two-terminal component as a special case of the multiterminal components.

We also require an appropriate set of current measurements for multiterminal components, but it is not immediately obvious which measurements are sufficient to yield a complete characterization of the component. However, if the component itself is considered as a vertex, one can intuitively see that the oriented

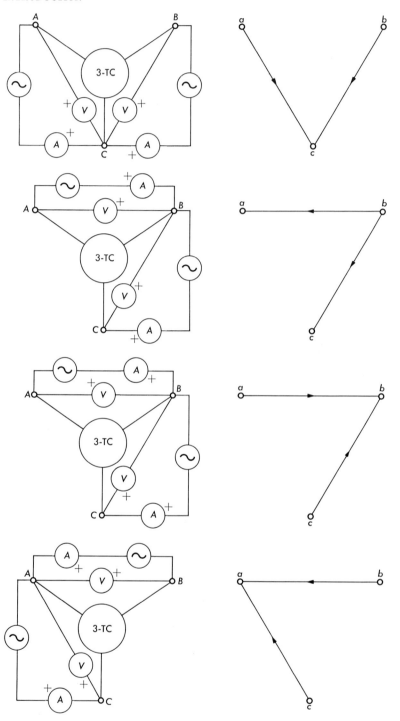

FIG. 1.9. Some possible terminal graphs for three-terminal components.

sum of the n terminal currents is zero. Hence, we need only $n - 1$ current measurements. It can be experimentally verified that any tree set of measurements is all that is required; the general results of this discussion are summarized in the following postulate.

Postulate 3. Any n-terminal component can be completely characterized by a set of $n - 1$ independent current measurements and $n - 1$ independent voltage measurements, defined by a tree graph connecting all its terminals.

Figure 1.9 shows several different possible arrangements of the voltage and current meters for a three-terminal component, and the graphs which are implied by these measurements. We call these tree graphs the terminal graphs of the multiterminal components.

1.12. THE TERMINAL EQUATIONS: COMPONENT MODELS

We have developed the relations that exist among the voltage measurements and among the current measurements for a given system graph. Thus there are $e - v + p$ independent circuit equations and $v - p$ independent cut-set equations. This gives a total of e linearly independent equations relating the $2e$ measurable variables for a given system. We therefore require in addition e linearly independent equations in order to specify the system completely. These e equations are made available through the relations between the voltages and currents for the components of the network, together with the specified functions for the voltage and current drivers. These, with the corresponding terminal graphs, complete the mathematical models of the components.

The volt-ampere relations mentioned above are called the terminal equations for the components of the system; for an n-terminal component, there are $n - 1$ terminal equations. To obtain these equations, it is necessary to make measurements in the laboratory and, on the basis of these measurements, to find equations describing the characteristics.

The procedure for determining the terminal equations of a component from the measured physical characteristics is called "modeling" the component. Component modeling is quite basic to network analysis and is, in general, a difficult subject, particularly when one is dealing with nonlinear devices, i.e., those whose physical characteristics cannot be correlated by linear mathematics. A full understanding of the problems associated with component modeling can be acquired only in the laboratory. Here, we shall be content to point out some of the techniques available for modeling components basic to the development of network theory.

In every case we may expect that these terminal equations are nonlinear, although very frequently it is possible to make "reasonable approximations" to the terminal characteristics using linear equations. In cases where this is not directly possible, a curvilinear relation can often be approximated by a set of straight lines which are tangents at appropriate points on the curve. These facts are

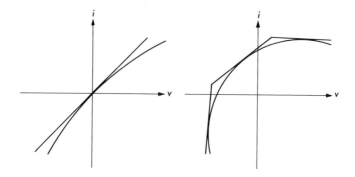

FIG. 1.10.   Approximation for terminal equations.   (a) Approximation of a nonlinear v-i characteristic by a linear relationship.   (b) Approximation of a nonlinear characteristic by a set of tangents (polygonal approximation).

illustrated in Fig. 1.10, and the method involved is known as *piecewise linear* or *polygonal* approximation.

A third form of approximation, which is very frequently encountered, is known as the *small-signal* approximation.   When we are interested in the operation of a device symmetrically about some point on its nonlinear characteristic, it is most convenient to use this method.   Since vacuum tubes and transistors are frequently described by means of the small-signal approximation, we shall give here a general method for forming the suitable equations.

Let us assume that some component may be characterized by nonlinear equations of the form

$$F(v_1, v_2, i_1, i_2) = \phi(E, I),\tag{1.19}$$

where v_1, v_2, i_1, i_2, E, I are functions of time, E and I being specified driving functions.   For some constant values of the variables, the system will eventually attain a steady state in which $v_1 = v_1^0$, $v_2 = v_2^0$, $i_1 = i_1^0$, $i_2 = i_2^0$, $E = E^0$, $I = I^0$.   Thus,

$$F(v_1^0, v_2^0, i_1^0, i_2^0) = \phi(E^0, I^0).\tag{1.20}$$

Our basic assumption is that in the process of operation of the component, the variations of v_1, v_2, i_1, i_2 are such that their deviations from the steady-state

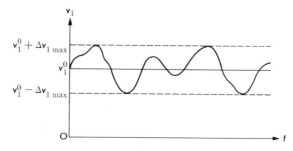

FIG. 1.11.   Variation of a variable about its steady-state value.

values $(v_1^0, v_2^0, i_1^0, i_2^0)$ remain sufficiently small, as shown, for example, in Fig. 1.11. Denoting these deviations by $\Delta v_1, \Delta v_2, \Delta i_1, \Delta i_2$, we have

$$
\begin{aligned}
v_1(t) &= v_1^0 + \Delta v_1(t), & i_1(t) &= i_1^0 + \Delta i_1(t), \\
v_2(t) &= v_2^0 + \Delta v_2(t), & i_2(t) &= i_2^0 + \Delta i_2(t).
\end{aligned}
\tag{1.21}
$$

We now expand the left-hand side of Eq. (1.19) in a power series in the deviations, obtaining

$$
\begin{aligned}
F(v_1, v_2, i_1, i_2) &= F(v_1^0, v_2^0, i_1^0, i_2^0) + \left(\frac{\partial F}{\partial v_1}\right)^0 \Delta v_1 \\
&\quad + \left(\frac{\partial F}{\partial v_2}\right)^0 \Delta v_2 + \left(\frac{\partial F}{\partial i_1}\right)^0 \Delta i_1 + \left(\frac{\partial F}{\partial i_2}\right)^0 \Delta i_2 \\
&\quad + \text{higher-order terms in the deviations} \\
&= \phi(E, I),
\end{aligned}
\tag{1.22}
$$

where $(\partial F/\partial v_1)^0$ is obtained by evaluating $\partial F/\partial v_1$ and replacing all the variables by their steady-state values. The other partial derivative terms are similarly obtained. Because of this, all the coefficients of the deviations are constant.

Finally, subtracting Eq. (1.20) from (1.22) and neglecting the higher-order terms, we have

$$
\left(\frac{\partial F}{\partial v_1}\right)^0 \Delta v_1 + \left(\frac{\partial F}{\partial v_2}\right)^0 \Delta v_2 + \left(\frac{\partial F}{\partial i_1}\right)^0 \Delta i_1 + \left(\frac{\partial F}{\partial i_2}\right)^0 \Delta i_2 = \phi(E, I) - \phi(E^0, I^0),
\tag{1.23}
$$

which, in order to emphasize the fact that the coefficients are constants, we may rewrite as

$$
a_1 \Delta v_1 + a_2 \Delta v_2 + a_3 \Delta i_1 + a_4 \Delta i_2 = \phi(E, I) - \phi(E^0, I^0).
\tag{1.24}
$$

Equation (1.24) is linear in the unknown deviations of the variables v_1, v_2, i_1, i_2 from their steady-state values, and is less precise than the original characteristic due to the fact that we have neglected the higher-order terms.

The above procedure may be carried out for every component of the system, and results in a set of linear terminal equations in the deviations of the voltages and currents from the operating point. Of course, for some components whose characteristics are very nearly linear, the range of application of the equations may be quite wide. For the more nonlinear components, however, we may be able to tolerate only small values of deviations. When time derivatives of the variables occur in the original nonlinear relation, they may themselves be treated as additional variables, and the resulting equation becomes a linear differential equation. We do not usually specify in our terminal equations that we are dealing with deviations from the steady-state values of the variables, but whenever a small-signal linear approximation is used, it is understood that the variables in the equations represent changes from the steady-state values.

Frequently it is possible to carry out this linearization graphically, without direct recourse to the mathematical detail following Eq. (1.19). As an example,

TABLE 1.1

Mathematical Models of Electrical Components

Schematic	Name	Terminal graph	Terminal equations
	Resistance		$v(t) = R\,i(t)$
	Inductance		$v(t) = L\dfrac{di(t)}{dt}$
	Capacitance		$i(t) = C\dfrac{dv(t)}{dt}$
	Voltage driver		$v(t) = E(t)$ (specified)
	Current driver		$i(t) = I(t)$ (specified)
	Ideal transformer		$\begin{bmatrix} v_2(t) \\ i_1(t) \end{bmatrix} = \begin{bmatrix} 0 & n \\ -n & 0 \end{bmatrix}\begin{bmatrix} i_2(t) \\ v_1(t) \end{bmatrix}$
	Vacuum tube		$\begin{bmatrix} i_1(t) \\ i_2(t) \end{bmatrix} = \begin{bmatrix} 0 & 0 \\ g_m & g_p \end{bmatrix}\begin{bmatrix} v_1(t) \\ v_2(t) \end{bmatrix}$ (small-signal linear approximation)
	Transistor		$\begin{bmatrix} v_1(t) \\ i_2(t) \end{bmatrix} = \begin{bmatrix} h_{11} & h_{12} \\ h_{21} & h_{22} \end{bmatrix}\begin{bmatrix} i_1(t) \\ v_2(t) \end{bmatrix}$ (small-signal linear approximation)

consider the nonlinear characteristic of Fig. 1.12, which is known as the plate characteristic for a vacuum triode. In this case, the left-hand side of (1.19) becomes

$$i_p = F(v_g, v_p),$$

and the point Q is the steady-state operating point at which

$$v_g = v_g^0, \quad v_p = v_p^0, \quad i_p = i_p^0.$$

The slope of the tangent at Q is $\tan \alpha$, and

$$(\partial i_p / \partial v_p)^0 = \tan \alpha = g_p.$$

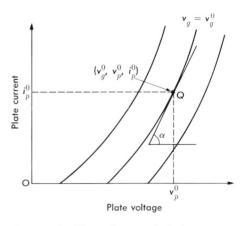

FIG. 1.12. Plate characteristic for a vacuum triode.

The substitutions equivalent to (1.21) and the resulting equation corresponding to (1.23) are here equivalent to a shift of the origin of coordinates to the point Q. We may use a similar graphical procedure to obtain

$$(\partial i_p / \partial v_g)^0 = g_m.$$

Thus, one of the small-signal approximations for terminal equations for a vacuum triode is

$$i_p = g_m v_g + g_p v_p. \tag{1.25}$$

We shall not go into any more detail here as to how the particular forms of the terminal equations are obtained for the components of electric networks; it is sufficient for our purposes to tabulate those corresponding to some of the more frequently encountered devices (Table 1.1). Of course, we shall not feel bound by these particular representations, and shall introduce alternatives whenever their use may be more fruitful.

1.13. GLOSSARY

We conclude this chapter with a glossary of the various terms introduced. The items are arranged on the list in the order in which they appear in the text. The number on the right refers to the section in which the term was first mentioned.

Term	Definition	Section
System	An orderly interconnection of parts into a meaningful whole	1–1
Natural system	A system whose operation is beyond man's control	1–1

Term	Definition	Section
Man-made system	A system which is devised and operated by man	1–1
Hybrid system	A system which is partially natural, and partially man-made	1–1
Linear system	A system which can be described by linear equations	1–2
Nonlinear system	A system which cannot be described by linear equations	1–2
Electric network	A physical system whose components have a finite number of terminals with respect to which it is fruitful to measure voltage and electrical current	1–3
Voltage	A variable which is represented by a measurement taken with a standard voltmeter	1–4
Electrical current	A variable which is represented by a measurement taken with a standard ammeter	1–4
Two-point oriented measurement	A measurement, taken between two terminals, which changes sign when the meter connections are reversed	1–5
Terminal variables	Variables which can be measured at the terminals of a component. In the electrical case, these are voltage and current.	1–5
Terminal graph	Oriented line segments which indicate the locations of pairs of measuring instruments, and the polarities of their connections	1–5
System graph	The union of all the terminal graphs for all the components of a system in one-to-one correspondence with their interconnection	1–6
Oriented linear graph	A collection of oriented line segments which intersect only at their endpoints	1–6
Element or edge	A line segment of a linear graph, together with its endpoints	1–6

Term	Definition	Section
Vertex or node	The endpoint of an element	1–6
Subgraph	A subset of the elements of a given graph	1–6
Complement of a subgraph	The subgraph which remains when a subgraph is removed from a given graph	1–6
Connected graph	A graph in which it is possible to trace at least one path along the elements and through every vertex	1–6
Part of a graph	A connected subgraph which has no vertex in common with its complement	1–6
Incidence	An element is incident on a vertex if that vertex is an endpoint of the element.	1–6
Circuit	A connected subgraph such that on every vertex there are incident exactly two elements	1–6
Forest	A subgraph which contains all the vertices of a given graph, is connected within each part, and contains no circuits	1–6
Coforest	The complement of a forest	1–6
Branch	An element of a forest	1–6
Chord	An element of a coforest	1–6
Tree	A forest of a connected graph	1–6
Cotree	The complement of a tree	1–6
Segregate set	If the vertices of a graph are divided into two mutually exclusive groups, the set of elements which are each incident on vertices in both groups form a segregate set.	1–8
Cut set	A segregate set which contains exactly one branch of a given forest	1–8
Formulation forest	A forest used to define cut sets	1–8
Fundamental circuit	A circuit which contains exactly one chord of a given forest (usually the formulation forest)	1–9

PROBLEMS

1.1. List several natural systems, man-made systems, and hybrid systems. For each system state what you would consider to be the components, and explain your choice.

1.2. Which of the following equations are linear, which are nonlinear, and which are algebraic?

(a) $x^2 + y^2 = a^2$

(b) $A \dfrac{dx}{dt} + Bx = C \sin Dt$

(c) $A \dfrac{dx}{dt} + Bx^t = C \sin Dt$

(d) $Ax + By = Ct$

(e) $A \cos x + B \sin y = C \tan Dt$

(f) $A \dfrac{d^3x}{dt^3} + B \dfrac{d^2x}{dt^2} + C \dfrac{dx}{dt} + Dx + E \int_0^t x \, dt = He^{Kt}$

(g) $Ax \int_0^t x \, dt = t$

(h) $\dfrac{dx_1}{dt} \dfrac{dx_2}{dt} + Ax_1 + Bx_2 = 0$

1.3. We have made the statement that an inquiry into the true meanings of the phenomena of electrical voltage and current would eventually result in a philosophical discussion. Can you think of any measurable quantities for which this would not be the case?

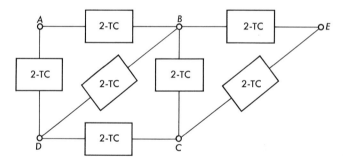

FIGURE 1.13

1.4. Figure 1.13 shows an electric network of two-terminal components. Draw a diagram for this network indicating voltmeter and ammeter locations necessary for measuring all the voltages and currents in the system.

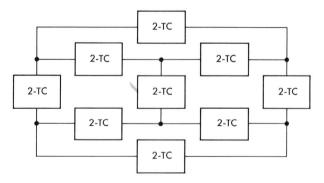

FIGURE 1.14

1.5. Repeat Problem 1.4 for the network of Fig. 1.14.

1.6. Draw the system graphs for the networks of Figs. 1.13 and 1.14, corresponding to the meter orientations you picked in the solutions of Problems 1.4 and 1.5.

1.7. Identify all the circuits in the graphs of Problem 1.6.

1.8. Identify as many forests as you can in the graphs of Problem 1.6, and for each forest, indicate the corresponding cut sets.

1.9. Figure 1.15 shows an oriented linear graph with two parts. Pick a forest and identify the corresponding fundamental circuits and cut sets.

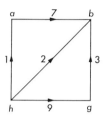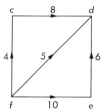

FIGURE 1.15

1.10. Figure 1.16 shows two connected oriented linear graphs. For each graph pick a tree and identify all the corresponding fundamental circuits and cut sets.

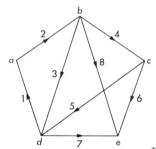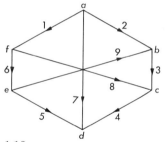

FIGURE 1.16

1.11. Consider the graph of Fig. 1.17. How many branches are there in any tree of this graph? How many chords are there in the corresponding cotree? Verify your answer by picking a typical tree and identifying the branches and chords.

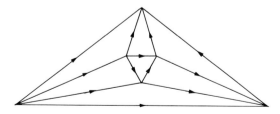

FIGURE 1.17

1.12. (a) Find as many trees as you can for the network of Fig. 1.5.
       (b) Write all the vertex and circuit equations for this network.

1.13. The following is the coefficient matrix for the vertex equations for an oriented linear graph. Draw the graph corresponding to this matrix (frequently called the *incidence matrix*).

$$
\begin{bmatrix}
1 & 0 & 0 & 0 & 0 & 0 & 0 & 0 & -1 & 1 \\
-1 & 1 & 1 & 0 & 0 & 0 & 0 & 0 & 0 & 0 \\
0 & -1 & 0 & -1 & 1 & 0 & 0 & 0 & 0 & 0 \\
0 & 0 & 0 & 0 & -1 & -1 & -1 & 0 & 0 & 0 \\
0 & 0 & 0 & 0 & 0 & 0 & 1 & 1 & 1 & 0 \\
0 & 0 & -1 & 1 & 0 & 1 & 0 & -1 & 0 & -1
\end{bmatrix}
$$

1.14. Corresponding to each forest picked in Problem 1.8, write a set of fundamental circuit and cut-set equations.

1.15. Write the equations for the fundamental circuits and cut sets chosen in Problems 1.9 and 1.10.

1.16. For each case of Problems 1.14 and 1.15 verify that Eq. (1.17) holds.

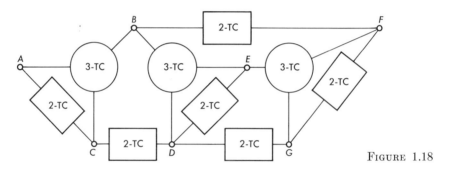

FIGURE 1.18

1.17. Figure 1.18 shows a network containing multiterminal components. Draw a possible system graph for this network, pick a formulation forest, and write the fundamental circuit and cut-set equations.

1.18. How many possible terminal graphs are there for a four-terminal component, for a five-terminal component, and for a six-terminal component?

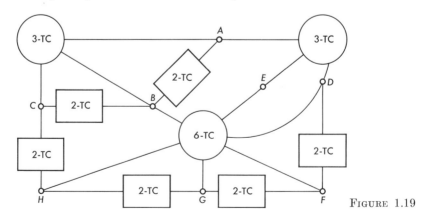

FIGURE 1.19

1.19. Repeat Problem 1.17 for the network of Fig. 1.19. Taking into account the possibilities for different terminal graphs for the multiterminal components, estimate the number of alternative system graphs that could be obtained for this network.

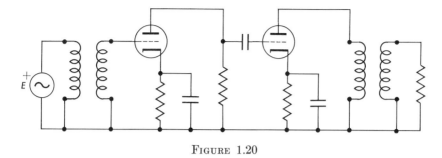

FIGURE 1.20

1.20. Figure 1.20 is a diagram which could be used to represent the small-signal linear operation of an electronic amplifier. Draw a system graph, and identify all the terminal equations. (The transformers are ideal.)

1.21. Figure 1.21 shows a simple network containing resistors, voltage drivers, and current drivers.

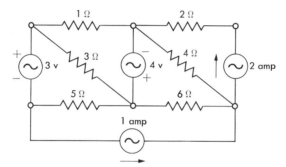

FIGURE 1.21

(a) Draw a system graph.
(b) Pick a formulation tree which includes the elements corresponding to the voltage drivers and excludes those corresponding to the current drivers.
(c) Write the fundamental circuit and cut-set equations.
(d) Write all the terminal equations.
(e) Substitute the terminal equations into the circuit equations and thus eliminate as many unknown voltages as possible.
(f) Use the cut-set equations to express the unknown branch currents in terms of the chord currents.
(g) Substitute the result of (f) into the result of (e) and obtain a set of equations whose unknowns are all chord currents.
(h) Solve the equations resulting from (g) for the chord currents, and by substituting in equations that you have already written, find all the currents and voltages in the network in terms of the known voltage and current drivers.

Chapter 2

FORMULATION TECHNIQUES FOR ANALYTICAL SOLUTIONS

In Chapter 1 we introduced the equations which characterize electric networks. For a network whose system graph contains e elements there are $2e$ of these equations, and it can be seen that for complex networks the direct solution of the $2e$ associated equations could be very cumbersome. In this chapter we shall show methods for solving the network equations analytically, taking advantage of the properties of the three sets of equations involved, namely the cut-set, circuit, and terminal equations.

We shall study only linear networks; some of the techniques of operational mathematics will later be shown to be most efficient in obtaining either a complete or a partial analysis of such networks. By a complete analysis we mean the solution for all the voltages and currents in the network.

2.1. THE BASIS OF THE FORMULATION PROCEDURES

The cut-set and fundamental circuit equations, combined with the component terminal equations, are basic to any form of analysis of electric networks. Our objective here is to eliminate variables among these systems of equations in such a way that a complete solution, which involves solving simultaneously the smallest possible number of equations, can be obtained. We have three possible courses of action. The first, known as the *branch* formulation, involves substituting successively the terminal equations and fundamental circuit equations into the cut-set equations. The second method, which is a technique dual to the branch formulation, is the substitution of the terminal equations and cut-set equations into the fundamental circuit equations, and is called the *chord* formulation. Lastly, the *branch-chord* formulation requires the substitution of both the cut-set and circuit equations into the terminal equations. In general, the branch-chord method of solution is more difficult than either the branch or chord techniques, and is to be avoided if possible.

2.2. SOME TOPOLOGICAL RESTRICTIONS

It is necessary to be able to recognize some simple restrictions on the types of components and their interconnections in an electric network. For example, we cannot arbitrarily specify all the voltages or all the currents corresponding to the measurements implied by a given system graph and expect to get a solution. In this section we shall indicate how many voltages and currents can be specified, and thus obtain the limits as to the numbers and locations of different kinds of components in a network.

Consider first, then, the fundamental circuit equations

$$[B \quad U] \begin{bmatrix} v_b(t) \\ v_c(t) \end{bmatrix} = [0] \tag{1.15}$$

or

$$[v_c(t)] = -[B][v_b(t)]. \tag{1.14}$$

These equations show that if we specify the branch voltages arbitrarily at any instant, the chord voltages are all determined at that instant. Therefore, we must be able to find a forest which contains all the voltage drivers if we wish to specify them arbitrarily.

In a similar manner, we can examine the cut-set equations

$$[i_b(t)] = -[A][i_c(t)], \tag{1.10}$$

and reach the conclusion that elements corresponding to current drivers should be consigned to the coforest.

Of course, networks can have more voltage drivers than there are branches or cut sets of current drivers, but in such cases we cannot specify the driving functions arbitrarily because we may violate the circuit and cut-set relations. It should also be mentioned that solutions are possible in which the formulation forest excludes some of the voltage drivers or includes some of the current drivers. However, it is advantageous to avoid such a choice, as will be evident later in this chapter.

It is always possible to specify the *initial* capacitor voltages and inductor currents in a given network. Therefore, if we wish to be sure that there are no inconsistencies among the cut-set, circuit, and terminal equations at every instant, it is necessary to include the capacitances in the forest and the inductors in the coforest. If the network contains circuits of capacitances or cut sets of inductors, an arbitrary specification of the initial voltages and currents in question may lead to difficulties in solution. On the other hand, so far as the formulation procedures which we shall study in this chapter are concerned, we would find no difficulty in placing the capacitors in the coforest or inductors in the forest. However, doing so may involve a slight complication in the solutions of the resulting equations.

Similar remarks can also be made concerning all those elements corresponding to multiterminal components for which time derivatives of the voltage or current variables may occur in the terminal equations. When the time derivative of a voltage appears in the terminal equations, it is most convenient to consign the corresponding element to the forest, whereas if the time derivative of a current appears, the corresponding element is most conveniently consigned to the coforest. Again we must stress that this choice of forest and coforest elements does not affect the formulation of the network equations, as in this chapter, but will slightly simplify their complete solution. In addition, as we shall see in a later chapter, when we investigate the characterization of networks by their *state equations*, it is highly advantageous to choose the forest according to the principles outlined above.

In summary, then, we may state:
(1) The forest should contain all the voltage drivers.
(2) The coforest should contain all the current drivers.
(3) Further restrictions that we have mentioned for other elements are unnecessary, but may lead to simplifications in the solutions of the network equations.

Finally we note that it can be proved that when a complete solution exists, we can always find a forest in the system graph such that it contains all the voltage drivers and none of the current drivers.

2.3. THE TERMINAL EQUATIONS

We have already mentioned that the branch-formulation technique requires the substitution of the terminal equations into the cut-set equations, while the chord method depends on the substitution of the terminal equations into the circuit equations. In general, some of the terminal relations appear as differential equations; in particular, from Table 1.1, we have, for the inductors and capacitors:

$$v_L(t) = L \frac{di_L(t)}{dt}, \tag{2.1}$$

$$i_C(t) = C \frac{dv_C(t)}{dt}. \tag{2.2}$$

Terminal equations of the form of (2.1) can easily be substituted into the circuit equations which are relations among the voltages in the network; similarly, terminal equations like (2.2) can be substituted into the cut-set equations. However, substitution of (2.1) into the cut-set equations, or (2.2) into the circuit equations, will require a further step. We must solve (2.1) for $i_L(t)$ and (2.2) for $v_C(t)$. This gives

$$i_L(t) = \frac{1}{L} \int_0^t v_L(x) \, dx + i_L(0+), \tag{2.3}$$

$$v_C(t) = \frac{1}{C} \int_0^t i_C(x) \, dx + v_C(0+). \tag{2.4}$$

Using (2.3) and (2.4), we can substitute the terminal equations for inductors into the cut-set equations, and those for capacitors into the circuit equations. Nevertheless, there is still one difficulty which arises from the fact that we intend to take advantage of the properties of matrix algebra in our substitution procedures. Although we can define matrix operations including integrals and derivatives, it is much more convenient for us to obtain all the terminal equations in the form of linear algebraic relations. We shall therefore make use of the Laplace transform to convert the differential and integral relations such as (2.1), (2.2), (2.3), and (2.4) into algebraic equations.

TABLE 2.1

LAPLACE TRANSFORMS OF THE TERMINAL EQUATIONS
CORRESPONDING TO THE TERMINAL GRAPHS OF TABLE 1.1

	Component	Terminal equations	Transformed terminal equations
1.	Resistance	$v(t) = Ri(t)$	$V(s) = RI(s)$ $I(s) = \frac{1}{R} V(s) = GV(s)$
2.	Inductance	$v(t) = L \frac{di(t)}{dt}$	$V(s) = LsI(s) - Li(0+)$ $I(s) = \frac{1}{Ls} V(s) + \frac{1}{s} i(0+)$
3.	Capacitance	$i(t) = C \frac{dv(t)}{dt}$	$I(s) = CsV(s) - Cv(0+)$ $V(s) = \frac{1}{Cs} I(s) + \frac{1}{s} v(0+)$
4.	Voltage source	$v(t) = E(t)$ (specified)	$V(s) = E(s)$ (specified)
5.	Current source	$i(t) = I(t)$ (specified)	$I(s) = I(s)$ (specified)
6.	Ideal trans-former	$\begin{bmatrix} v_2(t) \\ i_1(t) \end{bmatrix} = \begin{bmatrix} 0 & n \\ -n & 0 \end{bmatrix} \begin{bmatrix} i_2(t) \\ v_1(t) \end{bmatrix}$	$\begin{bmatrix} V_2(s) \\ I_1(s) \end{bmatrix} = \begin{bmatrix} 0 & n \\ -n & 0 \end{bmatrix} \begin{bmatrix} I_2(s) \\ V_1(s) \end{bmatrix}$
7.	Vacuum tube	$\begin{bmatrix} i_1(t) \\ i_2(t) \end{bmatrix} = \begin{bmatrix} 0 & 0 \\ g_m & g_p \end{bmatrix} \begin{bmatrix} v_1(t) \\ v_2(t) \end{bmatrix}$	$\begin{bmatrix} I_1(s) \\ I_2(s) \end{bmatrix} = \begin{bmatrix} 0 & 0 \\ g_m & g_p \end{bmatrix} \begin{bmatrix} V_1(s) \\ V_2(s) \end{bmatrix}$
8.	Transistor	$\begin{bmatrix} v_1(t) \\ i_2(t) \end{bmatrix} = \begin{bmatrix} h_{11} & h_{12} \\ h_{21} & h_{22} \end{bmatrix} \begin{bmatrix} i_1(t) \\ v_2(t) \end{bmatrix}$	$\begin{bmatrix} V_1(s) \\ I_2(s) \end{bmatrix} = \begin{bmatrix} h_{11} & h_{12} \\ h_{21} & h_{22} \end{bmatrix} \begin{bmatrix} I_1(s) \\ V_2(s) \end{bmatrix}$

The properties of the Laplace transform are given in Appendix A. Here, we only require the fact that this transform will convert integro-differential equations to algebraic relations as we wish. We shall leave the problem of solving the resulting transformed equations to the next chapter.

The Laplace transform of a function is given by

$$\mathcal{L}\{f(t)\} = \int_0^\infty e^{-st} f(t) \, dt = F(s), \tag{2.5}$$

and the Laplace transform of the time derivative of $f(t)$ is (see Appendix A)

$$\mathcal{L}\left\{\frac{d}{dt} f(t)\right\} = \int_0^\infty e^{-st} \frac{d}{dt} f(t) \, dt = s\mathcal{L}\{f(t)\} - f(0+) = sF(s) - f(0+), \tag{2.6}$$

where $f(0+)$ is the initial value of $f(t)$.

Using (2.5) and (2.6), we transform Eqs. (2.1) and (2.2) into

$$V_L(s) = LsI_L(s) - Li_L(0+), \tag{2.7}$$

$$I_C(s) = CsV_C(s) - Cv_C(0+). \tag{2.8}$$

Therefore, we also obtain

$$I_L(s) = \frac{1}{Ls} V_L(s) + \frac{1}{s} i_L(0+), \tag{2.9}$$

$$V_C(s) = \frac{1}{Cs} I_C(s) + \frac{1}{s} v_C(0+). \tag{2.10}$$

Note that we use capital letters to denote transformed variables, and lower-case letters for time functions.

When we apply the Laplace transform to the linear algebraic relations, the circuit equations, cut-set equations, and algebraic terminal equations, we merely change the voltages and currents from time functions into functions of the Laplace variable s. Thus, Laplace transforms really change only some terminal equations. Table 2.1 lists the transformed equations for the components of Table 1.1.

In the following sections we shall focus our attention on the formulation of the network equations, leaving the solution of the Laplace-transformed equations to the next chapter. We shall, however, show some examples in which all the equations are algebraic in the time domain.

2.4. THE BRANCH FORMULATION

We have shown how it is possible to rearrange the terminal equations for various components into a suitable form for substitution into either the circuit or the cut-set equations. In the branch-formulation method we shall follow the latter course, and continue by substituting the circuit equations into the resulting relations. First let us illustrate the procedure with an example; the conclusions about the resulting network equations which we shall draw will then be substantiated by means of a general symbolic development.

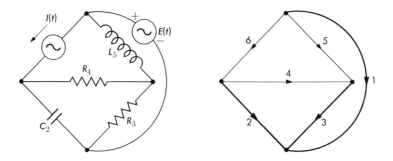

Fig. 2.1. A simple network and system graph.

EXAMPLE 2.1. Consider the network and system graph of Fig. 2.1. We select the tree for formulating the cut-set and circuit equations such that it includes the voltage driver and capacitance and excludes the current driver and inductance.

Thus either elements 1, 2, 3 or elements 1, 2, 4 form convenient formulation trees; we choose the former, for definiteness, as shown by the heavy lines in Fig. 2.1. Corresponding to this tree, then, the circuit equations are

$$\begin{bmatrix} 0 & -1 & 1 & 1 & 0 & 0 \\ -1 & 0 & 1 & 0 & 1 & 0 \\ -1 & 1 & 0 & 0 & 0 & 1 \end{bmatrix} \begin{bmatrix} V_1(s) \\ V_2(s) \\ V_3(s) \\ V_4(s) \\ V_5(s) \\ V_6(s) \end{bmatrix} = \begin{bmatrix} 0 \\ 0 \\ 0 \end{bmatrix}. \tag{2.11}$$

We also have the cut-set equations

$$\begin{bmatrix} 1 & 0 & 0 & 0 & 1 & 1 \\ 0 & 1 & 0 & 1 & 0 & -1 \\ 0 & 0 & 1 & -1 & -1 & 0 \end{bmatrix} \begin{bmatrix} I_1(s) \\ I_2(s) \\ I_3(s) \\ I_4(s) \\ I_5(s) \\ I_6(s) \end{bmatrix} = \begin{bmatrix} 0 \\ 0 \\ 0 \end{bmatrix}, \tag{2.12}$$

and the terminal relations

$$V_1(s) = E(s) \quad \text{(specified)}, \tag{2.13}$$

$$I_6(s) = I(s) \quad \text{(specified)}, \tag{2.14}$$

$$\begin{bmatrix} I_2(s) \\ I_3(s) \\ I_4(s) \\ I_5(s) \end{bmatrix} = \begin{bmatrix} C_2 s & 0 & 0 & 0 \\ 0 & G_3 & 0 & 0 \\ 0 & 0 & G_4 & 0 \\ 0 & 0 & 0 & \dfrac{1}{L_5 s} \end{bmatrix} \begin{bmatrix} V_2(s) \\ V_3(s) \\ V_4(s) \\ V_5(s) \end{bmatrix} + \begin{bmatrix} -C_2 v_2(0+) \\ 0 \\ 0 \\ \dfrac{1}{s} i_5(0+) \end{bmatrix}. \tag{2.15}$$

Let us rewrite the cut-set equations (2.12) so that we can conveniently eliminate I_2, I_3, I_4, I_5. First, we partition the matrices in (2.12) to give

$$\begin{bmatrix} 1 & | & 0 & 0 & 0 & 1 & | & 1 \\ 0 & | & 1 & 0 & 1 & 0 & | & -1 \\ 0 & | & 0 & 1 & -1 & -1 & | & 0 \end{bmatrix} \begin{bmatrix} I_1(s) \\ \text{-----} \\ I_2(s) \\ I_3(s) \\ I_4(s) \\ I_5(s) \\ \text{-----} \\ I_6(s) \end{bmatrix} = \begin{bmatrix} 0 \\ 0 \\ 0 \end{bmatrix}. \tag{2.16}$$

This may be rewritten as

$$\begin{bmatrix} 1 \\ 0 \\ 0 \end{bmatrix} [I_1(s)] + \begin{bmatrix} 0 & 0 & 0 & 1 \\ 1 & 0 & 1 & 0 \\ 0 & 1 & -1 & -1 \end{bmatrix} \begin{bmatrix} I_2(s) \\ I_3(s) \\ I_4(s) \\ I_5(s) \end{bmatrix} + \begin{bmatrix} 1 \\ -1 \\ 0 \end{bmatrix} [I_6(s)] = \begin{bmatrix} 0 \\ 0 \\ 0 \end{bmatrix}. \tag{2.17}$$

Note that the column matrix on the left-hand side of (2.15) appears explicitly in expression (2.17). We may therefore substitute directly from the terminal equations (2.15), into the cut-set equations (2.17). Thus we have

$$
\begin{bmatrix} 1 \\ 0 \\ 0 \end{bmatrix} [I_1(s)] + \begin{bmatrix} 0 & 0 & 0 & 1 \\ 1 & 0 & 1 & 0 \\ 0 & 1 & -1 & -1 \end{bmatrix} \begin{bmatrix} C_2s & 0 & 0 & 0 \\ 0 & G_3 & 0 & 0 \\ 0 & 0 & G_4 & 0 \\ 0 & 0 & 0 & \frac{1}{L_5 s} \end{bmatrix} \begin{bmatrix} V_2(s) \\ V_3(s) \\ V_4(s) \\ V_5(s) \end{bmatrix}
$$

$$
+ \begin{bmatrix} 1 \\ -1 \\ 0 \end{bmatrix} [I_6(s)] + \begin{bmatrix} 0 & 0 & 0 & 1 \\ 1 & 0 & 1 & 0 \\ 0 & 1 & -1 & -1 \end{bmatrix} \begin{bmatrix} -C_2 v_2(0+) \\ 0 \\ 0 \\ \frac{1}{s} i_5(0+) \end{bmatrix} = \begin{bmatrix} 0 \\ 0 \\ 0 \end{bmatrix}, \qquad (2.18)
$$

or, evaluating the last matrix product on the left-hand side of (2.18), we have

$$
\begin{bmatrix} 1 \\ 0 \\ 0 \end{bmatrix} [I_1(s)] + \begin{bmatrix} 0 & 0 & 0 & 1 \\ 1 & 0 & 1 & 0 \\ 0 & 1 & -1 & -1 \end{bmatrix} \begin{bmatrix} C_2s & 0 & 0 & 0 \\ 0 & G_3 & 0 & 0 \\ 0 & 0 & G_4 & 0 \\ 0 & 0 & 0 & \frac{1}{L_5 s} \end{bmatrix} \begin{bmatrix} V_2(s) \\ V_3(s) \\ V_4(s) \\ V_5(s) \end{bmatrix}
$$

$$
+ \begin{bmatrix} 1 \\ -1 \\ 0 \end{bmatrix} [I_6(s)] = \begin{bmatrix} -\frac{1}{s} i_5(0+) \\ C_2 v_2(0+) \\ \frac{1}{s} i_5(0+) \end{bmatrix}. \qquad (2.19)
$$

At this point we use the circuit equations (2.11) to eliminate the chord voltages which appear in (2.19). First (2.11) is rewritten in the form

$$
\begin{bmatrix} V_4(s) \\ V_5(s) \\ V_6(s) \end{bmatrix} = \begin{bmatrix} 0 & 1 & -1 \\ 1 & 0 & -1 \\ 1 & -1 & 0 \end{bmatrix} \begin{bmatrix} V_1(s) \\ V_2(s) \\ V_3(s) \end{bmatrix}, \qquad (2.20)
$$

from which we have

$$
\begin{bmatrix} V_4(s) \\ V_5(s) \end{bmatrix} = \begin{bmatrix} 0 & 1 & -1 \\ 1 & 0 & -1 \end{bmatrix} \begin{bmatrix} V_1(s) \\ V_2(s) \\ V_3(s) \end{bmatrix}. \qquad (2.21)
$$

We can also write the trivial equations

$$
\begin{bmatrix} V_2(s) \\ V_3(s) \end{bmatrix} = \begin{bmatrix} 0 & 1 & 0 \\ 0 & 0 & 1 \end{bmatrix} \begin{bmatrix} V_1(s) \\ V_2(s) \\ V_3(s) \end{bmatrix}, \qquad (2.22)
$$

and, combining (2.22) and (2.21), we obtain

$$
\begin{bmatrix} V_2(s) \\ V_3(s)^* \\ V_4(s) \\ V_5(s) \end{bmatrix} = \begin{bmatrix} 0 & 1 & 0 \\ 0 & 0 & 1 \\ 0 & 1 & -1 \\ 1 & 0 & -1 \end{bmatrix} \begin{bmatrix} V_1(s) \\ V_2(s) \\ V_3(s) \end{bmatrix}. \qquad (2.23)
$$

Now (2.23) may be immediately substituted into (2.19). This yields

$$
\begin{bmatrix} 1 \\ 0 \\ 0 \end{bmatrix} [I_1(s)] + \begin{bmatrix} 0 & 0 & 0 & 1 \\ 1 & 0 & 1 & 0 \\ 0 & 1 & -1 & -1 \end{bmatrix} \begin{bmatrix} C_2s & 0 & 0 & 0 \\ 0 & G_3 & 0 & 0 \\ 0 & 0 & G_4 & 0 \\ 0 & 0 & 0 & \dfrac{1}{L_5s} \end{bmatrix} \begin{bmatrix} 0 & 1 & 0 \\ 0 & 0 & 1 \\ 0 & 1 & -1 \\ 1 & 0 & -1 \end{bmatrix} \begin{bmatrix} V_1(s) \\ V_2(s) \\ V_3(s) \end{bmatrix}
$$

$$
+ \begin{bmatrix} 1 \\ -1 \\ 0 \end{bmatrix} [I_6(s)] = \begin{bmatrix} -\dfrac{1}{s}\, i_5(0+) \\ C_2 v_2(0+) \\ \dfrac{1}{s}\, i_5(0+) \end{bmatrix} . \qquad (2.24)
$$

In (2.24), the unknown quantities are $I_1(s)$, $V_2(s)$, $V_3(s)$. Thus this set of equations represents three equations in three unknowns. However, $I_1(s)$ appears only in the first equation. Therefore we can simultaneously solve the last two equations to obtain $V_2(s)$ and $V_3(s)$. These equations are

$$
\begin{bmatrix} 1 & 0 & 1 & 0 \\ 0 & 1 & -1 & -1 \end{bmatrix} \begin{bmatrix} C_2s & 0 & 0 & 0 \\ 0 & G_3 & 0 & 0 \\ 0 & 0 & G_4 & 0 \\ 0 & 0 & 0 & \dfrac{1}{L_5s} \end{bmatrix} \begin{bmatrix} 0 & 1 & 0 \\ 0 & 0 & 1 \\ 0 & 1 & -1 \\ 1 & 0 & -1 \end{bmatrix} \begin{bmatrix} V_1(s) \\ V_2(s) \\ V_3(s) \end{bmatrix}
$$

$$
= \begin{bmatrix} C_2 v_2(0+) \\ \dfrac{1}{s}\, i_5(0+) \end{bmatrix} + \begin{bmatrix} 1 \\ 0 \end{bmatrix} [I_6(s)], \qquad (2.25)
$$

or

$$
\begin{bmatrix} 0 & G_4 + C_2s & -G_4 \\ -\dfrac{1}{L_5s} & -G_4 & G_3 + G_4 + \dfrac{1}{L_5s} \end{bmatrix} \begin{bmatrix} V_1(s) \\ V_2(s) \\ V_3(s) \end{bmatrix} = \begin{bmatrix} C_2 v_2(0+) \\ \dfrac{1}{s}\, i_5(0+) \end{bmatrix} + \begin{bmatrix} 1 \\ 0 \end{bmatrix} [I_6(s)], \qquad (2.26)
$$

or

$$
\begin{bmatrix} G_4 + C_2s & -G_4 \\ -G_4 & G_3 + G_4 + \dfrac{1}{L_5s} \end{bmatrix} \begin{bmatrix} V_2(s) \\ V_3(s) \end{bmatrix} = \begin{bmatrix} C_2 v_2(0+) \\ \dfrac{1}{s}\, i_5(0+) \end{bmatrix} + \begin{bmatrix} 1 \\ 0 \end{bmatrix} [I_6(s)] + \begin{bmatrix} 0 \\ \dfrac{1}{L_5s} \end{bmatrix} [V_1(s)],
$$
$$
(2.27)
$$

where we have placed all the unknowns on the left and the known quantities on the right.

When we have solved (2.27) for $V_2(s)$, $V_3(s)$, we may immediately obtain $V_4(s)$, $V_5(s)$, and $V_6(s)$ from (2.20), and use these quantities in the terminal equations (2.15) to find $I_2(s)$, $I_3(s)$, $I_4(s)$, $I_5(s)$. Finally, $I_1(s)$ is obtained by substitution in the first cut-set equation, which may be written as

$$I_1(s) = -I_5(s) - I_6(s). \tag{2.28}$$

Note that these last operations do not require us to solve any equations; *as soon as we know the branch voltages we obtain the remaining currents and chord voltages by simple substitutions.* Furthermore, the number of simultaneous equations that we need to solve is one less than the number of cut-set equations. It is just equal to the number of nonspecified branch voltages.

The matrix triple product which appears in Eq. (2.24),

$$\begin{bmatrix} 0 & 0 & 0 & 1 \\ 1 & 0 & 1 & 0 \\ 0 & 1 & -1 & -1 \end{bmatrix} \begin{bmatrix} C_2 s & 0 & 0 & 0 \\ 0 & G_3 & 0 & 0 \\ 0 & 0 & G_4 & 0 \\ 0 & 0 & 0 & \dfrac{1}{L_5 s} \end{bmatrix} \begin{bmatrix} 0 & 1 & 0 \\ 0 & 0 & 1 \\ 0 & 1 & -1 \\ 1 & 0 & -1 \end{bmatrix},$$

has the remarkable property that the matrix on the right is the transpose of that on the left. We shall shortly show that this is a general property of the equations involved, so that once we have obtained the first matrix from the cut-set equations, we may immediately write down the third, without having to rearrange the circuit equations. The matrix which this triple product premultiplies is the column vector of the branch voltages.

Finally, the column matrix on the right-hand side of (2.24) depends only on the initial value of the capacitor voltage and the inductor current. In most practical cases these will be zero, so that this matrix will not appear.

Although we used matrix notation in Example 2.1, and shall do so throughout this book, it is certainly not necessary to do so. Matrix notation is most advantageous in setting forth the logical steps and the structure of the method of a problem solution, but its exploitation in small practical problems may not lead to any saving in time or effort. Therefore, in the following example, we repeat Example 2.1 without using matrices.

EXAMPLE 2.2. The circuit equations corresponding to the network and graph of Fig. 2.1 may be written as

$$\begin{aligned} -V_2(s) + V_3(s) + V_4(s) &= 0, \\ -V_1(s) + V_3(s) + V_5(s) &= 0, \\ -V_1(s) + V_2(s) + V_6(s) &= 0. \end{aligned} \tag{2.29}$$

The cut-set equations take the form

$$\begin{aligned} I_1(s) + I_5(s) + I_6(s) &= 0, \\ I_2(s) + I_4(s) - I_6(s) &= 0, \\ I_3(s) - I_4(s) - I_5(s) &= 0. \end{aligned} \tag{2.30}$$

and the terminal equations are

$$V_1(s) = E(s) \quad \text{(specified)}, \tag{2.13}$$

$$I_6(s) = I(s) \quad \text{(specified)}, \tag{2.14}$$

$$
\begin{aligned}
I_2(s) &= C_2 s V_2(s) - C_2 v_2(0+), \\
I_3(s) &= G_3 V_3(s), \\
I_4(s) &= G_4 V_4(s), \\
I_5(s) &= \frac{1}{L_5 s} V_5(s) + \frac{1}{s} i_5(0+).
\end{aligned}
\tag{2.31}
$$

We first substitute the terminal equations (2.31) into the cut-set equations (2.30), and obtain [equivalent to Eqs. (2.19)],

$$
\begin{aligned}
I_1(s) + \frac{1}{L_5 s} V_5(s) + I_6(s) &= -\frac{1}{s} i_5(0+), \\
C_2 s V_2(s) + G_4 V_4(s) - I_6(s) &= C_2 v_2(0+), \\
G_3 V_3(s) - G_4 V_4(s) - \frac{1}{L_5 s} V_5(s) &= \frac{1}{s} i_5(0+).
\end{aligned}
\tag{2.32}
$$

We next solve the circuit equations for the chord voltages in terms of the branch voltages. This yields

$$
\begin{aligned}
V_4(s) &= V_2(s) - V_3(s), \\
V_5(s) &= V_1(s) - V_3(s), \\
V_6(s) &= V_1(s) - V_2(s).
\end{aligned}
\tag{2.33}
$$

Substituting the first two equations of (2.33) into Eqs. (2.32), we eliminate the chord voltages and obtain

$$
\begin{aligned}
I_1(s) + \frac{1}{L_5 s} V_1(s) - \frac{1}{L_5 s} V_3(s) + I_6(s) &= -\frac{1}{s} i_5(0+), \\
(C_2 s + G_4) V_2(s) - G_4 V_3(s) - I_6(s) &= C_2 v_2(0+), \\
-\frac{1}{L_5 s} V_1(s) - G_4 V_2(s) + \left(G_3 + G_4 + \frac{1}{L_5 s}\right) V_3(s) &= \frac{1}{s} i_5(0+).
\end{aligned}
\tag{2.34}
$$

Examination of Eqs. (2.34), which are the same as (2.24), shows that only the last two need be solved simultaneously to obtain $V_2(s)$ and $V_3(s)$. When the known variables are moved to the right-hand side, these equations become

$$
\begin{aligned}
(C_2 s + G_4) V_2(s) - G_4 V_3(s) &= I_6(s) + C_2 v_2(0+), \\
-G_4 V_2(s) + \left(G_3 + G_4 + \frac{1}{L_5 s}\right) V_3(s) &= \frac{1}{L_5 s} V_1(s) + \frac{1}{s} i_5(0+),
\end{aligned}
\tag{2.35}
$$

which are equivalent to Eqs. (2.27).

When we have solved Eqs. (2.35) for $V_2(s)$ and $V_3(s)$, we can immediately find all the remaining variables by substitutions in the circuit, cut-set, and terminal equations. We first find $V_4(s)$, $V_5(s)$, and $V_6(s)$ from Eqs. (2.33), and this enables us to use Eqs. (2.31) to obtain $I_2(s)$, $I_3(s)$, $I_4(s)$, and $I_5(s)$. We may finally find $I_1(s)$ by substituting in the first cut-set equation of (2.30).

Although our solution of the network of Fig. 2.1 was somewhat shorter when we did not use matrix notation, it has the disadvantage that it is difficult to draw conclusions about the general method, which may be used in every case, from the equations which appeared in the solution. Indeed, we were able to present the solution as briefly as we did only because of the first method, which serves as a guide.

2.5. SYMBOLIC FORMULATION OF THE BRANCH EQUATIONS

We now embark on the symbolic formulation of the branch equations in order to give weight to our conclusions about the methods used in the previous section. Let us assume that a suitable formulation forest has been chosen for some system, so that we can write the cut-set equations

$$[U \quad A] \begin{bmatrix} I_b(s) \\ I_c(s) \end{bmatrix} = [0]. \tag{2.36}$$

It is convenient to partition the matrices on the left-hand side of this expression further, so that we can show the nonspecified currents explicitly. Accordingly, we write (2.36) in the form

$$\begin{bmatrix} U & 0 & A_{11} & A_{12} \\ 0 & U & A_{21} & A_{22} \end{bmatrix} \begin{bmatrix} I_{bd}(s) \\ I_{b2}(s) \\ I_{c1}(s) \\ I_{cd}(s) \end{bmatrix} = \begin{bmatrix} 0 \\ 0 \end{bmatrix}, \tag{2.37}$$

where $[I_{bd}(s)]$ is a column matrix of the branch currents for those branches whose voltages are specified; $[I_{b2}(s)]$, $[I_{c1}(s)]$ are column matrices of the current in the branches and chords, respectively, for which neither the voltages nor the currents are specified; and $[I_{cd}(s)]$ is the column matrix of specified currents.

Now (2.37) may be rearranged to give

$$\begin{bmatrix} U \\ 0 \end{bmatrix} [I_{bd}(s)] + \begin{bmatrix} 0 & A_{11} \\ U & A_{21} \end{bmatrix} \begin{bmatrix} I_{b2}(s) \\ I_{c1}(s) \end{bmatrix} + \begin{bmatrix} A_{12} \\ A_{22} \end{bmatrix} [I_{cd}(s)] = \begin{bmatrix} 0 \\ 0 \end{bmatrix}. \tag{2.38}$$

The branch formulation proceeds by the substitution of the terminal relations into the cut-set equations (2.38). This can be done only when it is possible to obtain the terminal equations in the explicit form:

$$\begin{aligned} [V_{bd}(s)] &= [F_1(s)] \quad \text{(specified)}, \\ [I_{cd}(s)] &= [F_2(s)] \quad \text{(specified)}, \end{aligned} \tag{2.39}$$

$$\begin{bmatrix} I_{b2}(s) \\ I_{c1}(s) \end{bmatrix} = \begin{bmatrix} Y_{11}(s) & Y_{12}(s) \\ Y_{21}(s) & Y_{22}(s) \end{bmatrix} \begin{bmatrix} V_{b2}(s) \\ V_{c1}(s) \end{bmatrix} + \begin{bmatrix} F_1(s, 0+) \\ F_2(s, 0+) \end{bmatrix}, \tag{2.40}$$

where $[V_{bd}]$, $[I_{cd}]$ represent column matrices of the specified branch voltages and chord currents; $[V_{b2}]$, $[V_{c1}]$ represent column matrices of the voltages in the branches and chords, respectively, for which neither the voltages nor the currents are specified; and $[F_1(s, 0+)]$, $[F_2(s, 0+)]$ are known matrices depending on the initial values of some of the voltages and currents. In such cases, we can substitute (2.40) into (2.38), and obtain

$$\begin{bmatrix} U \\ 0 \end{bmatrix} [I_{bd}(s)] + \begin{bmatrix} 0 & A_{11} \\ U & A_{21} \end{bmatrix} \begin{bmatrix} Y_{11}(s) & Y_{12}(s) \\ Y_{21}(s) & Y_{22}(s) \end{bmatrix} \begin{bmatrix} V_{b2}(s) \\ V_{c1}(s) \end{bmatrix}$$
$$+ \begin{bmatrix} A_{12} \\ A_{22} \end{bmatrix} [I_{cd}(s)] = - \begin{bmatrix} 0 & A_{11} \\ U & A_{21} \end{bmatrix} \begin{bmatrix} F_1(s, 0+) \\ F_2(s, 0+) \end{bmatrix}. \qquad (2.41)$$

We now intend to substitute the fundamental circuit equations into (2.41). For these equations we have

$$[B \quad U] \begin{bmatrix} V_b(s) \\ V_c(s) \end{bmatrix} = [0]. \qquad (2.42)$$

Partitioning these equations in the same fashion as (2.37), we obtain

$$\begin{bmatrix} B_{11} & B_{12} & U & 0 \\ B_{21} & B_{22} & 0 & U \end{bmatrix} \begin{bmatrix} V_{bd}(s) \\ V_{b2}(s) \\ V_{c1}(s) \\ V_{cd}(s) \end{bmatrix} = \begin{bmatrix} 0 \\ 0 \end{bmatrix}, \qquad (2.43)$$

so that we can write

$$[V_{c1}(s)] = [-B_{11} \quad -B_{12}] \begin{bmatrix} V_{bd}(s) \\ V_{b2}(s) \end{bmatrix}. \qquad (2.44)$$

We also use the trivial equation

$$[V_{b2}(s)] = [0 \quad U] \begin{bmatrix} V_{bd}(s) \\ V_{b2}(s) \end{bmatrix} \qquad (2.45)$$

and combining (2.44) and (2.45), we have

$$\begin{bmatrix} V_{b2}(s) \\ V_{c1}(s) \end{bmatrix} = \begin{bmatrix} 0 & U \\ -B_{11} & -B_{12} \end{bmatrix} \begin{bmatrix} V_{bd}(s) \\ V_{b2}(s) \end{bmatrix}. \qquad (2.46)$$

Equations (2.46) may easily be substituted into (2.41), and this operation yields

$$\begin{bmatrix} U \\ 0 \end{bmatrix} [I_{bd}(s)] + \begin{bmatrix} 0 & A_{11} \\ U & A_{21} \end{bmatrix} \begin{bmatrix} Y_{11}(s) & Y_{12}(s) \\ Y_{21}(s) & Y_{22}(s) \end{bmatrix} \begin{bmatrix} 0 & U \\ -B_{11} & -B_{12} \end{bmatrix} \begin{bmatrix} V_{bd}(s) \\ V_{b2}(s) \end{bmatrix}$$
$$+ \begin{bmatrix} A_{12}(s) \\ A_{22}(s) \end{bmatrix} [I_{cd}(s)] = - \begin{bmatrix} 0 & A_{11} \\ U & A_{21} \end{bmatrix} \begin{bmatrix} F_1(s, 0+) \\ F_2(s, 0+) \end{bmatrix}. \qquad (2.47)$$

At this point, we recall the relationship between the cut-set and fundamental circuit matrices, which is

$$[B] = -[A]', \qquad (1.18)$$

or

$$- \begin{bmatrix} B_{11} & B_{12} \\ B_{21} & B_{22} \end{bmatrix} = \begin{bmatrix} A_{11} & A_{12} \\ A_{21} & A_{22} \end{bmatrix}' = \begin{bmatrix} A'_{11} & A'_{21} \\ A'_{12} & A'_{22} \end{bmatrix}. \qquad (2.48)$$

From (2.48) we have

$$-[B_{11}] = [A'_{11}], \qquad -[B_{12}] = [A'_{21}], \tag{2.49}$$

so that (2.47) takes the form

$$\begin{bmatrix} U \\ 0 \end{bmatrix} [I_{bd}(s)] + \begin{bmatrix} 0 & A_{11} \\ U & A_{21} \end{bmatrix} \begin{bmatrix} Y_{11}(s) & Y_{12}(s) \\ Y_{21}(s) & Y_{22}(s) \end{bmatrix} \begin{bmatrix} 0 & U \\ A'_{11} & A'_{21} \end{bmatrix} \begin{bmatrix} V_{bd}(s) \\ V_{b2}(s) \end{bmatrix}$$

$$+ \begin{bmatrix} A_{12} \\ A_{22} \end{bmatrix} [I_{cd}(s)] = - \begin{bmatrix} 0 & A_{11} \\ U & A_{21} \end{bmatrix} \begin{bmatrix} F_1(s, 0+) \\ F_2(s, 0+) \end{bmatrix}. \tag{2.50}$$

Clearly, in (2.50) the third matrix of the triple product is the transpose of the first. *Thus, it becomes but a simple matter to write equations corresponding to (2.50) directly from the knowledge of the cut-set and terminal equations.* We do not need the fundamental circuit equations.

Equations (2.50) are called the *branch equations*, and their unknowns consist of $[I_{bd}(s)]$ and $[V_{b2}(s)]$. However, because of the nature of the matrix premultiplying $[I_{bd}(s)]$, we may divide the branch equations into two sets, the second of which involves only $[V_{b2}(s)]$. This second set is

$$[U \quad A_{21}] \begin{bmatrix} Y_{11}(s) & Y_{12}(s) \\ Y_{21}(s) & Y_{22}(s) \end{bmatrix} \begin{bmatrix} 0 & U \\ A'_{11} & A'_{21} \end{bmatrix} \begin{bmatrix} V_{bd}(s) \\ V_{b2}(s) \end{bmatrix} + [A_{22}] [I_{cd}(s)]$$

$$= -[U \quad A_{21}] \begin{bmatrix} F_1(s, 0+) \\ F_2(s, 0+) \end{bmatrix}. \tag{2.51}$$

We can rewrite (2.51) in the form

$$[U \quad A_{21}] \begin{bmatrix} Y_{11}(s) & Y_{12}(s) \\ Y_{21}(s) & Y_{22}(s) \end{bmatrix} \begin{bmatrix} U \\ A'_{21} \end{bmatrix} [V_{b2}(s)]$$

$$= -[U \quad A_{21}] \left\{ \begin{bmatrix} Y_{11}(s) & Y_{12}(s) \\ Y_{21}(s) & Y_{22}(s) \end{bmatrix} \begin{bmatrix} 0 \\ A'_{11} \end{bmatrix} [V_{bd}(s)] + \begin{bmatrix} F_1(s, 0+) \\ F_2(s, 0+) \end{bmatrix} \right\} - [A_{22}] [I_{cd}(s)], \tag{2.52}$$

and it can be seen that since the unknowns involved are the nonspecified branch voltages, they number exactly $v - p - n_V$, where v is the number of vertices in the system graph, n_V is the number of specified voltages, and p is the number of connected parts.

A point of particular interest is that *the matrix triple product involved in the branch equations (2.50) is symmetric whenever the coefficient matrix of the terminal equations is symmetric.* This follows from a theorem of matrix algebra which we leave as an exercise. The symmetry of this triple product is of great assistance to us in many cases, as we shall point out later.

For completeness, we note that when $[V_{b2}(s)]$ is found from (2.52), we can obtain the remaining voltages from the equations

$$\begin{bmatrix} V_{c1}(s) \\ V_{cd}(s) \end{bmatrix} = \begin{bmatrix} -B_{11} & -B_{12} \\ -B_{21} & -B_{22} \end{bmatrix} \begin{bmatrix} V_{bd}(s) \\ V_{b2}(s) \end{bmatrix}. \tag{2.53}$$

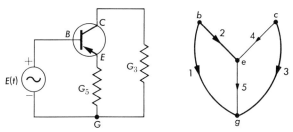

FIG. 2.2. Simple transistor network and system graph.

Then, substitution in (2.40) yields $[I_{b2}(s)]$ and $[I_{c1}(s)]$. We obtain $[I_{bd}(s)]$ by substitution into

$$[I_{bd}(s)] = [-A_{11} \quad -A_{12}] \begin{bmatrix} I_{c1}(s) \\ I_{cd}(s) \end{bmatrix}. \tag{2.54}$$

EXAMPLE 2.3. In this example we shall illustrate the use of the branch equations for finding all the voltages and currents involved in the network of Fig. 2.2. In this case, the terminal equations from Table 1.1 are

$$v_1(t) = E(t),$$
$$\begin{bmatrix} v_2(t) \\ i_4(t) \end{bmatrix} = \begin{bmatrix} h_{11} & h_{12} \\ h_{21} & h_{22} \end{bmatrix} \begin{bmatrix} i_2(t) \\ v_4(t) \end{bmatrix}, \qquad \begin{matrix} i_3(t) = G_3 v_3(t), \\ i_5(t) = G_5 v_5(t). \end{matrix} \tag{2.55}$$

Since all the equations are algebraic, it is unnecessary to use Laplace transforms; furthermore, the relations for the transistor must be rewritten to show $i_2(t)$ and $i_4(t)$ in terms of $v_2(t)$ and $v_4(t)$ in order to use the branch formulation. When this is done, we have

$$\begin{bmatrix} i_2(t) \\ i_4(t) \end{bmatrix} = \begin{bmatrix} g_{11} & g_{12} \\ g_{21} & g_{22} \end{bmatrix} \begin{bmatrix} v_2(t) \\ v_4(t) \end{bmatrix}, \tag{2.56}$$

where

$$g_{11} = 1/h_{11}, \qquad g_{12} = -h_{12}/h_{11},$$
$$g_{21} = h_{21}/h_{11}, \qquad g_{22} = (h_{11}h_{22} - h_{12}h_{21})/h_{11} = \Delta_h/h_{11}. \tag{2.57}$$

Thus we can easily rearrange the terminal relations (2.55) into the form

$$v_1(t) = E(t),$$
$$\begin{bmatrix} i_2(t) \\ i_3(t) \\ i_4(t) \\ i_5(t) \end{bmatrix} = \begin{bmatrix} g_{11} & 0 & g_{12} & 0 \\ 0 & G_3 & 0 & 0 \\ g_{21} & 0 & g_{22} & 0 \\ 0 & 0 & 0 & G_5 \end{bmatrix} \begin{bmatrix} v_2(t) \\ v_3(t) \\ v_4(t) \\ v_5(t) \end{bmatrix}. \tag{2.58}$$

The cut-set equations for this network are

$$\begin{bmatrix} 1 & 0 & 0 & -1 & 1 \\ 0 & 1 & 0 & 1 & -1 \\ 0 & 0 & 1 & 1 & 0 \end{bmatrix} \begin{bmatrix} i_1(t) \\ i_2(t) \\ i_3(t) \\ i_4(t) \\ i_5(t) \end{bmatrix} = 0. \tag{2.59}$$

We write (2.59) in a suitable form for substitution of the terminal equations (2.58), and obtain

$$
\begin{bmatrix} 1 \\ 0 \\ 0 \end{bmatrix} [i_1(t)] + \begin{bmatrix} 0 & 0 & -1 & 1 \\ 1 & 0 & 1 & -1 \\ 0 & 1 & 1 & 0 \end{bmatrix} \begin{bmatrix} i_2(t) \\ i_3(t) \\ i_4(t) \\ i_5(t) \end{bmatrix} = 0.
\tag{2.60}
$$

The substitution of (2.58) into (2.60) yields

$$
\begin{bmatrix} 1 \\ 0 \\ 0 \end{bmatrix} [i_1(t)] + \begin{bmatrix} 0 & 0 & -1 & 1 \\ 1 & 0 & 1 & -1 \\ 0 & 1 & 1 & 0 \end{bmatrix} \begin{bmatrix} g_{11} & 0 & g_{12} & 0 \\ 0 & G_3 & 0 & 0 \\ g_{21} & 0 & g_{22} & 0 \\ 0 & 0 & 0 & G_5 \end{bmatrix} \begin{bmatrix} v_2(t) \\ v_3(t) \\ v_4(t) \\ v_5(t) \end{bmatrix} = 0.
\tag{2.61}
$$

It remains for us to write the circuit equations in a suitable form for use in (2.61). However, we know in advance that this substitution will lead to

(a) a matrix triple product in which the first matrix is the transpose of the third,
(b) a set of equations whose variables are the branch voltages.

Therefore, we can immediately write the result of the substitution of the circuit equations into (2.61). This is

$$
\begin{bmatrix} 1 \\ 0 \\ 0 \end{bmatrix} [i_1(t)] + \begin{bmatrix} 0 & 0 & -1 & 1 \\ 1 & 0 & 1 & -1 \\ 0 & 1 & 1 & 0 \end{bmatrix} \begin{bmatrix} g_{11} & 0 & g_{12} & 0 \\ 0 & G_3 & 0 & 0 \\ g_{21} & 0 & g_{22} & 0 \\ 0 & 0 & 0 & G_5 \end{bmatrix} \begin{bmatrix} 0 & 1 & 0 \\ 0 & 0 & 1 \\ -1 & 1 & 1 \\ 1 & -1 & 0 \end{bmatrix} \begin{bmatrix} v_1(t) \\ v_2(t) \\ v_3(t) \end{bmatrix} = 0.
\tag{2.62}
$$

Equations (2.62) are the branch equations for this example. It can be seen that since $i_1(t)$ occurs only in the first equation, we need solve only the last two equations simultaneously in order to obtain all the voltages and currents in the network. This agrees with the expected number of equations $(v - 1 - n_V)$, since there are four vertices and one voltage driver.

The last two equations of (2.62) are

$$
\begin{bmatrix} 1 & 0 & 1 & -1 \\ 0 & 1 & 1 & 0 \end{bmatrix} \begin{bmatrix} g_{11} & 0 & g_{12} & 0 \\ 0 & G_3 & 0 & 0 \\ g_{21} & 0 & g_{22} & 0 \\ 0 & 0 & 0 & G_5 \end{bmatrix} \begin{bmatrix} 0 & 1 & 0 \\ 0 & 0 & 1 \\ -1 & 1 & 1 \\ 1 & -1 & 0 \end{bmatrix} \begin{bmatrix} v_1(t) \\ v_2(t) \\ v_3(t) \end{bmatrix} = 0.
\tag{2.63}
$$

Evaluating the triple product, we obtain

$$
\begin{bmatrix} -(g_{12}+g_{22}+G_5) & (g_{11}+g_{21}+g_{12}+g_{22}+G_5) & (g_{12}+g_{22}) \\ -g_{22} & (g_{21}+g_{22}) & (g_{22}+G_3) \end{bmatrix} \begin{bmatrix} v_1(t) \\ v_2(t) \\ v_3(t) \end{bmatrix} = 0,
\tag{2.64}
$$

or, since $v_1(t) = E(t)$,

$$
\begin{bmatrix} (g_{11}+g_{21}+g_{12}+g_{22}+G_5) & (g_{12}+g_{22}) \\ (g_{21}+g_{22}) & (g_{22}+G_3) \end{bmatrix} \begin{bmatrix} v_2(t) \\ v_3(t) \end{bmatrix} = \begin{bmatrix} g_{12}+g_{22}+G_5 \\ g_{22} \end{bmatrix} [E(t)].
\tag{2.65}
$$

We solve (2.65) for $v_2(t)$ and $v_3(t)$. This yields

$$\begin{bmatrix} v_2(t) \\ v_3(t) \end{bmatrix} = \begin{bmatrix} G_3(g_{12} + g_{22} + G_5) + g_{22}G_5 \\ g_{11}g_{22} - g_{21}g_{12} - g_{21}G_5 \end{bmatrix} \frac{E(t)}{\Delta}, \tag{2.66}$$

where

$$\Delta = g_{11}g_{22} - g_{21}g_{12} + G_3(g_{11} + g_{12} + g_{21} + g_{22}) + G_5(G_3 + g_{22}) \tag{2.67}$$

is the determinant of the coefficient matrix on the left of (2.65). We now know $v_1(t)$, $v_2(t)$, and $v_3(t)$, so that we can find the remaining voltages from the circuit equations

$$\begin{bmatrix} v_4(t) \\ v_5(t) \end{bmatrix} = \begin{bmatrix} -1 & 1 & 1 \\ 1 & -1 & 0 \end{bmatrix} \begin{bmatrix} v_1(t) \\ v_2(t) \\ v_3(t) \end{bmatrix}. \tag{2.68}$$

This is a simple substitution, and having obtained $v_4(t)$ and $v_5(t)$, we can find the currents $i_2(t)$, $i_3(t)$, $i_4(t)$, and $i_5(t)$, by substituting into the terminal relations (2.58). Finally, we obtain $i_1(t)$ by using the cut-set equation

$$i_1(t) = i_4(t) - i_5(t). \tag{2.69}$$

For completeness, we shall now show the application of the branch-formulation method without matrix notation for this example. The cut-set equations take the form,

$$\begin{aligned} i_1(t) - i_4(t) + i_5(t) &= 0, \\ i_2(t) + i_4(t) - i_5(t) &= 0, \\ i_3(t) + i_4(t) &= 0, \end{aligned} \tag{2.70}$$

and the terminal equations may be written as

$$\begin{aligned} v_1(t) &= E(t), \\ i_2(t) &= g_{11}v_2(t) + g_{12}v_4(t), \\ i_3(t) &= G_3v_3(t), \\ i_4(t) &= g_{21}v_2(t) + g_{22}v_4(t), \\ i_5(t) &= G_5v_5(t). \end{aligned} \tag{2.71}$$

We first substitute the terminal equations into the cut-set equations, and obtain

$$\begin{aligned} i_1(t) - g_{21}v_2(t) - g_{22}v_4(t) + G_5v_5(t) &= 0, \\ (g_{11} + g_{21})v_2(t) + (g_{12} + g_{22})v_4(t) - G_5v_5(t) &= 0, \\ g_{21}v_2(t) + G_3v_3(t) + g_{12}v_4(t) &= 0, \end{aligned} \tag{2.72}$$

which are equivalent to Eqs. (2.61). At this stage, we eliminate the chord voltages by substitution of the circuit equations into (2.72). The required circuit equations are

$$\begin{aligned} v_1(t) - v_2(t) - v_3(t) + v_4(t) &= 0, \\ - v_1(t) + v_2(t) + v_5(t) &= 0, \end{aligned} \tag{2.73}$$

and substitution of (2.73) into (2.72) yields

$$i_1(t) + (g_{22} + G_5)v_1(t) - (g_{21} + g_{22} + G_5)v_2(t) - g_{22}v_3(t) = 0,$$
$$-(g_{12} + g_{22} + G_5)v_1(t) + (g_{11} + g_{21} + g_{12} + g_{22} + G_5)v_2(t) + (g_{12} + g_{22})v_3(t) = 0,$$
$$-g_{22}v_1(t) + (g_{21} + g_{22})v_2(t) + (g_{22} + G_3)v_3(t) = 0,$$

$$(2.74)$$

which are the branch equations. Only the last two equations need to be solved simultaneously for $v_2(t)$ and $v_3(t)$; the remaining variables are then found by substitutions in Eqs. (2.73), (2.71), and (2.70). The details are left as an exercise.

This example shows one advantage of the use of matrix notation. We were able to write the branch equations (2.62) without direct recourse to the circuit equations; dispensing with the matrix notation necessitated the additional step of writing these equations. This arises, of course, because of the greater organization implicit in the matrix method.

We conclude this section by summarizing the salient points of the branch-formulation technique.

(1) To formulate the branch equations, the terminal relations must be written to express the currents explicitly in terms of the voltages.

(2) The cut-set equations are written in such a way as to facilitate the substitution of the terminal relations.

(3) The terminal relations are substituted into the cut-set equations.

(4) The fundamental circuit equations are used to eliminate all but the branch voltages from the result of step 3. The result is the branch equations.

(5) The matrix triple product which premultiplies the column vector of branch voltages in the branch equations has the property that the matrix on the right is the transpose of that on the left. This means that we can write the branch equations without explicitly using the circuit equations.

(6) The number of branch equations is equal to the number of branches, but we need solve simultaneously only those equations which do not contain the unknown currents through the voltage drivers. Thus, the number of simultaneous equations to be solved is just $v - p - n_V$, where v is the number of vertices in the system graph, n_V is the number of voltage drivers, and p is the number of connected parts.

2.6. THE CHORD FORMULATION

The chord-formulation technique is very similar in its details to the branch formulation. In this case, however, we substitute the terminal equations first into the fundamental circuit equations. We then use the cut-set equations in the resulting relations. We shall first illustrate the procedure with an example.

EXAMPLE 2.4. We shall here follow the chord-formulation technique for the network of Example 2.1. The network and its system graph are shown in Fig. 2.1, which we reproduce here as Fig. 2.3 for convenience.

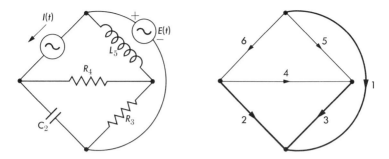

FIG. 2.3. A simple network and system graph.

The terminal equations (2.15), for this network may well be written as

$$\begin{bmatrix} V_2(s) \\ V_3(s) \\ V_4(s) \\ V_5(s) \end{bmatrix} = \begin{bmatrix} \dfrac{1}{C_2 s} & 0 & 0 & 0 \\ 0 & R_3 & 0 & 0 \\ 0 & 0 & R_4 & 0 \\ 0 & 0 & 0 & L_5 s \end{bmatrix} \begin{bmatrix} I_2(s) \\ I_3(s) \\ I_4(s) \\ I_5(s) \end{bmatrix} + \begin{bmatrix} \dfrac{1}{s} v_2(0+) \\ 0 \\ 0 \\ -L_5 i_5(0+) \end{bmatrix}. \tag{2.75}$$

The fundamental circuit equations are

$$\begin{bmatrix} 0 & -1 & 1 & 1 & 0 & 0 \\ -1 & 0 & 1 & 0 & 1 & 0 \\ -1 & 1 & 0 & 0 & 0 & 1 \end{bmatrix} \begin{bmatrix} V_1(s) \\ V_2(s) \\ V_3(s) \\ V_4(s) \\ V_5(s) \\ V_6(s) \end{bmatrix} = \begin{bmatrix} 0 \\ 0 \\ 0 \end{bmatrix}. \tag{2.11}$$

We wish to substitute (2.75) into (2.11), so that it is first necessary to rearrange (2.11) as

$$\begin{bmatrix} 0 \\ -1 \\ -1 \end{bmatrix} [V_1(s)] + \begin{bmatrix} -1 & 1 & 1 & 0 \\ 0 & 1 & 0 & 1 \\ 1 & 0 & 0 & 0 \end{bmatrix} \begin{bmatrix} V_2(s) \\ V_3(s) \\ V_4(s) \\ V_5(s) \end{bmatrix} + \begin{bmatrix} 0 \\ 0 \\ 1 \end{bmatrix} [V_6(s)] = \begin{bmatrix} 0 \\ 0 \\ 0 \end{bmatrix}. \tag{2.76}$$

Now the substitution of (2.75) into (2.76) is simple, and we obtain

$$\begin{bmatrix} 0 \\ -1 \\ -1 \end{bmatrix} [V_1(s)] + \begin{bmatrix} -1 & 1 & 1 & 0 \\ 0 & 1 & 0 & 1 \\ 1 & 0 & 0 & 0 \end{bmatrix} \begin{bmatrix} \dfrac{1}{C_2 s} & 0 & 0 & 0 \\ 0 & R_3 & 0 & 0 \\ 0 & 0 & R_4 & 0 \\ 0 & 0 & 0 & L_5 s \end{bmatrix} \begin{bmatrix} I_2(s) \\ I_3(s) \\ I_4(s) \\ I_5(s) \end{bmatrix}$$

$$+ \begin{bmatrix} 0 \\ 0 \\ 1 \end{bmatrix} [V_6(s)] + \begin{bmatrix} -1 & 1 & 1 & 0 \\ 0 & 1 & 0 & 1 \\ 1 & 0 & 0 & 0 \end{bmatrix} \begin{bmatrix} \dfrac{1}{s} v_2(0+) \\ 0 \\ 0 \\ L_5 i_5(0\,|\,) \end{bmatrix} = \begin{bmatrix} 0 \\ 0 \\ 0 \end{bmatrix}, \tag{2.77}$$

or, evaluating the last matrix product, we have

$$
\begin{bmatrix} 0 \\ -1 \\ -1 \end{bmatrix} [V_1(s)] +
\begin{bmatrix} -1 & 1 & 1 & 0 \\ 0 & 1 & 0 & 1 \\ 1 & 0 & 0 & 0 \end{bmatrix}
\begin{bmatrix} \frac{1}{C_2 s} & 0 & 0 & 0 \\ 0 & R_3 & 0 & 0 \\ 0 & 0 & R_4 & 0 \\ 0 & 0 & 0 & L_5 s \end{bmatrix}
\begin{bmatrix} I_2(s) \\ I_3(s) \\ I_4(s) \\ I_5(s) \end{bmatrix}
$$

$$
+ \begin{bmatrix} 0 \\ 0 \\ 1 \end{bmatrix} [V_6(s)] =
\begin{bmatrix} \frac{1}{s} v_2(0+) \\ L_5 i_5(0+) \\ -\frac{1}{s} v_2(0+) \end{bmatrix}. \tag{2.78}
$$

The next step is the substitution of the cut-set equations into (2.78). These equations are

$$
\begin{bmatrix} 1 & 0 & 0 & 0 & 1 & 1 \\ 0 & 1 & 0 & 1 & 0 & -1 \\ 0 & 0 & 1 & -1 & -1 & 0 \end{bmatrix}
\begin{bmatrix} I_1(s) \\ I_2(s) \\ I_3(s) \\ I_4(s) \\ I_5(s) \\ I_6(s) \end{bmatrix} =
\begin{bmatrix} 0 \\ 0 \\ 0 \end{bmatrix}. \tag{2.12}
$$

We rewrite (2.12) as

$$
\begin{bmatrix} I_1(s) \\ I_2(s) \\ I_3(s) \end{bmatrix} =
\begin{bmatrix} 0 & -1 & -1 \\ -1 & 0 & 1 \\ 1 & 1 & 0 \end{bmatrix}
\begin{bmatrix} I_4(s) \\ I_5(s) \\ I_6(s) \end{bmatrix}, \tag{2.79}
$$

and the last two of these equations are

$$
\begin{bmatrix} I_2(s) \\ I_3(s) \end{bmatrix} =
\begin{bmatrix} -1 & 0 & 1 \\ 1 & 1 & 0 \end{bmatrix}
\begin{bmatrix} I_4(s) \\ I_5(s) \\ I_6(s) \end{bmatrix}. \tag{2.80}
$$

Finally, noting that

$$
\begin{bmatrix} I_4(s) \\ I_5(s) \end{bmatrix} =
\begin{bmatrix} 1 & 0 & 0 \\ 0 & 1 & 0 \end{bmatrix}
\begin{bmatrix} I_4(s) \\ I_5(s) \\ I_6(s) \end{bmatrix}, \tag{2.81}
$$

we have

$$
\begin{bmatrix} I_2(s) \\ I_3(s) \\ I_4(s) \\ I_5(s) \end{bmatrix} =
\begin{bmatrix} -1 & 0 & 1 \\ 1 & 1 & 0 \\ 1 & 0 & 0 \\ 0 & 1 & 0 \end{bmatrix}
\begin{bmatrix} I_4(s) \\ I_5(s) \\ I_6(s) \end{bmatrix}. \tag{2.82}
$$

We may easily substitute (2.82) into (2.78). The result is

$$
\begin{bmatrix} 0 \\ -1 \\ -1 \end{bmatrix} [V_1(s)] +
\begin{bmatrix} -1 & 1 & 1 & 0 \\ 0 & 1 & 0 & 1 \\ 1 & 0 & 0 & 0 \end{bmatrix}
\begin{bmatrix} \frac{1}{C_2 s} & 0 & 0 & 0 \\ 0 & R_3 & 0 & 0 \\ 0 & 0 & R_4 & 0 \\ 0 & 0 & 0 & L_5 s \end{bmatrix}
\begin{bmatrix} -1 & 0 & 1 \\ 1 & 1 & 0 \\ 1 & 0 & 0 \\ 0 & 1 & 0 \end{bmatrix}
\begin{bmatrix} I_4(s) \\ I_5(s) \\ I_6(s) \end{bmatrix}
+ \begin{bmatrix} 0 \\ 0 \\ 1 \end{bmatrix} [V_6(s)] =
\begin{bmatrix} \frac{1}{s} v_2(0+) \\ L_5 i_5(0+) \\ -\frac{1}{s} v_2(0+) \end{bmatrix},
$$

$$
\tag{2.83}
$$

and (2.83) is the set of *chord equations* which we have sought. Note that here we have a matrix triple product similar to that which occurs in the branch equations; the third matrix is the transpose of the first. This means that it is unnecessary to write the cut-set equations explicitly in order to obtain the chord equations. Furthermore, in this case, the coefficient matrix of the terminal equations is symmetric, so that we can expect that the matrix triple product will also be symmetric. When we evaluate this triple product, we obtain

$$
\begin{bmatrix} 0 \\ -1 \\ -1 \end{bmatrix} [V_1(s)] +
\begin{bmatrix} R_3 + R_4 + (1/C_2 s) & R_3 & -1/C_2 s \\ R_3 & R_3 + L_5 s & 0 \\ -1/C_2 s & 0 & 1/C_2 s \end{bmatrix}
\begin{bmatrix} I_4(s) \\ I_5(s) \\ I_6(s) \end{bmatrix}
$$

$$
+ \begin{bmatrix} 0 \\ 0 \\ 1 \end{bmatrix} [V_6(s)] =
\begin{bmatrix} \dfrac{1}{s} v_2(0+) \\ L_5 i_5(0+) \\ -\dfrac{1}{s} v_2(0+) \end{bmatrix}. \qquad (2.84)
$$

The unknowns in (2.84) are $I_4(s)$, $I_5(s)$, and $V_6(s)$. However, we can solve the first two equations of this set for $I_4(s)$, $I_5(s)$, since $V_6(s)$ appears only in the third equation. These two equations may be written as

$$
\begin{bmatrix} R_3 + R_4 + (1/C_2 s) & R_3 \\ R_3 & R_3 + L_5 s \end{bmatrix}
\begin{bmatrix} I_4(s) \\ I_5(s) \end{bmatrix} =
\begin{bmatrix} 1/C_2 s \\ 0 \end{bmatrix} [I_6(s)] +
\begin{bmatrix} 0 \\ 1 \end{bmatrix} [V_1(s)]
$$

$$
+ \begin{bmatrix} \dfrac{1}{s} v_2(0+) \\ L_5 i_5(0+) \end{bmatrix}. \qquad (2.85)
$$

When $I_4(s)$ and $I_5(s)$ are found from (2.85), we may obtain $I_1(s)$, $I_2(s)$, $I_3(s)$ from (2.79) by a simple substitution. After this, we obtain $V_2(s)$, $V_3(s)$, $V_4(s)$, and $V_5(s)$ by substituting in (2.75) and $V_6(s)$ from the last equation of (2.11).

If we choose to avoid using matrices in the formulation, the results are very similar to those in the branch formulation. We first write the fundamental circuit equations:

$$
\begin{aligned}
-V_2(s) + V_3(s) + V_4(s) &= 0, \\
-V_1(s) + V_3(s) + V_5(s) &= 0, \\
-V_1(s) + V_2(s) + V_6(s) &= 0,
\end{aligned} \qquad (2.29)
$$

and the terminal relations

$$
\begin{aligned}
V_2(s) &= \frac{1}{C_2 s} I_2(s) + \frac{1}{s} v_2(0+), \\
V_3(s) &= R_3 I_3(s), \\
V_4(s) &= R_4 I_4(s), \\
V_5(s) &= L_5 s I_5(s) - L_5 i_5(0+).
\end{aligned} \qquad (2.86)
$$

We substitute (2.86) into (2.29), and eliminate all voltages except those corresponding to voltage or current drivers. The result is

$$-\frac{1}{C_2 s} I_2(s) + R_3 I_3(s) + R_4 I_4(s) = \frac{1}{s} v_2(0+),$$

$$-V_1(s) + R_3 I_3(s) + L_5 s I_5(s) = L_5 i_5(0+),$$ (2.87)

$$-V_1(s) + \frac{1}{C_2 s} I_2(s) + V_6(s) = -\frac{1}{s} v_2(0+),$$

which is equivalent to Eqs. (2.78). We now use the cut-set equations

$$I_1(s) + I_5(s) + I_6(s) = 0,$$
$$I_2(s) + I_4(s) - I_6(s) = 0,$$ (2.30)
$$I_3(s) - I_4(s) - I_5(s) = 0$$

to eliminate the branch currents which appear in (2.87). This results in

$$\left(\frac{1}{C_2 s} + R_3 + R_4\right) I_4(s) + R_3 I_5(s) = \frac{1}{C_2 s} I_6(s) + \frac{1}{s} v_2(0+),$$

$$R_3 I_4(s) + (L_5 s + R_3) I_5(s) = V_1(s) + L_5 i_5(0+),$$ (2.88)

$$-\frac{1}{C_2 s} I_4(s) + V_6(s) = V_1(s) - \frac{1}{C_2 s} I_6(s) - \frac{1}{s} v_2(0+),$$

which are the chord equations equivalent to Eqs. (2.83) or (2.84). It is necessary to solve only the first two of these equations in order to obtain all the variables by substitutions into the original network relations.

2.7. SYMBOLIC FORMULATION FOR THE CHORD EQUATIONS

In the following symbolic analysis we will place the chord formulation on a more general footing. We first write the fundamental circuit equations with respect to a suitable formulation forest for a given network:

$$[B \quad U] \begin{bmatrix} V_b(s) \\ V_c(s) \end{bmatrix} = [0].$$ (2.89)

As in the symbolic formulation for the branch equations, it is convenient here to partition the matrices in (2.89) further, and we accordingly write

$$\begin{bmatrix} B_{11} & B_{12} & U & 0 \\ B_{21} & B_{22} & 0 & U \end{bmatrix} \begin{bmatrix} V_{bd}(s) \\ V_{b2}(s) \\ V_{c1}(s) \\ V_{cd}(s) \end{bmatrix} = \begin{bmatrix} 0 \\ 0 \end{bmatrix},$$ (2.90)

which may be rearranged into the form

$$\begin{bmatrix} B_{11} \\ B_{21} \end{bmatrix} [V_{bd}(s)] + \begin{bmatrix} B_{12} & U \\ B_{22} & 0 \end{bmatrix} \begin{bmatrix} V_{b2}(s) \\ V_{c1}(s) \end{bmatrix} + \begin{bmatrix} 0 \\ U \end{bmatrix} [V_{cd}(s)] = \begin{bmatrix} 0 \\ 0 \end{bmatrix}.$$ (2.91)

To proceed further, we must be able to obtain the terminal relations, for those elements that do not have the voltage or current specified, in a form which shows the voltages explicitly in terms of the curents.   Thus we write the terminal equations as

$$[V_{bd}(s)] = [F_1(s)] \quad \text{(specified)},$$
$$[I_{cd}(s)] = [F_2(s)] \quad \text{(specified)},$$

(2.39)

$$\begin{bmatrix} V_{b2}(s) \\ V_{c1}(s) \end{bmatrix} = \begin{bmatrix} Z_{11}(s) & Z_{12}(s) \\ Z_{21}(s) & Z_{22}(s) \end{bmatrix} \begin{bmatrix} I_{b2}(s) \\ I_{c1}(s) \end{bmatrix} + \begin{bmatrix} F_1(s, 0+) \\ F_2(s, 0+) \end{bmatrix}.$$

(2.92)

$[F_1(s, 0+)]$, $[F_2(s, 0+)]$ are known matrices depending on the initial values of some of the currents and voltages.

When it is possible to obtain such a form for the terminal equations, we can substitute (2.92) into (2.91) to obtain

$$\begin{bmatrix} B_{11} \\ B_{21} \end{bmatrix} [V_{bd}(s)] + \begin{bmatrix} B_{12} & U \\ B_{22} & 0 \end{bmatrix} \begin{bmatrix} Z_{11}(s) & Z_{12}(s) \\ Z_{21}(s) & Z_{22}(s) \end{bmatrix} \begin{bmatrix} I_{b2}(s) \\ I_{c1}(s) \end{bmatrix}$$
$$+ \begin{bmatrix} 0 \\ U \end{bmatrix} [V_{cd}(s)] = - \begin{bmatrix} B_{12} & U \\ B_{22} & 0 \end{bmatrix} \begin{bmatrix} F_1(s, 0+) \\ F_2(s, 0+) \end{bmatrix}.$$

(2.93)

We now intend to substitute the cut-set equations into (2.93). It is quite easy to show that we can obtain these in the form

$$\begin{bmatrix} I_{b2}(s) \\ I_{c1}(s) \end{bmatrix} = \begin{bmatrix} -A_{21} & -A_{22} \\ U & 0 \end{bmatrix} \begin{bmatrix} I_{c1}(s) \\ I_{cd}(s) \end{bmatrix}.$$

(2.94)

This is suitable for substitution into (2.93) and the result is

$$\begin{bmatrix} B_{11} \\ B_{21} \end{bmatrix} [V_{bd}(s)] + \begin{bmatrix} B_{12} & U \\ B_{22} & 0 \end{bmatrix} \begin{bmatrix} Z_{11}(s) & Z_{12}(s) \\ Z_{21}(s) & Z_{22}(s) \end{bmatrix} \begin{bmatrix} -A_{21} & -A_{22} \\ U & 0 \end{bmatrix} \begin{bmatrix} I_{c1}(s) \\ I_{cd}(s) \end{bmatrix}$$
$$+ \begin{bmatrix} 0 \\ U \end{bmatrix} [V_{cd}(s)] = - \begin{bmatrix} B_{12} & U \\ B_{22} & 0 \end{bmatrix} \begin{bmatrix} F_1(s, 0+) \\ F_2(s, 0+) \end{bmatrix}.$$

(2.95)

We recall the relation between the fundamental circuit and the cut-set matrices [expression (2.48)], which allows us to write

$$-[A_{21}] = [B'_{12}], \qquad -[A_{22}] = [B'_{22}],$$

(2.96)

so that (2.95) becomes

$$\begin{bmatrix} B_{11} \\ B_{21} \end{bmatrix} [V_{bd}(s)] + \begin{bmatrix} B_{12} & U \\ B_{22} & 0 \end{bmatrix} \begin{bmatrix} Z_{11}(s) & Z_{12}(s) \\ Z_{21}(s) & Z_{22}(s) \end{bmatrix} \begin{bmatrix} B'_{12} & B'_{22} \\ U & 0 \end{bmatrix} \begin{bmatrix} I_{c1}(s) \\ I_{cd}(s) \end{bmatrix}$$
$$+ \begin{bmatrix} 0 \\ U \end{bmatrix} [V_{cd}(s)] = - \begin{bmatrix} B_{12} & U \\ B_{12} & 0 \end{bmatrix} \begin{bmatrix} F_1(s, 0+) \\ F_2(s, 0+) \end{bmatrix}.$$

(2.97)

Expression (2.97) is the set of equations which we call the *chord equations*.   As expected, it contains a matrix triple product such that the third matrix is the transpose of the first. The properties of this triple product are therefore such that it is unnecessary to write down the cut-set equations explicitly, and we note the fact that if the coefficient matrix of the terminal equations is symmetric, so will be the triple product itself.

The unknowns in the chord equations consist of $[I_{c1}(s)]$ and $[V_{cd}(s)]$. However, because of the zero matrix which premultiplies $[V_{cd}(s)]$, we are able to divide (2.97) into two sets of equations, the first of which is

$$[B_{11}][V_{bd}(s)] + [B_{12} \quad U] \begin{bmatrix} Z_{11}(s) & Z_{12}(s) \\ Z_{21}(s) & Z_{22}(s) \end{bmatrix} \begin{bmatrix} B'_{12} & B'_{22} \\ U & 0 \end{bmatrix} \begin{bmatrix} I_{c1}(s) \\ I_{cd}(s) \end{bmatrix} = -[B_{12} \quad U] \begin{bmatrix} F_1(s, 0+) \\ F_2(s, 0+) \end{bmatrix}$$

(2.98)

or

$$[B_{12} \quad U] \begin{bmatrix} Z_{11}(s) & Z_{12}(s) \\ Z_{21}(s) & Z_{22}(s) \end{bmatrix} \begin{bmatrix} B'_{12} \\ U \end{bmatrix} [I_{c1}(s)]$$

$$= -[B_{12} \quad U] \left\{ \begin{bmatrix} Z_{11}(s) & Z_{12}(s) \\ Z_{21}(s) & Z_{22}(s) \end{bmatrix} \begin{bmatrix} B'_{22} \\ 0 \end{bmatrix} [I_{cd}(s)] + \begin{bmatrix} F_1(s, 0+) \\ F_2(s, 0+) \end{bmatrix} \right\} - [B_{11}][V_{bd}(s)].$$

(2.99)

It is evident that the unknowns in (2.99) are the entries in $[I_{c1}(s)]$. The number of these unknowns is equal to that of the chords less that of the specified chord currents. Now, if there are e elements, v vertices, p connected parts, n_I specified chord currents, this number is $(e - v + p - n_I)$. Thus, the number of equations to be solved simultaneously when the chord equations are used is $(e - v + p - n_I)$.

Once the chord equations have been solved for $[I_{c1}(s)]$, we may obtain the branch currents by direct substitution into the cut-set equations:

$$\begin{bmatrix} I_{bd}(s) \\ I_{b2}(s) \end{bmatrix} = \begin{bmatrix} -A_{11} & -A_{12} \\ -A_{21} & -A_{22} \end{bmatrix} \begin{bmatrix} I_{c1}(s) \\ I_{cd}(s) \end{bmatrix}.$$

(2.100)

Next, we can substitute for $[I_{b2}(s)]$, $[I_{c1}(s)]$ into the terminal equations (2.92), and obtain $[V_{b2}(s)]$, $[V_{c1}(s)]$. Finally, $[V_{cd}(s)]$ is found by substitution in the fundamental circuit equations:

$$[V_{cd}(s)] = [-B_{21} \quad -B_{22}] \begin{bmatrix} V_{bd}(s) \\ V_{b2}(s) \end{bmatrix}.$$

(2.101)

EXAMPLE 2.5. In this example we shall obtain the chord equations for the simple transistor network of Fig. 2.2, which is repeated here for convenience (Fig. 2.4). For this network, we rewrite the terminal equations (2.55) in the form

$$\begin{bmatrix} v_2(t) \\ v_3(t) \\ v_4(t) \\ v_5(t) \end{bmatrix} = \begin{bmatrix} r_{11} & 0 & r_{12} & 0 \\ 0 & R_3 & 0 & 0 \\ r_{21} & 0 & r_{22} & 0 \\ 0 & 0 & 0 & R_5 \end{bmatrix} \begin{bmatrix} i_2(t) \\ i_3(t) \\ i_4(t) \\ i_5(t) \end{bmatrix},$$

(2.102)

where, for the transistor parameters, we have

$$r_{11} = (h_{11}h_{22} - h_{12}h_{21})/h_{22} = \Delta_h/h_{22}, \qquad r_{12} = h_{12}/h_{22},$$
$$r_{21} = -h_{21}/h_{22}, \qquad r_{22} = 1/h_{22}.$$

(2.103)

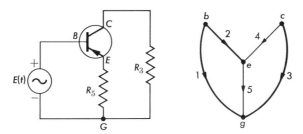

FIG. 2.4. Simple transistor network and system graph.

The fundamental circuit equations are

$$\begin{bmatrix} 1 & -1 & -1 & 1 & 0 \\ -1 & 1 & 0 & 0 & 1 \end{bmatrix} \begin{bmatrix} v_1(t) \\ v_2(t) \\ v_3(t) \\ v_4(t) \\ v_5(t) \end{bmatrix} = 0. \tag{2.104}$$

We rewrite (2.104) and substitute (2.102) into the result. This gives

$$\begin{bmatrix} 1 \\ -1 \end{bmatrix} [v_1(t)] + \begin{bmatrix} -1 & -1 & 1 & 0 \\ 1 & 0 & 0 & 1 \end{bmatrix} \begin{bmatrix} r_{11} & 0 & r_{12} & 0 \\ 0 & R_3 & 0 & 0 \\ r_{21} & 0 & r_{22} & 0 \\ 0 & 0 & 0 & R_5 \end{bmatrix} \begin{bmatrix} i_2(t) \\ i_3(t) \\ i_4(t) \\ i_5(t) \end{bmatrix} = 0. \tag{2.105}$$

Now, substitution of the cut-set equations into (2.105) will give rise to the familiar triple product expression. Thus, we obtain

$$\begin{bmatrix} 1 \\ -1 \end{bmatrix} [v_1(t)] + \begin{bmatrix} -1 & -1 & 1 & 0 \\ 1 & 0 & 0 & 1 \end{bmatrix} \begin{bmatrix} r_{11} & 0 & r_{12} & 0 \\ 0 & R_3 & 0 & 0 \\ r_{21} & 0 & r_{22} & 0 \\ 0 & 0 & 0 & R_5 \end{bmatrix} \begin{bmatrix} -1 & 1 \\ -1 & 0 \\ 1 & 0 \\ 0 & 1 \end{bmatrix} \begin{bmatrix} i_4(t) \\ i_5(t) \end{bmatrix} = 0, \tag{2.106}$$

or

$$\begin{bmatrix} r_{11} - r_{21} + R_3 - r_{12} + r_{22} & -r_{11} + r_{21} \\ -r_{11} + r_{12} & r_{11} + R_5 \end{bmatrix} \begin{bmatrix} i_4(t) \\ i_5(t) \end{bmatrix} = \begin{bmatrix} -1 \\ 1 \end{bmatrix} [v_1(t)], \tag{2.107}$$

which are the chord equations. We leave their formulation without using matrices as an exercise.

It is noteworthy that the chord formulation results in a set of two simultaneous equations in two unknowns, as did the branch formulation for the same example. Thus, we see that for this example, it is of no importance which equations are used for solution. However, since the branch formulation requires us to solve $v - p - n_V$ simultaneous equations, whereas the chord method requires the solution of $e - v + p - n_I$ equations, there will frequently be some advantage in using one or the other technique. We can forecast, *by a glance at the system graph*, which method is the most efficient in any given case.

In summary, the main points of the chord formulation are:

(1) To formulate the chord equations, the terminal relations must be written to express the voltages explicitly in terms of the currents.
(2) The fundamental circuit equations are written in such a way as to facilitate the substitution of the terminal relations.
(3) The terminal relations are substituted into the fundamental circuit equations.
(4) The cut-set equations are used to eliminate all but the chord currents from the result of step 3. The result is the chord equations.
(5) The matrix triple product which premultiplies the column vector of chord currents in the chord equations has the property that the matrix on the right is the transpose of that on the left. This means that we can write the chord equations without explicitly using the cut-set equations.
(6) The number of chord equations is equal to the number of chords, but we need solve simultaneously only those equations which do not contain the unknown voltages across the current drivers. Thus, the number of simultaneous equations to be solved is just $e - v + p - n_I$, where e is the number of elements, v is the number of vertices, p is the number of connected parts in the system graph, and n_I is the number of current drivers.

2.8. BRANCH AND CHORD EQUATIONS IN NETWORKS OF TWO-TERMINAL COMPONENTS

In the foregoing sections we have introduced the general properties of two techniques for the partial solution of electric networks. The methods are applicable for networks whose components have any number of terminals whatsoever, and we have nowhere taken into account the special properties of networks whose components have only two terminals. The subject of these networks has been very thoroughly investigated; it involves almost the complete range of what is usually called electric circuit theory, excluding only those circuits which contain transformers.

Networks whose components have two terminals (RLC networks) have the following outstanding features. First, both the branch formulation and the chord formulation are always applicable for their analysis; second, *the coefficient matrix of the terminal equations* used in their analysis by either the branch or the chord method is a *diagonal matrix* (we regard inductances with mutual inductance as multiterminal components). These properties enable us to reduce the work involved in formulating the branch or chord equations for such networks.

Let us recall that the general form of the branch equation is

$$\begin{bmatrix} U \\ 0 \end{bmatrix} [I_{bd}(s)] + \begin{bmatrix} 0 & A_{11} \\ U & A_{21} \end{bmatrix} \begin{bmatrix} Y_{11}(s) & Y_{12}(s) \\ Y_{21}(s) & Y_{22}(s) \end{bmatrix} \begin{bmatrix} 0 & U \\ A'_{11} & A'_{21} \end{bmatrix} \begin{bmatrix} V_{bd}(s) \\ V_{b2}(s) \end{bmatrix}$$
$$+ \begin{bmatrix} A_{12} \\ A_{22} \end{bmatrix} [I_{cd}(s)] = - \begin{bmatrix} 0 & A_{11} \\ U & A_{21} \end{bmatrix} \begin{bmatrix} F_1(s, 0+) \\ F_2(s, 0+) \end{bmatrix}, \quad (2.50)$$

and that of the chord equation is

$$\begin{bmatrix} B_{11} \\ B_{21} \end{bmatrix} [V_{bd}(s)] + \begin{bmatrix} B_{12} & U \\ B_{22} & 0 \end{bmatrix} \begin{bmatrix} Z_{11}(s) & Z_{12}(s) \\ Z_{21}(s) & Z_{22}(s) \end{bmatrix} \begin{bmatrix} B'_{12} & B'_{22} \\ U & 0 \end{bmatrix} \begin{bmatrix} I_{c1}(s) \\ I_{cd}(s) \end{bmatrix}$$

$$+ \begin{bmatrix} 0 \\ U \end{bmatrix} [V_{cd}] = - \begin{bmatrix} B_{12} & U \\ B_{22} & 0 \end{bmatrix} \begin{bmatrix} F_1(s, 0+) \\ F_2(s, 0+) \end{bmatrix}. \tag{2.97}$$

The most time-consuming part of the formulation of these equations is the calculation of the matrix triple products involved. In both cases, the triple product takes the form $[M][W][M]'$, where the entries in $[M]$ are all ± 1 or 0, and $[W]$ is a diagonal matrix. The following theorem, which we shall not digress to prove here, provides a quick method for evaluating these triple products, and will enable us to shorten the formulation procedures for RLC networks considerably.

Theorem 2.1. Let $[M]$ be a rectangular $p \times n$ matrix with entries $m_{ij} = \pm 1$ or 0, and let every subdeterminant of order 2 in $[M]$ be equal to ± 1 or 0. Furthermore, let $[W]$ be a diagonal matrix of order n, with all $w_{ii} > 0$. Then the entries in the matrix $[X] = [M][W][M]'$ are given by

$$x_{ij} = \sum_{k=1}^{n} m_{ik} m_{jk} w_{kk}. \tag{2.108}$$

Moreover, all the diagonal entries x_{ii} are positive, and every term in the summation (2.108) has the same sign.

It can be shown that the matrices involved in the triple products satisfy all the conditions of Theorem 2.1, and we shall now illustrate through an example how its use leads to a simplification of the formulation techniques.

EXAMPLE 2.6.   Consider the system graph of Fig. 2.5. We shall assume that $V_1(s)$, $V_2(s)$, $I_7(s)$, $I_8(s)$ are specified functions, and that the remaining elements correspond to two-terminal components. The terminal equations may, therefore, be written in either of the two forms:

$$\begin{bmatrix} V_3(s) \\ V_4(s) \\ V_5(s) \\ V_6(s) \end{bmatrix} = \begin{bmatrix} Z_3(s) & 0 & 0 & 0 \\ 0 & Z_4(s) & 0 & 0 \\ 0 & 0 & Z_5(s) & 0 \\ 0 & 0 & 0 & Z_6(s) \end{bmatrix} \begin{bmatrix} I_3(s) \\ I_4(s) \\ I_5(s) \\ I_6(s) \end{bmatrix}, \tag{2.109}$$

$$\begin{bmatrix} I_3(s) \\ I_4(s) \\ I_5(s) \\ I_6(s) \end{bmatrix} = \begin{bmatrix} Y_3(s) & 0 & 0 & 0 \\ 0 & Y_4(s) & 0 & 0 \\ 0 & 0 & Y_5(s) & 0 \\ 0 & 0 & 0 & Y_6(s) \end{bmatrix} \begin{bmatrix} V_3(s) \\ V_4(s) \\ V_5(s) \\ V_6(s) \end{bmatrix}, \tag{2.110}$$

where, for convenience, we have assumed that all the initial condition terms are identically zero. We shall first formulate the chord equations. This involves

Fig. 2.5. A typical system graph: $V_1(s)$, $V_2(s)$ specified; $I_7(s)$, $I_8(s)$ specified.

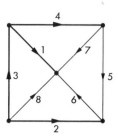

writing the fundamental circuit equations as follows:

$$
\begin{bmatrix} 0 & -1 \\ -1 & 1 \\ -1 & 0 \\ -1 & 0 \end{bmatrix} \begin{bmatrix} V_1(s) \\ V_2(s) \end{bmatrix} + \begin{bmatrix} 1 & 1 & 1 & 0 \\ -1 & 0 & 0 & 1 \\ 0 & 1 & 0 & 0 \\ -1 & 0 & 0 & 0 \end{bmatrix} \begin{bmatrix} V_3(s) \\ V_4(s) \\ V_5(s) \\ V_6(s) \end{bmatrix} + \begin{bmatrix} 0 & 0 \\ 0 & 0 \\ 1 & 0 \\ 0 & 1 \end{bmatrix} \begin{bmatrix} V_7(s) \\ V_8(s) \end{bmatrix} = 0.
$$

$$(2.111)$$

Our next step is the substitution of (2.109) into (2.111). This is followed by the substitution of the cut-set equations, and we obtain the matrix triple product

$$
\begin{bmatrix} 1 & 1 & 1 & 0 \\ -1 & 0 & 0 & 1 \\ 0 & 1 & 0 & 0 \\ -1 & 0 & 0 & 0 \end{bmatrix} \begin{bmatrix} Z_3(s) & 0 & 0 & 0 \\ 0 & Z_4(s) & 0 & 0 \\ 0 & 0 & Z_5(s) & 0 \\ 0 & 0 & 0 & Z_6(s) \end{bmatrix} \begin{bmatrix} 1 & -1 & 0 & -1 \\ 1 & 0 & 1 & 0 \\ 1 & 0 & 0 & 0 \\ 0 & 1 & 0 & 0 \end{bmatrix}.
$$

$$(2.112)$$

The complete product is specified as soon as the entries in the first two matrices are known, so that it is really unnecessary to write this product explicitly. Let us represent the matrix triple product (2.112) by the expression

$$
\begin{array}{cccc} Z_3(s) & Z_4(s) & Z_5(s) & Z_6(s) \end{array}
$$
$$
\begin{bmatrix} 1 & 1 & 1 & 0 \\ -1 & 0 & 0 & 1 \\ 0 & 1 & 0 & 0 \\ -1 & 0 & 0 & 0 \end{bmatrix}
$$

$$(2.113)$$

in which we have written the entries of the coefficient matrix $Z_i(s)$ above the appropriate columns of the first matrix in the triple product. That is, $Z_3(s)$ is above column 1, $Z_4(s)$ above column 2, etc.

Following this notation then, and remembering that the entries in the column matrix which postmultiplies the triple product are the chord currents, we can write directly from (2.111):

$$
\begin{array}{cccc} Z_3(s) & Z_4(s) & Z_5(s) & Z_6(s) \end{array}
$$
$$
\begin{bmatrix} 0 & -1 \\ -1 & 1 \\ -1 & 0 \\ -1 & 0 \end{bmatrix} \begin{bmatrix} V_1(s) \\ V_2(s) \end{bmatrix} + \begin{bmatrix} 1 & 1 & 1 & 0 \\ -1 & 0 & 0 & 1 \\ 0 & 1 & 0 & 0 \\ -1 & 0 & 0 & 0 \end{bmatrix} \begin{bmatrix} I_5(s) \\ I_6(s) \\ I_7(s) \\ I_8(s) \end{bmatrix} + \begin{bmatrix} 0 & 0 \\ 0 & 0 \\ 1 & 0 \\ 0 & 1 \end{bmatrix} \begin{bmatrix} V_7(s) \\ V_8(s) \end{bmatrix} = 0.
$$

$$(2.114)$$

We now use Theorem 2.1 to evaluate the triple product. If we call the resulting matrix $[W(s)]$, we have

$$w_{11}(s) = 1^2 Z_3(s) + 1^2 Z_4(s) + 1^2 Z_5(s),$$
$$w_{22}(s) = (-1)^2 Z_3(s) + 1^2 Z_6(s),$$
$$w_{33}(s) = 1^2 Z_4(s),$$
$$w_{44}(s) = (-1)^2 Z_3(s),$$
$$w_{12}(s) = w_{21}(s) = (-1)(1)Z_3(s),$$
$$w_{13}(s) = w_{31}(s) = (1)(1)Z_4(s),$$
$$w_{14}(s) = w_{41}(s) = (-1)(1)Z_3(s),$$
$$w_{23}(s) = w_{32}(s) = 0,$$
$$w_{24}(s) = w_{42}(s) = (-1)(-1)Z_3(s),$$
$$w_{34}(s) = w_{43}(s) = 0.$$

Thus, (2.114) becomes

$$\begin{bmatrix} 0 & -1 \\ -1 & 1 \\ -1 & 0 \\ -1 & 0 \end{bmatrix} \begin{bmatrix} V_1(s) \\ V_2(s) \end{bmatrix}$$

$$= \begin{bmatrix} Z_3(s) + Z_4(s) + Z_5(s) & -Z_3(s) & Z_4(s) & -Z_3(s) \\ -Z_3(s) & Z_3(s) + Z_6(s) & 0 & Z_3(s) \\ Z_4(s) & 0 & Z_4(s) & 0 \\ -Z_3(s) & Z_3(s) & 0 & Z_3(s) \end{bmatrix} \begin{bmatrix} I_5(s) \\ I_6(s) \\ I_7(s) \\ I_8(s) \end{bmatrix}$$

$$+ \begin{bmatrix} 0 & 0 \\ 0 & 0 \\ 1 & 0 \\ 0 & 1 \end{bmatrix} \begin{bmatrix} V_7(s) \\ V_8(s) \end{bmatrix}. \tag{2.115}$$

Thus, the entries in the ij and ji positions in the matrix triple product are obtained by multiplying the ith row of the first matrix into the jth row, with each term multiplied by the appropriate coefficient in the second matrix of the triple product, and summing. Moreover, our notation (2.113) is such that we write the appropriate coefficients above the entries which they multiply.

We now formulate the branch equations for the network of Fig. 2.5. To do this, we first write the cut-set equations in a form suitable for substitution. This defines the first matrix in the triple product. We can immediately write the final equations in the form (the column matrix which postmultiplies the triple product has the branch voltages for its entries)

$$\begin{bmatrix} 1 & 0 \\ 0 & 1 \\ 0 & 0 \\ 0 & 0 \end{bmatrix} \begin{bmatrix} I_1(s) \\ I_2(s) \end{bmatrix} + \begin{matrix} Y_3(s)\ \ Y_4(s)\ \ Y_5(s)\ \ Y_6(s) \\ \begin{bmatrix} 0 & 0 & 0 & 1 \\ 0 & 0 & 1 & -1 \\ 1 & 0 & -1 & 1 \\ 0 & 1 & -1 & 0 \end{bmatrix} \end{matrix} \begin{bmatrix} V_1(s) \\ V_2(s) \\ V_3(s) \\ V_4(s) \end{bmatrix} + \begin{bmatrix} 1 & 1 \\ 0 & 0 \\ 0 & 1 \\ -1 & 0 \end{bmatrix} \begin{bmatrix} I_7(s) \\ I_8(s) \end{bmatrix} = 0. \tag{2.116}$$

Now, evaluating the triple product by Theorem 2.1 or, equivalently, by the rule mentioned above, we have

$$
\begin{bmatrix} 1 & 0 \\ 0 & 1 \\ 0 & 0 \\ 0 & 0 \end{bmatrix} \begin{bmatrix} I_1(s) \\ I_2(s) \end{bmatrix}
$$

$$
+ \begin{bmatrix} Y_6(s) & -Y_6(s) & Y_6(s) & 0 \\ -Y_6(s) & Y_5(s) + Y_6(s) & -Y_5(s) - Y_6(s) & -Y_5(s) \\ Y_6(s) & -Y_5(s) - Y_6(s) & Y_3(s) + Y_5(s) + Y_6(s) & Y_5(s) \\ 0 & -Y_5(s) & Y_5(s) & Y_4(s) + Y_5(s) \end{bmatrix}
$$

$$
\times \begin{bmatrix} V_1(s) \\ V_2(s) \\ V_3(s) \\ V_4(s) \end{bmatrix} + \begin{bmatrix} 1 & 1 \\ 0 & 0 \\ 0 & 1 \\ -1 & 0 \end{bmatrix} \begin{bmatrix} I_7(s) \\ I_8(s) \end{bmatrix} = 0. \qquad (2.117)
$$

As can be seen from this example, we require only two lines of "work" to write either the branch or chord equations with the matrix triple products fully expanded. In fact, we have written more than we need for this example, since the solution of the network requires only either the first two equations of (2.115) or the last two of (2.117). Although it is a very simple matter, we need not calculate all the entries in the triple products.

It may seem that the above method for formulating the branch or chord equations is very simple, but we can go even further. We shall now demonstrate that it is possible to recognize the entries in the expanded matrix triple products *directly from the system graph*. Thus, since the fundamental circuit and cut-set equations are written by inspection of the system graph, *we are able to formulate the branch and chord equations by an inspection process*.

First, let us consider the entries on the main diagonal of the coefficient matrix of the branch equations for the network of Example 2.6 [expression (2.117)]. These are

$$
\begin{aligned}
w_{11}(s) &= Y_6(s), \\
w_{22}(s) &= Y_5(s) + Y_6(s), \\
w_{33}(s) &= Y_3(s) + Y_5(s) + Y_6(s), \\
w_{44}(s) &= Y_4(s) + Y_5(s).
\end{aligned}
$$

Inspection of the four cut sets corresponding to the tree of Fig. 2.5 shows that the elements included are:

> cut set 1:   elements 6; 1, 7, 8
> cut set 2:   elements 5, 6; 2
> cut set 3:   elements 3, 5, 6; 8
> cut set 4:   elements 4, 5; 7

Direct comparison shows that the entries on the diagonal of the coefficient matrix are the sums of the $Y_i(s)$ corresponding to all the elements of the associated cut sets. Since elements $1, 2, 7, 8$ correspond to voltage and current drivers, there are no coefficients $Y_1(s)$, $Y_2(s)$, $Y_7(s)$, $Y_8(s)$. Hence these are not included. That this is a general property of the main diagonal entries in the coefficient matrix follows directly from Theorem 2.1, as a little reflection will show.

Second, let us observe the off-diagonal elements of this coefficient matrix. Since the coefficient matrix is symmetric, we have $w_{ij} = w_{ji}$, for all i, j. Now in (2.117),

$$
\begin{aligned}
w_{12} &= -Y_6(s), \\
w_{13} &= Y_6(s), \\
w_{14} &= 0, \\
w_{23} &= -[Y_5(s) + Y_6(s)], \\
w_{24} &= -Y_5(s), \\
w_{34} &= Y_5(s),
\end{aligned}
$$

and the elements common to pairs of cut sets are

> cut sets 1, 2:   element 6
> cut sets 1, 3:   elements 6; 8
> cut sets 1, 4:   element 7
> cut sets 2, 3:   elements 5, 6
> cut sets 2, 4:   element 5
> cut sets 3, 4:   element 5

We may, therefore, directly observe that except for the sign, the entry in the ith row and jth column of the coefficient matrix is the sum of the $Y_k(s)$ coefficients for the elements common to cut sets i, j. In these sums, the $Y_k(s)$ are either all positive or all negative. We can decide which sign to use as follows. Let us consider an oriented path passing through the tree and including both elements 1 and 2. We observe that these two elements have opposite orientations with respect to this path, and that w_{12} is negative. Now consider an oriented tree path which includes both elements 1 and 3. Both elements have the same orientation with respect to this path, and w_{13} is positive. We can make similar comparisons for every off-diagonal entry, and generalize our findings; hence we can formulate the following rule (which can be substantiated through Theorem 2.1) for writing all the entries.

Rule 2.1. For networks whose components have two terminals, the entries in the coefficient matrix of the branch equations are as follows:
(a) The entries w_{ii} on the main diagonal are the sums of the $Y_k(s)$ coefficients corresponding to the elements in the ith cut set. If an element of the ith cut set is a voltage or current driver, it is omitted in the summation.
(b) The off-diagonal entries w_{ij} are $\pm$ the sums of the $Y_k(s)$ coefficients corresponding to the elements common to cut sets i, j. Again, elements corresponding to voltage or current drivers are omitted in the summations.
(c) The sign of the off-diagonal entry w_{ij} is positive if the defining branches of cut sets i, j have the same relative orientation with respect to a tree path containing these elements, and negative otherwise.

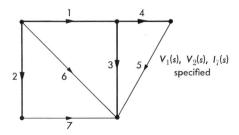

FIG. 2.6. A simple system graph.

EXAMPLE 2.7. Consider the system graph of Fig. 2.6. This represents a network of two-terminal components, and we assume that elements 1 and 2 correspond to voltage drivers, and element 7 to a current driver. We also assume that all the initial voltages and currents are zero. To formulate the branch equations, we write the expression

$$
\begin{bmatrix} 1 & 0 \\ 0 & 1 \\ 0 & 0 \\ 0 & 0 \end{bmatrix} \begin{bmatrix} I_1(s) \\ I_2(s) \end{bmatrix} + \begin{bmatrix} \text{to be} \\ \text{found} \end{bmatrix} \begin{bmatrix} V_1(s) \\ V_2(s) \\ V_3(s) \\ V_4(s) \end{bmatrix} + \begin{bmatrix} 1 \\ -1 \\ 1 \\ 0 \end{bmatrix} [I_7(s)] = 0, \qquad (2.118)
$$

which is obtained by omitting, in the cut-set equations, the matrix product that is not associated with voltage or current drivers. This product is replaced by the matrix of branch voltages and its associated coefficient matrix, which is to be found. To determine the entries in the coefficient matrix we simply use Rule 2.1. This immediately gives

$$
\begin{bmatrix} 1 & 0 \\ 0 & 1 \\ 0 & 0 \\ 0 & 0 \end{bmatrix} \begin{bmatrix} I_1(s) \\ I_2(s) \end{bmatrix} + \begin{bmatrix} Y_6(s) & 0 & Y_6(s) & 0 \\ 0 & 0 & 0 & 0 \\ Y_6(s) & 0 & Y_3(s) + Y_5(s) + Y_6(s) & -Y_5(s) \\ 0 & 0 & -Y_5(s) & Y_4(s) + Y_5(s) \end{bmatrix} \begin{bmatrix} V_1(s) \\ V_2(s) \\ V_3(s) \\ V_4(s) \end{bmatrix}
$$

$$
+ \begin{bmatrix} 1 \\ -1 \\ 1 \\ 0 \end{bmatrix} [I_7(s)] = 0. \qquad (2.119)
$$

Following a line of reasoning which is very similar to that leading to Rule 2.1, we find that the chord equations may be written directly from the system graph. This is done by means of the following rule.

Rule 2.2. For networks whose components have two terminals, the entries in the coefficient matrix of the chord equations are as follows:
(a) The entries w_{ii} on the main diagonal are the sums of the $Z_k(s)$ coefficients corresponding to the elements in the ith fundamental circuit. If an element of the ith fundamental circuit is a voltage or current driver, it is omitted in this summation.

(b) The off-diagonal entries, w_{ij}, are $\pm$ the sums of the $Zk(s)$ coefficients corresponding to the elements common to fundamental circuits i, j. Again elements corresponding to voltage or current drivers are omitted in the summations.

(c) The sign of the off-diagonal entry w_{ij} is positive if the relative orientations of the common parts of the tree paths of fundamental circuits i and j are the same, and negative otherwise.

EXAMPLE 2.8. Here, we shall write the chord equations for the network of Example 2.7. To do this, we use the fundamental circuit equations to write the expression

$$\begin{bmatrix} 0 & 0 \\ -1 & 0 \\ -1 & 1 \end{bmatrix}\begin{bmatrix} V_1(s) \\ V_2(s) \end{bmatrix} + \begin{bmatrix} \text{to be} \\ \text{found} \end{bmatrix}\begin{bmatrix} I_5(s) \\ I_6(s) \\ I_7(s) \end{bmatrix} + \begin{bmatrix} 0 \\ 0 \\ 1 \end{bmatrix}[V_7(s)] = \begin{bmatrix} 0 \\ 0 \\ 0 \end{bmatrix}. \tag{2.120}$$

All that remains is to fill in the coefficient matrix, using Rule 2.2. This gives

$$\begin{bmatrix} 0 & 0 \\ -1 & 0 \\ -1 & 1 \end{bmatrix}\begin{bmatrix} V_1(s) \\ V_2(s) \end{bmatrix} + \begin{bmatrix} Z_3(s)+Z_4(s)+Z_5(s) & Z_3(s) & Z_3(s) \\ Z_3(s) & Z_3(s)+Z_6(s) & Z_3(s) \\ Z_3(s) & Z_3(s) & Z_3(s) \end{bmatrix}\begin{bmatrix} I_5(s) \\ I_6(s) \\ I_7(s) \end{bmatrix}$$
$$+ \begin{bmatrix} 0 \\ 0 \\ 1 \end{bmatrix}[V_7(s)] = \begin{bmatrix} 0 \\ 0 \\ 0 \end{bmatrix}, \tag{2.121}$$

which are the chord equations.

Of course, in Examples 2.7 and 2.8, it is not necessary to write expressions (2.118), (2.120). *The final equations are written directly from the graph.*

It is important for the reader to realize that *the "shortcuts" introduced in this section apply only to networks whose components have but two terminals.* For networks with multiterminal components, we have no option but to calculate the entries in the triple product matrices by the ordinary rules of matrix algebra. In any case, it is more important that one should be aware of the underlying methods than that one should memorize, by rote, the "shortcut" rules.

Finally, we note that there was no compelling need to use matrix notation in obtaining the rules for writing network equations by inspection. However, the derivation and presentation of such rules without this notation requires the same degree of organization as that which occurs naturally when matrices are used. Moreover, our method leads to the most succinct statement of the results. There is, therefore, nothing to be gained by rewording the rules to eliminate reference to matrices.

2.9. THE MESH AND NODE SYSTEMS OF EQUATIONS

Any discussion of the formulation of network equations is incomplete without a mention of what are usually called the *loop* or *mesh system* and the *node system* of equations. These equations have for a long time formed the basis of much of what is in network theory, and hence it is only reasonable that we establish how they are related to the chord and branch equations which we have discussed so far.

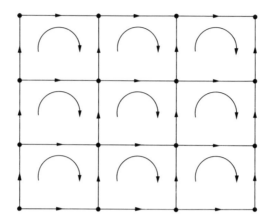

FIG. 2.7. A system graph showing a set of independent circuits
which are not associated with any tree.

The chord equations result from the choice of fundamental circuits. But there
are other criteria which can be established for selecting $e - v + p$ independent
circuits from a system graph. For example, the $e - v + p$ circuits or loops shown
in Fig. 2.7 are independent and form the basis for the loop system of equations.

The criterion for selecting the above circuits is simple. First select a loop. Each
succeeding loop must contain at least one element not contained in the preceding
loops. Note that the circuits of Fig. 2.7 do not form a set of fundamental circuits
of any tree in the graph. In general, there may or may not exist a tree in the graph
for which the loops are also fundamental circuits.

The mesh system of equations is a set of $e - v + p$ linearly independent equations whose unknowns are $e - v + p$ mesh currents defined for each set of $e -
v + p$ independent circuits. The current in any element of a network is the oriented
sum of mesh currents for the circuits which contain the given element. The standard orientation for this sum is the orientation of the element current in question.
Since the unknowns of the mesh equations correspond to a set of independent
circuits, there always exists a nonsingular transformation linking the mesh currents
and the chord currents corresponding to any given forest of the network. As a
special case, when the fundamental circuits are chosen for the circuits of the mesh
system of equations, we have

$$[I_m] = [I_c], \qquad (2.122)$$

and the mesh equations are identical to the chord equations.

There exist rules for writing the mesh system of equations, and these are similar
to Rule 2.2. Here, however, we shall only give a simple example which establishes
the tie between the mesh and chord systems of equations.

EXAMPLE 2.9. For the bridge network and graph of Fig. 2.8, we have designated
three circuits to define corresponding mesh currents I_I, I_{II}, I_{III}.

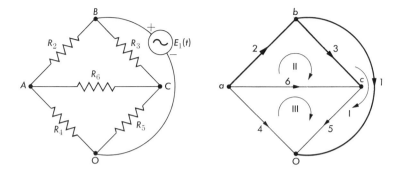

FIG. 2.8. A bridge network and system graph.

In terms of the chord currents $i_4(t)$, $i_5(t)$, and $i_6(t)$, we can write

$$
\begin{bmatrix} i_4(t) \\ i_5(t) \\ i_6(t) \end{bmatrix} = \begin{bmatrix} 0 & 0 & -1 \\ -1 & 0 & 1 \\ 0 & -1 & 1 \end{bmatrix} \begin{bmatrix} I_\mathrm{I}(t) \\ I_\mathrm{II}(t) \\ I_\mathrm{III}(t) \end{bmatrix},
\tag{2.123}
$$

$$
\begin{bmatrix} I_\mathrm{I}(t) \\ I_\mathrm{II}(t) \\ I_\mathrm{III}(t) \end{bmatrix} = \begin{bmatrix} -1 & -1 & 0 \\ -1 & 0 & -1 \\ -1 & 0 & 0 \end{bmatrix} \begin{bmatrix} i_4(t) \\ i_5(t) \\ i_6(t) \end{bmatrix}.
\tag{2.124}
$$

Writing the chord equations, we obtain

$$
\begin{bmatrix} R_2 + R_4 & 0 & R_2 \\ 0 & R_3 + R_5 & -R_3 \\ R_2 & -R_3 & R_2 + R_3 + R_6 \end{bmatrix} \begin{bmatrix} i_4(t) \\ i_5(t) \\ i_6(t) \end{bmatrix} = \begin{bmatrix} 1 \\ 1 \\ 0 \end{bmatrix} [E_1(t)].
\tag{2.125}
$$

To obtain the loop equations, we merely substitute (2.123) into (2.125), and premultiply both sides of the equation by the transpose of the coefficient matrix of (2.123) to obtain symmetry:

$$
\begin{bmatrix} R_3 + R_5 & -R_3 & -R_5 \\ -R_3 & (R_2 + R_3 + R_6) & -R_6 \\ -R_5 & -R_6 & (R_4 + R_5 + R_6) \end{bmatrix} \begin{bmatrix} I_\mathrm{I}(t) \\ I_\mathrm{II}(t) \\ I_\mathrm{III}(t) \end{bmatrix} = \begin{bmatrix} -1 \\ 0 \\ 0 \end{bmatrix} [E_1(t)].
\tag{2.126}
$$

We leave it to the reader to obtain the rule for writing (2.126) directly from the graph, or even more directly, from the network.

The important conclusion is that the mesh and chord equations are related by a nonsingular transformation. The advantage of writing the chord equations in preference to the mesh equations emanates from the fact that the former gives the element variables directly; these are, after all, the quantities in which we are finally interested.

On the other hand, the node system of equations is a set of $v - 1$ linearly independent equations whose unknowns are the voltages of $v - 1$ vertices with respect to the remaining vertex of the system graph corresponding to a given network. The voltages corresponding to the elements of any tree of the system graph can be obtained by a nonsingular transformation from these $v - 1$ node voltages (we assume that the graph has only one part; however, the result can be generalized for a graph with p parts). Thus, when the formulation tree is such that every branch is incident on and directed toward a single node (a *Lagrangian tree*), and when the node voltages are taken with respect to this node (datum node), we have

$$[V_m] = [V_b], \tag{2.127}$$

and the node equations are identical to the branch equations.

We shall not investigate the general rules for writing the node system of equations for reasons similar to those which we mentioned in the case of the mesh equations. We therefore conclude our discussion of these equations with the following examples.

EXAMPLE 2.10. For the network and graph of Fig. 2.8, the node voltages with respect to node O are $v_{ao}(t)$, $v_{bo}(t)$, $v_{co}(t)$. In terms of the branch voltages $v_1(t)$, $v_2(t)$, $v_3(t)$, we have

$$\begin{bmatrix} v_1(t) \\ v_2(t) \\ v_3(t) \end{bmatrix} = \begin{bmatrix} 0 & 1 & 0 \\ 1 & -1 & 0 \\ 0 & 1 & -1 \end{bmatrix} \begin{bmatrix} v_{ao}(t) \\ v_{bo}(t) \\ v_{co}(t) \end{bmatrix}, \tag{2.128}$$

or

$$\begin{bmatrix} v_{ao}(t) \\ v_{bo}(t) \\ v_{co}(t) \end{bmatrix} = \begin{bmatrix} 1 & 1 & 0 \\ 1 & 0 & 0 \\ 1 & 0 & -1 \end{bmatrix} \begin{bmatrix} v_1(t) \\ v_2(t) \\ v_3(t) \end{bmatrix}. \tag{2.129}$$

When we write the branch equations, we have

$$\begin{bmatrix} 1 \\ 0 \\ 0 \end{bmatrix} [i_1(t)] + \begin{bmatrix} G_4 + G_5 & G_4 & -G_5 \\ G_4 & G_2 + G_4 + G_6 & G_6 \\ -G_5 & G_6 & G_3 + G_5 + G_6 \end{bmatrix} \begin{bmatrix} v_1(t) \\ v_2(t) \\ v_3(t) \end{bmatrix} = 0. \tag{2.130}$$

Substituting (2.128) into (2.130), we obtain

$$\begin{bmatrix} 1 \\ 0 \\ 0 \end{bmatrix} [i_1(t)] + \begin{bmatrix} G_4 & 0 & G_5 \\ G_2 + G_4 + G_6 & -G_2 & -G_6 \\ G_6 & G_3 & -(G_3 + G_5 + G_6) \end{bmatrix} \begin{bmatrix} v_{ao}(t) \\ v_{bo}(t) \\ v_{co}(t) \end{bmatrix} = 0. \tag{2.131}$$

Premultiplying by the transpose of the coefficient matrix of (2.128) and noting that

$$v_{bo}(t) = E_1(t), \tag{2.132}$$

we have

$$\begin{bmatrix} G_2 + G_4 + G_6 & -G_6 \\ -G_2 & -G_3 \\ -G_6 & G_3 + G_5 + G_6 \end{bmatrix} \begin{bmatrix} v_{ao} \\ v_{co} \end{bmatrix} = \begin{bmatrix} G_2 \\ -(G_2 + G_3) \\ G_3 \end{bmatrix} [E_1(t)] - \begin{bmatrix} 0 \\ 1 \\ 0 \end{bmatrix} [i_1(t)]. \tag{2.133}$$

Now, we extract the first and third equations of (2.133), so that

$$\begin{bmatrix} G_2 + G_4 + G_6 & -G_6 \\ -G_6 & G_3 + G_5 + G_6 \end{bmatrix} \begin{bmatrix} v_{ao} \\ v_{co} \end{bmatrix} = \begin{bmatrix} G_2 \\ G_3 \end{bmatrix} [E_1(t)]. \tag{2.134}$$

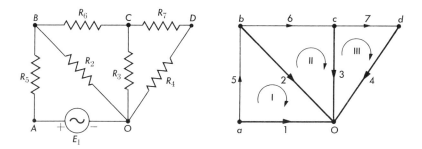

Fig. 2.9. Network and system graph for Example 2.11.

Equations (2.134) are called the node equations. Again, the conclusion is that the branch equations and node equations are related by a nonsingular transformation.

Example 2.11. For the simple network of Fig. 2.9, we define mesh currents as indicated, and the node voltages $v_{ao}(t)$, $v_{bo}(t)$, $v_{co}(t)$, $v_{do}(t)$. Here we have

$$
\begin{aligned}
v_{ao}(t) &= v_1(t), & v_{co}(t) &= v_3(t), & I_I(t) &= i_5(t), & I_{III}(t) &= i_7(t). \\
v_{bo}(t) &= v_2(t), & v_{do}(t) &= v_4(t), & I_{II}(t) &= i_6(t),
\end{aligned}
$$

Thus, for the particular choice of tree (a Lagrangian tree) and for the particular element orientations as shown in the graph, the chord equations are identical to the mesh equations, and the branch equations are identical to the node equations.

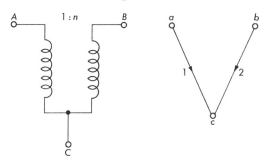

Fig. 2.10. Ideal transformer and terminal graph.

2.10. THE BRANCH-CHORD FORMULATION TECHNIQUE

So far we have discussed two formulation techniques which effect a partial solution for electric networks. Each of these requires that the terminal relations be written in a special way; in the branch technique we need the equations showing the currents explicitly in terms of the voltages, whereas in the chord method the voltages should be expressed explicitly in terms of the currents. However, it is not always possible to obtain the terminal equations in either form. Consider the terminal relations for an ideal transformer (Fig. 2.10). These are

$$
\begin{bmatrix} v_2 \\ i_1 \end{bmatrix} - \begin{bmatrix} 0 & n \\ -n & 0 \end{bmatrix} \begin{bmatrix} i_2 \\ v_1 \end{bmatrix}.
\tag{2.135}
$$

It is impossible to rewrite these equations in either of the explicit forms required for the branch and chord techniques. Therefore, when such devices are included in a network, we must use another method, the branch-chord formulation.

There is one extra restriction which arises in networks containing ideal transformers. Reference to Eqs. (2.135) shows that specification of v_2 and i_1 automatically specifies i_2 and v_1, and conversely. However, we know that the chord voltages are linear combinations of the branch voltages, and the branch currents are linear combinations of the chord currents. Therefore, we must be able to choose a formulation forest such that in Fig. 2.10, either element 1 or element 2 is a branch, but not both. If we cannot choose such a forest, we shall find that some of the voltages and currents are doubly specified, so that there may not be a solution to the network.

Bearing this factor in mind, we shall now illustrate the branch-chord formulation technique with an example.

EXAMPLE 2.12. Let us consider the simple network of Fig. 2.11, which contains an ideal transformer and a vacuum tube. Note that we pick the formulation tree so that element 1 is a chord and element 2 is a branch. This satisfies the restriction mentioned above. Also, element 4 is picked as a chord, since the terminal equations for the vacuum tube specify that $I_4(s)$ is equal to zero. Furthermore, element 6 represents the parallel RC cathode circuit. The terminal equations for this network can easily be written in the form

$$
\begin{bmatrix}
1 & 0 & 0 & 0 & 0 & 0 & 0 & 0 & 0 \\
0 & 1 & 0 & 0 & 0 & 0 & 0 & -n & 0 \\
0 & 0 & C_6 s + G_6 & 0 & 0 & 0 & 0 & 0 & 0 \\
0 & 0 & 0 & C_8 s & 0 & 0 & 0 & 0 & 0 \\
0 & 0 & 0 & 0 & G_9 & 0 & 0 & 0 & 0 \\
0 & 0 & 0 & 0 & 0 & g_p & 0 & 0 & g_m \\
0 & 0 & 0 & 0 & 0 & 0 & G_7 & 0 & 0 \\
0 & 0 & 0 & 0 & 0 & 0 & 0 & 0 & 0 \\
0 & 0 & 0 & 0 & 0 & 0 & 0 & 0 & 0
\end{bmatrix}
\begin{bmatrix}
V_3(s) \\ V_2(s) \\ V_6(s) \\ V_8(s) \\ V_9(s) \\ V_5(s) \\ V_7(s) \\ V_1(s) \\ V_4(s)
\end{bmatrix}
$$

$$
=
\begin{bmatrix}
0 & 0 & 0 & 0 & 0 & 0 & 0 & 0 & 0 \\
0 & 0 & 0 & 0 & 0 & 0 & 0 & 0 & 0 \\
0 & 0 & 1 & 0 & 0 & 0 & 0 & 0 & 0 \\
0 & 0 & 0 & 1 & 0 & 0 & 0 & 0 & 0 \\
0 & 0 & 0 & 0 & 1 & 0 & 0 & 0 & 0 \\
0 & 0 & 0 & 0 & 0 & 1 & 0 & 0 & 0 \\
0 & 0 & 0 & 0 & 0 & 0 & 1 & 0 & 0 \\
0 & n & 0 & 0 & 0 & 0 & 0 & 1 & 0 \\
0 & 0 & 0 & 0 & 0 & 0 & 0 & 0 & 1
\end{bmatrix}
\begin{bmatrix}
I_3(s) \\ I_2(s) \\ I_6(s) \\ I_8(s) \\ I_9(s) \\ I_5(s) \\ I_7(s) \\ I_1(s) \\ I_4(s)
\end{bmatrix}
+
\begin{bmatrix}
E(s) \\ 0 \\ C_6 v_6(0+) \\ C_8 v_8(0+) \\ 0 \\ 0 \\ 0 \\ 0 \\ 0
\end{bmatrix},
$$

$$(2.136)$$

where the terminal equation for the parallel RC cathode network is given by the third equation,

$$(C_6 s + G_6) V_6(s) = I_6(s) + C_6 v_6(0+).$$

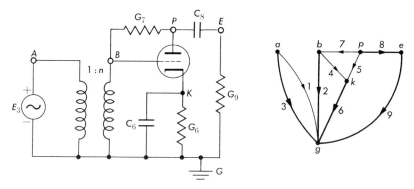

Fɪɢ. 2.11. A simple network and system graph.

For this network, the cut-set and fundamental circuit equations are

$$
\begin{bmatrix} I_3(s) \\ I_2(s) \\ I_6(s) \\ I_8(s) \\ I_9(s) \end{bmatrix} =
\begin{bmatrix} 0 & 0 & -1 & 0 \\ 0 & 1 & 0 & -1 \\ 1 & 0 & 0 & 1 \\ -1 & -1 & 0 & 0 \\ -1 & -1 & 0 & 0 \end{bmatrix}
\begin{bmatrix} I_5(s) \\ I_7(s) \\ I_1(s) \\ I_4(s) \end{bmatrix} ;
\tag{2.137}
$$

$$
\begin{bmatrix} V_5(s) \\ V_7(s) \\ V_1(s) \\ V_4(s) \end{bmatrix} =
\begin{bmatrix} 0 & 0 & -1 & 1 & 1 \\ 0 & -1 & 0 & 1 & 1 \\ 1 & 0 & 0 & 0 & 0 \\ 0 & 1 & -1 & 0 & 0 \end{bmatrix}
\begin{bmatrix} V_3(s) \\ V_2(s) \\ V_6(s) \\ V_8(s) \\ V_9(s) \end{bmatrix} .
\tag{2.138}
$$

Our first step is the rearrangement of (2.137) and (2.138) into a suitable form for substitution into (2.136). This gives

$$
\begin{bmatrix} I_3(s) \\ I_2(s) \\ I_6(s) \\ I_8(s) \\ I_9(s) \\ I_5(s) \\ I_7(s) \\ I_1(s) \\ I_4(s) \end{bmatrix} =
\begin{bmatrix} 0 & 0 & -1 & 0 \\ 0 & 1 & 0 & -1 \\ 1 & 0 & 0 & 1 \\ -1 & -1 & 0 & 0 \\ -1 & -1 & 0 & 0 \\ 1 & 0 & 0 & 0 \\ 0 & 1 & 0 & 0 \\ 0 & 0 & 1 & 0 \\ 0 & 0 & 0 & 1 \end{bmatrix}
\begin{bmatrix} I_5(s) \\ I_7(s) \\ I_1(s) \\ I_4(s) \end{bmatrix} ;
\tag{2.139}
$$

$$
\begin{bmatrix} V_3(s) \\ V_2(s) \\ V_6(s) \\ V_8(s) \\ V_9(s) \\ V_5(s) \\ V_7(s) \\ V_1(s) \\ V_4(s) \end{bmatrix} =
\begin{bmatrix} 1 & 0 & 0 & 0 & 0 \\ 0 & 1 & 0 & 0 & 0 \\ 0 & 0 & 1 & 0 & 0 \\ 0 & 0 & 0 & 1 & 0 \\ 0 & 0 & 0 & 0 & 1 \\ 0 & 0 & -1 & 1 & 1 \\ 0 & -1 & 0 & 1 & 1 \\ 1 & 0 & 0 & 0 & 0 \\ 0 & 1 & -1 & 0 & 0 \end{bmatrix}
\begin{bmatrix} V_3(s) \\ V_2(s) \\ V_6(s) \\ V_8(s) \\ V_9(s) \end{bmatrix} .
\tag{2.140}
$$

Substituting (2.139) and (2.140) into (2.136), we obtain

$$
\begin{bmatrix}
1 & 0 & 0 & 0 & 0 & 0 & 0 & 0 & 0 \\
0 & 1 & 0 & 0 & 0 & 0 & 0 & -n & 0 \\
0 & 0 & C_6 s + G_6 & 0 & 0 & 0 & 0 & 0 & 0 \\
0 & 0 & 0 & C_8 s & 0 & 0 & 0 & 0 & 0 \\
0 & 0 & 0 & 0 & G_9 & 0 & 0 & 0 & 0 \\
0 & 0 & 0 & 0 & 0 & g_p & 0 & 0 & g_m \\
0 & 0 & 0 & 0 & 0 & 0 & G_7 & 0 & 0 \\
0 & 0 & 0 & 0 & 0 & 0 & 0 & 0 & 0 \\
0 & 0 & 0 & 0 & 0 & 0 & 0 & 0 & 0
\end{bmatrix}
\begin{bmatrix}
1 & 0 & 0 & 0 & 0 \\
0 & 1 & 0 & 0 & 0 \\
0 & 0 & 1 & 0 & 0 \\
0 & 0 & 0 & 1 & 0 \\
0 & 0 & 0 & 0 & 1 \\
0 & 0 & -1 & 1 & 1 \\
0 & -1 & 0 & 1 & 1 \\
1 & 0 & 0 & 0 & 0 \\
0 & 1 & -1 & 0 & 0
\end{bmatrix}
\begin{bmatrix}
V_3(s) \\
V_2(s) \\
V_6(s) \\
V_8(s) \\
V_9(s)
\end{bmatrix}
$$

$$
=
\begin{bmatrix}
0 & 0 & 0 & 0 & 0 & 0 & 0 & 0 & 0 \\
0 & 0 & 0 & 0 & 0 & 0 & 0 & 0 & 0 \\
0 & 0 & 1 & 0 & 0 & 0 & 0 & 0 & 0 \\
0 & 0 & 0 & 1 & 0 & 0 & 0 & 0 & 0 \\
0 & 0 & 0 & 0 & 1 & 0 & 0 & 0 & 0 \\
0 & 0 & 0 & 0 & 0 & 1 & 0 & 0 & 0 \\
0 & 0 & 0 & 0 & 0 & 0 & 1 & 0 & 0 \\
0 & n & 0 & 0 & 0 & 0 & 0 & 1 & 0 \\
0 & 0 & 0 & 0 & 0 & 0 & 0 & 0 & 1
\end{bmatrix}
\begin{bmatrix}
0 & 0 & -1 & 0 \\
0 & 1 & 0 & -1 \\
1 & 0 & 0 & 1 \\
-1 & -1 & 0 & 0 \\
-1 & -1 & 0 & 0 \\
1 & 0 & 0 & 0 \\
0 & 1 & 0 & 0 \\
0 & 0 & 1 & 0 \\
0 & 0 & 0 & 1
\end{bmatrix}
\begin{bmatrix}
I_5(s) \\
I_7(s) \\
I_1(s) \\
I_4(s)
\end{bmatrix}
+
\begin{bmatrix}
E(s) \\
0 \\
C_6 v_6(0+) \\
C_8 v_8(0+) \\
0 \\
0 \\
0 \\
0 \\
0
\end{bmatrix},
$$

$$(2.141)$$

and, performing the indicated multiplications, we find that (2.141) reduces to

$$
\begin{bmatrix}
1 & 0 & 0 & 0 & 0 \\
-n & 1 & 0 & 0 & 0 \\
0 & 0 & C_6 s + G_6 & 0 & 0 \\
0 & 0 & 0 & C_8 s & 0 \\
0 & 0 & 0 & 0 & G_9 \\
0 & g_m & -(g_p + g_m) & g_p & g_p \\
0 & -G_7 & 0 & G_7 & G_7 \\
0 & 0 & 0 & 0 & 0 \\
0 & 0 & 0 & 0 & 0
\end{bmatrix}
\begin{bmatrix}
V_3(s) \\
V_2(s) \\
V_6(s) \\
V_8(s) \\
V_9(s)
\end{bmatrix}
$$

$$
=
\begin{bmatrix}
0 & 0 & 0 & 0 \\
0 & 0 & 0 & 0 \\
1 & 0 & 0 & 1 \\
-1 & -1 & 0 & 0 \\
-1 & -1 & 0 & 0 \\
1 & 0 & 0 & 0 \\
0 & 1 & 0 & 0 \\
0 & n & 1 & -n \\
0 & 0 & 0 & 1
\end{bmatrix}
\begin{bmatrix}
I_5(s) \\
I_7(s) \\
I_1(s) \\
I_4(s)
\end{bmatrix}
+
\begin{bmatrix}
E(s) \\
0 \\
C_6 v_6(0+) \\
C_8 v_8(0+) \\
0 \\
0 \\
0 \\
0 \\
0
\end{bmatrix}.
$$

$$(2.142)$$

Now (2.142) is a set of nine equations whose variables are the branch voltages and chord currents. Since the first equation is merely

$$V_3(s) = E(s), \qquad (2.143)$$

and the last,

$$I_4(s) = 0, \qquad (2.144)$$

we can easily reduce (2.142) to

$$
\begin{bmatrix}
1 & 0 & 0 & 0 \\
0 & C_6s + G_6 & 0 & 0 \\
0 & 0 & C_8s & 0 \\
0 & 0 & 0 & G_9 \\
g_m & -(g_m + g_p) & g_p & g_p \\
-G_7 & 0 & G_7 & G_7 \\
0 & 0 & 0 & 0
\end{bmatrix}
\begin{bmatrix}
V_2(s) \\
V_6(s) \\
V_8(s) \\
V_9(s)
\end{bmatrix}
=
\begin{bmatrix}
0 & 0 & 0 \\
1 & 0 & 0 \\
-1 & -1 & 0 \\
-1 & -1 & 0 \\
1 & 0 & 0 \\
0 & 1 & 0 \\
0 & n & 1
\end{bmatrix}
\begin{bmatrix}
I_5(s) \\
I_7(s) \\
I_1(s)
\end{bmatrix}
+
\begin{bmatrix}
nE(s) \\
C_6v_6(0+) \\
C_8v_8(0+) \\
0 \\
0 \\
0 \\
0
\end{bmatrix},
$$

$$(2.145)$$

or, placing all the unknowns on the left-hand side, we have

$$
\begin{bmatrix}
1 & 0 & 0 & 0 & 0 & 0 & 0 \\
0 & C_6s + G_6 & 0 & 0 & -1 & 0 & 0 \\
0 & 0 & C_8s & 0 & 1 & 1 & 0 \\
0 & 0 & 0 & G_9 & 1 & 1 & 0 \\
g_m & -(g_m + g_p) & g_p & g_p & -1 & 0 & 0 \\
-G_7 & 0 & G_7 & G_7 & 0 & -1 & 0 \\
0 & 0 & 0 & 0 & 0 & -n & -1
\end{bmatrix}
\begin{bmatrix}
V_2(s) \\
V_6(s) \\
V_8(s) \\
V_9(s) \\
I_5(s) \\
I_7(s) \\
I_1(s)
\end{bmatrix}
=
\begin{bmatrix}
nE(s) \\
C_6v_6(0+) \\
C_8v_8(0+) \\
0 \\
0 \\
0 \\
0
\end{bmatrix}.
\qquad (2.146)
$$

Equations (2.146) are the *branch-chord equations*. It can be seen that there are as many equations in this set as there are nonspecified branch voltages and non-specified chord currents.

The matrix method used in this example indicates clearly the substitution procedures involved in the branch-chord formulation. However, because of the high proportion of zero entries in the matrices that appear, some time can be saved, in this case, when matrix notation is not used. Equations (2.136) are readily written as

$$
\begin{aligned}
&V_3(s) = E(s), \qquad V_2(s) - nV_1(s) = 0, \\
&(C_6s + G_6)V_6(s) = I_6(s) + C_6v_6(0+), \\
&C_8sV_8(s) = I_8(s) + C_8v_8(0+), \qquad\qquad\qquad (2.147) \\
&G_9V_9(s) = I_9(s), \qquad g_pV_5(s) + g_mV_4(s) = I_5(s), \\
&G_7V_7(s) = I_7(s), \qquad 0 = nI_2(s) + I_1(s), \qquad 0 = I_4(s),
\end{aligned}
$$

where we have grouped the voltages on the left-hand side, and the currents, specified functions, and initial condition terms on the right-hand side. The fundamental circuit equations (2.138) take the form

$$
\begin{aligned}
V_5(s) &= -V_6(s) + V_8(s) + V_9(s), \\
V_7(s) &= -V_2(s) + V_8(s) + V_9(s), \qquad\qquad (2.148) \\
V_1(s) &= V_3(s), \qquad V_4(s) = V_2(s) - V_6(s),
\end{aligned}
$$

and the cut-set equations (2.137) are

$$
\begin{aligned}
I_3(s) &= -I_1(s), \\
I_2(s) &= I_7(s) - I_4(s), \\
I_6(s) &= I_5(s) + I_4(s), \\
I_8(s) &= -I_5(s) - I_7(s), \\
I_9(s) &= -I_5(s) - I_7(s).
\end{aligned}
\tag{2.149}
$$

Equations (2.148) express the chord voltages in terms of the branch voltages, while Eqs. (2.149) show the branch currents in terms of the chord currents. Hence, we can eliminate the chord voltages and branch currents by substituting (2.148) into the left-hand side of (2.147) and (2.149) into the right-hand side of the same equations. The result, equivalent to Eqs. (2.141) or (2.142), is

$$
\begin{aligned}
V_3(s) &= E(s), \\
-nV_3(s) + V_2(s) &= 0, \\
(C_6 s + G_6)V_6(s) &= I_5(s) + I_4(s) + C_6 v_6(0+), \\
C_8 s V_8(s) &= -I_5(s) - I_7(s) + C_8 v_8(0+), \\
G_9 V_9(s) &= -I_5(s) - I_7(s), \\
g_m V_2(s) - (g_p + g_m)V_6(s) + g_p V_8(s) + g_p V_9(s) &= I_5(s), \\
-G_7 V_2(s) + G_7 V_8(s) + G_7 V_9(s) &= I_7(s), \\
0 &= nI_7(s) + I_1(s) - nI_4(s), \\
0 &= I_4(s).
\end{aligned}
\tag{2.150}
$$

We eliminate $V_3(s)$ and $I_4(s)$ by using the first and last of these equations, and obtain

$$
\begin{aligned}
V_2(s) &= nE(s), \\
(C_6 s + G_6)V_6(s) - I_5(s) &= C_6 v_6(0+), \\
C_8 s V_8(s) + I_5(s) + I_7(s) &= C_8 v_8(0+), \\
G_9 V_9(s) + I_5(s) + I_7(s) &= 0, \\
g_m V_2(s) - (g_m + g_p)V_6(s) + g_p V_8(s) + g_p V_9(s) - I_5(s) &= 0, \\
-G_7 V_2(s) + G_7 V_8(s) + G_7 V_9(s) - I_7(s) &= 0, \\
-nI_7(s) - I_1(s) &= 0,
\end{aligned}
\tag{2.151}
$$

which are the same equations as (2.146), the branch-chord equations.

There is an alternative method for arriving at the branch-chord equations. This arises because we can write the terminal relations in a slightly different way. In Example 2.12 we arranged the terminal equations so that all the voltages appeared on one side, and the currents on the other. Another way of writing these equations is to express the chord currents and branch voltages explicitly in terms of the branch currents and chord voltages. We illustrate the formulation technique for this case in Example 2.13.

EXAMPLE 2.13. Here we shall find the branch-chord equations for the same network as Example 2.12, starting with the terminal equations written in the form which follows:

$$
\begin{bmatrix} V_3(s) \\ V_2(s) \\ V_6(s) \\ V_8(s) \\ V_9(s) \\ I_5(s) \\ I_7(s) \\ I_1(s) \\ I_4(s) \end{bmatrix}
=
\begin{bmatrix}
0 & 0 & 0 & 0 & 0 & 0 & 0 & 0 & 0 \\
0 & 0 & 0 & 0 & 0 & 0 & 0 & n & 0 \\
0 & 0 & \dfrac{1}{C_6 s + G_6} & 0 & 0 & 0 & 0 & 0 & 0 \\
0 & 0 & 0 & \dfrac{1}{C_8 s} & 0 & 0 & 0 & 0 & 0 \\
0 & 0 & 0 & 0 & R_9 & 0 & 0 & 0 & 0 \\
0 & 0 & 0 & 0 & 0 & g_p & 0 & 0 & g_m \\
0 & 0 & 0 & 0 & 0 & 0 & G_7 & 0 & 0 \\
0 & -n & 0 & 0 & 0 & 0 & 0 & 0 & 0 \\
0 & 0 & 0 & 0 & 0 & 0 & 0 & 0 & 0
\end{bmatrix}
\begin{bmatrix} I_3(s) \\ I_2(s) \\ I_6(s) \\ I_8(s) \\ I_9(s) \\ V_5(s) \\ V_7(s) \\ V_1(s) \\ V_4(s) \end{bmatrix}
+
\begin{bmatrix} E(s) \\ 0 \\ \dfrac{C_6 v_6(0+)}{C_6 s + G_6} \\ \dfrac{1}{s} v_8(0+) \\ 0 \\ 0 \\ 0 \\ 0 \\ 0 \end{bmatrix} ,
$$

$$(2.152)$$

in which the branch voltages and chord currents are shown as explicit functions of the remaining variables. In this case, it is convenient to write the cut-set and circuit equations together as one set, as follows (from Eqs. 2.137 and 2.138):

$$
\begin{bmatrix} I_3(s) \\ I_2(s) \\ I_6(s) \\ I_8(s) \\ I_9(s) \\ V_5(s) \\ V_7(s) \\ V_1(s) \\ V_4(s) \end{bmatrix}
=
\begin{bmatrix}
0 & 0 & 0 & 0 & 0 & 0 & 0 & -1 & 0 \\
0 & 0 & 0 & 0 & 0 & 0 & 1 & 0 & -1 \\
0 & 0 & 0 & 0 & 0 & 1 & 0 & 0 & 1 \\
0 & 0 & 0 & 0 & 0 & -1 & -1 & 0 & 0 \\
0 & 0 & 0 & 0 & 0 & -1 & -1 & 0 & 0 \\
0 & 0 & -1 & 1 & 1 & 0 & 0 & 0 & 0 \\
0 & -1 & 0 & 1 & 1 & 0 & 0 & 0 & 0 \\
1 & 0 & 0 & 0 & 0 & 0 & 0 & 0 & 0 \\
0 & 1 & -1 & 0 & 0 & 0 & 0 & 0 & 0
\end{bmatrix}
\begin{bmatrix} V_3(s) \\ V_2(s) \\ V_6(s) \\ V_8(s) \\ V_9(s) \\ I_5(s) \\ I_7(s) \\ I_1(s) \\ I_4(s) \end{bmatrix} .
$$

$$(2.153)$$

Substituting (2.153) into (2.152), we obtain

$$
\begin{bmatrix} V_3(s) \\ V_2(s) \\ V_6(s) \\ V_8(s) \\ V_9(s) \\ I_5(s) \\ I_7(s) \\ I_1(s) \\ I_4(s) \end{bmatrix}
=
\begin{bmatrix}
0 & 0 & 0 & 0 & 0 & 0 & 0 & 0 & 0 \\
0 & 0 & 0 & 0 & 0 & 0 & 0 & n & 0 \\
0 & 0 & \dfrac{1}{C_6 s + G_6} & 0 & 0 & 0 & 0 & 0 & 0 \\
0 & 0 & 0 & \dfrac{1}{C_8 s} & 0 & 0 & 0 & 0 & 0 \\
0 & 0 & 0 & 0 & R_9 & 0 & 0 & 0 & 0 \\
0 & 0 & 0 & 0 & 0 & g_p & 0 & 0 & g_m \\
0 & 0 & 0 & 0 & 0 & 0 & G_7 & 0 & 0 \\
0 & -n & 0 & 0 & 0 & 0 & 0 & 0 & 0 \\
0 & 0 & 0 & 0 & 0 & 0 & 0 & 0 & 0
\end{bmatrix}
$$

$$
\times
\begin{bmatrix}
0 & 0 & 0 & 0 & 0 & 0 & 0 & -1 & 0 \\
0 & 0 & 0 & 0 & 0 & 0 & 1 & 0 & -1 \\
0 & 0 & 0 & 0 & 0 & 1 & 0 & 0 & 1 \\
0 & 0 & 0 & 0 & 0 & -1 & -1 & 0 & 0 \\
0 & 0 & 0 & 0 & 0 & -1 & -1 & 0 & 0 \\
0 & 0 & -1 & 1 & 1 & 0 & 0 & 0 & 0 \\
0 & -1 & 0 & 1 & 1 & 0 & 0 & 0 & 0 \\
1 & 0 & 0 & 0 & 0 & 0 & 0 & 0 & 0 \\
0 & 1 & -1 & 0 & 0 & 0 & 0 & 0 & 0
\end{bmatrix}
\begin{bmatrix} V_3(s) \\ V_2(s) \\ V_6(s) \\ V_8(s) \\ V_9(s) \\ I_5(s) \\ I_7(s) \\ I_1(s) \\ I_4(s) \end{bmatrix}
+
\begin{bmatrix} E(s) \\ 0 \\ \dfrac{C_6 v_6(0+)}{C_6 s + G_6} \\ \dfrac{1}{s} v_8(0+) \\ 0 \\ 0 \\ 0 \\ 0 \\ 0 \end{bmatrix} ,
$$

$$(2.154)$$

or

$$
\begin{bmatrix} V_3(s) \\ V_2(s) \\ V_6(s) \\ V_8(s) \\ V_9(s) \\ I_5(s) \\ I_7(s) \\ I_1(s) \\ I_4(s) \end{bmatrix} =
\begin{bmatrix}
0 & 0 & 0 & 0 & 0 & 0 & 0 & 0 & 0 \\
n & 0 & 0 & 0 & 0 & 0 & 0 & 0 & 0 \\
0 & 0 & 0 & 0 & 0 & \dfrac{1}{C_6 s + G_6} & 0 & 0 & \dfrac{1}{C_6 s + G_6} \\
0 & 0 & 0 & 0 & 0 & \dfrac{-1}{C_8 s} & \dfrac{-1}{C_8 s} & 0 & 0 \\
0 & 0 & 0 & 0 & 0 & -R_9 & -R_9 & 0 & 0 \\
0 & g_m & -(g_m + g_p) & g_p & g_p & 0 & 0 & 0 & 0 \\
0 & -G_7 & 0 & G_7 & G_7 & 0 & 0 & 0 & 0 \\
0 & 0 & 0 & 0 & 0 & 0 & -n & 0 & n \\
0 & 0 & 0 & 0 & 0 & 0 & 0 & 0 & 0
\end{bmatrix}
\begin{bmatrix} V_3(s) \\ V_2(s) \\ V_6(s) \\ V_8(s) \\ V_9(s) \\ I_5(s) \\ I_7(s) \\ I_1(s) \\ I_4(s) \end{bmatrix}
$$

$$
+ \begin{bmatrix} E(s) \\ 0 \\ \dfrac{C_6 v_6(0+)}{C_6 s + G_6} \\ \dfrac{1}{s} v_8(0+) \\ 0 \\ 0 \\ 0 \\ 0 \\ 0 \end{bmatrix}. \qquad (2.155)
$$

Now the column matrices of variables in (2.155) are identical, so we may simplify these equations to read

$$
\begin{bmatrix}
1 & 0 & 0 & 0 & 0 & 0 & 0 & 0 & 0 \\
-n & 1 & 0 & 0 & 0 & 0 & 0 & 0 & 0 \\
0 & 0 & 1 & 0 & 0 & \dfrac{-1}{C_6 s + G_6} & 0 & 0 & \dfrac{-1}{C_6 s + G_6} \\
0 & 0 & 0 & 1 & 0 & \dfrac{1}{C_8 s} & \dfrac{1}{C_8 s} & 0 & 0 \\
0 & 0 & 0 & 0 & 1 & R_9 & R_9 & 0 & 0 \\
0 & -g_m & (g_m + g_p) & -g_p & -g_p & 1 & 0 & 0 & 0 \\
0 & G_7 & 0 & -G_7 & -G_7 & 0 & 1 & 0 & 0 \\
0 & 0 & 0 & 0 & 0 & 0 & n & 1 & -n \\
0 & 0 & 0 & 0 & 0 & 0 & 0 & 0 & 1
\end{bmatrix}
\begin{bmatrix} V_3(s) \\ V_2(s) \\ V_6(s) \\ V_8(s) \\ V_9(s) \\ I_5(s) \\ I_7(s) \\ I_1(s) \\ I_4(s) \end{bmatrix}
$$

$$
= \begin{bmatrix} E(s) \\ 0 \\ \dfrac{C_6 v_6(0+)}{C_6 s + G_6} \\ \dfrac{1}{s} v_8(0+) \\ 0 \\ 0 \\ 0 \\ 0 \\ 0 \end{bmatrix}, \qquad (2.156)
$$

and, since $I_4(s)$ is zero, and $V_3(s) = E(s)$, we finally obtain

$$
\begin{bmatrix}
1 & 0 & 0 & 0 & 0 & 0 & 0 \\
0 & 1 & 0 & 0 & \dfrac{-1}{C_6 s + G_6} & 0 & 0 \\
0 & 0 & 1 & 0 & \dfrac{1}{C_8 s} & \dfrac{1}{C_8 s} & 0 \\
0 & 0 & 0 & 1 & R_9 & R_9 & 0 \\
-g_m & (g_m + g_p) & -g_p & -g_p & 1 & 0 & 0 \\
G_7 & 0 & -G_7 & -G_7 & 0 & 1 & 0 \\
0 & 0 & 0 & 0 & 0 & n & 1
\end{bmatrix}
\begin{bmatrix}
V_2(s) \\
V_6(s) \\
V_8(s) \\
V_9(s) \\
I_5(s) \\
I_7(s) \\
I_1(s)
\end{bmatrix}
=
\begin{bmatrix}
nE(s) \\
\dfrac{C_6 v_6(0+)}{C_6 s + G_6} \\
\dfrac{1}{s} v_8(0+) \\
0 \\
0 \\
0 \\
0
\end{bmatrix},
$$

$$(2.157)$$

which are essentially the same equations as (2.146) or (2.151). Again, the solution is somewhat shorter when we dispense with matrices. Equations (2.152) become

$$
\begin{aligned}
&V_3(s) = E(s), \qquad V_2(s) = nV_1(s), \\
&V_6(s) = \frac{I_6(s)}{C_6 s + G_6} + \frac{C_6 v_6(0+)}{C_6 s + G_6}, \\
&V_8(s) = \frac{I_8(s)}{C_8 s} + \frac{v_8(0+)}{s}, \qquad V_9(s) = R_9 I_9(s), \\
&I_5(s) = g_p V_5(s) + g_m V_4(s), \\
&I_7(s) = G_7 V_7(s), \qquad I_1(s) = -nI_2(s), \qquad I_4(s) = 0.
\end{aligned}
$$

$$(2.158)$$

The fundamental circuit and cut-set equations (2.148) and (2.149) are substituted into the right-hand side of (2.158). This immediately yields

$$
\begin{aligned}
&V_2(s) = nE(s), \\
&V_6(s) - \frac{I_5(s)}{C_6 s + G_6} = \frac{C_6 v_6(0+)}{C_6 s + G_6}, \\
&V_8(s) + \frac{I_5(s)}{C_8 s} + \frac{I_7(s)}{C_8 s} = \frac{v_8(0+)}{s}, \\
&V_9(s) + R_9 I_5(s) + R_9 I_7(s) = 0, \\
&-g_m V_2(s) + (g_m + g_p) V_6(s) - g_p V_8(s) - g_p V_9(s) + I_5(s) = 0, \\
&G_7 V_2(s) - G_7 V_8(s) - G_7 V_9(s) + I_7(s) = 0, \\
&nI_7(s) + I_1(s) = 0,
\end{aligned}
$$

$$(2.159)$$

which are again the branch-chord equations.

There is no particular advantage in using either of the substitution procedures; one chooses the method only by the convenience of writing the terminal equations in the form of (2.136) or (2.147) or in the form of (2.152) or (2.158).

We leave the symbolic formulation of the branch-chord equations as an exercise. We only state here that the branch-chord technique can be applied to any network, and that the number of simultaneous equations to be solved when this method is used is equal to the number of elements in the system graph, less the number of specified voltages and currents. Also, once the branch-chord equations are solved, the chord voltages and branch currents can easily be found by substitution into the circuit and cut-set equations.

2.11. THE RELATIVE MERITS OF THE FORMULATION TECHNIQUES

In the previous sections we developed the branch, chord, and branch-chord formulation techniques. In each case it is possible to predict the number of simultaneous equations that must be solved. For a network whose graph contains v vertices, e elements, p connected parts, n_V voltage drivers, and n_I current drivers, these numbers are shown in Table 2.2. This table shows that the number of branch-chord equations is equal to the sum of the numbers of chord equations and branch equations for any particular network. Thus, there is usually *much more labor involved* in the analysis of a network by the branch-chord method than by either of the others. Furthermore, we can tell at the outset of our analysis which of the techniques will lead to the smallest number of equations.

TABLE 2.2

Formulation technique	Number of simultaneous equations
Branch	$v - p - n_V$
Chord	$e - v + p - n_I$
Branch-Chord	$e - n_V - n_I$

Because of these facts, it might be thought that there is little point in developing the branch-chord technique. However, there are cases in which we have little or no choice. For example, we have seen that the terminal equations for ideal transformers *cannot* be arranged in a suitable form for either the branch or the chord techniques, so that the branch-chord method must be used. Similarly, the equations for the transistor are most conveniently obtained in the hybrid form (2.55); since $h_{22} \sim 5 \times 10^{-5}$ for many transistors, and the product $h_{22}v_2 \sim 0$, as a first approximation we might take $h_{22} = 0$. Under these circumstances, we cannot apply the chord technique for transistor circuits. Finally, because of the form of the small-signal equations for a vacuum tube, it is impossible to apply the chord method directly for circuits including these devices.

We are thus left with the fact that we must occasionally use the branch-chord method. However, when there is a choice, it is always better to use either the branch or the chord formulation, and inspection of the system graph will inform us as to which of these two is more efficient.

PROBLEMS

2.1. For each of the networks in Fig. 2.12 write the system graph and find a forest which contains all the voltage drivers and no current drivers.

2.2. Formulate the branch equations for the networks of Fig. 2.12.

2.3. Complete the detailed solution for all the voltages and currents of Example 2.3.

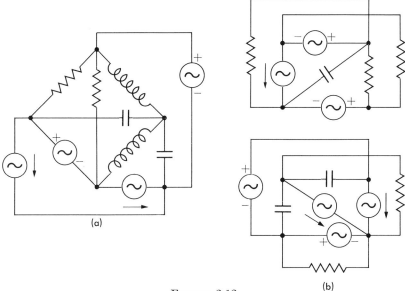

(a)

FIGURE 2.12

(b)

2.4 Formulate the branch equations for the network of Fig. 2.13.

2.5 For each of the networks of Fig. 2.14 state the number of equations that need to be solved when the branch method is used.

2.6. Without using matrix notation, formulate the chord equations for the network of Fig. 2.4.

2.7. Formulate the chord equations for the networks of Fig. 2.12.

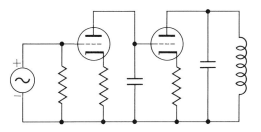

FIGURE 2.13

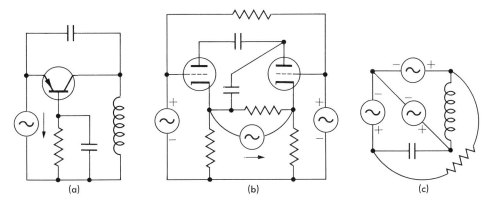

(a)   (b)   (c)

FIGURE 2.14

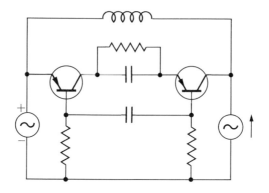

FIGURE 2.15

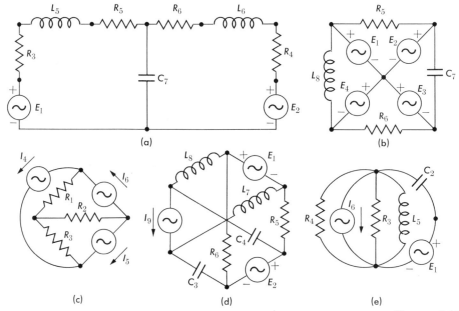

FIGURE 2.16

2.8. Complete the details of the solution for all the voltages and currents in Example 2.5. Verify that your answers agree with your solution of Problem 2.3.

2.9. Formulate the chord equations for the network of Fig. 2.15.

2.10. For each of the networks of Fig. 2.14, state the number of equations that need to be solved when the chord method is used.

2.11. For the networks of Fig. 2.14, formulate the set of network equations which will lead to the most efficient solution.

2.12. Prove the following theorem:

If A is a rectangular $m \times n$ matrix, and B is a symmetric square matrix of order n, then $W = ABA'$ is a symmetric matrix.

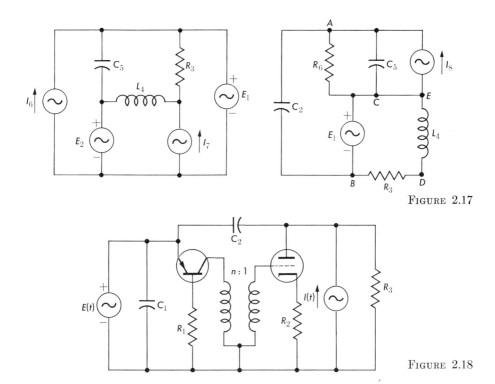

FIGURE 2.17

FIGURE 2.18

2.13. Formulate the branch and chord equations for each of the networks of Fig. 2.16 by inspection.

2.14. For the networks of Fig. 2.17, which formulation method will lead to the most efficient solution? Write, by inspection, the equations corresponding to this technique.

2.15. Assume that the terminal equations for an arbitrary network are $[V_{bd}(s)] = [F_1(s)]$, $[I_{cd}(s)] = [F_2(s)]$,

$$\begin{bmatrix} V_{b2}(s) \\ I_{c1}(s) \end{bmatrix} = \begin{bmatrix} H_{11}(s) & H_{12}(s) \\ H_{21}(s) & H_{22}(s) \end{bmatrix} \begin{bmatrix} I_{b2}(s) \\ V_{c1}(s) \end{bmatrix} + \begin{bmatrix} F_1(s, 0+) \\ F_2(s, 0+) \end{bmatrix}.$$

Give a symbolic derivation of the branch-chord equations.

2.16. Assume that the terminal equations for an arbitrary network are $[V_{bd}(s)] = [F_1(s)]$, $[I_{cd}(s)] = [F_2(s)]$,

$$\begin{bmatrix} Y_{11}(s) & Y_{12}(s) \\ Y_{21}(s) & Y_{22}(s) \end{bmatrix} \begin{bmatrix} V_{b2}(s) \\ V_{c1}(s) \end{bmatrix} = \begin{bmatrix} Z_{11}(s) & Z_{12}(s) \\ Z_{21}(s) & Z_{22}(s) \end{bmatrix} \begin{bmatrix} I_{b2}(s) \\ I_{c1}(s) \end{bmatrix} + \begin{bmatrix} F_1(s, 0+) \\ F_2(s, 0+) \end{bmatrix}.$$

Give a symbolic derivation of the branch-chord equations.

2.17. Formulate a set of branch-chord equations for the network of Fig. 2.18. Write the terminal equations for the vacuum tube and transistor in the hybrid form.

Chapter 3

ANALYTICAL SOLUTIONS OF THE NETWORK EQUATIONS

In Chapter 2 we developed methods for formulating sets of equations which characterize electric networks. In this chapter, we shall show how these equations may be solved analytically, and derive some of the useful properties and techniques connected with their solutions. As we previously mentioned, it is not necessary to use Laplace transform methods in the formulation of the network equations; there is likewise no compelling need for the use of such methods in their solutions. Indeed, Laplace transform techniques are conspicuously absent from the Russian literature. However, two considerations justify the Laplace method. The first, which we have already encountered, is that linear integro-differential equations are thereby converted into linear algebraic equations. The second, and more important consideration, is that almost the whole theory of network synthesis is based on the properties of the network functions which appear when this method is used. We shall assume in this chapter that the reader is equipped with all the basic knowledge of Laplace transforms contained in Appendix A.

3.1. GENERAL SOLUTIONS TO THE NETWORK EQUATIONS

In order to put our developments into a proper perspective, we begin this chapter with a symbolic treatment of a general set of network equations. To do this, we first recall from Chapter 2 the general form of the branch equations as a representative of the three formulation procedures. This general symbolic form is

$$[U \quad A_{21}] \begin{bmatrix} Y_{11}(s) & Y_{12}(s) \\ Y_{21}(s) & Y_{22}(s) \end{bmatrix} \begin{bmatrix} U \\ A'_{21} \end{bmatrix} [V_{b2}(s)]$$

$$= -[U \quad A_{21}] \begin{bmatrix} Y_{11}(s) & Y_{12}(s) \\ Y_{21}(s) & Y_{22}(s) \end{bmatrix} \begin{bmatrix} 0 \\ A'_{11} \end{bmatrix} [V_{bd}(s)]$$

$$-[A_{22}][I_{cd}(s)] - [U \quad A_{21}] \begin{bmatrix} F_1(s, 0+) \\ F_2(s, 0+) \end{bmatrix}. \tag{2.52}$$

If we calculate the matrix products in the coefficients, (2.52) may be reduced to

$$[W_b(s)][V_{b2}(s)] = [M(s)][V_{bd}(s)] - [A_{22}][I_{cd}(s)] + [F(s, 0+)], \tag{3.1}$$

76

where

$$[W_b(s)] = [U \quad A_{21}] \begin{bmatrix} Y_{11}(s) & Y_{12}(s) \\ Y_{21}(s) & Y_{22}(s) \end{bmatrix} \begin{bmatrix} U \\ A'_{21} \end{bmatrix}, \tag{3.2}$$

$$[M(s)] = -[U \quad A_{21}] \begin{bmatrix} Y_{11}(s) & Y_{12}(s) \\ Y_{21}(s) & Y_{22}(s) \end{bmatrix} \begin{bmatrix} 0 \\ A'_{11} \end{bmatrix}, \tag{3.3}$$

$$[F(s, 0+)] = -[U \quad A_{21}] \begin{bmatrix} F_1(s, 0+) \\ F_2(s, 0+) \end{bmatrix}, \tag{3.4}$$

and $[W_b(s)]$, $[M(s)]$, $[A_{22}]$, and $[F(s, 0+)]$ are all known matrices. Since $[V_{bd}(s)]$ and $[I_{cd}(s)]$ are column matrices of specified functions, let us write

$$[M(s)][V_{bd}(s)] - [A_{22}][I_{cd}(s)] = [F(s)], \tag{3.5}$$

and $[F(s)]$ will itself be a column matrix of specified functions. Also $[F(s, 0+)]$ depends only on the initial values of some of the voltages and currents in the network. We have therefore reduced the branch equations to the form

$$[W_b(s)][V_{b2}(s)] = [F(s)] + [F(s, 0+)], \tag{3.6}$$

where the right-hand side consists of two terms; the first depends on the voltage and current drivers, and the second on the initial conditions in the network.

Clearly, by a similar line of reasoning the chord equations can be written as

$$[W_c(s)][I_{c1}(s)] = [F(s)] + [F(s, 0+)], \tag{3.7}$$

where

$$[W_c(s)] = [B_{12} \quad U] \begin{bmatrix} Z_{11}(s) & Z_{12}(s) \\ Z_{21}(s) & Z_{22}(s) \end{bmatrix} \begin{bmatrix} B'_{12} \\ U \end{bmatrix}. \tag{3.8}$$

The branch-chord equations can also be reduced to a similar form. Therefore, in general, we must solve sets of equations which appear as

$$[W(s)][X(s)] = [F(s)] + [F(s, 0+)], \tag{3.9}$$

where

$[W(s)]$ is a known coefficient matrix,
$[F(s)]$ is a column matrix of specified functions,
$[F(s, 0+)]$ is a column matrix of initial conditions, and
$[X(s)]$ is a column matrix of unknowns. This may contain branch voltages or chord currents or, in the case of the branch-chord equations, both branch voltages and chord currents.

EXAMPLE 3.1. Consider the branch equations obtained in Example 2.1:

$$\begin{bmatrix} G_4 + C_2 s & -G_4 \\ -G_4 & G_3 + G_4 + \dfrac{1}{L_5 s} \end{bmatrix} \begin{bmatrix} V_2(s) \\ V_3(s) \end{bmatrix} = \begin{bmatrix} 1 \\ 0 \end{bmatrix} [I_6(s)] + \begin{bmatrix} 0 \\ \dfrac{1}{L_5 s} \end{bmatrix} [V_1(s)] + \begin{bmatrix} C_2 v_2(0+) \\ \dfrac{1}{s} i_5(0+) \end{bmatrix}. \tag{2.27}$$

These are immediately put into the same form as Eqs. (3.9) by combining the first two terms on the right. We obtain

$$
\begin{bmatrix} G_4 + C_2 s & -G_4 \\ -G_4 & G_3 + G_4 + \dfrac{1}{L_5 s} \end{bmatrix} \begin{bmatrix} V_2(s) \\ V_3(s) \end{bmatrix} = \begin{bmatrix} I_6(s) \\ \dfrac{1}{L_5 s} V_1(s) \end{bmatrix} + \begin{bmatrix} C_2 v_2(0+) \\ \dfrac{1}{s} i_5(0+) \end{bmatrix}, \tag{3.10}
$$

where the coefficient matrix

$$
\begin{bmatrix} G_4 + C_2 s & -G_4 \\ -G_4 & G_3 + G_4 + \dfrac{1}{L_5 s} \end{bmatrix}
$$

corresponds to $[W(s)]$ in (3.9), and the column matrices

$$
\begin{bmatrix} V_2(s) \\ V_3(s) \end{bmatrix}, \qquad \begin{bmatrix} I_6(s) \\ \dfrac{1}{L_5 s} V_1(s) \end{bmatrix}, \qquad \text{and} \qquad \begin{bmatrix} C_2 v_2(0+) \\ \dfrac{1}{s} i_5(0+) \end{bmatrix}
$$

correspond to $[X(s)]$, $[F(s)]$, $[F(s, 0+)]$, respectively.

EXAMPLE 3.2. The chord equations obtained in Example 2.4,

$$
\begin{bmatrix} R_3 + R_4 + \dfrac{1}{C_2 s} & R_3 \\ R_3 & R_3 + L_5 s \end{bmatrix} \begin{bmatrix} I_4(s) \\ I_5(s) \end{bmatrix} = \frac{1}{C_2 s} [I_6(s)] + \begin{bmatrix} 0 \\ 1 \end{bmatrix} [V_1(s)] + \begin{bmatrix} \dfrac{1}{s} v_2(0+) \\ L_5 i_5(0+) \end{bmatrix}, \tag{2.85}
$$

may be written as

$$
\begin{bmatrix} R_3 + R_4 + \dfrac{1}{C_2 s} & R_3 \\ R_3 & R_3 + L_5 s \end{bmatrix} \begin{bmatrix} I_4(s) \\ I_5(s) \end{bmatrix} = \begin{bmatrix} \dfrac{1}{C_2 s} I_6(s) \\ V_1(s) \end{bmatrix} + \begin{bmatrix} \dfrac{1}{s} v_2(0+) \\ L_5 i_5(0+) \end{bmatrix}, \tag{3.11}
$$

which is in the same form as (3.9).

Both Eqs. (3.10) and (3.11) are sets of two linear algebraic equations in two unknowns, with a parameter s. We can therefore solve (3.10) for V_2 and V_3 or (3.11) for I_4 and I_5, as functions of s. This solution is quite simple; we have, from (3.11), that

$$
\begin{bmatrix} I_4(s) \\ I_5(s) \end{bmatrix} = \begin{bmatrix} R_3 + R_4 + \dfrac{1}{C_2 s} & R_3 \\ R_3 & R_3 + L_5 s \end{bmatrix}^{-1} \left\{ \begin{bmatrix} \dfrac{1}{C_2 s} I_6(s) \\ V_1(s) \end{bmatrix} + \begin{bmatrix} \dfrac{1}{s} v_2(0+) \\ L_5 i_5(0+) \end{bmatrix} \right\} \tag{3.12}
$$

$$
= \frac{\begin{bmatrix} R_3 + L_5 s & -R_3 \\ -R_3 & R_3 + R_4 + \dfrac{1}{C_2 s} \end{bmatrix} \left\{ \begin{bmatrix} \dfrac{1}{C_2 s} I_6(s) \\ V_1(s) \end{bmatrix} + \begin{bmatrix} \dfrac{1}{s} v_2(0+) \\ L_5 i_5(0+) \end{bmatrix} \right\}}{\begin{vmatrix} R_3 + R_4 + \dfrac{1}{C_2 s} & R_3 \\ R_3 & R_3 + L_5 s \end{vmatrix}} \tag{3.13}
$$

so that

$$
\begin{bmatrix} I_4(s) \\ I_5(s) \end{bmatrix} = \frac{\begin{bmatrix} R_3 + L_5 s & -R_3 \\ -R_3 & R_3 + R_4 + \dfrac{1}{C_2 s} \end{bmatrix}}{(R_3 + R_4)L_5 s + \left(\dfrac{L_5}{C_2} + R_3 R_4\right) + \dfrac{R_3}{C_2 s}} \left\{ \begin{bmatrix} \dfrac{1}{C_2 s} I_6(s) \\ V_1(s) \end{bmatrix} + \begin{bmatrix} \dfrac{1}{s} v_2(0+) \\ L_5 i_5(0+) \end{bmatrix} \right\},
\qquad (3.14)
$$

or

$$
\begin{bmatrix} I_4(s) \\ I_5(s) \end{bmatrix} = \frac{\begin{bmatrix} R_3 + L_5 s & -R_3 \\ -R_3 & R_3 + R_4 + \dfrac{1}{C_2 s} \end{bmatrix}}{(R_3 + R_4)L_5 s^2 + \left(\dfrac{L_5}{C_2} + R_3 R_4\right) s + \dfrac{R_3}{C_2}} \left\{ \begin{bmatrix} \dfrac{1}{C_2} I_6(s) \\ s V_1(s) \end{bmatrix} + \begin{bmatrix} v_2(0+) \\ L_5 s i_5(0+) \end{bmatrix} \right\}.
$$

$$(3.15)$$

We cannot proceed further with the solution of these equations until we are given the specifications of $V_1(s)$ and $I_6(s)$, the voltage and current drivers. However, we observe that the entries in the coefficient matrix are at most rational functions of s, as are the entries in the column matrix of initial conditions. Therefore, if $I_6(s)$ and $V_1(s)$ are rational functions of s, we are assured that $I_4(s)$ and $I_5(s)$ will also be rational functions. We can therefore find the inverse Laplace transforms, or the time response of the network, $i_4(t)$ and $i_5(t)$, quite easily by expanding the rational functions in terms of partial fractions (see Appendix A for further information).

In general terms, then, from (3.9) we have

$$[X(s)] = [W(s)]^{-1}\{[F(s)] + [F(s, 0+)]\} \qquad (3.16)$$

or

$$[X(s)] = \frac{[W_1(s)]}{\det W(s)} \{[F(s)] + [F(s, 0+)]\}, \qquad (3.17)$$

where $\det W(s)$ is the determinant of $[W(s)]$, and $[W_1(s)]$ is the adjoint of $[W(s)]$. The adjoint of a matrix is the transposed matrix of the cofactors of its entries. All the entries in $[W(s)]$ are at most rational functions of s, so that $\det W(s)$ is, accordingly, a rational function of s. Thus, if the specified functions $[F(s)]$ are rational functions, all the entries in $[X(s)]$ will be rational, and we have a simple method for finding $[x(t)]$.

Since it is necessary to know exactly what the driving functions of a given network are, we cannot proceed further with the solution in general terms without using the convolution. In the following sections therefore we shall deal with two important special cases. These are, first, the case in which all the specified functions are step functions, and second, the case in which all the driving functions are sinusoidal, with the same frequency. Two other situations, in which the driving functions consist of general exponentials and of impulse functions, are left as exercises.

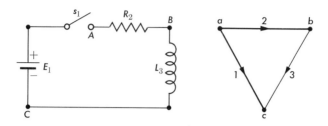

FIG. 3.1. A series RL network and system graph.

3.2. STEP-FUNCTION RESPONSE

We shall begin our discussion of the response of networks to step driving functions with a simple example which will illustrate most of the salient points.

EXAMPLE 3.3.   Consider the simple network of Fig. 3.1.   In this network we assume that the switch S_1 is closed at $t = 0$ and that the initial current through the inductance is

$$i_3(0+) = \frac{E}{2R_2}. \tag{3.18}$$

(Note that the sign of $i_3(0+)$ is reversed when the orientation of element 3 is reversed.)   This initial current can be realized by connecting a resistance equal to R_2 across the switch S_1.   For all $t > 0$, we can write the chord equation

$$(R_2 + sL_3)I_3(s) = V_1(s) + L_3 i_3(0+) \tag{3.19}$$

in terms of Laplace transformed variables; or, in the time domain,

$$v_1(t) = R_2 i_3(t) + L_3 \frac{di_3(t)}{dt}. \tag{3.20}$$

The solution of (3.19) is

$$I_3(s) = \frac{1}{R_2 + L_3 s} \{V_1(s) + L_3 i_3(0+)\}; \tag{3.21}$$

and since

$$v_1(t) = \begin{cases} E & \text{for } t > 0, \\ 0 & \text{for } t < 0, \end{cases} \tag{3.22}$$

or

$$v_1(t) = Eu(t),$$

where

$$u(t) = \begin{cases} 1 & \text{for } t > 0, \\ 0 & \text{for } t < 0, \end{cases}$$

is the unit step function, we have

$$V_1(s) = E/s. \tag{3.23}$$

Thus

$$I_3(s) = \frac{1}{R_2 + L_3 s}\left\{\frac{E}{s} + \frac{EL_3}{2R_2}\right\} = \frac{E}{R_2 + L_3 s}\left\{\frac{1}{s} + \frac{L_3}{2R_2}\right\}, \qquad (3.24)$$

or

$$I_3(s) = \frac{E\{1 + s(L_3/2R_2)\}}{(R_2 + L_3 s)s} = \frac{E\{1/L_3 + s/2R_2\}}{s(s + R_2/L_3)}. \qquad (3.25)$$

We can now expand the right-hand side of (3.25) in partial fractions to obtain

$$I_3(s) = \frac{-E/2R_2}{s + R_2/L_3} + \frac{E/R_2}{s}. \qquad (3.26)$$

The time response therefore is $(t > 0)$

$$i_3(t) = -\frac{E}{2R_2}e^{-(R_2/L_3)t} + \frac{E}{R_2}. \qquad (3.27)$$

There are several things to be noted about the solution for $i_3(t)$. It consists of two terms: the first of these is a decreasing exponential, and the second is constant. The exponential term is called the *transient* part of the solution, while the constant is called the *steady-state* or *dc-solution*.

We observe that the transient is of the form

$$i_3(t)_t = ke^{-t/\tau}, \qquad (3.28)$$

where $\tau = L_3/R_3$ has the dimension of time and is called the *time constant* of the circuit. Note that this constant appears in the partial-fraction expansion in the term

$$\frac{-(E/2R_2)}{s + R_2/L_3}.$$

The denominator of this term is merely $1/L_3$ times the coefficient of $I_3(s)$ in the chord equation (3.19). This coefficient in turn depends only on the characteristics and interconnections of the components in the network, and not on $V_1(s)$. *Thus the time variation of the transient depends only on the network and not on the driving functions.*

The coefficient $(R_2 + sL_3)$ in (3.19), which forms the denominator of the Laplace transform of the transient response, is called the *characteristic polynomial*. We may therefore state that the time variation of the transient response is *given by the zeros of the characteristic polynomial*. [The zeros of a polynomial $P(s)$ are the values of s which satisfy the equation $P(s) = 0$.] Note that this coefficient takes the place of $[W(s)]$ in (3.9); when we are dealing with more than one equation, the characteristic polynomial is strongly related to det $W(s)$; it is frequently referred to as the *determinantal polynomial*. We shall make no distinction between these terms.

Now consider the constant multiplier for the transient term:

$$k = -E/2R_2, \qquad (3.29)$$

which is obtained by partial-fraction expansion. That is,

$$k = \left\{ \left(s + \frac{R_2}{L_3} \right) I_3(s) \right\} \Bigg|_{s=-(R_2/L_3)}, \tag{3.30}$$

or, from (3.21),

$$k = \frac{1}{L_3} V_1(s) \Bigg|_{s=-(R_2/L_3)} + i_3(0+). \tag{3.31}$$

We conclude therefore that the constant multiplier in the transient depends not only on the network, but also on the driving function and the *initial conditions*.

On the other hand, the steady-state solution is

$$i_3(t)_{ss} = E/R_2. \tag{3.32}$$

This is merely the inverse Laplace transform of $(E/R_2)/s$, which appears in the partial-fraction expansion (3.26). The denominator of this term, s, first became evident in (3.24) when we substituted the specific form of the driving function into the chord equation. Thus, the time variation of the steady-state solution is prescribed by the driving function $V_1(s)$ and not by the remaining components and their interconnection in the network. Alternatively, we may state that the steady-state solution depends on the driving functions and not on the determinantal polynomial.

As to the constant (E/R_2), it was obtained in the partial-fraction expansion as

$$sI_3(s) \Bigg|_{s=0} = \left(\frac{1}{R_2 + L_3 s} \{ E + s i_3(0+) \} \right) \Bigg|_{s=0} = \frac{E}{R_2}. \tag{3.33}$$

We observe that the initial condition term has no effect on the steady-state solution. Further, we may obtain the steady-state solution directly from the chord equation (3.19) by

(1) deleting the initial condition term;
(2) replacing $V_1(s) = E/s$ by E;
(3) putting $s = 0$ wherever it occurs in the remainder of the equation.

This process reduces (3.19) to

$$R_2 I_{3_{ss}} = E. \tag{3.34}$$

Another important point of view is that since the driving function is a constant for $t > 0$, the steady-state solution must be a constant. Hence all time derivatives must be zero, and the steady-state solution may be obtained directly from the differential equation by making this assumption. That is, in (3.20) we write $di_3(t)/dt = 0$, so that

$$v_1(t) = R_2 i_3(t)_{ss} = E,$$

and

$$i_3(t)_{ss} = E/R_2. \tag{3.32}$$

Now let us consider a slightly more complicated example in which it is necessary to solve more than one equation.

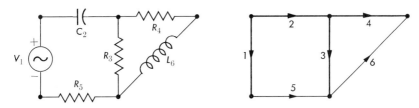

FIG. 3.2. Simple network and graph.

EXAMPLE 3.4. Consider the simple network of Fig. 3.2. For this network the chord equations are

$$\begin{bmatrix} V_1(s) \\ 0 \end{bmatrix} + \begin{bmatrix} R_3 + R_5 + \dfrac{1}{C_2 s} & -R_3 \\ -R_3 & R_3 + R_4 + L_6 s \end{bmatrix} \begin{bmatrix} I_5(s) \\ I_6(s) \end{bmatrix} + \begin{bmatrix} \dfrac{-1}{s} v_2(0+) \\ -L_6 i_6(0+) \end{bmatrix} = \begin{bmatrix} 0 \\ 0 \end{bmatrix}, \quad (3.35)$$

or

$$\begin{bmatrix} R_3 + R_5 + \dfrac{1}{C_2 s} & -R_3 \\ -R_3 & R_3 + R_4 + L_6 s \end{bmatrix} \begin{bmatrix} I_5(s) \\ I_6(s) \end{bmatrix} = \begin{bmatrix} -1 \\ 0 \end{bmatrix} [V_1(s)] + \begin{bmatrix} \dfrac{1}{s} v_2(0+) \\ L_6 i_6(0+) \end{bmatrix}. \quad (3.36)$$

In this example, let us assume for ease of calculation that $C_2 = \frac{1}{2}$ f, $R_3 = 3\,\Omega$, $R_4 = 4\,\Omega$, $R_5 = 5\,\Omega$, $L_6 = 6$ h, $v_2(0+) = 2$ v, $i_6(0+) = \frac{1}{6}$ amp, $v_1(t) = u(t)$. Then (3.36) reduces to

$$\begin{bmatrix} 8 + \dfrac{2}{s} & -3 \\ -3 & 7 + 6s \end{bmatrix} \begin{bmatrix} I_5(s) \\ I_6(s) \end{bmatrix} = \begin{bmatrix} -1 \\ 0 \end{bmatrix} [V_1(s)] + \begin{bmatrix} \dfrac{2}{s} \\ 1 \end{bmatrix}. \quad (3.37)$$

Before going through a formal solution, let us try to find the steady-state currents I_5, I_6 by the procedure mentioned above. That is, we neglect the initial conditions, replace $V_1(s)$ by the magnitude of the step (in this case, unity), and set $s = 0$. This immediately gives rise to difficulties because of the expression $2/s$ in one entry of the coefficient matrix. Allowing s to approach zero makes this term infinite. To bypass this difficulty, we multiply the first equation by s on both sides. This gives

$$\begin{bmatrix} 8s + 2 & -3s \\ -3 & 7 + 6s \end{bmatrix} \begin{bmatrix} I_5(s) \\ I_6(s) \end{bmatrix} = \begin{bmatrix} -1 \\ 0 \end{bmatrix} s[V_1(s)] + \begin{bmatrix} 2 \\ 1 \end{bmatrix}. \quad (3.38)$$

Now, writing unity for $V_1(s)$, neglecting the initial conditions, and setting $s = 0$, we obtain

$$\begin{bmatrix} 2 & 0 \\ -3 & 7 \end{bmatrix} \begin{bmatrix} I_{5_{ss}} \\ I_{6_{ss}} \end{bmatrix} = \begin{bmatrix} 0 \\ 0 \end{bmatrix}, \quad (3.39)$$

which are immediately solved to give $I_{5_{ss}} = I_{6_{ss}} = 0$, the steady-state solution.

We now show the development of the complete solution. From (3.37) we obtain

$$
\begin{bmatrix} I_5(s) \\ I_6(s) \end{bmatrix} = \begin{bmatrix} 8 + \dfrac{2}{s} & -3 \\ -3 & 6s + 7 \end{bmatrix}^{-1} \left\{ \begin{bmatrix} -1 \\ 0 \end{bmatrix} \dfrac{1}{s} + \begin{bmatrix} \dfrac{2}{s} \\ 1 \end{bmatrix} \right\} \tag{3.40}
$$

$$
= \frac{\begin{bmatrix} 6s + 7 & 3 \\ 3 & 8 + \dfrac{2}{s} \end{bmatrix}}{\left(8 + \dfrac{2}{s}\right)(6s + 7) - 9} \left\{ \begin{bmatrix} -1 \\ 0 \end{bmatrix} \dfrac{1}{s} + \begin{bmatrix} \dfrac{2}{s} \\ 1 \end{bmatrix} \right\} \tag{3.41}
$$

$$
= \frac{\begin{bmatrix} 6s + 7 & 3 \\ 3 & 8 + \dfrac{2}{s} \end{bmatrix} \left\{ \begin{bmatrix} -1 \\ 0 \end{bmatrix} \dfrac{1}{s} + \begin{bmatrix} \dfrac{2}{s} \\ 1 \end{bmatrix} \right\}}{59 + 48s + \dfrac{14}{s}}, \tag{3.42}
$$

or, multiplying the numerator and denominator by s, we have

$$
\begin{bmatrix} I_5(s) \\ I_6(s) \end{bmatrix} = \frac{\begin{bmatrix} 6s^2 + 7s & 3s \\ 3s & 8s + 2 \end{bmatrix}}{(48s^2 + 59s + 14)} \left\{ \frac{1}{s} \begin{bmatrix} -1 \\ 0 \end{bmatrix} + \frac{1}{s} \begin{bmatrix} 2 \\ s \end{bmatrix} \right\}. \tag{3.43}
$$

The determinantal polynomial in (3.43) is $48s^2 + 59s + 14$. To proceed further, we factor this and rearrange the equations slightly. We obtain

$$
\begin{bmatrix} I_5(s) \\ I_6(s) \end{bmatrix} = \frac{\begin{bmatrix} 6s^2 + 7s & 3s \\ 3s & 8s + 2 \end{bmatrix} \left\{ \begin{bmatrix} -1 \\ 0 \end{bmatrix} + \begin{bmatrix} 2 \\ s \end{bmatrix} \right\}}{48s(s + 0.321)(s + 0.908)} = \frac{\begin{bmatrix} 9s^2 + 7s \\ 8s^2 + 5s \end{bmatrix}}{48s(s + 0.321)(s + 0.908)}, \tag{3.44}
$$

and, expanding in partial fractions, we have

$$
\begin{bmatrix} I_5(s) \\ I_6(s) \end{bmatrix} = \frac{[A]}{(s + 0.321)} + \frac{[B]}{(s + 0.908)} + \frac{[C]}{s}, \tag{3.45}
$$

where

$$
[A] = \frac{\begin{bmatrix} 9(-0.321)^2 + 7(-0.321) \\ 8(-0.321)^2 + 5(-0.321) \end{bmatrix}}{-48(0.321)(0.908 - 0.321)} = \begin{bmatrix} 0.135 \\ 0.0863 \end{bmatrix}. \tag{3.46}
$$

Similarly,

$$
[B] = \begin{bmatrix} 0.0427 \\ 0.0813 \end{bmatrix}, \tag{3.47}
$$

and

$$
[C] = \begin{bmatrix} 0 \\ 0 \end{bmatrix}. \tag{3.48}
$$

Thus we have

$$\begin{bmatrix} I_5(s) \\ I_6(s) \end{bmatrix} = \frac{\begin{bmatrix} 0.135 \\ 0.0863 \end{bmatrix}}{s + 0.321} + \frac{\begin{bmatrix} 0.0427 \\ 0.0813 \end{bmatrix}}{s + 0.908} + \frac{\begin{bmatrix} 0 \\ 0 \end{bmatrix}}{s}, \tag{3.49}$$

and taking the inverse Laplace transform yields

$$\begin{bmatrix} i_5(t) \\ i_6(t) \end{bmatrix} = \begin{bmatrix} 0.135 \\ 0.0863 \end{bmatrix} e^{-0.321t} + \begin{bmatrix} 0.0427 \\ 0.0813 \end{bmatrix} e^{-0.908t} + \begin{bmatrix} 0 \\ 0 \end{bmatrix}. \tag{3.50}$$

The first two terms in (3.50) represent the transient part of the solution, because their time dependence is related only to zeros of the determinantal polynomial; the third term is the steady state. We can readily verify this fact by noting the position of the capacitor in the network which is excited by a dc-source.

The conclusion to be drawn from the above example is that in finding the steady-state solution of the network equations in cases when some entries of the coefficient matrix contain terms like k/s, we must multiply both sides of the appropriate equations by s before setting $s = 0$.

Although, in finding the steady-state solution, we were able to set $s = 0$ before inverting the coefficient matrix in both of the previous examples, this is not always the case. Sometimes it is necessary to invert the matrix before setting s equal to zero; in fact, it is the general procedure.

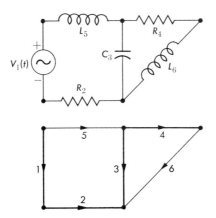

FIG. 3.3. Simple network and graph.

EXAMPLE 3.5. In this example, we find the steady-state currents I_5, I_6 for the network of Fig. 3.3, in which we assume that

$$V_1(t) = u(t), \qquad V_1(s) = 1/s,$$

$$R_2 = 2\,\Omega, \qquad C_3 = \tfrac{1}{3}\,\text{f}, \qquad R_4 = 4\,\Omega, \qquad L_5 = 5\,\text{h}, \qquad L_6 = 6\,\text{h}, \tag{3.51}$$

$$v_3(0+) = 3\,\text{v}, \qquad i_5(0+) = \tfrac{1}{5}\,\text{amp}, \qquad i_6(0+) = \tfrac{1}{6}\,\text{amp}.$$

The chord equations are

$$
\begin{bmatrix} -1 \\ 0 \end{bmatrix} [V_1(s)] + \begin{bmatrix} R_2 + L_5 s + \dfrac{1}{C_3 s} & -\dfrac{1}{C_3 s} \\ -\dfrac{1}{C_3 s} & R_4 + L_6 s + \dfrac{1}{C_3 s} \end{bmatrix} \begin{bmatrix} I_5(s) \\ I_6(s) \end{bmatrix}
$$

$$
= - \begin{bmatrix} -1 & 1 & 0 & 1 & 0 \\ 0 & -1 & 1 & 0 & 1 \end{bmatrix} \begin{bmatrix} 0 \\ \dfrac{1}{s} v_3(0+) \\ 0 \\ -L_5 i_5(0+) \\ -L_6 i_6(0+) \end{bmatrix},
$$

(3.52)

or, substituting the numerical values and rearranging, we have

$$
\begin{bmatrix} 2 + 5s + \dfrac{3}{s} & -\dfrac{3}{s} \\ -\dfrac{3}{s} & 4 + 6s + \dfrac{3}{s} \end{bmatrix} \begin{bmatrix} I_5(s) \\ I_6(s) \end{bmatrix} = \begin{bmatrix} 1/s \\ 0 \end{bmatrix} + \begin{bmatrix} 1 - \dfrac{3}{s} \\ 1 + \dfrac{3}{s} \end{bmatrix}.
$$

(3.53)

Since every entry in the coefficient matrix contains a term $\pm 3/s$, we multiply both equations by s. This gives

$$
\begin{bmatrix} 5s^2 + 2s + 3 & -3 \\ -3 & 6s^2 + 4s + 3 \end{bmatrix} \begin{bmatrix} I_5(s) \\ I_6(s) \end{bmatrix} = s \begin{bmatrix} 1/s \\ 0 \end{bmatrix} + \begin{bmatrix} s - 3 \\ s + 3 \end{bmatrix}.
$$

(3.54)

Now, if we attempt to find the steady-state currents I_5, I_6 by the procedure mentioned in the previous examples, we obtain

$$
\begin{bmatrix} 3 & -3 \\ -3 & 3 \end{bmatrix} \begin{bmatrix} I_5 \\ I_6 \end{bmatrix} = \begin{bmatrix} 1 \\ 0 \end{bmatrix},
$$

(3.55)

which cannot be solved for I_5, I_6, since the determinant of the coefficient matrix is zero. However, we know that the initial conditions have no effect on the steady-state solution; so we shall neglect them and write, for the equations to be solved,

$$
\begin{bmatrix} 5s^2 + 2s + 3 & -3 \\ -3 & 6s^2 + 4s + 3 \end{bmatrix} \begin{bmatrix} I_5(s) \\ I_6(s) \end{bmatrix} = s \begin{bmatrix} 1/s \\ 0 \end{bmatrix}.
$$

(3.56)

The solution is given by

$$
\begin{bmatrix} I_5(s) \\ I_6(s) \end{bmatrix} = \frac{\begin{bmatrix} 6s^2 + 4s + 3 & 3 \\ 3 & 5s^2 + 2s + 3 \end{bmatrix} s \begin{bmatrix} 1/s \\ 0 \end{bmatrix}}{30s^4 + 32s^3 + 41s^2 + 18s}
$$

$$
= \frac{\begin{bmatrix} 6s^2 + 4s + 3 & 3 \\ 3 & 5s^2 + 2s + 3 \end{bmatrix} \begin{bmatrix} 1 \\ 0 \end{bmatrix} \dfrac{1}{s}}{30s^3 + 32s^2 + 41s + 18},
$$

so that we obtain

$$\begin{bmatrix} I_5(s) \\ I_6(s) \end{bmatrix} = \frac{\frac{1}{18}\begin{bmatrix} 3 & 3 \\ 3 & 3 \end{bmatrix}\begin{bmatrix} 1 \\ 0 \end{bmatrix}}{s} + \text{other terms in the partial-fraction expansion,}$$

and

$$\begin{bmatrix} i_5(t) \\ i_6(t) \end{bmatrix} = \frac{1}{18}\begin{bmatrix} 3 & 3 \\ 3 & 3 \end{bmatrix}\begin{bmatrix} 1 \\ 0 \end{bmatrix} + \text{other terms} = \begin{bmatrix} \frac{1}{6} \\ \frac{1}{6} \end{bmatrix} + \cdots \tag{3.57}$$

The steady state is the part of the complete solution which has the same time variation as the driving function. Therefore, the term written is the steady-state solution, and it has been obtained by inverting the coefficient matrix before setting $s = 0$.

The general procedure for finding the steady-state step function response is therefore:

(1) Write the network equations neglecting the initial condition term.
(2) If there are any equations with coefficients containing terms like k/s, multiply the appropriate equations on both sides by s.
(3) Replace the step-function drivers by their magnitudes.
(4) Set $s = 0$. If the determinant of the resulting coefficient matrix is nonzero, the equations may be solved, giving the steady-state solution.
(5) If in step 4 the determinant is zero, invert the coefficient matrix before setting $s = 0$. The result is again the steady-state solution.

As to the transient solution, it is seen that there is no short-cut method. When we wish to find the transient, we must solve the equations and find the determinantal polynomial; this must be factored, and we then expand in terms of partial fractions. It is not, however, necessary to find the steady-state solution when we only wish to obtain the transient.

In the foregoing examples, we consistently chose to solve the equations by premultiplying each side by the inverse of the coefficient matrix. This is a simple enough procedure in the few examples that we chose, but finding the inverse of a fourth- or higher-order matrix can be a very tedious job. In such cases, and especially when one is only interested in one of the network variables, it is often more expedient to use other methods, such as Cramer's rule, or "successive elimination," to solve the equations. The solutions obtained by any method will, of course, contain the same characteristic polynomials, etc., that appeared in our examples, and the procedure for finding the transient and steady-state parts of the response is unaltered. In any case, a lengthy process is always involved in the solution of large sets of equations; in Chapter 4 we shall indicate methods by which the number of equations to be dealt with at any one time can be reduced.

3.3. SYMBOLIC DEVELOPMENT OF THE STEP-FUNCTION RESPONSE

In this section we shall give, in general terms, a development of the procedures which we introduced by examples in Section 3.2. Our starting point is the representative set of network equations,

$$[W(s)][X(s)] = [F(s)] + [F(s, 0+)]. \tag{3.9}$$

Here, we assume that all the driving functions are step functions, so that

$$[F(s)] = \frac{1}{s} [F], \tag{3.58}$$

where $[F]$ is a column matrix of constants, and (3.9) becomes

$$[W(s)][X(s)] = \frac{1}{s} [F] + [F(s, 0+)]. \tag{3.59}$$

We have already written the solution of (3.9) as

$$[X(s)] = \frac{[W_1(s)]}{\det W(s)} \{[F(s)] + [F(s, 0+)]\}, \tag{3.17}$$

so that, in this case, we have

$$[X(s)] = \frac{[W_1(s)]}{\det W(s)} \left\{ \frac{1}{s} [F] + [F(s, 0+)] \right\}. \tag{3.60}$$

However, in this form of the solution, the entries in $[W_1(s)]$ may be rational functions of s, as may $\det W(s)$. We would rather deal with polynomial expressions. We therefore examine $[W(s)]$ and find in each row the lowest common multiple of the denominators of the entries. We then multiply each row on both sides of the equation by this factor. This can be accomplished symbolically by premultiplying both sides of (3.59) by a diagonal matrix $[P(s)]$, where the entry in the ith row and column of $[P(s)]$ is the lowest common multiple of the denominators of the entries in the ith row of $[W(s)]$. In the case of RLC networks the entries of $P(s)$ will be either 1 or s. We thus obtain

$$[P(s)][W(s)][X(s)] = [P(s)] \left\{ \frac{1}{s} [F] + [F(s, 0+)] \right\}. \tag{3.61}$$

Let us write

$$[P(s)][W(s)] = [A(s)], \tag{3.62}$$

so that $[A(s)]$ is a matrix whose entries are polynomials in s. The solution of (3.61) may now be written as

$$[X(s)] = [A(s)]^{-1}[P(s)] \left\{ \frac{1}{s} [F] + [F(s, 0+)] \right\} \tag{3.63}$$

$$= \frac{[A_1(s)][P(s)] \left\{ \frac{1}{s} [F] + [F(s, 0+)] \right\}}{\det A(s)}, \tag{3.64}$$

where $[A_1(s)]$ is the adjoint of $[A(s)]$ and $\det A(s)$ is the determinant of $[A(s)]$.

Since all the entries in $[A(s)]$ are polynomials in s, det $A(s)$ is also a polynomial. It is the *determinantal* or *characteristic polynomial* which we saw in the previous examples. Det $A(s)$ may be factored and written in the form

$$\det A(s) = K(s - s_1)(s - s_2) \cdots (s - s_n), \qquad (3.65)$$

where $s_1, s_2, \ldots, s_n$ are its zeros and K is the coefficient of the highest power of s. Using (3.65) in (3.64), we have

$$[X(s)] = \frac{[A_1(s)][P(s)] \left\{ \frac{1}{s} [F] + [F(s, 0+)] \right\}}{K(s - s_1)(s - s_2) \cdots (s - s_n)}, \qquad (3.66)$$

or

$$[X(s)] = \frac{[A_1(s)][P(s)]\{[F] + s[F(s, 0+)]\}}{sK(s - s_1)(s - s_2) \cdots (s - s_n)}. \qquad (3.67)$$

The right-hand side of (3.67) may be expanded in partial fractions. For ease of manipulation, we shall assume that all the s_i are distinct; that is, no $s_i = s_j$ $(i \neq j)$, $i, j = 1, 2, \ldots, n$. In this case, we have

$$[X(s)] = \frac{[X_1]}{s - s_1} + \frac{[X_2]}{s - s_2} + \cdots + \frac{[X_n]}{s - s_n} + \frac{[X_s]}{s}$$

$$= \sum_{i=1}^{n} \frac{[X_i]}{s - s_i} + \frac{[X_s]}{s}, \qquad (3.68)$$

where

$$[X_i] = \lim_{s \to s_i} (s - s_i)[X(s)], \qquad i = 1, 2, \ldots, n, \qquad (3.69)$$

and

$$[X_s] = \lim_{s \to 0} s[X(s)]. \qquad (3.70)$$

When det $A(s)$ contains multiple zeros, there is only a slight complication in the partial-fraction expansion of (3.67). (See Appendix A.)

The final time solution is obtained by taking the inverse Laplace transform of (3.68), which yields

$$[x(t)] = \sum_{i=1}^{n} [X_i]e^{s_i t} + [X_s], \qquad t > 0. \qquad (3.71)$$

In (3.69) the term $\sum_{i=1}^{n} [X_i] e^{s_i t}$ is the transient, and it is clear that the exponential time variation depends only on the zeros, s_i, of the determinantal polynomial. The steady state is $[X_s]$; its time dependence is that of the driving functions.

Let us first examine the steady state. We have

$$[X_s] = \lim_{s \to 0} s[X(s)], \qquad (3.70)$$

and, using (3.64), this may be written as

$$[X_s] = \lim_{s \to 0} s \frac{[A_1(s)][P(s)]\left\{\frac{1}{s}[F] + [F(s, 0+)]\right\}}{\det A(s)}$$

$$= \lim_{s \to 0} \frac{[A_1(s)][P(s)][F]}{\det A(s)} + \lim_{s \to 0} \frac{s[A_1(s)][P(s)][F(s, 0+)]}{\det A(s)}. \qquad (3.72)$$

Except in a few possible trivial cases the second limit on the right-hand side of (3.72) is always zero even when $\det A(0) = 0$. Therefore, we have

$$[X_s] = \lim_{s \to 0} \frac{[A_1(s)][P(s)][F]}{\det A(s)}. \qquad (3.73)$$

When $\lim_{s \to 0} \det A(s) \neq 0$, (3.73) becomes

$$[X_s] = \frac{[A_1(0)][P(0)][F]}{\det A(0)} = [A(0)]^{-1}[P(0)][F], \qquad (3.74)$$

and if $[P(s)]$ is a unit matrix, that is, when all the entries of $W(s)$ are polynomials, the steady-state solution is reduced to

$$[X_s] = [W(0)]^{-1}[F]. \qquad (3.75)$$

Equations (3.75), (3.74), (3.73) apply to the three cases encountered in Examples 3.3, 3.4, and 3.5, respectively.

We now examine the transient part of the solution, which is given by

$$[x_t(t)] = \sum_{i=1}^{n} [X_i]e^{s_i t}. \qquad (3.76)$$

The numbers s_i are the zeros of the determinantal polynomial. They may be real, imaginary, or complex numbers. Since the determinantal polynomial has real coefficients, we know from ordinary algebra that any complex s_i must occur in complex conjugate pairs. That is, if $s_i = \sigma_i + j\omega_i$ (where $j = \sqrt{-1}$), then there must exist some $s_k = \sigma_k + j\omega_k$ such that $\sigma_i = \sigma_k$ and $\omega_i = -\omega_k$, or $s_i = s_k^*$, where the * indicates the complex conjugate. Now

$$[X_i] = \lim_{s \to s_i} (s - s_i)[X(s)], \qquad (3.69)$$

$$[X_k] = \lim_{s \to s_k} (s - s_k)[X(s)], \qquad (3.77)$$

and we can write

$$[X(s)] = \frac{[A_1(s)][P(s)]\{[F] + s[F(s, 0+)]\}}{(s - s_i)(s - s_k)N(s)} = \frac{[M(s)]}{(s - s_i)(s - s_k)N(s)} \qquad (3.78)$$

or

$$[X(s)] = \frac{[Q(s)]}{(s - s_i)(s - s_k)},$$

where $[Q(s)]$ is a column matrix of rational functions of s. Thus, we can write

$$[X_i] = \frac{[Q(s_i)]}{s_i - s_k} = \frac{[Q(s_i)]}{2j\omega_i},$$

$$[X_k] = \frac{[Q(s_k)]}{s_k - s_i} = \frac{[Q(s_k)]}{2j\omega_k} = \frac{[Q(s_i^*)]}{-2j\omega_i} = \frac{[Q^*(s_i)]}{-2j\omega_i},$$

or

$$[X_k] = [X_i^*]. \tag{3.79}$$

We now write the part of the transient given by s_i and s_k in the form

$$[X_i]e^{s_it} + [X_k]e^{s_kt} = [X_i]e^{\sigma_it}e^{j\omega_it} + [X_i^*]e^{\sigma_it}e^{-j\omega_it}$$

$$= e^{\sigma_it}\{[X_i]e^{j\omega_it} + [X_i^*]e^{-j\omega_it}\}$$

$$= e^{\sigma_it}\left\{\begin{bmatrix} X_{i1} \\ X_{i2} \\ \vdots \\ X_{in} \end{bmatrix}e^{j\omega_it} + \begin{bmatrix} X_{i1}^* \\ X_{i2}^* \\ \vdots \\ X_{in}^* \end{bmatrix}e^{-j\omega_it}\right\}$$

$$= e^{\sigma_it}\left\{\begin{bmatrix} |X_{i1}|e^{j\theta_1} \\ |X_{i2}|e^{j\theta_2} \\ \vdots \\ |X_{in}|e^{j\theta_n} \end{bmatrix}e^{j\omega_it} + \begin{bmatrix} |X_{i1}|e^{-j\theta_1} \\ |X_{i2}|e^{-j\theta_2} \\ \vdots \\ |X_{in}|e^{-j\theta_n} \end{bmatrix}e^{-j\omega_it}\right\}$$

$$= e^{\sigma_it}\begin{bmatrix} |X_{i1}|(e^{j(\omega_it+\theta_1)} + e^{-j(\omega_it+\theta_1)}) \\ |X_{i2}|(e^{j(\omega_it+\theta_2)} + e^{-j(\omega_it+\theta_2)}) \\ \vdots \\ |X_{in}|(e^{j(\omega_it+\theta_n)} + e^{-j(\omega_it+\theta_n)}) \end{bmatrix},$$

and finally

$$[X_i]e^{s_it} + [X_k]e^{s_kt} = 2e^{\sigma_it}\begin{bmatrix} |X_{i1}|\cos(\omega_it + \theta_1) \\ |X_{i2}|\cos(\omega_it + \theta_2) \\ \vdots \\ |X_{in}|\cos(\omega_it + \theta_n) \end{bmatrix}. \tag{3.80}$$

Similarly, we can combine all the pairs of terms in the transient which have complex exponential time variation. When the s_i are pure imaginaries, the result is similar, except that the e^{σ_it} on the right-hand side of (3.80) is missing. Thus the transient is composed of terms like (3.80) and ordinary exponential terms corresponding to real s_i.

It is necessary to take note of the fact that when any of the real s_i are positive, the entries in $[X_i]e^{s_it}$ represent increasing exponentials; as t increases, the transient grows without bound, as illustrated in Fig. 3.4(a). A similar situation occurs when the complex s_i have positive real parts; this gives rise to exponentially increasing sinusoids, as shown in Fig. 3.4(b). When some of the s_i are purely imaginary, the transient contains purely sinusoidal terms as in Fig. 3.4(c). When, however, the

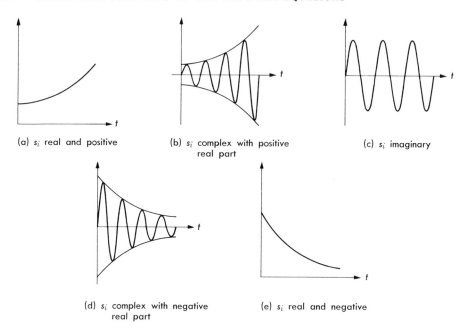

(a) s_i real and positive

(b) s_i complex with positive real part

(c) s_i imaginary

(d) s_i complex with negative real part

(e) s_i real and negative

FIG. 3.4. Illustration of the typical forms of the transient response.

real parts of the complex s_i are negative, the transient contains exponentially decreasing sinusoids, as in Fig. 3.4(d); if any s_i are real and negative, the corresponding terms of the transient are decreasing exponentials, as is illustrated above in Fig. 3.4(e).

We say that a network is stable if the transient decreases with time, and unstable otherwise. Therefore, since the numbers s_i are the zeros of the determinantal polynomial, we can state that a network is stable if the real parts of the zeros of the determinantal polynomial are all negative. This type of stability, called *asymptotic stability*, is of practical interest in most cases.

3.4. SINUSOIDAL RESPONSE

We shall introduce the sinusoidal response in the same way as that in which we discussed the step-function response, through examples. In this case we are interested in networks whose driving functions are all sinusoidal *with the same frequency*.

EXAMPLE 3.6. Consider the network and graph of Fig. 3.5. When we use the branch equations to obtain the capacitor voltages, we have

$$\begin{bmatrix} I_1(s) \\ 0 \\ 0 \end{bmatrix} + \begin{bmatrix} 2 & 2 & -1 \\ 2 & 2+s & -1 \\ -1 & -1 & 1+2s \end{bmatrix} \begin{bmatrix} V_1(s) \\ V_2(s) \\ V_3(s) \end{bmatrix} = \begin{bmatrix} 0 \\ v_2(0+) \\ 2v_3(0+) \end{bmatrix}, \tag{3.81}$$

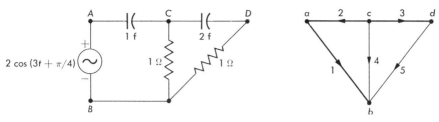

Fig. 3.5. Simple network and graph.

so that the equations to be solved are

$$\begin{bmatrix} 2+s & -1 \\ -1 & 1+2s \end{bmatrix} \begin{bmatrix} V_2(s) \\ V_3(s) \end{bmatrix} = \begin{bmatrix} -2 \\ 1 \end{bmatrix} [V_1(s)] + \begin{bmatrix} v_2(0+) \\ 2v_3(0+) \end{bmatrix}. \tag{3.82}$$

In (3.82),

$$V_1(s) = \mathcal{L}2 \cos\left(3t + \frac{\pi}{4}\right) = \mathcal{L}\{e^{j(3t+\pi/4)} + e^{-j(3t+\pi/4)}\}, \tag{3.83}$$

$$V_1(s) = \frac{e^{j(\pi/4)}}{s - 3j} + \frac{e^{-j(\pi/4)}}{s + 3j} = \frac{1}{\sqrt{2}}\left(\frac{1+j}{s-3j} + \frac{1-j}{s+3j}\right)$$

$$= \frac{\sqrt{2}(s-3)}{(s+3j)(s-3j)} = \frac{\sqrt{2}(s-3)}{(s^2+9)}. \tag{3.84}$$

We solve (3.82) and insert the expression for $V_1(s)$ from (3.84). This yields

$$\begin{bmatrix} V_2(s) \\ V_3(s) \end{bmatrix} = \frac{\begin{bmatrix} 1+2s & 1 \\ 1 & 2+s \end{bmatrix}\left\{\begin{bmatrix} -2 \\ 1 \end{bmatrix}\sqrt{2}(s-3) + (s^2+9)\begin{bmatrix} v_2(0+) \\ 2v_3(0+) \end{bmatrix}\right\}}{\{(2s+1)(s+2)-1\}(s+3j)(s-3j)} \tag{3.85}$$

$$= \frac{\begin{bmatrix} 2s+1 & 1 \\ 1 & s+2 \end{bmatrix}\left\{\begin{bmatrix} -2 \\ 1 \end{bmatrix}\sqrt{2}(s-3) + (s^2+9)\begin{bmatrix} v_2(0+) \\ 2v_3(0+) \end{bmatrix}\right\}}{2(s^2 + \frac{5}{2}s + \frac{1}{2})(s^2+9)}. \tag{3.86}$$

The determinantal polynomial is

$$2(s^2 + \tfrac{5}{2}s + \tfrac{1}{2}) = 2(s+2.28)(s+0.219). \tag{3.87}$$

For the transient solution (that part of the total solution whose time dependence is given by the characteristic polynomial), we can therefore find

$$\begin{bmatrix} V_2(s) \\ V_3(s) \end{bmatrix}_t = \frac{[A]}{s+2.28} + \frac{[B]}{s+0.219}, \tag{3.88}$$

where $[A]$ and $[B]$ are, of course, obtained in the usual way for partial-fraction expansions:

$$[A] = \frac{\begin{bmatrix} 1-2(2.28) & 1 \\ 1 & 2-2.28 \end{bmatrix}\left\{\begin{bmatrix} -2 \\ 1 \end{bmatrix}\sqrt{2}(-2.28-3) + \{(2.28)^2+9\}\begin{bmatrix} v_2(0+) \\ 2v_3(0+) \end{bmatrix}\right\}}{2\{0.219-2.28\}\{(2.28)^2+9\}}. \tag{3.89}$$

We assume that $v_2(0+) = 1$, $v_3(0+) = -1$, and (3.89) reduces to

$$[A] = \begin{bmatrix} 2.40 \\ -0.674 \end{bmatrix}. \tag{3.90}$$

Similarly,

$$[B] = \begin{bmatrix} -0.334 \\ -0.425 \end{bmatrix}, \tag{3.91}$$

so that the transient response is

$$\begin{bmatrix} v_2(t) \\ v_3(t) \end{bmatrix}_t = \begin{bmatrix} 2.40 \\ -0.674 \end{bmatrix} e^{-2.28t} + \begin{bmatrix} -0.334 \\ -0.425 \end{bmatrix} e^{-0.219t}. \tag{3.92}$$

Note that the form of the transient solution for the sinusoidal drivers is the same as that which we obtained in the case of step functions. Furthermore, there is no difference in the computation for the two situations. Of course, the actual functions will be different, but regardless of the types of voltage and current drivers, the transient calculation is unchanged.

To calculate the sinusoidal steady-state response, we note that

$$\begin{bmatrix} V_2(s) \\ V_3(s) \end{bmatrix} = \begin{bmatrix} V_2(s) \\ V_3(s) \end{bmatrix}_t + \begin{bmatrix} V_2(s) \\ V_3(s) \end{bmatrix}_{ss}, \tag{3.93}$$

which, in this case, becomes

$$\begin{bmatrix} V_2(s) \\ V_3(s) \end{bmatrix} = \frac{[A]}{s + 2.28} + \frac{[B]}{s + 0.219} + \frac{[C]}{s - j3} + \frac{[D]}{s + j3}, \tag{3.94}$$

so that

$$\begin{bmatrix} V_2(s) \\ V_3(s) \end{bmatrix}_{ss} = \frac{[C]}{s - 3j} + \frac{[D]}{s + 3j}, \tag{3.95}$$

where

$$[C] = \frac{\begin{bmatrix} 1 + 6j & 1 \\ 1 & 2 + 3j \end{bmatrix} \left\{ \begin{bmatrix} -2 \\ 1 \end{bmatrix} \frac{1}{\sqrt{2}} (1 + j) \right\}}{-17 + 15j} = \begin{bmatrix} 0.541 e^{j(\pi - \tan^{-1} 0.146)} \\ 0.132 e^{-j(\tan^{-1} 0.0625)} \end{bmatrix}. \tag{3.96}$$

To find $[D]$ we note that both $V_2(s)$ and $V_3(s)$ (Eqs. 3.86) are rational functions of s with real coefficients. Since $[D]$ is determined by setting $s = -3j$ instead of $s = +3j$ as in the calculation of $[C]$, we conclude that

$$[D] = [C^*]. \tag{3.97}$$

Therefore,

$$\begin{bmatrix} V_2(s) \\ V_3(s) \end{bmatrix}_{ss} = \frac{\begin{bmatrix} 0.541 e^{j(\pi - \tan^{-1} 0.146)} \\ 0.132 e^{-j\tan^{-1} 0.0625} \end{bmatrix}}{s - 3j} + \frac{\begin{bmatrix} 0.541 e^{-j(\pi - \tan^{-1} 0.146)} \\ 0.132 e^{j\tan^{-1} 0.0625} \end{bmatrix}}{s + 3j}. \tag{3.98}$$

To obtain the time domain solution, we take the inverse Laplace transform of (3.98), which yields

$$\begin{bmatrix} v_2(t) \\ v_3(t) \end{bmatrix}_{ss} = \begin{bmatrix} 0.541e^{j(\pi-\tan^{-1}0.146)} \\ 0.132e^{-j\tan^{-1}0.0625} \end{bmatrix} e^{3jt} + \begin{bmatrix} 0.541e^{-j(\pi-\tan^{-1}0.146)} \\ 0.132e^{j\tan^{-1}0.0625} \end{bmatrix} e^{-3jt}$$

$$= \begin{bmatrix} 0.541(e^{j(3t+\pi-\tan^{-1}0.146)} + e^{-j(3t+\pi-\tan^{-1}0.146)}) \\ 0.132(e^{j(3t-\tan^{-1}0.0625)} + e^{-j(3t-\tan^{-1}0.0625)}) \end{bmatrix},$$

and finally,

$$\begin{bmatrix} v_2(t) \\ v_3(t) \end{bmatrix}_{ss} = \begin{bmatrix} 1.082 \cos(3t + \pi - \tan^{-1}0.146) \\ 0.264 \cos(3t - \tan^{-1}0.0625) \end{bmatrix}. \quad (3.99)$$

Note that the steady-state solution is sinusoidal; $v_2(t)$ and $v_3(t)$ differ only by their amplitudes and phase angles from $v_1(t)$. Also, these amplitudes and phase angles are completely determined by the numerator of the first term on the right of (3.98), or the matrix $[C]$, expression (3.96). The amplitudes are just twice the magnitudes of the entries in $[C]$, and the phase angles are the corresponding arguments. We observe that $[C]$ was obtained by multiplying the right-hand side of (3.86) by $s - 3j$, and replacing s by $3j$ in the result. Tracing back through our development, we see that $[C]$ may equally well have been found by replacing $V_1(s)$ in (3.82), by the expression $\frac{1}{2}(2e^{j(\pi/4)})$, neglecting the initial condition term, and setting $s = 3j$ in the remaining expression. This procedure yields

$$\begin{bmatrix} 2+3j & -1 \\ -1 & 1+6j \end{bmatrix} \begin{bmatrix} C_1 \\ C_2 \end{bmatrix} = \begin{bmatrix} -2 \\ 1 \end{bmatrix} \tfrac{1}{2}(2e^{j(\pi/4)}), \quad (3.100)$$

from which

$$[C] = \begin{bmatrix} C_1 \\ C_2 \end{bmatrix} = \begin{bmatrix} 2+3j & -1 \\ -1 & 1+6j \end{bmatrix}^{-1} \begin{bmatrix} -2 \\ 1 \end{bmatrix} \tfrac{1}{2}(2e^{j(\pi/4)}) \quad (3.101)$$

$$= \begin{bmatrix} 0.541e^{j(\pi-\tan^{-1}0.146)} \\ 0.132e^{-j\tan^{-1}0.0625} \end{bmatrix}. \quad (3.96)$$

Thus the steady-state solution may be found by replacing the Laplace transform of the driving function by a complex number whose magnitude is half the amplitude of the original sinusoidal driving function, and whose argument is the corresponding phase angle. When we neglect the initial conditions and set $s = j\omega$, where ω is the angular frequency of the sinusoid, and solve, we obtain a column matrix of complex numbers whose magnitudes are half the amplitudes of the response sinusoids and whose arguments are the corresponding phase angles. We started with half the amplitude of the driving function and obtained half the amplitude of the response. So far as the steady state is concerned, we may just as well have dispensed with this factor $\frac{1}{2}$, and obtained the solution more directly.

EXAMPLE 3.7.   To illustrate the ease with which the sinusoidal steady-state response can be found, let us consider the network of Fig. 3.6. For this network,

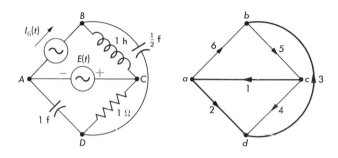

FIGURE 3.6

we assume that

$$E(t) = \cos t,$$
$$I_6(t) = -\sin t = \cos (t + \pi/2). \tag{3.102}$$

We write the chord equations, neglecting the initial conditions, and obtain

$$\begin{bmatrix} -1 \\ 1 \\ 0 \end{bmatrix} [V_1(s)] + \begin{bmatrix} 1 + \dfrac{1}{s} & -\dfrac{1}{s} & \dfrac{1}{s} \\ -\dfrac{1}{s} & s + \dfrac{3}{s} & -\dfrac{3}{s} \\ \dfrac{1}{s} & -\dfrac{3}{s} & \dfrac{3}{s} \end{bmatrix} \begin{bmatrix} I_4(s) \\ I_5(s) \\ I_6(s) \end{bmatrix} + \begin{bmatrix} 0 \\ 0 \\ 1 \end{bmatrix} [V_6(s)] = \begin{bmatrix} 0 \\ 0 \\ 0 \end{bmatrix}, \tag{3.103}$$

so that we must solve

$$\begin{bmatrix} 1 + \dfrac{1}{s} & -\dfrac{1}{s} \\ -\dfrac{1}{s} & s + \dfrac{3}{s} \end{bmatrix} \begin{bmatrix} I_4(s) \\ I_5(s) \end{bmatrix} = \begin{bmatrix} 1 \\ -1 \end{bmatrix} [V_1(s)] + \begin{bmatrix} -\dfrac{1}{s} \\ \dfrac{3}{s} \end{bmatrix} I_6(s). \tag{3.104}$$

In (3.104) we replace $V_1(s)$ by 1 and $I_6(s)$ by $e^{j(\pi/2)} = j$ and set $s = j\omega = j$, so that we obtain

$$\begin{bmatrix} 1 + \dfrac{1}{j} & -\dfrac{1}{j} \\ -\dfrac{1}{j} & j + \dfrac{3}{j} \end{bmatrix} \begin{bmatrix} \bar{I}_4 \\ \bar{I}_5 \end{bmatrix} = \begin{bmatrix} 1 \\ -1 \end{bmatrix} + \begin{bmatrix} -\dfrac{1}{j} \\ \dfrac{3}{j} \end{bmatrix} j \tag{3.105}$$

or

$$\begin{bmatrix} 1 - j & j \\ j & -2j \end{bmatrix} \begin{bmatrix} \bar{I}_4 \\ \bar{I}_5 \end{bmatrix} = \begin{bmatrix} 0 \\ 2 \end{bmatrix}, \tag{3.106}$$

where the variables $\bar{I}_4$ and $\bar{I}_5$ are complex numbers whose magnitudes and arguments constitute the steady-state solution. The solution is

$$\begin{bmatrix} \bar{I}_4 \\ \bar{I}_5 \end{bmatrix} = \begin{bmatrix} 1 - j & j \\ j & -2j \end{bmatrix}^{-1} \begin{bmatrix} 0 \\ 2 \end{bmatrix} = \frac{1}{-1 \;\; -2j} \begin{bmatrix} -2j \\ 2 - 2j \end{bmatrix} = \frac{2}{5} \begin{bmatrix} 2 + j \\ 1 + 3j \end{bmatrix}. \tag{3.107}$$

Finally,

$$\begin{bmatrix} \bar{I}_4 \\ \bar{I}_5 \end{bmatrix} = \begin{bmatrix} (2/\sqrt{5})e^{j\tan^{-1}1/2} \\ (2\sqrt{2}/\sqrt{5})e^{j\tan^{-1}3} \end{bmatrix}, \tag{3.108}$$

so that the steady-state time response is

$$\begin{bmatrix} i_4(t) \\ i_5(t) \end{bmatrix}_{ss} = \begin{bmatrix} (2/\sqrt{5}) \cos (t + \tan^{-1}1/2) \\ (4/\sqrt{10}) \cos (t + \tan^{-1}3) \end{bmatrix} = \begin{bmatrix} (2/\sqrt{5}) \cos (t + 0.46) \\ (4/\sqrt{10}) \cos (t + 1.25) \end{bmatrix}. \tag{3.109}$$

Note that it would have been simple to write Eqs. (3.105) directly, and that the solution from this point is merely an exercise in complex number algebra. The complex numbers with which we replaced $V_1(s)$ and $I_6(s)$ are frequently called the *phasor* representations of the voltage and current drivers; (3.109) is correspondingly the phasor solution, or alternatively, the sinusoidal steady-state solution. We shall consistently identify the phasors by superscript bars, such as $\bar{I}$, $\bar{E}$. The terminology arises from the fact that complex numbers can be represented as vectors.

As a result of the above examples, we can state that the sinusoidal response may be obtained by the procedure outlined below.

A. *Transient*
(1) Write the network equations (Laplace domain).
(2) Invert the coefficient matrix and obtain the determinantal polynomial.
(3) Factor the determinantal polynomial.
(4) Find those terms of the partial fraction expansion whose denominators are the factors of the determinantal polynomial.
(5) The inverse Laplace transform of step 4 is the transient.

B. *Sinusoidal steady state*
(1) Write the network equations, neglecting the initial conditions.
(2) Replace the Laplace transforms of the drivers by their corresponding phasors.
(3) Set $s = j\omega$, where ω is the angular frequency of the applied sinusoids.
(4) The solution of the resulting set of linear algebraic equations is the sinusoidal steady-state solution of the network equations.

It is possible that for the particular value of ω, say ω_0, that we require, the determinant of the coefficient matrix, for $s = j\omega_0$, is zero. In such cases, we must invert the coefficient matrix before setting $s = j\omega_0$. Finally, the complete solution is just the sum of the transient and the steady state.

3.5. SYMBOLIC DEVELOPMENT OF THE SINUSOIDAL RESPONSE

In this section, we shall generalize the procedures introduced in Section 3.4 for finding the sinusoidal response. As in the case of the step-function response, we start with the representative set of network equations in the form

$$[W(s)][X(s)] = [F(s)] + [F(s, 0+)]. \tag{3.9}$$

In this case $[F(s)]$ is the Laplace transform of a column matrix of sinusoidal functions of the same frequency. Thus $[F(s)] = \mathcal{L}[f(t)]$, where

$$[f(t)] = \begin{bmatrix} F_1 \cos(\omega t + \phi_1) \\ F_2 \cos(\omega t + \phi_2) \\ \vdots \\ F_n \cos(\omega t + \phi_n) \end{bmatrix} \tag{3.110}$$

$$= \frac{1}{2} \begin{bmatrix} F_1 e^{j(\omega t + \phi_1)} \\ F_2 e^{j(\omega t + \phi_2)} \\ \vdots \\ F_n e^{j(\omega t + \phi_n)} \end{bmatrix} + \frac{1}{2} \begin{bmatrix} F_1 e^{-j(\omega t + \phi_1)} \\ F_2 e^{-j(\omega t + \phi_2)} \\ \vdots \\ F_n e^{-j(\omega t + \phi_n)} \end{bmatrix}, \tag{3.111}$$

$$= \frac{1}{2} \begin{bmatrix} F_1 e^{j\phi_1} \\ F_2 e^{j\phi_2} \\ \vdots \\ F_n e^{j\phi_n} \end{bmatrix} e^{j\omega t} + \frac{1}{2} \begin{bmatrix} F_1 e^{-j\phi_1} \\ F_2 e^{-j\phi_2} \\ \vdots \\ F_n e^{-j\phi_n} \end{bmatrix} e^{-j\omega t}, \tag{3.112}$$

or

$$[f(t)] = \begin{bmatrix} \overline{F}_1 \\ \overline{F}_2 \\ \vdots \\ \overline{F}_n \end{bmatrix} e^{j\omega t} + \begin{bmatrix} \overline{F}_1^* \\ \overline{F}_2^* \\ \vdots \\ \overline{F}_n^* \end{bmatrix} e^{-j\omega t} = [\overline{F}]e^{j\omega t} + [\overline{F}^*]e^{-j\omega t}, \tag{3.113}$$

where $\overline{F}_i = \frac{1}{2}F_i e^{j\phi_i}$.

Taking the Laplace transform of (3.113), we can write

$$[F(s)] = \mathcal{L}[f(t)] = \frac{[\overline{F}]}{s - j\omega} + \frac{[\overline{F}^*]}{s + j\omega}. \tag{3.114}$$

We substitute (3.114) into (3.9) and obtain

$$[W(s)][X(s)] = \frac{[\overline{F}]}{s - j\omega} + \frac{[\overline{F}^*]}{s + j\omega} + [F(s, 0+)]. \tag{3.115}$$

Since the entries of $[W(s)]$ are, in general, rational functions of s, we premultiply both sides of (3.115) by the diagonal matrix $[P(s)]$ whose entries are the lowest common multiples of the denominators of the corresponding rows of $[W(s)]$. This gives

$$[A(s)][X(s)] = [P(s)] \left\{ \frac{[\overline{F}]}{s - j\omega} + \frac{[\overline{F}^*]}{s + j\omega} + [F(s, 0+)] \right\}, \tag{3.116}$$

where

$$[A(s)] = [P(s)][W(s)] \tag{3.62}$$

is a matrix whose entries are polynomials in s. The solution of (3.116) is

$$[X(s)] = \frac{[A_1(s)][P(s)] \left\{ \dfrac{[\overline{F}]}{s - j\omega} + \dfrac{[\overline{F}^*]}{s + j\omega} + [F(s, 0+)] \right\}}{k(s - s_1)(s - s_2) \cdots (s - s_n)}, \tag{3.117}$$

where $[A_1(s)]$ is the adjoint of $[A(s)]$, and $k(s - s_1)(s - s_2) \cdots (s - s_n) = \det A(s)$ is the determinantal polynomial.

Expanding the right-hand side of (3.117) in terms of partial fractions, assuming that all s_i are distinct, we have

$$[X(s)] = \sum_{i=1}^{n} \frac{[X_i]}{s - s_i} + \frac{[\overline{X}_s]}{s - j\omega} + \frac{[\overline{X}_s^*]}{s + j\omega}, \tag{3.118}$$

where

$$[X_i] = \lim_{s \to s_i} (s - s_i)[X(s)], \tag{3.119}$$

$$[\overline{X}_s] = \lim_{s \to j\omega} (s - j\omega)[X(s)], \tag{3.120}$$

and

$$[\overline{X}_s^*] = \lim_{s \to -j\omega} (s + j\omega)[X(s)]. \tag{3.121}$$

It is useful to refer to the development of the step-function response in Section 3.3 to see how similar it is to the derivation in this section. This previous development will also help in proving that the two matrices $[\overline{X}_s]$ and $[\overline{X}_s^*]$ are, in fact, complex conjugates, as the notation shows.

The final time solution is given, for the sinusoidal case, by taking the inverse Laplace transform of (3.118). This yields

$$[x(t)] = \sum_{i=1}^{n} [X_i]e^{s_i t} + [\overline{X}_s]e^{j\omega t} + [\overline{X}_s^*]e^{-j\omega t}. \tag{3.122}$$

Here, the term $\sum_{i=1}^{n} [X_i]e^{s_i t}$ is the transient, and all our remarks in Section 3.3 again apply; if the real parts of any s_i are positive, the transient increases without bound; if any s_i are purely imaginary, the transient contains components which represent a sustained oscillation; if the real parts of all the s_i are negative, the transient decays exponentially. The numbers $s_1, s_2, \ldots, s_n$ are given once again by the zeros of the determinantal polynomial, and the column matrices $[X_i]$ are given by expression (3.119).

The sinusoidal steady-state response is given by

$$[x_s(t)] = [\overline{X}_s]e^{j\omega t} + [\overline{X}_s^*]e^{-j\omega t} \tag{3.123}$$

$$= \begin{bmatrix} \overline{X}_{s_1} \\ \overline{X}_{s_2} \\ \vdots \\ \overline{X}_{s_n} \end{bmatrix} e^{j\omega t} + \begin{bmatrix} \overline{X}_{s_1}^* \\ \overline{X}_{s_2}^* \\ \vdots \\ \overline{X}_{s_n}^* \end{bmatrix} e^{-j\omega t}$$

$$= \begin{bmatrix} |\overline{X}_{s_1}|(e^{j(\omega t+\theta_1)} + e^{-j(\omega t+\theta_1)}) \\ |\overline{X}_{s_2}|(e^{j(\omega t+\theta_2)} + e^{-j(\omega t+\theta_2)}) \\ \vdots \\ |\overline{X}_{s_n}|(e^{j(\omega t+\theta_n)} + e^{-j(\omega t+\theta_n)}) \end{bmatrix}, \tag{3.124}$$

where

$$\overline{X}_{s_i} = |\overline{X}_{s_i}| e^{j\theta_i}.$$

Finally,

$$[x_s(t)] = 2 \begin{bmatrix} |X_{s_1}| \cos (\omega t + \theta_1) \\ |X_{s_2}| \cos (\omega t + \theta_2) \\ \vdots \\ |X_{s_n}| \cos (\omega t + \theta_n) \end{bmatrix}. \tag{3.125}$$

Thus the sinusoidal steady-state solution is sinusoidal with the same frequency as that of the drivers. The phase angles and amplitudes are, of course, not the same. However, the amplitudes of the response functions are merely twice the magnitudes of the entries in $[\overline{X}_s]$, and the phase angles are the arguments of the same entries. Thus, once $[\overline{X}_s]$ is known, we can easily write the time functions representing the response. However, $[\overline{X}_s]$ is given by

$$[\overline{X}_s] = \lim_{s \to j\omega} (s - j\omega)[X(s)] \tag{3.120}$$

and, from (3.115),

$$[X(s)] = [W(s)]^{-1} \left\{ \frac{[\overline{F}]}{s - j\omega} + \frac{[\overline{F}^*]}{s + j\omega} + [F(s, 0+)] \right\}, \tag{3.126}$$

so that

$$[\overline{X}_s] = \lim_{s \to j\omega} (s - j\omega)[W(s)]^{-1} \frac{[\overline{F}]}{s - j\omega} + \lim_{s \to j\omega} (s - j\omega)[W(s)]^{-1} \left\{ \frac{[\overline{F}^*]}{s + j\omega} + [F(s, 0+)] \right\}. \tag{3.127}$$

Now the second limit on the right of (3.127) is zero, leaving

$$[\overline{X}_s] = \lim_{s \to j\omega} [W(s)]^{-1}[\overline{F}], \tag{3.128}$$

and, provided det $W(j\omega) \neq 0$, we have

$$[\overline{X}_s] = [W(j\omega)]^{-1}[\overline{F}]. \tag{3.129}$$

Thus $[\overline{X}_s]$ is the solution of the equations

$$[W(j\omega)][\overline{X}_s] = [\overline{F}]. \tag{3.130}$$

These are just the network equations with the driving functions replaced by the entries in $[\overline{F}]$, the initial conditions omitted, and $s = j\omega$. The magnitudes of the entries in $[\overline{F}]$ are exactly half the amplitudes of the original sinusoidal drivers, and the magnitudes of the entries in $[\overline{X}_s]$ are half the amplitudes of the response functions. Since we may multiply both sides of (3.130) by 2, we may use the amplitudes of the drivers to obtain the actual amplitudes of the response. The matrix $[\overline{F}]$ is called the phasor representation of the sinusoidal drivers, and $[\overline{X}_s]$ is the phasor representation of the response. The whole process of finding the sinusoidal steady-state solution is seen to be reduced to the solution of a set of linear algebraic equations whose coefficients are a set of complex numbers.

The above development has substantiated all the conclusions which we drew from our examples in Section 3.4, including the procedure for finding the solutions which we summarized at the end of that section.

3.6. POWER IN ELECTRIC NETWORKS

We have not so far made any reference to considerations of power and energy in electric networks. In this section, we shall show that the vertex and circuit postulates imply the principle of conservation of energy; we shall also introduce some of the terminology which is associated with power in alternating current networks.

For a two-terminal component the *instantaneous power* is defined as the product of the instantaneous terminal voltage and current. That is,

$$P(t) = v(t)i(t) \tag{3.131}$$

where $P(t)$ is the instantaneous power. The electric *energy* associated with the component is defined by

$$W(t) = \int_0^t P(t)\, dt. \tag{3.132}$$

For multiterminal components the definition of instantaneous power, expression (3.131), is generalized to read

$$P(t) = [v(t)]'[i(t)], \tag{3.133}$$

where $[v(t)]$, $[i(t)]$ are column matrices of the voltage and current associated with each of the elements of the terminal graph corresponding to the component, and the prime denotes the transpose.

Note that $P(t)$ is a scalar quantity. This is indicated in (3.133), since, for an $(n + 1)$-terminal component $[v(t)]'$ is a $1 \times n$ matrix, while $[i(t)]$ is an $n \times 1$ matrix. The product is therefore a 1×1 matrix or a scalar. It is also worth while mentioning that (3.131) is merely a special case of (3.133); that is, for a two-terminal component expression (3.133) reduces to (3.131).

The total instantaneous power in a given network is clearly the sum of the power for each component. Thus,

$$P_T(t) = \sum_k P_k(t) = \sum_k [v(t)]_k'[i(t)]_k. \tag{3.134}$$

This expression may be simplified by noting that it is merely the sum of the products of each of the element voltages in the network with their corresponding currents. We may therefore write

$$P_T(t) = \sum_{p=1}^e v_p(t)i_p(t) = [V(t)]'[I(t)], \tag{3.135}$$

where $[V(t)]$, $[I(t)]$ are, respectively, column matrices of all the voltages and currents in the network.

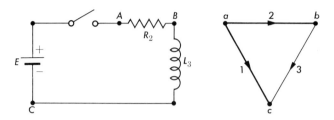

Fɪɢ. 3.7. A series RL network and system graph.

EXAMPLE 3.8. Consider the network of Fig. 3.7. This is the same as Fig. 3.1, and from Example 3.3, we have

$$i_2(t) = i_3(t) = -i_1(t) = \frac{E}{R_2}(1 - \tfrac{1}{2}e^{-(R_2/L_3)t}),$$

$$v_1(t) = E,$$

$$v_2(t) = E(1 - \tfrac{1}{2}e^{-(R_2/L_3)t}), \tag{3.136}$$

$$v_3(t) = \frac{E}{2}e^{-(R_2/L_3)t}.$$

The instantaneous powers associated with the various components are

$$P_R(t) = v_2(t)i_2(t) = \frac{E^2}{R_2}(1 - \tfrac{1}{2}e^{-(R_2/L_3)t})^2 \quad \text{(resistance)} \tag{3.137}$$

$$P_L(t) = v_3(t)i_3(t) = \frac{E^2}{2R_2}(1 - \tfrac{1}{2}e^{-(R_2/L_3)t})e^{-(R_2/L_3)t} \quad \text{(inductance)} \tag{3.138}$$

$$P_E(t) = v_1(t)i_1(t) = -\frac{E^2}{R_2}(1 - \tfrac{1}{2}e^{-(R_2/L_3)t}) \quad \text{(voltage driver)} \tag{3.139}$$

The total power is

$$
\begin{aligned}
P_T(t) &= [V(t)]'[I(t)] \\
&= v_1(t)i_1(t) + v_2(t)i_2(t) + v_3(t)i_3(t) \\
&= P_R(t) + P_L(t) + P_E(t) \\
&= (1 - \tfrac{1}{2}e^{-(R_2/L_3)t})\left\{\frac{E^2}{R_2}(1 - \tfrac{1}{2}e^{-(R_2/L_3)t}) + \frac{E^2}{2R_2}e^{-(R_2/L_3)t} - \frac{E^2}{R_2}\right\} \\
&= (1 - \tfrac{1}{2}e^{-(R_2/L_3)t})\frac{E^2}{R_2}\{(1 - \tfrac{1}{2}e^{-(R_2/L_3)t}) + \tfrac{1}{2}e^{-(R_2/L_3)t} - 1\} \\
&= 0. \tag{3.140}
\end{aligned}
$$

The fact that the total power is zero is no accident. It is merely a statement that the power required to operate some of the components is produced by others. Since power is the time derivative of energy, the total rate of change of energy is zero, and the energy is constant.

In order to show that this fact is implied by the network equations, let us partition the column matrices of the voltages and currents into

$$[V(t)] = \begin{bmatrix} V_b(t) \\ V_c(t) \end{bmatrix}, \tag{3.141}$$

$$[I(t)] = \begin{bmatrix} I_b(t) \\ I_c(t) \end{bmatrix}, \tag{3.142}$$

in order to show the branch and chord variables explicitly. With this partitioning, (3.135) becomes

$$P_T(t) = [V'_b(t)\ V'_c(t)] \begin{bmatrix} I_b(t) \\ I_c(t) \end{bmatrix}. \tag{3.143}$$

From the fundamental circuit equations, we have

$$\begin{bmatrix} V_b(t) \\ V_c(t) \end{bmatrix} = \begin{bmatrix} U \\ -B \end{bmatrix} [V_b(t)], \tag{3.144}$$

so that

$$[V'_b(t)\ V'_c(t)] = [V_b(t)]'[U\ -B']. \tag{3.145}$$

Similarly, from the cut-set equations,

$$\begin{bmatrix} I_b(t) \\ I_c(t) \end{bmatrix} = \begin{bmatrix} -A \\ U \end{bmatrix} [I_c(t)], \tag{3.146}$$

and, substituting (3.145) and (3.146) into (3.143), we obtain

$$P_T(t) = [V_b(t)]'[U\ -B'] \begin{bmatrix} -A \\ U \end{bmatrix} [I_c(t)] \tag{3.147}$$

$$= [V_b(t)]'[(-A\ -B')][I_c(t)]. \tag{3.148}$$

However, in Chapter 1 we noted that

$$-[B]' = [A], \tag{1.14}$$

or

$$[(-A\ -B')] = [0]. \tag{3.149}$$

Thus

$$P_T(t) = [V_b(t)]'[0][I_c(t)] = 0. \tag{3.150}$$

As we have already mentioned, this result is a statement of the fact that the total electric energy of any network is constant; whatever is removed by some components is replaced by others. In many fields, it is the practice to postulate this principle (conservation of energy) as fundamental. Had we done so, we would have initiated our discussion with three postulates:

(1) the vertex postulate,
(2) the circuit postulate,
(3) conservation of energy.

However, it can be shown that any two of these three will imply the third. We have chosen to use the vertex and circuit postulates, so that voltage and current are our fundamental variables. All other variables are defined in terms of these. In the area of mechanics, however, it has been the custom to use the vertex postulate and conservation of energy as the fundamentals, although this is not necessary, and in some cases, may not even be desirable.

We now turn our attention to power in networks under steady-state conditions. For these conditions we may neglect all the transient voltages and currents. Thus, for networks driven by dc-sources, only those components whose terminal equations contain algebraic terms can supply or dissipate energy. More particularly, the steady-state dc-power for inductances and capacitances is zero. The sinusoidal case, however, deserves more discussion. Suppose, for example, that the sinusoidal steady-state current through an inductance is

$$i_L(t) = I_0 \sin(\omega t + \phi). \tag{3.151}$$

The corresponding voltage will be

$$v_L(t) = L \frac{di_L(t)}{dt} = \omega L I_0 \cos(\omega t + \phi), \tag{3.152}$$

and the instantaneous power,

$$P_L(t) = i_L(t)v_L(t) = \omega L I_0 \sin(\omega t + \phi) \cos(\omega t + \phi)$$

$$= \frac{\omega L I_0}{2} \sin 2(\omega t + \phi). \tag{3.153}$$

The instantaneous power varies sinusoidally; it is sometimes positive and sometimes negative. We are more interested in the long-term question of whether or not energy will be dissipated by a component. The answer to this question is given by the *average power* which is defined by

$$P_{\text{ave}} = \frac{1}{t_2 - t_1} \int_{t_1}^{t_2} P(t) \, dt. \tag{3.154}$$

If the average power is positive, energy is dissipated in the interval $t_1 < t < t_2$, while if it is negative, energy is supplied. Note that in the steady-state dc-case, the average power is equal to the instantaneous power. For the sinusoidal case, the average power is a meaningful quantity if $t_2 - t_1 = 2\pi/\omega$, the period of the sinusoid, so that

$$P_{\text{ave}} = \frac{\omega}{2\pi} \int_0^{2\pi/\omega} P(t) \, dt. \tag{3.155}$$

For inductances and capacitances in the sinusoidal steady state, it may easily be verified that $P_{\text{ave}} = 0$.

Consider the sinusoidal steady-state voltage and current through a resistor R:

$$i(t) = I_0 \cos (\omega t + \phi),$$
$$v(t) = R I_0 \cos (\omega t + \phi). \tag{3.156}$$

We therefore have

$$P_R(t) = v(t) i(t) = R I_0^2 \cos^2 (\omega t + \phi) \tag{3.157}$$

for the instantaneous power, and

$$
\begin{aligned}
P_{R_{\text{ave}}} &= \frac{\omega}{2\pi} \int_0^{2\pi/\omega} R I_0^2 \cos^2 (\omega t + \phi)\, dt \\
&= \frac{\omega}{2\pi} R I_0^2 \int_0^{2\pi/\omega} \tfrac{1}{2}\{1 + \cos 2(\omega t + \phi)\}\, dt \\
&= \frac{\omega}{2\pi} R I_0^2 \frac{1}{2} \frac{2\pi}{\omega} = \frac{1}{2} R I_0^2.
\end{aligned}
\tag{3.158}
$$

On the other hand, when the same resistor is used under steady-state dc-conditions, we obtain

$$i(t) = I_0, \qquad v(t) = R I_0, \qquad P_R(t) = P_{R_{\text{ave}}}(t) = R I_0^2.$$

Thus the energy dissipated by a resistance in the sinusoidal steady-state is just half that dissipated under dc-conditions when the magnitude of the direct current is equal to the amplitude of the sinusoid. This leads us to the notion of the *effective value* of a sinusoidal current.

The *effective value of a sinusoidal current* is defined as the magnitude of the corresponding direct current which will give rise to an identical power in a unit resistance. A similar definition applies to the effective value of a voltage.

The effective value of a current or voltage is also called the *rms value*. It is the square root of the mean of the square of the given function. That is,

$$V_{\text{eff}} = V_{\text{rms}} = \left\{ \frac{1}{t_2 - t_1} \int_{t_1}^{t_2} (v(t))^2\, dt \right\}^{1/2}. \tag{3.159}$$

For sinusoids this becomes

$$
\begin{aligned}
I_{\text{rms}} &= \left\{ \frac{\omega}{2\pi} \int_0^{2\pi/\omega} I_0^2 \cos^2 (\omega t + \phi)\, dt \right\}^{1/2} \\
&= \left\{ \frac{\omega I_0^2}{2\pi} \frac{1}{2} \int_0^{2\pi/\omega} [1 + \cos 2(\omega t + \phi)]\, dt \right\}^{1/2} \\
&= \left\{ \frac{\omega I_0^2}{2\pi} \frac{1}{2} \frac{2\pi}{\omega} \right\}^{1/2} = \frac{I_0}{\sqrt{2}}.
\end{aligned}
$$

Thus we have

$$V_{\text{rms}} = V_{\text{eff}} = V_0/\sqrt{2},$$
$$I_{\text{rms}} = I_{\text{eff}} = I_0/\sqrt{2} \tag{3.160}$$

for sinusoids. For other waveforms, the ratio of the amplitude to the effective value is not necessarily $\sqrt{2}$.

To close this section we shall discuss an example of a power calculation for the sinusoidal steady state in a simple RLC network which contains exactly one voltage driver. This example will also serve to introduce the concepts of driving-point impedance and admittance. In Chapter 4 we shall discuss these topics more thoroughly; however, for the present, we define the *driving-point impedance* $Z(j\omega)$ of a network containing only one voltage driver as the ratio of the Laplace transform of the voltage across the source to that of the total current taken from the source, with $s = j\omega$. The *driving-point admittance* $Y(j\omega)$ is defined as the reciprocal of the driving-point impedance. Thus,

$$Z(j\omega) = V(j\omega)/I(j\omega), \tag{3.161}$$

$$Y(j\omega) = 1/Z(j\omega) = I(j\omega)/V(j\omega), \tag{3.162}$$

where $V(j\omega)$, $I(j\omega)$ are the Laplace transforms ($s = j\omega$) of the source voltage and the current taken from the source, respectively.

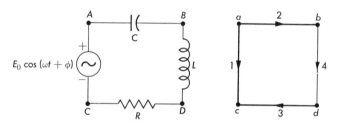

Fig. 3.8. An RLC series network and system graph.

EXAMPLE 3.9. Let us consider the simple network of Fig. 3.8. For this network we note that

$$-i_1(t) = i_2(t) = i_3(t) = i_4(t) = i(t), \tag{3.163}$$

where $i(t)$ is the total current drawn from the source.

We know that the average power in the inductance and capacitance is zero, and that the energy in the network is dissipated by the resistance and supplied by the source. Hence we could find the power by merely evaluating the average power in the resistance. However, for more complicated networks, we would need to add the power connected with all the resistances, so that another method may be more efficient. Our alternative is to find the power corresponding to the source. This must be equal in magnitude and opposite in sign to the sum of the powers connected with the resistances. We shall follow this approach.

The instantaneous power we wish to find is

$$-P_E(t) = -v_1(t)i_1(t) = v_1(t)i(t). \tag{3.164}$$

Now, for the sinusoidal steady state, we can find $i(t)$ by solving the chord equation

$$E_0 e^{j\phi} = \overline{E}_0 = (R + j\omega L + 1/j\omega C)\overline{I}, \tag{3.165}$$

where $\overline{E}_0$, $\overline{I}$ are the phasors corresponding to $E_0 \cos(\omega t + \phi)$ and $i(t)$, respectively. Using our definitions of impedance and admittance, we can write (3.165) in the form

$$\overline{E}_0 = Z(j\omega)\overline{I} = \overline{I}/Y(j\omega), \tag{3.166}$$

where

$$Z(j\omega) = R + j(\omega L - 1/\omega C),$$

and

$$Y(j\omega) = \frac{1}{R + j(\omega L - 1/\omega C)}. \tag{3.167}$$

From (3.166), we obtain

$$\overline{I} = \overline{E}_0 Y(j\omega), \tag{3.168}$$

or

$$i(t) = E_0 |Y| \cos(\omega t + \phi + \psi), \tag{3.169}$$

where ψ is the argument of Y.

Thus, from (3.164) and (3.169),

$$\begin{aligned} P_E(t) &= E_0 \cos(\omega t + \phi) E_0 |Y| \cos(\omega t + \phi + \psi) \\ &= E_0^2 |Y| \cos(\omega t + \phi) \cos(\omega t + \phi + \psi), \end{aligned} \tag{3.170}$$

and the average power,

$$\begin{aligned} P_{\text{ave}} &= E_0^2 |Y| \frac{\omega}{2\pi} \int_0^{2\pi/\omega} \cos(\omega t + \phi) \cos(\omega t + \phi + \psi)\, dt \\ &= E_0^2 |Y| \frac{\omega}{2\pi} \frac{1}{2} \int_0^{2\pi/\omega} \{\cos(2\omega t + 2\phi + \psi) + \cos\psi\}\, dt \\ &= E_0^2 |Y| \frac{\omega}{2\pi} \frac{1}{2} \frac{2\pi}{\omega} \cos\psi = \frac{E_0^2}{2} |Y| \cos\psi. \end{aligned} \tag{3.171}$$

An alternative procedure for the sinusoidal steady state is to define the average power as

$$P_{\text{ave}} = \tfrac{1}{2} \operatorname{Re}(\overline{E}_0 \overline{I}^*), \tag{3.172}$$

where the symbol Re indicates the real part of a complex number. This is entirely equivalent to our approach, since

$$\overline{I} = \overline{E}_0 Y(j\omega),$$

so that

$$\overline{E}_0 \overline{I}^* = |\overline{E}_0|e^{j\phi}|\overline{E}_0 Y(j\omega)|e^{-j(\phi+\psi)} = |\overline{E}_0|^2|Y|e^{-j\psi},$$

and

$$\mathrm{Re}\,(\overline{E}_0 \overline{I}^*) = |\overline{E}_0|^2|Y|\cos\psi. \tag{3.173}$$

Had we used the effective or rms-values of the sinusoidal quantities in place of the amplitudes for defining the phasor quantities, that is,

$$\overline{E}_{0_{\mathrm{rms}}} = \frac{1}{\sqrt{2}}\,\overline{E}_0, \qquad \overline{I}_{\mathrm{rms}} = \frac{1}{\sqrt{2}}\,\overline{I},$$

we would have obtained

$$P_{\mathrm{ave}} = \mathrm{Re}(\overline{E}_{0_{\mathrm{rms}}}\overline{I}^*_{\mathrm{rms}}). \tag{3.174}$$

This expression may also be written in any of the following forms by substitutions of Eqs. (3.162) and (3.169). Thus,

$$P_{\mathrm{ave}} = \mathrm{Re}\,(\overline{E}_{0_{\mathrm{rms}}}\overline{I}^*_{\mathrm{rms}}), \tag{3.174}$$

$$P_{\mathrm{ave}} = \mathrm{Re}\,Z(j\omega)|\overline{I}_{\mathrm{rms}}|^2 = \mathrm{Re}\,\frac{|\overline{I}_{\mathrm{rms}}|^2}{Y(j\omega)}, \tag{3.175}$$

$$P_{\mathrm{ave}} = \mathrm{Re}\,\frac{|\overline{E}_{0_{\mathrm{rms}}}|^2}{Z(j\omega)} = \mathrm{Re}\,Y(j\omega)|\overline{E}_{0_{\mathrm{rms}}}|^2, \tag{3.176}$$

$$P_{\mathrm{ave}} = |\overline{E}_{0_{\mathrm{rms}}}|^2|Y(j\omega)|\cos\psi = \frac{|\overline{E}_{0_{\mathrm{rms}}}|^2}{|Z(j\omega)|}\cos\psi, \tag{3.172}$$

$$P_{\mathrm{ave}} = |\overline{I}_{\mathrm{rms}}|^2|Z(j\omega)|\cos\psi = \frac{|I_{\mathrm{rms}}|^2}{|Y(j\omega)|}\cos\psi. \tag{3.177}$$

Note that $\cos\psi = 1$ when $Z(j\omega)$ and $Y(j\omega)$ are purely real. This situation occurs when the network is purely resistive, or when $\omega L = 1/\omega C$; $\cos\psi$ is less than unity for other frequencies. The quantity $\cos\psi$ is called the *power factor* of the network; since ψ is the difference between the phase angles of the current and voltage, we have the following definition. The *power factor* of a given two-terminal network is the cosine of the difference in phase between the voltage and current applied to the network.

The driving-point impedance $Z(j\omega)$ may be expanded as

$$Z(j\omega) = \mathrm{Re}\,[Z(j\omega)] + j\,\mathrm{Im}\,[Z(j\omega)] = R(\omega) + jX(\omega), \tag{3.178}$$

where the symbol Im denotes the imaginary part of a complex number. In (3.178) $R(\omega)$ is called the resistive part of the impedance, and $X(\omega)$ is called the *reactance*. Thus the reactance is the imaginary part of the impedance.

Similarly, the driving point admittance may be expanded as

$$Y(j\omega) = \mathrm{Re}\,[Y(j\omega)] + j\,\mathrm{Im}\,[Y(j\omega)] = G(\omega) + jB(\omega). \tag{3.179}$$

Here $G(\omega)$ is the *conductance*, and $B(\omega)$ the *susceptance*. Note that the power factor is given by

$$\cos \psi = \frac{G(\omega)}{\sqrt{G^2(\omega) + B^2(\omega)}} = \frac{R(\omega)}{\sqrt{R^2(\omega) + X^2(\omega)}}, \qquad (3.180)$$

and

$$\psi = \tan^{-1} \frac{B(\omega)}{G(\omega)} = -\tan^{-1} \frac{X(\omega)}{R(\omega)}. \qquad (3.181)$$

3.7. THE PRINCIPLE OF SUPERPOSITION

If our methods were useful only in cases where the voltage and current drivers were all pure sinusoids with the same frequency, they would not be very fruitful. Indeed, it is very seldom that voltage or current sources of such an idealized nature are encountered. More frequently, the driving functions can be written in the form

$$F(t) = B_0 + B_1 \cos \omega t + B_2 \cos 2\omega t + \cdots + B_n \cos n\omega t, \qquad (3.182)$$

in which there are components not only of the fundamental frequency ω but also of the harmonic frequencies 2ω, 3ω, etc.

To show how the techniques of the previous sections can be adapted for such cases, we shall use the *principle of superposition*, which can be expressed in the following theorem.

Theorem 3.1. (Superposition). Let $[A][X] = [F]$ be a set of linear equations in which $[A]$ is a square nonsingular matrix of constants, $[X]$ is a column matrix of unknowns, and $[F]$ is a known column matrix. Furthermore, let

$$[F] = [F_1] + [F_2] + \cdots + [F_n], \qquad (3.183)$$

where $[F_i]$, $i = 1, 2, \ldots, n$, are all known column matrices. Then,

$$[X] = [X_1] + [X_2] + \cdots + [X_n], \qquad (3.184)$$

where $[X_i]$, $i = 1, 2, \ldots, n$, are the solutions of the sets of equations $[A][X_i] = [F_i]$.

To prove this theorem, we merely note that

$$[X] = [A]^{-1}[F], \qquad (3.185)$$

and

$$[X_i] = [A]^{-1}[F_i]. \qquad (3.186)$$

Then

$$\sum_{i=1}^{n} [X_i] = \sum_{i=1}^{n} [A]^{-1}[F_i] = [A]^{-1} \sum_{i=1}^{n} [F_i]. \qquad (3.187)$$

But

$$\sum_{i=1}^{n} [F_i] = [F]. \tag{3.188}$$

Therefore,

$$\sum_{i=1}^{n} [X_i] = [A]^{-1}[F] = [X]. \tag{3.189}$$

We now observe how the principle of superposition can be of service to us. First, let us suppose that there is only one driving function for our network. The network equations are

$$[W(s)][X(s)] = [F(s)] + [F(s, 0+)], \tag{3.9}$$

in which $[F(s)] = [F]G(s)$, where $[F]$ is a column matrix of constants, and $G(s)$ represents the single driving function. If

$$G(s) = \mathcal{L}\{B_0 + B_1 \cos \omega t + B_2 \cos 2\omega t + \cdots + B_n \cos n\omega t\} \tag{3.190}$$

$$= \frac{B_0}{s} + \frac{B_1 s}{s^2 + \omega^2} + \frac{B_2 s}{s^2 + (2\omega)^2} + \cdots + \frac{B_n s}{s^2 + (n\omega)^2}, \tag{3.191}$$

we have

$$[W(s)][X(s)] = \frac{B_0}{s}[F] + \sum_{k=1}^{n} \frac{[F]B_k s}{s^2 + (k\omega)^2} + [F(s, 0+)]. \tag{3.192}$$

Equations (3.192) are in exactly the same form as those used in our statement of the superposition theorem. Therefore, to find the complete solution, we solve

$$[W(s)][X_0(s)] = \frac{B_0[F]}{s},$$

$$[W(s)][X_k(s)] = \frac{B_k s[F]}{s^2 + (k\omega)^2}, \qquad k = 1, 2, \ldots, n, \tag{3.193}$$

$$[W(s)][X_{n+1}(s)] = [F(s, 0+)].$$

The complete solution is

$$[X(s)] = [X_0(s)] + [X_1(s)] + \cdots + [X_n(s)] + [X_{n+1}(s)], \tag{3.194}$$

and the final time solution is the inverse Laplace transform of (3.194).

We can, of course, separate the transient and the steady-state solutions from the equations we solve. The total steady-state solution will be the sum of the individual steady-state terms, and the complete transient will be the sum of the individual transients.

EXAMPLE 3.10. In this example we shall calculate the steady-state current through the inductance in the network of Fig. 3.9 when

$$E_1(t) = 1 + \cos t + \cos 3t. \tag{3.195}$$

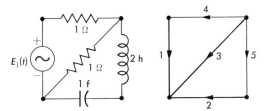

FIG. 3.9. Simple network and graph.

First, the chord equations are

$$\begin{bmatrix} 2 & 1 \\ 1 & 1 + 2s + 1/s \end{bmatrix} \begin{bmatrix} I_4(s) \\ I_5(s) \end{bmatrix} = \begin{bmatrix} -V_1(s) \\ 0 \end{bmatrix}, \tag{3.196}$$

where we have omitted the initial conditions because we are interested only in the steady state.

We first solve for the steady-state dc-term; that is, we replace $V_1(s)$ by 1 and set $s = 0$. This gives

$$\begin{bmatrix} I_4 \\ I_5 \end{bmatrix}_{dc} = \begin{bmatrix} 2 & 1 \\ 0 & 1 \end{bmatrix}^{-1} \begin{bmatrix} -1 \\ 0 \end{bmatrix} = \tfrac{1}{2} \begin{bmatrix} 1 & -1 \\ 0 & 2 \end{bmatrix} \begin{bmatrix} -1 \\ 0 \end{bmatrix}, \tag{3.197}$$

from which

$$I_{5dc} = 0. \tag{3.198}$$

Next, we solve for a typical sinusoidal steady-state response; we replace $V_1(s)$ by 1, and set $s = j\omega$. Thus,

$$\begin{bmatrix} 2 & 1 \\ j\omega & -2\omega^2 + j\omega + 1 \end{bmatrix} \begin{bmatrix} \bar{I}_4 \\ \bar{I}_5 \end{bmatrix} = \begin{bmatrix} -1 \\ 0 \end{bmatrix}, \tag{3.199}$$

or

$$\begin{bmatrix} \bar{I}_4 \\ \bar{I}_5 \end{bmatrix} = \frac{1}{-4\omega^2 + j\omega + 2} \begin{bmatrix} -2\omega^2 + j\omega + 1 & -1 \\ -j\omega & 2 \end{bmatrix} \begin{bmatrix} -1 \\ 0 \end{bmatrix},$$

so that

$$\begin{aligned}
\bar{I}_5 &= \frac{j\omega}{2 - 4\omega^2 + j\omega} \\
&= \frac{\omega}{\sqrt{4(1 - 2\omega^2)^2 + \omega^2}} \exp\left[j\left(\frac{\pi}{2} - \tan^{-1} \frac{\omega}{2 - 4\omega^2} \right) \right]. \tag{3.200}
\end{aligned}$$

Therefore,

$$\begin{aligned}
I_5(t) &= \frac{\omega}{\sqrt{4(1 - 2\omega^2)^2 + \omega^2}} \cos\left(\omega t + \frac{\pi}{2} - \tan^{-1} \frac{\omega}{2 - 4\omega^2} \right) \\
&= \frac{\omega}{\sqrt{4(1 - 2\omega^2)^2 + \omega^2}} \cos\left(\omega t + \tan^{-1} \frac{2 - 4\omega^2}{\omega} \right). \tag{3.201}
\end{aligned}$$

For this example we have to evaluate two terms corresponding to $\omega = 1$ and $\omega = 3$. When $\omega = 1$,

$$I_{5_1}(t) = \frac{1}{\sqrt{5}} \cos [t + \tan^{-1} (-2)]. \tag{3.202}$$

When $\omega = 3$,

$$I_{5_3}(t) = \frac{3}{\sqrt{1165}} \cos \left(3t + \tan^{-1} - \frac{34}{3} \right). \tag{3.203}$$

Therefore, the complete steady-state response is

$$I_5(t) = I_{5_{dc}} + I_{5_1}(t) + I_{5_3}(t)$$

$$= 0 + \frac{1}{\sqrt{5}} \cos [t + \tan^{-1} (-2)] + \frac{3}{\sqrt{1165}} \cos \left(3t + \tan^{-1} - \frac{34}{3} \right).$$

$$\tag{3.204}$$

The principle of superposition may also be applied when there are many voltage and current drivers, each of which can be expressed as combinations of step functions and sinusoids of various frequencies. We first calculate the response to the step-function drivers acting alone, and later to each set of sinusoidal drivers with common frequencies. The total response is merely the sum of all these individual components.

Finally, it is unnecessary for us to consider only applications of the superposition theorem to sinusoidal and step driving functions. However, as we shall show in the next section, most periodic driving functions can be expressed in terms of functions of those two types, so that they are of particular interest.

3.8. FOURIER SERIES REPRESENTATION OF SIGNALS

As we mentioned in Section 3.7, the driving functions for practical networks can frequently be written in terms of sums of sinusoids. This is done by means of the *Fourier series*, whose elementary details are explained in Appendix B.

We shall not find it necessary in our development to refer frequently to the Fourier series representation of signals; we include this section in order to provide one method for dealing with general periodic driving functions. We shall only state the important results from Appendix B, and follow them by illustrative examples.

Suppose we are given a function $f(t)$, such that $f(t + 2L) = f(t)$; that is, $f(t)$ is periodic with period $2L$. This may be a representative periodic voltage or current driver. We may expand $f(t)$ by the *trigonometric Fourier series*,

$$f(t) = \frac{a_0}{2} + \sum_{n=1}^{\infty} a_n \cos \frac{n\pi t}{L} + \sum_{n=1}^{\infty} b_n \sin \frac{n\pi t}{L} \tag{3.205}$$

or

$$f(t) = \frac{a_0}{2} + \sum_{n=1}^{\infty} a_n \cos n\omega t + \sum_{n=1}^{\infty} b_n \sin n\omega t, \tag{3.206}$$

where

$$\omega = \pi/L \tag{3.207}$$

and the *Fourier coefficients* are given by

$$a_0 = \frac{1}{L} \int_{-L}^{L} f(t) \, dt = \frac{\omega}{\pi} \int_{-\pi/\omega}^{\pi/\omega} f(t) \, dt, \tag{3.208}$$

$$a_n = \frac{1}{L} \int_{-L}^{L} f(t) \cos \frac{n\pi t}{L} \, dt = \frac{\omega}{\pi} \int_{-\pi/\omega}^{\pi/\omega} f(t) \cos n\omega t \, dt, \tag{3.209}$$

$$b_n = \frac{1}{L} \int_{-L}^{L} f(t) \sin \frac{n\pi t}{L} \, dt = \frac{\omega}{\pi} \int_{-\pi/\omega}^{\pi/\omega} f(t) \sin n\omega t \, dt. \tag{3.210}$$

If $f(t)$ is an *even function*, that is, if $f(t) = f(-t)$, the Fourier trigonometric series reduces to

$$f(t) = \frac{a_0}{2} + \sum_{n=1}^{\infty} a_n \cos \frac{n\pi t}{L}, \tag{3.211}$$

or

$$f(t) = \frac{a_0}{2} + \sum_{n=1}^{\infty} a_n \cos n\omega t, \qquad \text{where} \qquad \omega = \frac{\pi}{L}, \tag{3.212}$$

which is the *Fourier cosine* series. The coefficients are in this case given by

$$a_0 = \frac{2}{L} \int_{0}^{L} f(t) \, dt = \frac{2\omega}{\pi} \int_{0}^{\pi/\omega} f(t) \, dt, \tag{3.213}$$

$$a_n = \frac{2}{L} \int_{0}^{L} f(t) \cos \frac{n\pi t}{L} \, dt = \frac{2\omega}{\pi} \int_{0}^{\pi/\omega} f(t) \cos n\omega t \, dt. \tag{3.214}$$

The Fourier cosine series may also be used to expand the function $f_1(t) = E_v\{f(t)\}$, the even part of $f(t)$.

If $f(t)$ is an *odd function*, that is, if $f(t) = -f(-t)$, the Fourier trigonometric series reduces to

$$f(t) = \sum_{n=1}^{\infty} b_n \sin \frac{n\pi t}{L}, \tag{3.215}$$

or

$$f(t) = \sum_{n=1}^{\infty} b_n \sin n\omega t, \qquad \text{where} \qquad \omega = \frac{\pi}{L}, \tag{3.216}$$

which is the *Fourier sine series*. In this case the coefficients are given by

$$b_n = \frac{2}{L} \int_{0}^{L} f(t) \sin \frac{n\pi t}{L} \, dt = \frac{2\omega}{\pi} \int_{0}^{\pi/\omega} f(t) \sin n\omega t \, dt. \tag{3.217}$$

The Fourier sine series may also be used to expand $f_2(t) = O_d\{f(t)\}$, the odd part of $f(t)$.

We may also observe that each term in the Fourier trigonometric series may be expanded in terms of exponentials; this leads to the *exponential Fourier series*:

$$f(t) = \sum_{n=-\infty}^{\infty} c_n e^{jn\pi t/L} = \sum_{n=-\infty}^{\infty} c_n e^{jn\omega t}, \tag{3.218}$$

where

$$c_n = \frac{1}{2L} \int_{-L}^{L} f(t)e^{-jn\pi t/L} \, dt = \frac{\omega}{2\pi} \int_{-\pi/\omega}^{\pi/\omega} f(t)e^{-jn\omega t} \, dt. \tag{3.219}$$

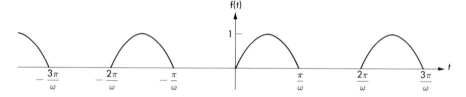

FIG. 3.10. Half-wave rectified sine wave.

EXAMPLE 3.11.   We shall evaluate the Fourier trigonometrical series for the "Halfwave rectified sine wave" of Fig. 3.10. This function may be expressed as

$$f(t) = \begin{cases} \sin \omega t & 0 < t < \pi/\omega, \\ 0 & -\pi/\omega < t < 0, \end{cases} \tag{3.220}$$

$$f(t) = f\left(t + \frac{2\pi}{\omega}\right).$$

We calculate,

$$a_0 = \frac{\omega}{\pi} \int_{-\pi/\omega}^{\pi/\omega} f(t) \, dt = \frac{\omega}{\pi} \int_{0}^{\pi/\omega} \sin \omega t \, dt = \frac{\omega}{\pi}\left(-\frac{1}{\omega}\right)[\cos \omega t]_0^{\pi/\omega}$$

$$= -\frac{1}{\pi}\{-1 \quad -1\} = \frac{2}{\pi}, \tag{3.221}$$

$$a_n = \frac{\omega}{\pi} \int_{-\pi/\omega}^{\pi/\omega} f(t) \cos n\omega t \, dt = \frac{\omega}{\pi} \int_{0}^{\pi/\omega} \sin \omega t \cos n\omega t \, dt$$

$$= \frac{\omega}{2\pi} \int_{0}^{\pi/\omega} \{\sin (n + 1)\omega t - \sin (n - 1)\omega t\} \, dt$$

$$= \frac{\omega}{2\pi}\left[\frac{\cos (n - 1)\omega t}{(n - 1)\omega} - \frac{\cos (n+1)\omega t}{(n+1)\omega}\right]_0^{\pi/\omega} \quad (n \neq 1)$$

$$= \frac{1}{2\pi}\left\{\frac{\cos (n - 1)\pi}{n - 1} - \frac{\cos (n+1)\pi}{n+1} + \frac{1}{n+1} - \frac{1}{n-1}\right\}.$$

Now, for $n = 2m$,

$$\cos (n \pm 1)\pi = \cos (2m \pm 1)\pi = -1$$

and, for $n = 2m + 1$,

$$\cos (n + 1)\pi = \cos (2m + 2)\pi = 1,$$
$$\cos (n - 1)\pi = \cos (2m\pi) = 1.$$

Therefore,

$$a_{2m} = \frac{1}{2\pi} \left\{ \frac{-1}{2m - 1} + \frac{1}{2m + 1} + \frac{1}{2m + 1} - \frac{1}{2m - 1} \right\} = \frac{-2}{\pi(4m^2 - 1)}, \tag{3.222}$$

$$a_{2m+1} = \frac{1}{2\pi} \left\{ \frac{1}{2m} - \frac{1}{2m + 2} + \frac{1}{2m + 2} - \frac{1}{2m} \right\} = 0, \tag{3.223}$$

and

$$a_1 = \frac{\omega}{\pi} \int_0^{\pi/\omega} \sin \omega t \cos \omega t \, dt = 0. \tag{3.224}$$

Finally,

$$b_n = \frac{\omega}{\pi} \int_{-\pi/\omega}^{\pi/\omega} f(t) \sin n\omega t \, dt = \frac{\omega}{\pi} \int_0^{\pi/\omega} \sin \omega t \sin n\omega t \, dt$$

$$= \frac{\omega}{2\pi} \int_0^{\pi/\omega} \{ \cos (n - 1)\omega t - \cos (n + 1)\omega t \} \, dt$$

$$= \frac{\omega}{2\pi} \left[\frac{\sin (n - 1)\omega t}{(n - 1)\omega} - \frac{\sin (n + 1)\omega t}{(n + 1)\omega} \right]_0^{\pi/\omega} \quad (n \neq 1)$$

$$= \frac{1}{2\pi} \left\{ \frac{\sin (n - 1)\pi}{n - 1} - \frac{\sin (n + 1)\pi}{n + 1} \right\}. \tag{3.225}$$

Hence

$$b_n = 0 \quad \text{for} \quad n \neq 1,$$

and

$$b_1 = \frac{\omega}{\pi} \int_0^{\pi/\omega} \sin^2 \omega t \, dt = \frac{\omega}{\pi} \frac{1}{2} \int_0^{\pi/\omega} (1 - \cos 2\omega t) \, dt$$

$$= \frac{\omega}{2\pi} \left[t - \frac{1}{2\omega} \sin 2\omega t \right]_0^{\pi/\omega} = \frac{\omega}{2\pi} \left\{ \frac{\pi}{\omega} \right\} = \frac{1}{2}. \tag{3.226}$$

Thus, the trigonometrical Fourier series is

$$f(t) = \frac{1}{\pi} + \frac{1}{2} \sin \omega t - \frac{2}{\pi} \sum_{m=1}^{\infty} \frac{1}{4m^2 - 1} \cos 2m\omega t. \tag{3.227}$$

Further examples of the calculation of Fourier series appear in Appendix B.

The application of Fourier series to the solution of networks with arbitrary periodic drivers is very similar to the method used in Example 3.10; we merely evaluate the solution for each term in the Fourier series, and sum. By virtue of the superposition principle, the resulting series is the complete solution. A single example will suffice to show the method.

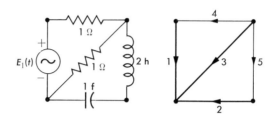

FIG. 3.11. Simple network and graph.

EXAMPLE 3.12. Consider the network of Fig. 3.11. This is the same as Fig. 3.9, and we shall find the steady-state current through the inductance when $E_1(t)$ is the "full wave rectified sine wave" defined by:

$$E_1(t) = \sin \omega t, \quad 0 < t < \pi/\omega,$$
$$E_1(t + \pi/\omega) = E_1(t). \tag{3.228}$$

The Fourier series for this function is

$$E_1(t) = \frac{2}{\pi} - \frac{4}{\pi} \sum_{n=1}^{\infty} \frac{1}{(4n^2 - 1)} \cos 2n\omega t, \tag{3.229}$$

and the chord equations are

$$\begin{bmatrix} 2 & 1 \\ 1 & 1 + 2s + \frac{1}{s} \end{bmatrix} \begin{bmatrix} I_4(s) \\ I_5(s) \end{bmatrix} = \begin{bmatrix} -V_1(s) \\ 0 \end{bmatrix}. \tag{3.196}$$

We solve for the dc-term by replacing $V_1(s)$ by $2/\pi$ and setting $s = 0$. This gives

$$I_{5\mathrm{dc}} = 0. \tag{3.230}$$

For the sinusoidal terms, we replace $V_1(s)$ by the phasor

$$\overline{V}_{1,n} = \frac{-4}{\pi(4n^2 - 1)}, \tag{3.231}$$

and set $s = j\omega_n = 2jn\omega$.

The solution is given by

$$\begin{bmatrix} 2 & 1 \\ j\omega_n & -2\omega_n^2 + j\omega_n + 1 \end{bmatrix} \begin{bmatrix} \overline{I}_{4n} \\ \overline{I}_{5n} \end{bmatrix} = \begin{bmatrix} 4/\pi(4n^2 - 1) \\ 0 \end{bmatrix}, \tag{3.232}$$

from which we obtain

$$\bar{I}_{5n} = \frac{-4j\omega_n}{\pi(4n^2 - 1)(2 - 4\omega_n^2 + j\omega_n)}$$

$$= -\frac{4\omega_n}{\pi(4n^2 - 1)\sqrt{4(1 - 2\omega_n^2)^2 + \omega_n^2}} \exp\left[j\left(\frac{\pi}{2} - \tan^{-1}\frac{\omega_n}{2 - 4\omega_n^2}\right)\right]. \qquad (3.233)$$

Therefore,

$$i_{5n}(t) = \frac{-4\omega_n}{\pi(4n^2 - 1)\sqrt{4(1 - 2\omega_n^2)^2 + \omega_n^2}} \cos\left(\omega_n t + \frac{\pi}{2} - \tan^{-1}\frac{\omega_n}{2 - 4\omega_n^2}\right),$$

and since $\omega_n = 2n\omega$,

$$i_{5n}(t) = \frac{-8n\omega}{\pi(4n^2 - 1)\sqrt{4(1 - 8n^2\omega^2)^2 + 4n^2\omega^2}} \cos\left(2n\omega t + \frac{\pi}{2} - \tan^{-1}\frac{n\omega}{1 - 8n^2\omega^2}\right). \qquad (3.234)$$

Thus the complete solution is

$$i_5(t) = i_{5_{dc}} + \sum_{n=1}^{\infty} i_{5n}(t) = -\frac{8\omega}{\pi} \sum_{n=1}^{\infty} \frac{n \cos\left(2n\omega t + \frac{\pi}{2} - \tan^{-1}\frac{n\omega}{1 - 8n^2\omega^2}\right)}{(4n^2 - 1)\{4(1 - 8n^2\omega^2)^2 + 4n^2\omega^2\}^{1/2}}. \qquad (3.235)$$

3.9. SUMMARY

In this chapter we have shown general methods for the complete solution of the branch, chord, and branch-chord equations when the driving functions are either all step functions or all sinusoids with a single frequency. We have seen that for these cases the steady-state solution can always be obtained through a very simple procedure; the transient solutions, in general, require a little more algebra, but the method of finding them is well defined and is simple in principle.

We have also introduced the concepts of power and energy in networks, and have shown how Fourier series and the principle of superposition can together extend our methods to the solution of networks when the sources are arbitrary periodic functions.

PROBLEMS

1. Use the branch equations to find all the voltages and currents for the network of Example 3.4 (Fig. 3.2.)

2. Find the transient currents $i_5(t)$ and $i_6(t)$ for the network of Example 3.5 (Fig. 3.3).

3. Use the branch equations to find the steady-state voltage across the capacitance in the network of Example 3.5.

4. For the network of Fig. 3.3, assume that the driving function is changed to $V_1(t) = \cos 5t$. Find all the voltages and currents in the network (transient and steady state). Use the chord equations.

5. Repeat Problem 4 for the network of Fig. 3.2.

6. Use the chord equations to find the steady-state voltages and currents in the network of Fig. 3.5.

7. Find the magnitude and phase of the steady-state current through R_L for the network of Fig. 3.12.

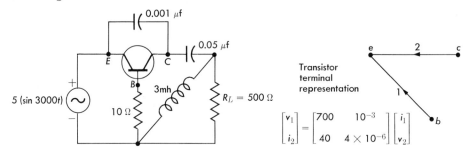

FIGURE 3.12

8. Find the driving-point impedance of the network connected between points A, B in Fig. 3.5.

9. Find the average power supplied by the source (steady state) in the network of Fig. 3.5.

10. Use the branch equations to obtain the steady-state capacitor voltages in the network of Fig. 3.6.

11. Assume that the voltage source of the network of Fig. 3.7 is sinusoidal. What is the driving-point impedance of the remaining network? the driving-point admittance? the steady-state average power dissipation?

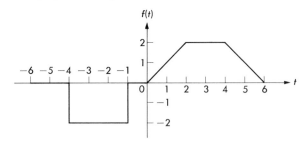

FIGURE 3.13

12. Find the Fourier trigonometric series for the function shown in Fig. 3.13.

13. Find the Fourier exponential series for the function shown in Fig. 3.13.

14. Find the Fourier sine and cosine series for the function shown in Fig. 3.14. Sketch the periodic functions which these series represent.

15. Consider the function shown in Fig. 3.15 described by

$$\begin{aligned} f(t) &= 0, & t < 0, \\ f(t) &= 1/a, & 0 \le t \le a, \\ f(t) &= 0, & t > a. \end{aligned}$$

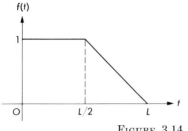

FIGURE 3.14

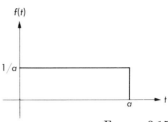

FIGURE 3.15

(a) Find $\int_{-\infty}^{\infty} f(t)\, dt$.

(b) Find the Laplace transform of this function.

(c) Let a tend to zero. The resulting function is called a unit impulse. What is the Laplace transform of this new function? How can you relate it to the unit step function?

16. Assume that all the driving functions of a network are impulse functions. What form does the column matrix $[F(s)]$ in Eq. (3.16) take in this case? If the initial conditions were all zero, how would you relate the impulse-function response and the coefficient matrix of the network equations?

17. What relation is there between the impulse-function response and the driving-point impedance of a network?

18. Consider networks whose driving functions all have the form $Fe^{s_0 t}$, where s_0 is a constant which may be complex. Find the general characteristics of the network response.

19. When $s_0 = 0$ in Problem 18, the exponential driving functions all reduce to constants. Show that in this case the response reduces to the step-function response.

20. For Problem 18 consider the cases $s_0 = j\omega$, $s_0 = -j\omega$. Use the theorem of superposition to derive the sinusoidal response from the general exponential response. Comment on the relation between the sinusoidal steady-state phasor response and the exponential steady-state response.

21. How would you relate the impulse response and the general exponential response?

Chapter 4

SOLUTION OF LARGE NETWORKS THROUGH SUBNETWORKS

We have developed methods for the formulation and solution of the equations characterizing electric networks. However, for some networks the number of equations involved may be so large that direct application of our methods, or any others, is impractical. Our techniques are so systematic that we could, for these cases, turn immediately to the digital computer not only for the solution but also for the formulation of the network equations. However, this procedure would not take into account the increased efficiency in solution which arises when we have a procedure for solving the network in stages. Such a method could also take advantage of the fact that many networks, such as multistage amplifiers, contain several identical subnetworks. This chapter is therefore devoted to the problem of representation of subnetworks as being in themselves components of networks. We shall see that this representation will effectively simplify the analysis of networks, so that we can obtain our solution as a series of partial solutions. Our method will reduce the number of equations which must be solved simultaneously in order to obtain complete solutions. We shall also introduce some network functions and discuss their characteristics.

4.1. TERMINAL REPRESENTATIONS

Let us suppose that we are given an n-terminal component which is to be used in a larger network. When we connect this component into the network we are interested only in the external terminal voltages and currents; its inner workings are of no concern to us. However, in order to calculate these external voltages and currents, we must know the terminal equations corresponding to the terminal graph we choose to represent the component. That is, we must know its *terminal representation*.

One way of finding the terminal representation of a given component is to determine by measurements in the laboratory the coefficients of the terminal equations corresponding to a chosen terminal graph. For example, let us consider a four-terminal component as shown in Fig. 4.1(a). Let the terminal graph be that shown in Fig. 4.1(b). In order to determine the terminal equations we need to use three voltage drivers or three current drivers, or any combination of voltage and current drivers with a total of three. These drivers are connected in one-to-one correspondence with the three elements of the terminal graph.

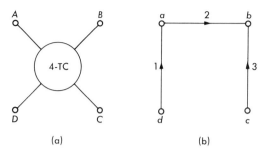

Fig. 4.1. A four-terminal component and terminal graph.

Thus we might set up a system similiar to that shown in Fig. 4.2(a); the corresponding system graph is shown in Fig. 4.2(b). For this system graph, elements 1, 2, and 3 form the terminal graph for the four-terminal component, and elements 4, 5, and 6 correspond to the applied voltage drivers. In the laboratory we measure i_4, i_5, and i_6 for various values of v_4, v_5, and v_6, and obtain the three equations relating them. Now, from the system graph [Fig. 4.2(b)] we have

$$\begin{bmatrix} v_4 \\ v_5 \\ v_6 \end{bmatrix} = \begin{bmatrix} v_1 \\ v_2 \\ v_3 \end{bmatrix} \quad \text{(fundamental circuit equations)}, \tag{4.1}$$

and

$$\begin{bmatrix} i_4 \\ i_5 \\ i_6 \end{bmatrix} = - \begin{bmatrix} i_1 \\ i_2 \\ i_3 \end{bmatrix} \quad \text{(cut-set equations)}, \tag{4.2}$$

so that as soon as we have found the relations between v_4, v_5, v_6 and i_4, i_5, i_6, we can immediately obtain the terminal equations which relate v_1, v_2, v_3 to i_1, i_2, i_3.

Let us now suppose that the given component is made up of an interconnection of other subcomponents. This will certainly make no difference to our procedure in the laboratory, which is still well represented by Fig. 4.2. However, the knowl-

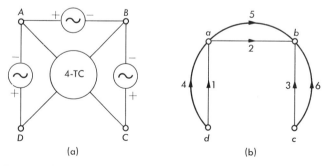

Fig. 4.2. Schematic diagram and system graph for the laboratory determination of the terminal equations for a four-terminal component.

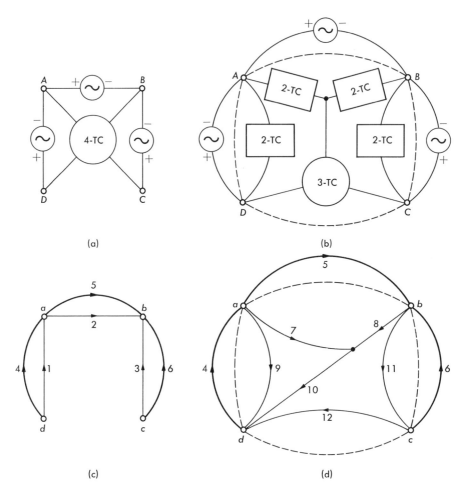

FIG. 4.3. Schematic diagrams and system graphs used in the analytical derivation of the terminal representation.

edge of the internal structure of the subassembly gives us an alternative way of representing the system on which we are making measurements.

Suppose that the four-terminal component of Fig. 4.3(a) is actually composed of an interconnection of four two-terminal components and a three-terminal component as shown in Fig. 4.3(b). The test system which we set up in the laboratory by applying three voltage drivers to the four-terminal component may be as well represented by the system graph of Fig. 4.3(d) as it is by that of Fig. 4.3(c). The voltage-current relations for elements 4, 5, and 6 must be the same in both cases; they correspond to the same voltage drivers applied to the same system.

We know how to calculate the voltage-current relations for elements 1, 2, and 3 of Fig. 4.3(c) as soon as we obtain the relationships for elements 4, 5, and 6 [Eqs. (4.1), (4.2)]. However, Fig. 4.3(d) is a simple system graph. If we know the terminal equations for the four two-terminal components and the three-terminal component of Fig. 4.3(b), that is, the voltage-current relations for elements 7, 8, 9, 10, 11, and 12 of Fig. 4.3(d), we can certainly calculate i_4, i_5, and i_6 in terms of v_4, v_5, and v_6, using any one of the methods, chord, branch, or branch-chord, which we developed in Chapter 2. We can thus derive the terminal relations corresponding to elements 1, 2, and 3 directly from the knowledge of the components and their interconnection. This is the essence of the terminal representation method.

So far we have illustrated our ideas only with a four-terminal component. Of course, the number of terminals is inconsequential; everything we have said could equally well be applied to two-, three-, five-, or n-terminal components. Similarly, there is no reason why we should have chosen voltage drivers instead of current drivers for our test systems; the method is essentially the same whichever we choose; we may even use both voltage and current-drivers. The choice of the drivers determines the form of the terminal equations.

4.2. ILLUSTRATIVE EXAMPLES

In this section we shall give three examples of the terminal representation technique.

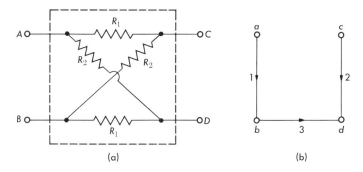

(a)   (b)

FIG. 4.4.   A four-terminal resistive subnetwork and its terminal graph.

EXAMPLE 4.1.   Consider the four-terminal component of Fig. 4.4(a). When this subnetwork is to be connected arbitrarily at terminals A, B, C, and D into a network, it might be well represented by the terminal graph of Fig. 4.4(b) and a set of associated terminal equations. To find these terminal equations we apply three voltage drivers to the subassembly as shown in Fig. 4.5(a). This gives us the two alternative system graphs shown in Fig. 4.5(b) and (c). From the system schematic [Fig. 4.5(a)] and system graph [Fig. 4.5(c)], we write down the following branch equations:

$$\begin{bmatrix} G_1 + G_2 & -G_1 & G_1 + G_2 \\ -G_1 & G_1 + G_2 & -(G_1 + G_2) \\ G_1 + G_2 & -(G_1 + G_2) & 2(G_1 + G_2) \end{bmatrix} \begin{bmatrix} V_4(s) \\ V_5(s) \\ V_6(s) \end{bmatrix} = - \begin{bmatrix} I_4(s) \\ I_5(s) \\ I_6(s) \end{bmatrix} . \qquad (4.3)$$

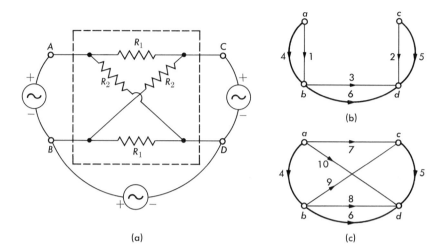

FIG. 4.5. Schematic diagram and system graphs used in the derivation of a four-terminal representation for the subnetwork of Fig. 4.4.

Now, from Fig. 4.5(b),

$$\begin{bmatrix} V_4(s) \\ V_5(s) \\ V_6(s) \end{bmatrix} = \begin{bmatrix} V_1(s) \\ V_2(s) \\ V_3(s) \end{bmatrix}, \tag{4.4}$$

$$-\begin{bmatrix} I_4(s) \\ I_5(s) \\ I_6(s) \end{bmatrix} = \begin{bmatrix} I_1(s) \\ I_2(s) \\ I_3(s) \end{bmatrix}. \tag{4.5}$$

Therefore, substituting (4.4) and (4.5) into (4.3), we obtain the terminal relations corresponding to the terminal graph of Fig. 4.4(b):

$$\begin{bmatrix} G_1 + G_2 & -G_1 & G_1 + G_2 \\ -G_1 & G_1 + G_2 & -(G_1 + G_2) \\ G_1 + G_2 & -(G_1 + G_2) & 2(G_1 + G_2) \end{bmatrix} \begin{bmatrix} V_1(s) \\ V_2(s) \\ V_3(s) \end{bmatrix} = \begin{bmatrix} I_1(s) \\ I_2(s) \\ I_3(s) \end{bmatrix}. \tag{4.6}$$

Note that we applied voltage drivers, and obtained the terminal relations in the form

$$[I(s)] = [Y(s)][V(s)]. \tag{4.7}$$

We shall see that this is a general result, and the entries in $[Y(s)]$ are called the *short-circuit parameters* of the component since they are measured by short-circuit tests. Terminal equations in the form of (4.7) are said to be in the "short-circuit form."

EXAMPLE 4.2. In this example we shall find a three-terminal representation of the symmetric T-network shown in Fig. 4.6(a). When this subnetwork is to be connected into a system at terminals A, B, and C, but *not* at terminal D, it may well be represented by the terminal graph of Fig. 4.6(b) and a pair of corresponding

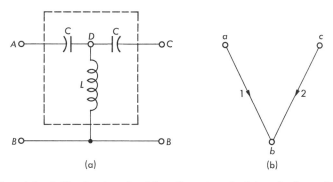

Fig. 4.6. A T-subnetwork with a three-terminal terminal graph.

terminal equations. To find the terminal equations, we apply two current drivers
as shown in Fig. 4.7(a), and obtain the two system graphs of Fig. 4.7(b) and (c).
We write down the chord equations corresponding to Fig. 4.7(a) and (c), which,
assuming zero initial conditions, are

$$\begin{bmatrix} 1/sC + sL & sL \\ sL & 1/sC + sL \end{bmatrix} \begin{bmatrix} I_3(s) \\ I_4(s) \end{bmatrix} = - \begin{bmatrix} V_3(s) \\ V_4(s) \end{bmatrix}. \tag{4.8}$$

Noting from Fig. 4.7(b) that

$$\begin{bmatrix} V_3(s) \\ V_4(s) \end{bmatrix} = \begin{bmatrix} V_1(s) \\ V_2(s) \end{bmatrix}, \tag{4.9}$$

$$\begin{bmatrix} I_3(s) \\ I_4(s) \end{bmatrix} = - \begin{bmatrix} I_1(s) \\ I_2(s) \end{bmatrix}, \tag{4.10}$$

we immediately obtain the terminal equations corresponding to the system graph
of Fig. 4.6(b) as

$$\begin{bmatrix} V_1(s) \\ V_2(s) \end{bmatrix} = \begin{bmatrix} 1/sC + sL & sL \\ sL & 1/sC + sL \end{bmatrix} \begin{bmatrix} I_1(s) \\ I_2(s) \end{bmatrix}. \tag{4.11}$$

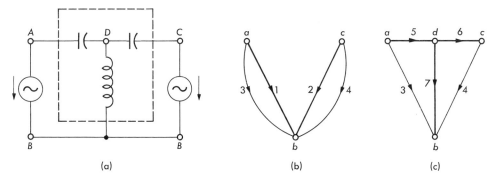

Fig. 4.7. Schematic diagram and system graphs used in the derivation of a three-terminal
representation of the network of Fig. 4.6.

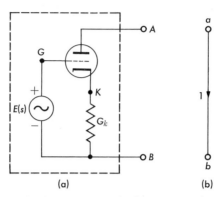

FIG. 4.8. A subnetwork whose two-terminal representation is to be obtained.

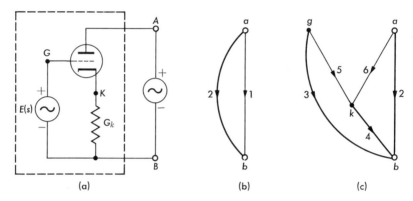

FIG. 4.9. Schematic diagram and system graphs used in the derivation of the two-terminal representation of the network of Fig. 4.8.

Here we note that the equations are in the *open-circuit form*,

$$[V(s)] = [Z(s)][I(s)]. \qquad (4.12)$$

This is analogous to the results that we would expect if we were to apply current generators to the subassembly in a laboratory test. The entries in the matrix $[Z(s)]$ are called the *open-circuit parameters* since they are obtained by open-circuit tests.

EXAMPLE 4.3. If the simple network of Fig. 4.8(a) is to be connected into a system only at terminals A and B, it is appropriate to use a two-terminal representation with the terminal graph of Fig. 4.8(b). To find the terminal equation corresponding to this graph, we apply a voltage generator as shown in Fig. 4.9(a), and obtain the system graphs of Fig. 4.9(b) and (c). We write the branch equations

$$\begin{bmatrix} I_2(s) \\ I_3(s) \\ 0 \end{bmatrix} + \begin{bmatrix} 0 & 0 & 1 \\ 0 & 1 & 0 \\ 1 & -1 & -1 \end{bmatrix} \begin{bmatrix} G_k & 0 & 0 \\ 0 & 0 & 0 \\ 0 & g_m & g_p \end{bmatrix} \begin{bmatrix} 0 & 0 & 1 \\ 0 & 1 & -1 \\ 1 & 0 & -1 \end{bmatrix} \begin{bmatrix} V_2(s) \\ V_3(s) \\ V_4(s) \end{bmatrix} = \begin{bmatrix} 0 \\ 0 \\ 0 \end{bmatrix}$$

or, equivalently,

$$
\begin{bmatrix}
g_p & g_m & -(g_m + g_p) \\
0 & 0 & 0 \\
-g_p & -g_m & G_k + g_m + g_p
\end{bmatrix}
\begin{bmatrix}
V_2(s) \\
V_3(s) \\
V_4(s)
\end{bmatrix}
= -
\begin{bmatrix}
I_2(s) \\
I_3(s) \\
0
\end{bmatrix},
\tag{4.13}
$$

and solve the last equation of (4.13) for $V_4(s)$. This gives

$$
V_4(s) = \frac{1}{G_k + g_m + g_p} \{g_p V_2(s) + g_m V_3(s)\}.
\tag{4.14}
$$

Now, substituting (4.14) into the first equation of (4.13), we obtain

$$
-I_2(s) = \frac{g_p G_k V_2(s)}{g_m + g_p + G_k} + \frac{g_m G_k E(s)}{g_m + g_p + G_k}
\tag{4.15}
$$

since $V_3(s) = E(s)$.

From Fig. 4.9(b) we have

$$
V_2(s) = V_1(s), \qquad -I_2(s) = I_1(s),
$$

so that the required terminal equation is

$$
I_1(s) = \frac{g_p G_k}{g_m + g_p + G_k} V_1(s) + \frac{g_m G_k E(s)}{g_m + g_p + G_k}.
\tag{4.16}
$$

This equation is in the short-circuit form

$$
I(s) = Y(s) V(s) + I_0(s).
\tag{4.17}
$$

We shall indicate that the terminal equation corresponding to the two-terminal representation of any linear network can be written in both the form of (4.17) and the open-circuit form

$$
V(s) = Z(s) I(s) + E_0(s).
\tag{4.18}
$$

Equations (4.17) and (4.18) correspond respectively to the Norton and Thevenin two-terminal equivalent circuits.

It is noteworthy that in Examples 4.1 and 4.2 we did not need to invert any matrices in finding the terminal equations, while in Example 4.3 we were required to solve one equation. Since we have used the branch and chord techniques only, depending on the form of the terminal equations of the components, we can always predict how many equations must be solved in finding the required relations. We can therefore decide whether we should apply voltage or current drivers to obtain our terminal relations with the least labor. For instance, in Example 4.1, had we applied current drivers and found the open-circuit form of the terminal equations, we would have needed to solve one equation. Whenever the applied voltage drivers form a complete tree of the system graph, or the applied current drivers form a complete cotree, we do not need to solve any equations, or equivalently, to invert any matrices.

Finally, note that in Example 4.2, we assumed that the initial voltages and currents in the network were zero. This was merely a simplifying assumption, and there is no reason why nonzero initial conditions should not be retained. However, to avoid the possibility that the additional symbols involved in the initial condition terms might obscure the simplicity of our methods, we shall henceforth assume that all initial voltages and currents that should appear in the network equations are zero.

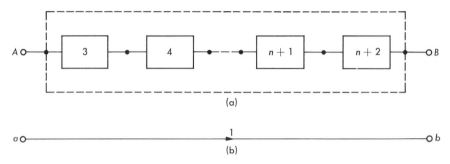

(a)

(b)

FIG. 4.10. A series assemblage whose two-terminal representation is to be obtained.

4.3. SOME INTERESTING TWO-TERMINAL REPRESENTATIONS

In this section we shall use the concept of terminal representations to investigate series, parallel, and series-parallel networks. We shall also define the driving-point impedance and admittance of a two-terminal network, and illustrate the Thevenin and Norton network equivalences.

First, let us consider the series connection of n two-terminal components whose terminal equations are given by

$$V_k(s) = Z_k(s)I_k(s), \qquad k = 3, 4, \ldots, n + 2. \tag{4.19}$$

We shall consider a two-terminal representation of these components as illustrated in Fig. 4.10. The series assemblage is to be connected into a network only at terminals A and B [Fig. 4.10(a)] so that it can be represented by the terminal graph of Fig. 4.10(b). We shall find the open-circuit form of the terminal equation corresponding to this terminal graph. This is done by applying a current driver as shown in Fig. 4.11(a), so that we obtain the system graphs of Fig. 4.11(b) and (c). We write the chord equation

$$\left(\sum_k Z_k(s)\right) I_2(s) = -V_2(s), \tag{4.20}$$

and note that

$$V_2(s) = V_1(s),$$
$$I_2(s) = -I_1(s),$$

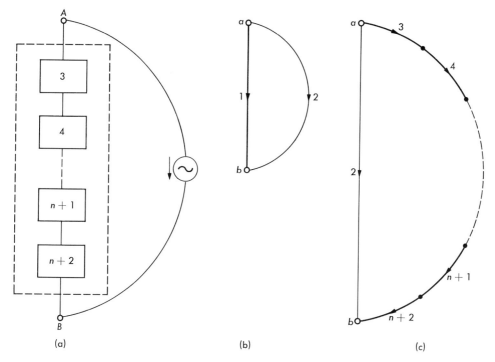

FIG. 4.11. Schematic diagram and system graphs used in the derivation of the two-terminal representation of a series assemblage.

so that the terminal equation is

$$V_1(s) = \left(\sum_k Z_k(s)\right) I_1(s).\tag{4.21}$$

Thus the series assemblage of Fig. 4.10 may be regarded as a two-terminal component with terminal equation

$$V_1(s) = Z_1(s)I_1(s),\tag{4.22}$$

where

$$Z_1(s) = \sum_{k=3}^{n+2} \left(Z_k(s)\right).\tag{4.23}$$

If all $Z_k(s) = R_k$, we note that

$$Z_1(s) = R_1(s) = \sum_{k=3}^{n+2} R_k,\tag{4.24}$$

which is the well-known result that n resistances connected in series are equivalent to a single resistance whose value is the sum of the individual resistances.

Similarly, if all $Z_k(s) = sL_k$, we have

$$Z_1(s) = \sum_{k=3}^{n+2} sL_k = s \sum_{k=3}^{n+2} L_k = sL_1, \tag{4.25}$$

which is the summation rule for inductances connected in series.

Again, if all $Z_k(s) = 1/sC_k$, we have

$$Z_1(s) = \sum_{k=3}^{n+2} \frac{1}{sC_k} = \frac{1}{s} \sum_{k=3}^{n+2} \frac{1}{C_k} = \frac{1}{sC_1}, \tag{4.26}$$

which shows that when n capacitors are connected in series they are equivalent to a single capacitor the reciprocal of whose capacitance is the sum of the reciprocals of the individual capacitances.

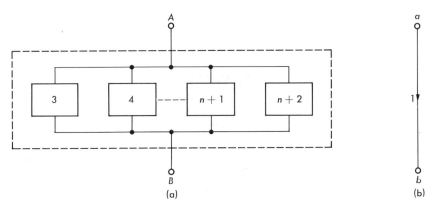

FIG. 4.12. A parallel assemblage whose two-terminal representation is to be obtained.

We now consider the parallel connection of n two-terminal components when the terminal equations are given by

$$I_k(s) = Y_k(s)V_k(s), \qquad k = 3, 4, \ldots, n + 2. \tag{4.27}$$

We shall obtain the two-terminal representation of this assemblage as illustrated in Fig. 4.12. In order to obtain the terminal equation in the short-circuit form, we apply a voltage driver as shown in Fig. 4.13(a), and obtain the two system graphs shown in parts (b) and (c) of the figure. The branch equation corresponding to Fig. 4.13(c) is

$$\left(\sum_k Y_k(s) \right) V_2(s) = -I_2(s), \tag{4.28}$$

and since

$$V_2(s) = V_1(s),$$
$$-I_2(s) = I_1(s),$$

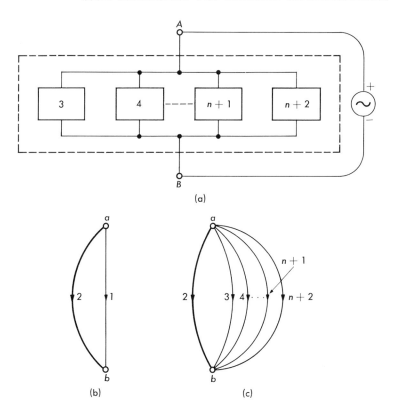

FIG. 4.13. Schematic diagram and system graphs used in the derivation of the two-terminal representation of a parallel assemblage.

we immediately have the terminal equation

$$I_1(s) = \left(\sum_k Y_k(s)\right) V_1(s). \tag{4.29}$$

Thus the parallel assemblage of Fig. 4.12(a) may be considered as a two-terminal component whose terminal equation is

$$I_1(s) = Y_1(s)V_1(s), \tag{4.30}$$

where

$$Y_1(s) = \sum_{k=3}^{n+2} Y_k(s). \tag{4.31}$$

When the n components are all conductances, (4.31) reduces to the summation rule for parallel conductances; that is, the equivalent conductance of n conductances connected in parallel is the sum of the individual conductances.

   Similarly, for inductors we find that the reciprocal of the equivalent inductance of n inductors connected in parallel is the sum of the reciprocals of the individual inductances.

Also, for capacitors, the equivalent capacitance of n capacitors connected in parallel is the sum of the individual capacitances.

In order to give a general statement of the results of the series and parallel combinations, we shall define the *driving-point impedance* and *driving-point admittance* of a two-terminal network.

When the terminal equation corresponding to a two-terminal component is written in the open-circuit form,

$$V(s) = Z(s)I(s) + E_0(s), \tag{4.32}$$

the function $Z(s)$ is defined as the driving-point impedance of the two-terminal component; $E_0(s)$ is called the *open-circuit voltage* of the component.

Similarly, when the terminal equation corresponding to a two-terminal component is written in the short-circuit form,

$$I(s) = Y(s)V(s) + I_0(s), \tag{4.33}$$

the function $Y(s)$ is called the driving-point admittance of the two-terminal component; $I_0(s)$ is called the *short-circuit current* of the component.

It is easy to verify the fact that the driving-point admittance of a component is the reciprocal of its driving-point impedance. That is

$$Y(s) = \frac{1}{Z(s)}. \tag{4.34}$$

Further, when $E_0(s) = I_0(s) = 0$, and $s = j\omega$, the above definitions reduce to those of Section 3.6.

Using the concepts of impedance and admittance, we can immediately state from Eqs. (4.23) and (4.31) the rules for the combination of impedances in series, and admittances in parallel. Thus, n impedances connected in series are equivalent to a single impedance whose value is the sum of the individual impedances, and n admittances connected in parallel are equivalent to a single admittance whose value is the sum of the individual admittances.

We reserve the letter Z for impedances. Whenever we have previously used it, we have conformed to this convention; the letter Y is similarly used to refer to admittances.

EXAMPLE 4.4. In this example we shall find the driving-point impedance and admittance of the two-terminal network shown in Fig. 4.14(a). In this network we can combine the elements of three subnetworks, enclosed by dashed lines in the figure, by considering them as series assemblies. We thus reduce Fig. 4.14(a) to the network of Fig. 4.14(b), in which

$$Z_9 = R_2 + 1/sC_3 + sL_4, \tag{4.35}$$

$$Z_{10} = 1/sC_5 + R_6, \tag{4.36}$$

$$Z_{11} = sL_7 + 1/sC_8. \tag{4.37}$$

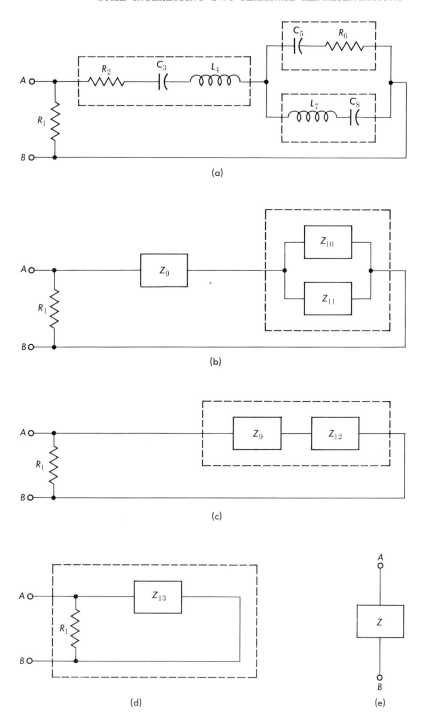

FIG. 4.14. Reduction of a series-parallel network.

In Fig. 4.14(b), we can consider Z_{10} and Z_{11} connected in parallel as a single two-terminal subnetwork. This reduces the network to that of Fig. 4.14(c). In this diagram

$$Z_{12} = \frac{1}{Y_{12}} \qquad (4.38)$$

and

$$Y_{12} = Y_{10} + Y_{11} = \frac{1}{Z_{10}} + \frac{1}{Z_{11}}, \qquad (4.39)$$

or

$$Z_{12} = \frac{Z_{10}Z_{11}}{Z_{10} + Z_{11}}. \qquad (4.40)$$

At this point we regard the series connection of Z_9 and Z_{12} as a single two-terminal component, and thereby reduce the network to that shown in Fig. 4.14(d), where

$$Z_{13} = Z_9 + Z_{12}. \qquad (4.41)$$

Now Z_{13} is in parallel with R_1, so that we can consider their combination as the simple two-terminal device of Fig. 4.14(e). We have

$$Z = \frac{R_1 Z_{13}}{R_1 + Z_{13}} \qquad (4.42)$$

and

$$Y = \frac{1}{Z} = \frac{1}{R_1} + \frac{1}{Z_{13}} = G_1 + Y_{13}. \qquad (4.43)$$

Equations (4.42) and (4.43) can easily be written in terms of the original network parameters. They are ratios of two fourth-degree polynomials in s.

Example 4.4 shows the method which we may apply when dealing with series-parallel networks; whenever we encounter a network in which there exist series or parallel connections of two-terminal components, we can immediately reduce its complexity by considering these assemblages as being two-terminal components in themselves.

Consider the two-terminal network of Fig. 4.15(a). It is very easy to show that when it is represented by the terminal graph of Fig. 4.15(b), the terminal equation is

$$V(s) = Z(s)I(s) + E_0(s). \qquad (4.18)$$

This equation, however, is the general open-circuit form for the two-terminal representation of any network. Hence the network of Fig. 4.15(a) may be regarded as a pictorial description of two-terminal representations; it is the Thevenin equivalent network.

Similarly, the network of Fig. 4.15(c) has for its two-terminal representation the terminal graph of Fig. 4.15(d) and the terminal equation

$$I(s) = Y(s)V(s) + I_0(s). \qquad (4.17)$$

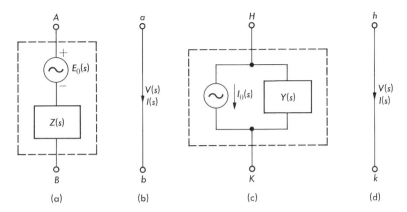

FIG. 4.15. Simple two-terminal representations; the Thevenin and Norton equivalents.

Since this equation is the general short-circuit form for the two-terminal representation of any network, the network of Fig. 4.15(c) is an alternative pictorial description of two-terminal representations. It is called the Norton equivalent network.

Another pair of interesting two-terminal representations is shown in Fig. 4.16. When we connect an impedance in *series* with a current driver, as in Fig. 4.16(a), it is easy to show that the terminal equation corresponding to the graph of Fig. 4.16(b) is

$$I_1(s) = I(s) \quad \text{(specified)}, \tag{4.44}$$

whatever $Z(s)$ may be. Thus, when we are not interested in the voltage developed across an impedance connected in series with a current driver, we may completely disregard the impedance.

Similarly, for the two-terminal representation of an impedance connected in parallel with a voltage driver [Fig. 4.16(c)], we obtain the terminal graph of Fig.

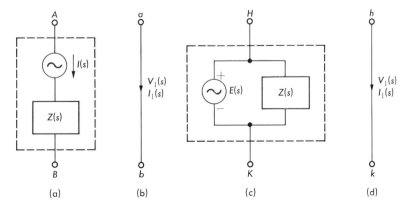

FIG. 4.16. Simple two-terminal representations.

4.16(d) with the terminal equation

$$V_1(s) = E(s) \quad \text{(specified).} \tag{4.45}$$

Hence we may ignore an impedance connected in parallel with a voltage driver when we have no interest in the current associated with it.

4.4. TERMINAL REPRESENTATIONS OF COUPLED COILS

We have already seen that an n-vertex tree terminal graph is sufficient to characterize an n-terminal component. A set of n magnetically coupled coils, which is considered as a $2n$-terminal component, merits some further consideration. Because there is no electric connection between the pairs of coils, we shall see that the terminal graph of this multiterminal component is not necessarily a tree.

EXAMPLE 4.5.   Let us consider three magnetically coupled coils, as shown in Fig. 4.17(a). Since this set of coils constitutes a six-terminal component, it may well be represented by the terminal graph of Fig. 4.17(b). The terminal equations associated with this component and graph, neglecting the initial conditions, are

$$\begin{bmatrix} V_1(s) \\ V_2(s) \\ V_3(s) \\ I_4(s) \\ I_5(s) \end{bmatrix} = \begin{bmatrix} sL_{11} & sL_{12} & sL_{13} & 0 & 0 \\ sL_{12} & sL_{22} & sL_{23} & 0 & 0 \\ sL_{13} & sL_{23} & sL_{33} & 0 & 0 \\ 0 & 0 & 0 & 0 & 0 \\ 0 & 0 & 0 & 0 & 0 \end{bmatrix} \begin{bmatrix} I_1(s) \\ I_2(s) \\ I_3(s) \\ V_4(s) \\ V_5(s) \end{bmatrix}. \tag{4.46}$$

Here we note that the last two equations are merely

$$\begin{bmatrix} I_4(s) \\ I_5(s) \end{bmatrix} = \begin{bmatrix} 0 \\ 0 \end{bmatrix}, \tag{4.47}$$

and because of the two zero columns in the coefficient matrix of Eq. (4.46), $V_1(s)$, $V_2(s)$, and $V_3(s)$ do not depend in any way on $V_4(s)$ and $V_5(s)$. Hence we may delete the last two equations, and $V_4(s)$ and $V_5(s)$, from Eqs. (4.46), together with elements 4 and 5 of the terminal graph. Thus we are left with the three-part

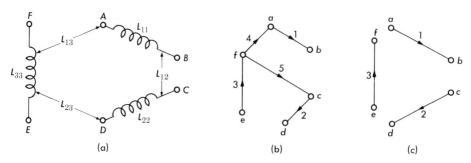

FIG. 4.17.   Three magnetically coupled coils, with two of their possible terminal graphs.

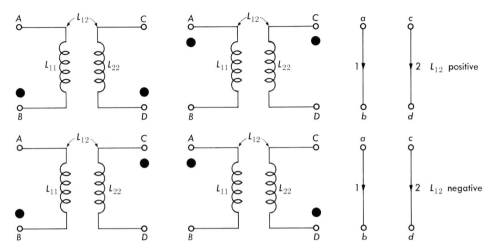

FIG. 4.18. Polarity symbols for magnetically coupled coils.

terminal graph of Fig. 4.17(c) and the associated terminal equations

$$\begin{bmatrix} V_1(s) \\ V_2(s) \\ V_3(s) \end{bmatrix} = \begin{bmatrix} sL_{11} & sL_{12} & sL_{13} \\ sL_{12} & sL_{22} & sL_{23} \\ sL_{13} & sL_{23} & sL_{33} \end{bmatrix} \begin{bmatrix} I_1(s) \\ I_2(s) \\ I_3(s) \end{bmatrix}. \tag{4.48}$$

In Eqs. (4.48) the numbers L_{11}, L_{22}, and L_{33} are the *self-inductances* of the three coils, and the magnitudes of the numbers L_{12}, L_{13}, and L_{23} are the *mutual inductances* between coils 1 and 2, 1 and 3, and 2 and 3, respectively. Thus L_{11}, L_{22}, and L_{33} are positive, while L_{12}, L_{13}, and L_{23} may be either positive or negative quantities. Whether or not a particular coefficient is positive may be ascertained in the laboratory; the sign depends on the relative polarity of the magnetic fields associated with the physical coils. In order to indicate this sign on schematic diagrams, we use the following convention. One terminal of each coil of a pair of magnetically coupled coils is marked with a distinctive symbol. This is shown in Fig. 4.18, which also illustrates the sign convention. When the polarity markings are both at the terminal identified by the vertices toward (or away from) which the elements of the terminal graph are directed, the mutual inductance term, L_{12}, is positive; otherwise it is negative.

When several coils are magnetically coupled, a different polarity symbol must be used for each pair. Manufacturers of multiwinding transformers invariably use this method for indicating the magnetic polarities involved in their products. The three coils of Fig. 4.17 are all magnetically coupled. Therefore, we require three different sets of magnetic polarity markings. If these are as shown in Fig. 4.19(a), in which we have used a circle to indicate the relative magnetic polarity between coils 1 and 2, a square for that between coils 1 and 3, and a diamond for the relative polarity between coils 2 and 3, we find that L_{12} is positive, L_{13} is negative, and L_{23} is positive, with respect to the terminal graph of Fig. 4.19(b).

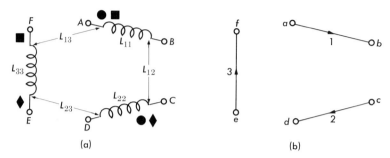

FIG. 4.19. Polarity symbols for the coils of Fig. 4.17.

In summary, we can now make the general statement that n magnetically coupled coils may be characterized by an n-element, $2n$-vertex terminal graph, together with a set of n terminal relations. When these equations are written in the open-circuit form, the coefficient matrix is symmetrical, and the off-diagonal terms are given by

$$Z_{ij}(s) = \pm s M_{ij}, \tag{4.49}$$

where M_{ij} is the mutual inductance between coils i and j, and the sign is determined by the procedure discussed above. As to the terms on the main diagonal, they are given by the self-inductances of the coils, and are always positive.

In our subsequent development, we shall write the terminal equations of coupled coils without regard to the signs of mutual inductance terms. These could take either positive or negative values, as the case may be.

4.5. SYMBOLIC DEVELOPMENT

Having discussed some special cases in the last two sections, we shall now return to a general symbolic procedure for deriving terminal representations. However, since our method merely amounts to the solution of one of the sets of branch, chord, or branch-chord equations for the currents associated with voltage drivers and voltages across current drivers, we shall not supply all the details. All our remarks in Chapter 2 about the general application of these methods and the required forms of the component terminal equations apply equally well here.

We shall consider only the development of the open circuit form of the terminal equations for an n-terminal representation of a network; the methods for obtaining other forms of the equations are entirely similar.

When we wish to obtain the open-circuit form of the terminal equations for a given n-terminal representation, we must apply $n - 1$ current drivers to the given network in a one-to-one correspondence with the given terminal graph. We represent the currents associated with these drivers and the voltages across them by $[I_m(s)]$ and $[V_m(s)]$, respectively. If the voltages and currents corresponding to the required terminal graph are given by $[V(s)]$ and $[I(s)]$, respectively, we have

$$[V(s)] = [V_m(s)], \tag{4.50}$$

$$[I(s)] = -[I_m(s)]. \tag{4.51}$$

We represent the voltages and currents for the components as

$$[V_{bd}(s)], \quad [I_{bd}(s)] \quad \text{(voltage drivers)},$$
$$[V_{b2}(s)], \quad [I_{b2}(s)] \quad \text{(nonspecified branch variables)},$$
$$[V_{c1}(s)], \quad [I_{c1}(s)] \quad \text{(nonspecified chord variables)},$$
$$[V_{cd}(s)], \quad [I_{cd}(s)] \quad \text{(current drivers)}.$$

The chord equations for the system which includes the n-terminal network and the extra applied current drivers may be written as

$$\begin{bmatrix} B_{11} \\ B_{21} \\ B_{31} \end{bmatrix} [V_{bd}(s)] + \begin{bmatrix} Z_{11}(s) & Z_{12}(s) & Z_{13}(s) \\ Z_{21}(s) & Z_{22}(s) & Z_{23}(s) \\ Z_{31}(s) & Z_{32}(s) & Z_{33}(s) \end{bmatrix} \begin{bmatrix} I_{c1}(s) \\ I_{cd}(s) \\ I_m(s) \end{bmatrix} = - \begin{bmatrix} 0 \\ V_{cd}(s) \\ V_m(s) \end{bmatrix}. \qquad (4.52)$$

To find the required terminal equations, we merely eliminate $[I_{c1}(s)]$ and $[V_{cd}(s)]$ from (4.52). We set aside the second row of (4.52), since $[V_{cd}(s)]$ only occurs there, and rewrite the remaining equations in the form

$$\begin{bmatrix} B_{11} \\ B_{31} \end{bmatrix} [V_{bd}(s)] + \begin{bmatrix} Z_{11}(s) & Z_{13}(s) \\ Z_{31}(s) & Z_{33}(s) \end{bmatrix} \begin{bmatrix} I_{c1}(s) \\ I_m(s) \end{bmatrix} + \begin{bmatrix} Z_{12}(s) \\ Z_{32}(s) \end{bmatrix} [I_{cd}(s)] = - \begin{bmatrix} 0 \\ V_m(s) \end{bmatrix}. \qquad (4.53)$$

We can conveniently eliminate $[I_{c1}(s)]$ from (4.53) by premultiplying both sides of the equations by the matrix

$$\begin{bmatrix} U & 0 \\ -Z_{31}(s)Z_{11}^{-1}(s) & U \end{bmatrix}.$$

After some rearrangement, this gives

$$\begin{bmatrix} Z_{11}(s) & Z_{13}(s) \\ 0 & Z_{33}(s) - Z_{31}(s)Z_{11}^{-1}(s)Z_{13}(s) \end{bmatrix} \begin{bmatrix} I_{c1}(s) \\ I_m(s) \end{bmatrix} = - \begin{bmatrix} 0 \\ V_m(s) \end{bmatrix}$$
$$+ \begin{bmatrix} -Z_{12}(s)I_{cd}(s) - B_{11}V_{bd}(s) \\ Z_{31}(s)Z_{11}^{-1}(s)\{Z_{12}(s)I_{cd}(s) + B_{11}V_{bd}(s)\} - Z_{32}(s)I_{cd}(s) - B_{31}V_{bd}(s) \end{bmatrix}. \qquad (4.54)$$

Into the second set of equations of (4.54) we substitute (4.50) and (4.51). The result is

$$\{[Z_{33}(s)] - [Z_{31}(s)][Z_{11}(s)]^{-1}[Z_{13}(s)]\}[I(s)]$$
$$= [V(s)] - [Z_{31}(s)][Z_{11}(s)]^{-1}\{[Z_{12}(s)][I_{cd}(s)] + [B_{11}][V_{bd}(s)]\}$$
$$+ [Z_{32}(s)][I_{cd}(s)] + [B_{31}][V_{bd}(s)]. \qquad (4.55)$$

This may be written as

$$[V(s)] = [Z(s)][I(s)] + [E_0(s)], \qquad (4.56)$$

where

$$[Z(s)] = [Z_{33}(s)] - [Z_{31}(s)][Z_{11}(s)]^{-1}[Z_{13}(s)] \qquad (4.57)$$

and

$$[E_0(s)] = [Z_{31}(s)][Z_{11}(s)]^{-1}\{[Z_{12}(s)][I_{cd}(s)] + [B_{11}][V_{bd}(s)]\}$$
$$- [Z_{32}(s)][I_{cd}(s)] - [B_{31}][V_{bd}(s)]. \qquad (4.58)$$

Note that, when we are dealing with a two-terminal representation and there is only one equation in (4.56), the above result reduces to the Thevenin equivalent.

For complete generality, we should derive Eqs. (4.56) using the branch and branch-chord techniques; this is left as an exercise; the methods are trivially different from the above.

Some further results, which we shall not digress to discuss in detail, are as follows. To obtain the open-circuit form of the n-terminal representation, we are required to apply current drivers in one-to-one correspondence with the chosen terminal graph for our component. If the component itself contains current drivers or ideal transformers, it may happen that it is impossible to find a formulation tree (forest) such that all the current drivers are located in the cotree (coforest). Hence, for such a network, it is impossible to obtain the open-circuit form of the terminal equations for the chosen terminal graph. (It may, however, be possible to do so for some other terminal graph).

Similarly, for the short-circuit form of the terminal equations, it is necessary for us to find a formulation tree which contains all the voltage drivers. If this is not possible, we cannot obtain the short-circuit equations for the chosen terminal graph.

For some components and terminal graphs, it is impossible to locate all the elements corresponding to our external drivers in either the tree or the cotree. In these cases we can obtain the terminal equations in the *hybrid form*,

$$\begin{bmatrix} V_1(s) \\ I_2(s) \end{bmatrix} = \begin{bmatrix} H_{11}(s) & H_{12}(s) \\ H_{21}(s) & H_{22}(s) \end{bmatrix} \begin{bmatrix} I_1(s) \\ V_2(s) \end{bmatrix} + \begin{bmatrix} E_0(s) \\ I_0(s) \end{bmatrix}. \tag{4.59}$$

This is done by applying some voltage drivers and some current drivers; in the laboratory, these correspond to open- and short-circuit tests. The analytical derivation of the hybrid form of the terminal equations is somewhat tedious. For this reason, and because components for which this method is a necessity are infrequently encountered, we shall not discuss the development of the hybrid form of the terminal equations further. In any case, we can obtain the hybrid form from either the open- or short-circuit forms, whenever they exist.

4.6. SOLUTION OF LARGE NETWORKS

In this section we shall illustrate the procedure for solving large networks through easy stages. However, due to space limitations, we shall restrict ourselves to simple examples.

EXAMPLE 4.6.   Consider the network of Fig. 4.20 for which we shall find the voltage across the resistance R_L. This can be done by formulating a set of network equations following the methods of Chapter 2, a process which involves drawing the system graph of Fig. 4.21. This graph contains 7 vertices and 11 elements, two of which correspond to voltage drivers. Hence, the solution requires the solution of nine equations if the branch-chord method is used, five equations if the chord formulation is chosen, or four equations when we wish to apply the

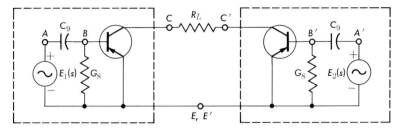

FIG. 4.20. A transistorized difference amplifier.

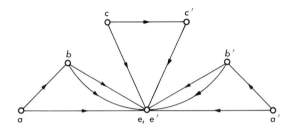

FIG. 4.21. System graph for the network of Fig. 4.20.

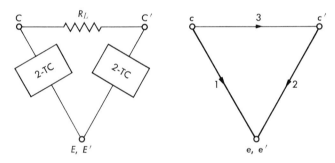

FIG. 4.22. Reduction of the network of Fig. 4.20 obtained by identifying two two-terminal subnetworks.

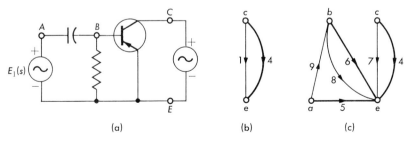

FIG. 4.23. Schematic diagram and system graphs used in deriving the terminal equations for the subnetworks in Example 4.6.

branch technique. Thus, even the branch formulation, which is the easiest to apply, would involve the inversion of a relatively large matrix.

We shall begin the analysis of this network by recognizing the two two-terminal subnetworks enclosed by dashed lines in Fig. 4.20. When we have found their two-terminal representations, we need only analyze the simple network of Fig. 4.22. Here, we see that the chord technique requires the solution of only one equation. If the terminal equations for the two-terminal subnetworks are obtained in the form,

$$V_1(s) = Z_1(s)I_1(s) + E_{01}(s),$$
$$V_2(s) = Z_2(s)I_2(s) + E_{02}(s),$$

(4.60)

the required chord equation is

$$(Z_1(s) + Z_2(s) + R_L)I_3(s) = E_{02}(s) - E_{01}(s),$$

(4.61)

or, since $V_3(s) = R_L I_3(s)$,

$$V_3(s) = \frac{(E_{02}(s) - E_{01}(s))R_L}{Z_1(s) + Z_2(s) + R_L}.$$

(4.62)

It remains only to determine the quantities $Z_1(s)$, $Z_2(s)$, $E_{01}(s)$, and $E_{02}(s)$. To do this, we find the two-terminal representations of the subnetworks in question by means of the branch formulation. This method is more appropriate for networks containing transistors. The procedure will involve the solution of only one equation for each subnetwork; this is a great simplification. Furthermore, in this case, the two subnetworks under consideration differ only in their voltage drivers. Hence there is a further simplification, and we need only perform one calculation to obtain terminal representations for both subnetworks. We therefore isolate one of the subnetworks, and apply a voltage driver as shown in Fig. 4.23(a). This gives the system graphs of Fig. 4.23(b) and (c). To apply the branch formulation, we must first write the transistor equations in the short-circuit form:

$$\begin{bmatrix} I_6(s) \\ I_7(s) \end{bmatrix} = \begin{bmatrix} g_{66} & g_{67} \\ g_{76} & g_{77} \end{bmatrix} \begin{bmatrix} V_6(s) \\ V_7(s) \end{bmatrix}.$$

(4.63)

The branch equations corresponding to Fig. 4.23(c) are

$$- \begin{bmatrix} I_4(s) \\ I_5(s) \\ 0 \end{bmatrix} = \begin{bmatrix} 0 & 1 & 0 & 0 \\ 0 & 0 & 0 & 1 \\ 1 & 0 & 1 & -1 \end{bmatrix} \begin{bmatrix} g_{66} & g_{67} & 0 & 0 \\ g_{76} & g_{77} & 0 & 0 \\ 0 & 0 & G_8 & 0 \\ 0 & 0 & 0 & sC_9 \end{bmatrix} \begin{bmatrix} 0 & 0 & 1 \\ 1 & 0 & 0 \\ 0 & 0 & 1 \\ 0 & 1 & -1 \end{bmatrix} \begin{bmatrix} V_4(s) \\ V_5(s) \\ V_6(s) \end{bmatrix}$$

(4.64)

or

$$- \begin{bmatrix} I_4(s) \\ I_5(s) \\ 0 \end{bmatrix} = \begin{bmatrix} g_{77} & 0 & g_{76} \\ 0 & sC_9 & -sC_9 \\ g_{67} & -sC_9 & g_{66} + G_8 + sC_9 \end{bmatrix} \begin{bmatrix} V_4(s) \\ V_5(s) \\ V_6(s) \end{bmatrix}.$$

(4.65)

From the last equation of (4.65), we have

$$V_6(s) = \frac{1}{g_{66} + G_8 + sC_9}\left(-g_{67}V_4(s) + sC_9V_5(s)\right), \qquad (4.66)$$

and substituting (4.66) into the first equation of (4.65),

$$-I_4(s) = \left(g_{77} - \frac{g_{67}g_{76}}{g_{66} + G_8 + sC_9}\right)V_4(s) + \frac{sC_9g_{76}}{g_{66} + G_8 + sC_9}V_5(s) \qquad (4.67)$$

or, since $-I_4(s) = I_1(s)$, $V_4(s) = V_1(s)$, $V_5(s) = E_1(s)$,

$$I_1(s) = \left(g_{77} - \frac{g_{67}g_{76}}{g_{66} + G_8 + sC_9}\right)V_1(s) + \frac{sC_9g_{76}E_1(s)}{g_{66} + G_8 + sC_9}. \qquad (4.68)$$

This is the terminal equation for the subnetwork containing the voltage driver $E_1(s)$; the other subnetwork has the same terminal equation, with $E_1(s)$ replaced by $E_2(s)$. Therefore, in Eqs. (4.60), we may identify

$$Z_1(s) = Z_2(s) = \frac{g_{66} + G_8 + sC_9}{g_{77}(g_{66} + G_8 + sC_9) - g_{67}g_{76}},$$

$$E_{01}(s) = \frac{-sC_9g_{76}E_1(s)}{g_{77}(g_{66} + G_8 + sC_9) - g_{67}g_{76}}, \qquad (4.69)$$

$$E_{02}(s) = \frac{-sC_9g_{76}E_2(s)}{g_{77}(g_{66} + G_8 + sC_9) - g_{67}g_{76}}.$$

Hence, (4.62) becomes

$$V_3(s) = \frac{sC_9g_{76}R_L\left(E_1(s) - E_2(s)\right)}{(2 + R_Lg_{77})(g_{66} + G_8 + sC_9) - R_Lg_{67}g_{76}}. \qquad (4.70)$$

In this solution we were never required to solve more than one equation at a time; this is a very considerable advantage over the direct method.

EXAMPLE 4.7. In this example we shall find the output voltage of the three-stage amplifier of Fig. 4.24. The direct solution, using the branch technique, requires

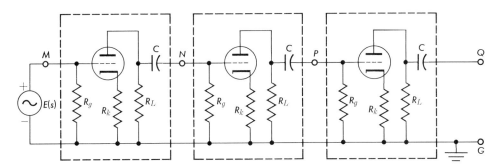

FIG. 4.24. A three-stage vacuum tube amplifier.

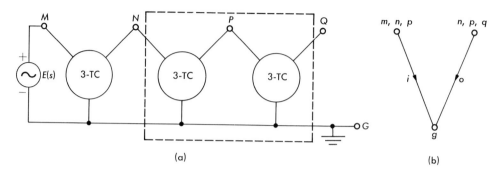

Fɪɢ. 4.25. Reduction of the network of Fig. 4.24 obtained by identifying three three-terminal subnetworks.

the solution of ten simultaneous equations. However, the network can be regarded as an interconnection of three-terminal subnetworks, as shown in Fig. 4.25(a). The terminal graph for each of these subnetworks is of the form shown in Fig. 4.25(b), and the corresponding terminal equations may be obtained by the branch formulation in the normal manner. This involves the inversion of only a 2×2 matrix, and the result is

$$\begin{bmatrix} I_i(s) \\ I_0(s) \end{bmatrix} = \begin{bmatrix} Y_{11}(s) & 0 \\ Y_{21}(s) & Y_{22}(s) \end{bmatrix} \begin{bmatrix} V_i(s) \\ V_0(s) \end{bmatrix}, \tag{4.71}$$

where

$$Y_{11}(s) = G_g = \frac{1}{R_g}, \qquad Y_{21}(s) = \frac{sCg_mG_k}{\Delta},$$

$$Y_{22}(s) = \frac{sC}{\Delta} \left((G_k + g_m + g_p)G_L + G_kg_p \right), \tag{4.72}$$

$$\Delta = (G_k + g_m + g_p)(sC + G_L) + G_kg_p.$$

The direct solution of the network of Fig. 4.25 requires the solution of three simultaneous equations. To avoid this, we first find the three-terminal representation of a subnetwork containing two of the three-terminal components enclosed in the dashed lines in Fig. 4.25. This requires the solution of one equation, and there remains the problem of obtaining the terminal representation of the network of Fig. 4.26(a). The terminal graph corresponding to the new component is shown in Fig. 4.26(b), and the associated terminal equations are

$$\begin{bmatrix} I_2(s) \\ I_3(s) \end{bmatrix} = \begin{bmatrix} Y_{11}(s) & 0 \\ Y'_{21}(s) & Y_{22}(s) \end{bmatrix} \begin{bmatrix} V_2(s) \\ V_3(s) \end{bmatrix}, \tag{4.73}$$

where

$$Y'_{21}(s) = \frac{-(Y_{21}(s))^2}{Y_{11}(s) + Y_{22}(s)}. \tag{4.74}$$

The solution of the network of Fig. 4.26(a) by the branch method requires only

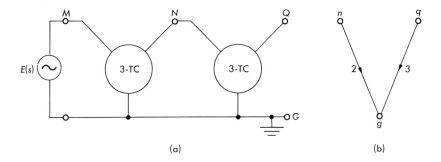

FIG. 4.26. Further reduction of the amplifier network.

the solution of one equation, and we obtain

$$V_{\text{out}}(s) = V_3(s) = \frac{-Y_{21}^3(s)E(s)}{Y_{22}(s)(Y_{11}(s) + Y_{22}(s))^2}.$$ (4.75)

Thus the use of terminal representations has allowed us to solve the given network problem in stages, where the largest matrix to be inverted is of order 2. This is to be compared with the inversion of a 10×10 matrix when the direct method is used.

In the above solution we considered three identical subnetworks of the given system. In order to find the three-terminal representations it was necessary for us to invert a 2×2 matrix. We may, however, choose to consider smaller subnetworks in our analysis. For example, the three-terminal representation of the assemblage of Fig. 4.27, which was required in the above example, may itself be obtained in stages. The process requires the solution of only one equation at a time.

We first find the three-terminal representation of the vacuum tube combined with the resistor R_k, as indicated in Fig. 4.28(a), corresponding to the terminal graph of Fig. 4.28(b). This allows the subnetwork to be depicted as shown in

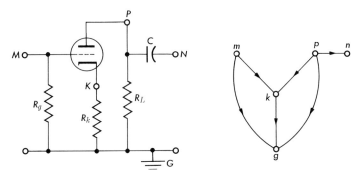

FIG. 4.27. A three-terminal subnetwork of the amplifier of Fig. 4.24.

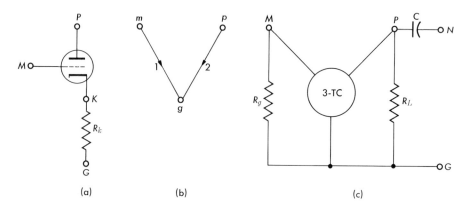

FIG. 4.28. Identification of a subnetwork of the assembly of Fig. 4.27.

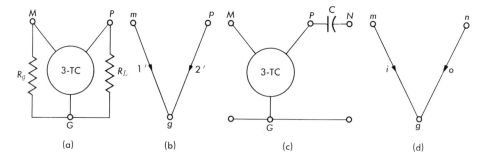

FIG. 4.29. Reduction of the assembly of Fig. 4.28(c) through its subnetworks.

Fig. 4.28(c). We obtain the required terminal relations in the normal manner through the branch formulation; the procedure involves the solution of one equation, and the result is

$$
\begin{bmatrix} I_1(s) \\ I_2(s) \end{bmatrix} = \frac{1}{g_p + g_m + G_k} \begin{bmatrix} 0 & 0 \\ g_m G_k & g_p G_k \end{bmatrix} \begin{bmatrix} V_1(s) \\ V_2(s) \end{bmatrix}.
\tag{4.76}
$$

We next consider the three-terminal representation of the subnetwork illustrated in Fig. 4.29(a), whose terminal graph is given by Fig. 4.29(b). When we have obtained the associated terminal equations, we may consider the assemblage of Fig. 4.27 as that shown in Fig. 4.29(c). The use of the branch equations for finding these terminal relations does not involve the solution of any equations, and we obtain

$$
\begin{bmatrix} I_1'(s) \\ I_2'(s) \end{bmatrix} = \frac{1}{g_m + g_p + G_k} \begin{bmatrix} G_g(g_m + g_p + G_k) & 0 \\ g_m G_k & g_p G_k + G_L(g_m + g_p + G_k) \end{bmatrix} \begin{bmatrix} V_1'(s) \\ V_2'(s) \end{bmatrix}.
$$

$$\tag{4.77}$$

At this point we have only to find the three-terminal representation of the subnetwork of Fig. 4.29(c). The associated terminal graph is that shown in Fig. 4.29(d), and the corresponding terminal relations are found through the branch formulation. This involves the solution of one equation; we finally obtain

$$\begin{bmatrix} I_i(s) \\ I_0(s) \end{bmatrix} = \frac{sC}{\Delta} \begin{bmatrix} \Delta G_g/sC & 0 \\ g_m G_k & g_p g_k + G_L(G_k + g_m + g_p) \end{bmatrix} \begin{bmatrix} V_i(s) \\ V_0(s) \end{bmatrix}, \tag{4.78}$$

where

$$\Delta = G_k g_p + (sC + G_L)(G_k + g_m + g_p). \tag{4.79}$$

Of course, Eqs. (4.79) are exactly the same as (4.71), since they are the terminal relations for the same representation of the same subnetwork.

The choice of subnetworks is seen to have a considerable influence on our solutions. If we choose to find terminal representations of large subnetworks, we may solve the network in few stages, at the expense of a possible requirement of the inversion of large matrices. On the other hand, when we choose small subnetworks involving only two or three components, the number of steps in the solution is increased, but the number of equations to be solved at each state is correspondingly decreased. We can say, however, that the total number of equations to be solved remains the same, regardless of the method of solution. Nevertheless, the choice of suitable subassemblies allows us to solve these equations one or two at a time in succession, obviating the need for inverting large matrices. The method also allows us to take into account the simplifications which arise through the existence of similar subnetworks in a given network, as is very frequently the case in large systems.

4.7. TREE TRANSFORMATIONS

We have frequently mentioned the fact that any n-vertex tree graph can be used for the terminal graph corresponding to an n-terminal component. The terminal equations will, of course, differ from one terminal graph to another; furthermore, different forms of terminal equations may be associated with the same terminal graph. From the theory of linear graphs, it is known that there are $2^{(n-1)}n^{(n-2)}$ different trees connecting n vertices when the orientation of the elements is taken into account. Therefore, for an n-terminal component there are many different n-terminal representations.

It may happen, in some cases, that one representation is more helpful than another; in this section we shall illustrate the transformation of a given n-terminal representation into an alternative one. The techniques involved are nothing more than simple applications of the methods of previous sections; we shall see that no matrix inversion is involved in the transformation. The method consists of nonsingular transformations of the variables associated with one tree to those with another; thus it also results in a nonsingular transformation of the terminal equations. The technique is therefore called a *tree transformation*.

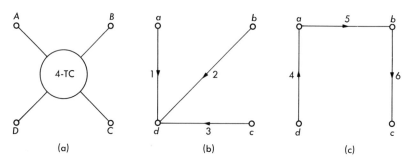

FIG. 4.30. A four-terminal component and two possible terminal graphs.

Consider a typical four-terminal component as shown in Fig. 4.30(a). Let us assume that its terminal relations, corresponding to the terminal graph of Fig. 4.30(b) are given in the open-circuit form

$$\begin{bmatrix} V_1(s) \\ V_2(s) \\ V_3(s) \end{bmatrix} = \begin{bmatrix} Z_{11}(s) & Z_{12}(s) & Z_{13}(s) \\ Z_{21}(s) & Z_{22}(s) & Z_{23}(s) \\ Z_{31}(s) & Z_{32}(s) & Z_{33}(s) \end{bmatrix} \begin{bmatrix} I_1(s) \\ I_2(s) \\ I_3(s) \end{bmatrix} + \begin{bmatrix} E_1(s) \\ E_2(s) \\ E_3(s) \end{bmatrix} \tag{4.80}$$

or

$$[V_b(s)] = [Z(s)][I_b(s)] + [E_0(s)]. \tag{4.81}$$

We wish to find the terminal equations corresponding to the terminal graph of Fig. 4.30(c), also in the open-circuit form. We therefore apply three current generators, as shown in Fig. 4.31(a), and obtain the two system graphs of Fig. 4.31(b) and (c). From Fig. 4.31(b), we have

$$\begin{bmatrix} V_7(s) \\ V_8(s) \\ V_9(s) \end{bmatrix} = \begin{bmatrix} -1 & 0 & 0 \\ 1 & -1 & 0 \\ 0 & 1 & -1 \end{bmatrix} \begin{bmatrix} V_1(s) \\ V_2(s) \\ V_3(s) \end{bmatrix} \tag{4.82}$$

or, symbolically,

$$[V_c(s)] = -[B][V_b(s)], \tag{4.83}$$

and

$$\begin{bmatrix} I_1(s) \\ I_2(s) \\ I_3(s) \end{bmatrix} = \begin{bmatrix} 1 & -1 & 0 \\ 0 & 1 & -1 \\ 0 & 0 & 1 \end{bmatrix} \begin{bmatrix} I_7(s) \\ I_8(s) \\ I_9(s) \end{bmatrix} \tag{4.84}$$

or

$$[I_b(s)] = -[A][I_c(s)] = [B]'[I_c(s)]. \tag{4.85}$$

Also, from Fig. 4.31(c),

$$\begin{bmatrix} I_7(s) \\ I_8(s) \\ I_9(s) \end{bmatrix} = - \begin{bmatrix} I_4(s) \\ I_5(s) \\ I_6(s) \end{bmatrix} \tag{4.86}$$

or

$$[I_c(s)] = -[I(s)], \tag{4.87}$$

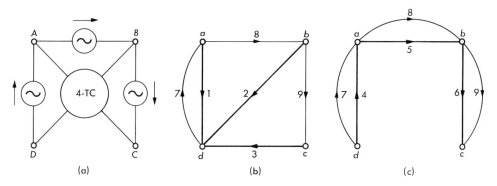

Fig. 4.31. Schematic and graphs used in a tree transformation.

and

$$\begin{bmatrix} V_7(s) \\ V_8(s) \\ V_9(s) \end{bmatrix} = \begin{bmatrix} V_4(s) \\ V_5(s) \\ V_6(s) \end{bmatrix}\qquad(4.88)$$

or

$$[V_c(s)] = [V(s)].\qquad(4.89)$$

Now, substituting successively (4.82), (4.80), (4.84), and (4.86) into (4.88), we obtain the terminal equations

$$\begin{bmatrix} V_4(s) \\ V_5(s) \\ V_6(s) \end{bmatrix} = \begin{bmatrix} -1 & 0 & 0 \\ 1 & -1 & 0 \\ 0 & 1 & -1 \end{bmatrix}\begin{bmatrix} Z_{11}(s) & Z_{12}(s) & Z_{13}(s) \\ Z_{21}(s) & Z_{22}(s) & Z_{23}(s) \\ Z_{31}(s) & Z_{32}(s) & Z_{33}(s) \end{bmatrix}\begin{bmatrix} -1 & 1 & 0 \\ 0 & -1 & 1 \\ 0 & 0 & -1 \end{bmatrix}\begin{bmatrix} I_4(s) \\ I_5(s) \\ I_6(s) \end{bmatrix}$$
$$+ \begin{bmatrix} -1 & 0 & 0 \\ 1 & -1 & 0 \\ 0 & 1 & -1 \end{bmatrix}\begin{bmatrix} E_1(s) \\ E_2(s) \\ E_3(s) \end{bmatrix}.\qquad(4.90)$$

Symbolically, the general form of (4.90) is obtained by substituting (4.83), (4.81), (4.85), and (4.87) into (4.89), as

$$[V(s)] = [B][Z(s)][B]'[I(s)] - [B][E_0(s)].\qquad(4.91)$$

There is no matrix inversion involved in obtaining (4.90) or (4.91) from (4.80) or (4.81). This is to be expected, since the elements corresponding to the applied current drivers form a complete cotree of the system graph of Fig. 4.31(b). They also constitute a tree. Even if we had started with the terminal equations in the short-circuit form, we could have obtained the short-circuit form of our new representation without taking an inverse. This is, of course, quite general, since the tree transformation always involves the superposition of one tree graph over another; it is of no consequence which of these graphs should be considered as the tree of the resulting system graph.

EXAMPLE 4.8. Consider the three-terminal networks of Fig. 4.32(a), (b), and (c). They are known respectively as *grounded-cathode*, *grounded grid*, and *grounded-*

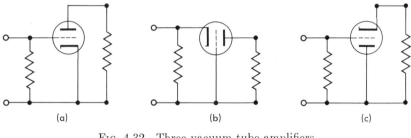

FIG. 4.32. Three vacuum tube amplifiers.

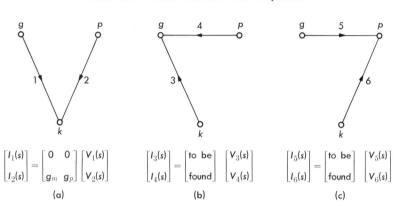

FIG. 4.33.   Three-terminal representations for a vacuum tube which are useful for: (a) grounded cathode; (b) grounded grid; (c) grounded plate connection.

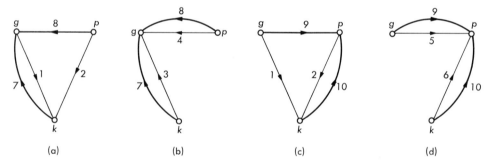

FIG. 4.34. System graphs required in finding the terminal relations associated with the terminal graphs of Fig. 4.33(b) and (c) by tree transformations.

plate vacuum-tube amplifiers. For the grounded-cathode amplifier, it is most convenient to represent the vacuum tube by the usual graph and equations of Fig. 4.33(a). For the grounded-grid amplifier, however, it may be more convenient to use the terminal representation of Fig. 4.33(b), while that of Fig. 4.33(c) is most suitable for use with the grounded-plate network. Should we attempt to obtain the coefficients in the terminal equations for these alternative representations by laboratory methods, we would find considerable difficulty associated with the grid-to-plate measurements. Therefore, the most convenient method for obtaining the terminal representations of Fig. 4.33(b) and (c) is the use of tree transformations from the representation of Fig. 4.33(a).

This is done by applying voltage drivers and obtaining the system graphs of Fig. 4.34. Figures 4.34(a) and (b) correspond to the representation of Fig. 4.33(b), while Fig. 4.34(c) and (d) correspond to that of Fig. 4.33(c).

For the system graphs of Fig. 4.34(a) and (b), we have

$$
-\begin{bmatrix} I_7(s) \\ I_8(s) \end{bmatrix} = \begin{bmatrix} I_3(s) \\ I_4(s) \end{bmatrix} = \begin{bmatrix} -1 & -1 \\ 0 & 1 \end{bmatrix} \begin{bmatrix} I_1(s) \\ I_2(s) \end{bmatrix}
$$
$$
= \begin{bmatrix} -1 & -1 \\ 0 & 1 \end{bmatrix} \begin{bmatrix} 0 & 0 \\ g_m & g_p \end{bmatrix} \begin{bmatrix} V_1(s) \\ V_2(s) \end{bmatrix}
$$
$$
= \begin{bmatrix} -1 & -1 \\ 0 & 1 \end{bmatrix} \begin{bmatrix} 0 & 0 \\ g_m & g_p \end{bmatrix} \begin{bmatrix} -1 & 0 \\ -1 & 1 \end{bmatrix} \begin{bmatrix} V_7(s) \\ V_8(s) \end{bmatrix}
$$
$$
= \begin{bmatrix} -1 & -1 \\ 0 & 1 \end{bmatrix} \begin{bmatrix} 0 & 0 \\ g_m & g_p \end{bmatrix} \begin{bmatrix} -1 & 0 \\ -1 & 1 \end{bmatrix} \begin{bmatrix} V_3(s) \\ V_4(s) \end{bmatrix}, \tag{4.92}
$$

so that the terminal equations corresponding to the graph of Fig. 4.33(b) are

$$
\begin{bmatrix} I_3(s) \\ I_4(s) \end{bmatrix} = \begin{bmatrix} g_m + g_p & -g_p \\ -(g_m + g_p) & g_p \end{bmatrix} \begin{bmatrix} V_3(s) \\ V_4(s) \end{bmatrix}. \tag{4.93}
$$

Similarly, for the system graphs of Fig. 4.34(c) and (d), we have

$$
-\begin{bmatrix} I_9(s) \\ I_{10}(s) \end{bmatrix} = \begin{bmatrix} I_5(s) \\ I_6(s) \end{bmatrix} = \begin{bmatrix} 1 & 0 \\ -1 & -1 \end{bmatrix} \begin{bmatrix} I_1(s) \\ I_2(s) \end{bmatrix}
$$
$$
= \begin{bmatrix} 1 & 0 \\ -1 & -1 \end{bmatrix} \begin{bmatrix} 0 & 0 \\ g_m & g_p \end{bmatrix} \begin{bmatrix} V_1(s) \\ V_2(s) \end{bmatrix}
$$
$$
= \begin{bmatrix} 1 & 0 \\ -1 & -1 \end{bmatrix} \begin{bmatrix} 0 & 0 \\ g_m & g_p \end{bmatrix} \begin{bmatrix} 1 & -1 \\ 0 & -1 \end{bmatrix} \begin{bmatrix} V_9(s) \\ V_{10}(s) \end{bmatrix}
$$
$$
= \begin{bmatrix} 1 & 0 \\ -1 & -1 \end{bmatrix} \begin{bmatrix} 0 & 0 \\ g_m & g_p \end{bmatrix} \begin{bmatrix} 1 & -1 \\ 0 & -1 \end{bmatrix} \begin{bmatrix} V_5(s) \\ V_6(s) \end{bmatrix}, \tag{4.94}
$$

and the terminal relations for the representation of Fig. 4.33(c) are

$$
\begin{bmatrix} I_5(s) \\ I_6(s) \end{bmatrix} = \begin{bmatrix} 0 & 0 \\ -g_m & g_m + g_p \end{bmatrix} \begin{bmatrix} V_5(s) \\ V_6(s) \end{bmatrix}. \tag{4.95}
$$

EXAMPLE 4.9. In this example, we illustrate a tree transformation for a component whose terminal equations are given in the hybrid form. Hitherto we have consistently used the tree-graph representation shown in Fig. 4.35(a) and its corresponding hybrid parameters for representing a transistor. This is most useful for the so-called "common-emitter" connection, whereas when we use the "common-base" configuration, it is most convenient that we use the hybrid parameters corresponding to the terminal graph of Fig. 4.35(b). In order to obtain this repre-

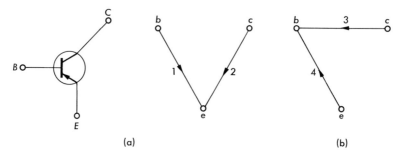

FIG. 4.35. A transistor and two possible terminal graphs.

sentation, we apply drivers, and set up the system graphs of Fig. 4.36. We are given the terminal equations

$$V_1(s) = h_{11}I_1(s) + h_{12}V_2(s),$$
$$I_2(s) = h_{21}I_1(s) + h_{22}V_2(s). \tag{4.96}$$

We note from Fig. 4.36(a) and (b) that

$$V_1(s) = -V_6(s) = -V_4(s), \tag{4.97}$$
$$V_2(s) = V_5(s) - V_6(s) = V_3(s) - V_4(s), \tag{4.98}$$

and

$$I_1(s) = I_5(s) + I_6(s) = -I_3(s) - I_4(s), \tag{4.99}$$
$$I_2(s) = -I_5(s) = I_3(s). \tag{4.100}$$

The substitution of (4.97), (4.98), (4.99), and (4.100) into (4.96) gives

$$-h_{12}V_3(s) + (h_{12} - 1)V_4(s) = -h_{11}I_3(s) - h_{11}I_4(s),$$
$$-h_{22}V_3(s) + h_{22}V_4(s) = -(1 + h_{21})I_3(s) - h_{21}I_4(s). \tag{4.101}$$

To transform these terminal equations into the hybrid form we rewrite (4.101) as

$$-h_{12}V_3(s) + h_{11}I_4(s) = -h_{11}I_3(s) + (1 - h_{12})V_4(s),$$
$$-h_{22}V_3(s) + h_{21}I_4(s) = -(1 + h_{21})I_3(s) - h_{22}V_4(s), \tag{4.102}$$

and solving (4.103) for $V_3(s)$ and $I_4(s)$ in terms of $I_3(s)$ and $V_4(s)$, we obtain

$$V_3(s) = \frac{1}{\Delta_h}\left(h_{11}I_3(s) + (h_{21} + \Delta_h)V_4(s)\right),$$
$$\tag{4.103}$$
$$I_4(s) = \frac{1}{\Delta_h}\left((h_{12} - \Delta_h)I_3(s) + h_{22}V_4(s)\right),$$

where

$$\Delta_h = h_{11}h_{22} - h_{12}h_{21}. \tag{4.104}$$

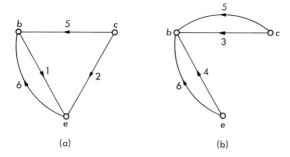

FIG. 4.36. System graphs used in tree transformation for the transistor.

Note that the tree transformation did not involve the solution of any simultaneous equations; it was only in expressing the transformed equations (4.101) in the hybrid form (4.103) that we were required to do this.

In summary, then, we have discussed a simple method for obtaining the terminal equations associated with one tree graph from those associated with another. This tree transformation never involves a matrix inverse, and can frequently simplify the analysis of a network. It allows us to derive terminal representations, which may not easily be obtained in the laboratory, for every possible terminal graph associated with a given component.

4.8. TWO-PORTS

In this section we shall consider four-terminal networks which are connected into systems in such a way that there is no external connection between two pairs of terminals, as shown in Fig. 4.37. When a four-terminal network is connected in this way, it is called a *two-port*, or *two-terminal-pair network*. Two-ports are of central importance in the theory of linear control systems and network synthesis. The two pairs of terminals AB and CD are called, respectively, the input and output terminal pairs, and the corresponding voltages and currents are called the input and output variables. We shall show that two-ports can be represented by

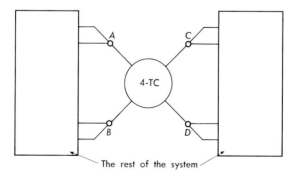

FIG. 4.37. A four-terminal network connected as a two-port.

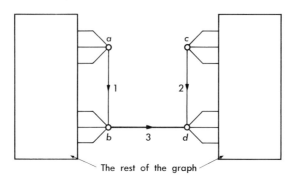

FIG. 4.38. System graph for Fig. 4.37.

separated terminal graphs with only two elements and sets of associated terminal equations; thus a two-port representation is similar to that of a pair of coupled coils, which we discussed in Section 4.4. Through the study of two-port terminal equations, we shall introduce the concept of *transfer functions*; such functions are of considerable interest in many applications.

Consider the linear graph corresponding to the system of Fig. 4.37. This is shown in Fig. 4.38, in which we have shown explicitly only the terminal graph associated with the four-terminal component. We immediately notice that element 3 constitutes the only path connecting vertices b and d; it must therefore be a branch of any tree of the system graph. Hence it is a cut set and we have the equation

$$I_3(s) = 0. \tag{4.105}$$

Further, $V_3(s)$ will not appear in any circuit equation, so that if the terminal equations for the four-terminal component are

$$
\begin{bmatrix} V_1(s) \\ V_2(s) \\ V_3(s) \end{bmatrix} =
\begin{bmatrix} Z_{11}(s) & Z_{12}(s) & Z_{13}(s) \\ Z_{21}(s) & Z_{22}(s) & Z_{23}(s) \\ Z_{31}(s) & Z_{32}(s) & Z_{33}(s) \end{bmatrix}
\begin{bmatrix} I_1(s) \\ I_2(s) \\ I_3(s) \end{bmatrix} +
\begin{bmatrix} E_1(s) \\ E_2(s) \\ E_3(s) \end{bmatrix}, \tag{4.106}
$$

none of the voltages and currents in the network will depend on $Z_{13}(s)$, $Z_{23}(s)$, or $Z_{33}(s)$, and $V_3(s)$ is the only variable which depends on $Z_{31}(s)$, $Z_{32}(s)$, and $E_3(s)$. Therefore, when $V_3(s)$ is not of interest, we are at liberty to dispense with element 3 of the terminal graph and the third equation of the terminal relations (4.106).

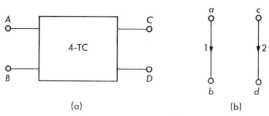

FIG. 4.39. A four-terminal component and its two-port terminal graph.

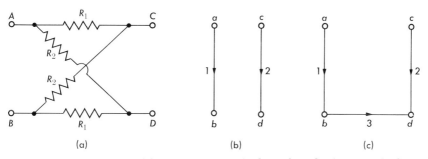

FIG. 4.40. A lattice network with a two-port terminal graph and a four-terminal terminal graph.

Note the similarity between the above development and the case of pairs of coupled coils. In both cases we can represent the component by a two-element separated terminal graph, as illustrated in Fig. 4.39, and a pair of terminal equations. However, the two-port representation applies only when the subnetwork is loaded only at its input and output terminal pairs; there is no such restriction in the case of coupled coils.

EXAMPLE 4.10. In this example we shall find a two-port representation of the lattice network of Fig. 4.4 (Example 4.1). We shall use this network to illustrate the fact that two-port representations can be obtained directly from an analysis of the given network as well as from its four-terminal representation. Figure 4.40 shows the lattice network in question, together with a two-port terminal graph and a four-terminal tree graph. The four-terminal representation of this network, corresponding to the graph of Fig. 4.40(c) was obtained in Example 4.1; the terminal equations are

$$\begin{bmatrix} G_1 + G_2 & -G_1 & G_1 + G_2 \\ -G_1 & G_1 + G_2 & -(G_1 + G_2) \\ G_1 + G_2 & -(G_1 + G_2) & 2(G_1 + G_2) \end{bmatrix} \begin{bmatrix} V_1(s) \\ V_2(s) \\ V_3(s) \end{bmatrix} = \begin{bmatrix} I_1(s) \\ I_2(s) \\ I_3(s) \end{bmatrix}. \tag{4.6}$$

In order to obtain the two-port representation from (4.6), we merely set $I_3(s) = 0$, and eliminate $V_3(s)$. This procedure yields

$$V_3(s) = -\tfrac{1}{2}V_1(s) + \tfrac{1}{2}V_2(s), \qquad I_3(s) = 0, \tag{4.107}$$

so that

$$\begin{bmatrix} I_1(s) \\ I_2(s) \end{bmatrix} = \begin{bmatrix} G_1 + G_2 & -G_1 \\ -G_1 & G_1 + G_2 \end{bmatrix} \begin{bmatrix} V_1(s) \\ V_2(s) \end{bmatrix} + \begin{bmatrix} G_1 + G_2 \\ -(G_1 + G_2) \end{bmatrix} [V_3(s)]$$

$$= \tfrac{1}{2} \begin{bmatrix} G_1 + G_2 & G_2 - G_1 \\ G_2 - G_1 & G_1 + G_2 \end{bmatrix} \begin{bmatrix} V_1(s) \\ V_2(s) \end{bmatrix}. \tag{4.108}$$

Equations (4.108) are the terminal equations associated with the two-port graph of Fig. 4.40(b); together, the equations and graph are a two-port characterization of the network of Fig. 4.40(a).

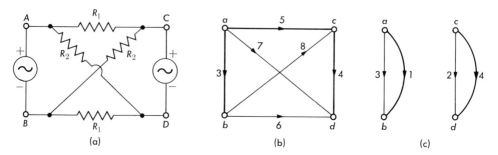

FIG. 4.41. Schematic diagram and graphs used in finding a two-port representation.

We have obtained the two-port representation of the given network from a four-terminal representation; it is, however, possible, and frequently convenient, to use a more direct method. We follow the same principles as in any terminal representation, and apply two voltage drivers in one-to-one correspondence with the two-port graph, as shown in Fig. 4.41(a). This gives the two system graphs of Fig. 4.41(b) and (c). We obtain the relations between $I_3(s)$, $I_4(s)$ and $V_3(s)$, $V_4(s)$ through the branch equations, which are

$$-\begin{bmatrix} I_3(s) \\ I_4(s) \\ 0 \end{bmatrix} = \begin{bmatrix} G_1 + G_2 & -G_1 & -(G_1 + G_2) \\ -G_1 & G_1 + G_2 & G_1 + G_2 \\ -(G_1 + G_2) & G_1 + G_2 & 2(G_1 + G_2) \end{bmatrix} \begin{bmatrix} V_3(s) \\ V_4(s) \\ V_5(s) \end{bmatrix}. \qquad (4.109)$$

From the third equation of (4.109), we have

$$V_5(s) = \tfrac{1}{2} V_3(s) - \tfrac{1}{2} V_4(s), \qquad (4.110)$$

and substituting (4.110) into the first two equations of (4.109),

$$-\begin{bmatrix} I_3(s) \\ I_4(s) \end{bmatrix} = \tfrac{1}{2} \begin{bmatrix} G_1 + G_2 & G_2 - G_1 \\ G_2 - G_1 & G_1 + G_2 \end{bmatrix} \begin{bmatrix} V_3(s) \\ V_4(s) \end{bmatrix}. \qquad (4.111)$$

Finally, we note that

$$\begin{bmatrix} I_1(s) \\ I_2(s) \end{bmatrix} = -\begin{bmatrix} I_3(s) \\ I_4(s) \end{bmatrix}, \qquad \begin{bmatrix} V_1(s) \\ V_2(s) \end{bmatrix} = \begin{bmatrix} V_3(s) \\ V_4(s) \end{bmatrix},$$

and obtain the required terminal relations (Eqs. 4.108).

In general, the two-port terminal relations consist of two equations expressing two of the variables $V_1(s)$, $V_2(s)$, $I_1(s)$, and $I_2(s)$ explicitly in terms of the remainder. Hence there are six possible different forms which these equations may take. When there are no specified functions in the terminal equations, the six different forms, all of which are associated with the terminal graph of Fig. 4.42, are:
(a) open-circuit form,

$$\begin{bmatrix} V_1(s) \\ V_2(s) \end{bmatrix} = \begin{bmatrix} z_{11}(s) & z_{12}(s) \\ z_{21}(s) & z_{22}(s) \end{bmatrix} \begin{bmatrix} I_1(s) \\ I_2(s) \end{bmatrix}; \qquad (4.112)$$

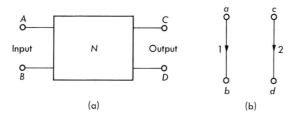

FIG. 4.42. A two-port and its terminal graph.

(b) short-circuit form,

$$\begin{bmatrix} I_1(s) \\ I_2(s) \end{bmatrix} = \begin{bmatrix} y_{11}(s) & y_{12}(s) \\ y_{21}(s) & y_{22}(s) \end{bmatrix} \begin{bmatrix} V_1(s) \\ V_2(s) \end{bmatrix};$$ (4.113)

(c) hybrid form,

$$\begin{bmatrix} V_1(s) \\ I_2(s) \end{bmatrix} = \begin{bmatrix} h_{11}(s) & h_{12}(s) \\ h_{21}(s) & h_{22}(s) \end{bmatrix} \begin{bmatrix} I_1(s) \\ V_2(s) \end{bmatrix};$$ (4.114)

(d) inverse hybrid form,

$$\begin{bmatrix} I_1(s) \\ V_2(s) \end{bmatrix} = \begin{bmatrix} g_{11}(s) & g_{12}(s) \\ g_{21}(s) & g_{22}(s) \end{bmatrix} \begin{bmatrix} V_1(s) \\ I_2(s) \end{bmatrix};$$ (4.115)

(e) "cascade" form,

$$\begin{bmatrix} V_1(s) \\ I_1(s) \end{bmatrix} = \begin{bmatrix} A(s) & B(s) \\ C(s) & D(s) \end{bmatrix} \begin{bmatrix} V_2(s) \\ -I_2(s) \end{bmatrix};$$ (4.116)

(f) "inverse-cascade" form,

$$\begin{bmatrix} V_2(s) \\ I_2(s) \end{bmatrix} = \frac{1}{AD - BC} \begin{bmatrix} D(s) & B(s) \\ C(s) & A(s) \end{bmatrix} \begin{bmatrix} V_1(s) \\ -I_1(s) \end{bmatrix}.$$ (4.117)

Note that in the cascade form, we have assigned a negative sign for the output current variable. As we shall observe in the next section, this introduces some simplicity in the cascade, or A, B, C, D, parameters for networks whose subnetworks are also represented by cascade parameters.

Clearly, when all six different forms of the two-port terminal equations exist for a given network, they are very simply interrelated. For example, if we wish to obtain the open-circuit parameters z_{ij} from the hybrid parameters h_{ij}, we may rewrite (4.114) in the form

$$\begin{bmatrix} 1 & -h_{12} & -h_{11} & 0 \\ 0 & -h_{22} & -h_{21} & 1 \end{bmatrix} \begin{bmatrix} V_1(s) \\ V_2(s) \\ I_1(s) \\ I_2(s) \end{bmatrix} = \begin{bmatrix} 0 \\ 0 \end{bmatrix}$$ (4.118)

or

$$\begin{bmatrix} 1 & -h_{12} \\ 0 & -h_{22} \end{bmatrix} \begin{bmatrix} V_1(s) \\ V_2(s) \end{bmatrix} = -\begin{bmatrix} -h_{11} & 0 \\ -h_{21} & 1 \end{bmatrix} \begin{bmatrix} I_1(s) \\ I_2(s) \end{bmatrix},$$ (4.119)

TABLE 4.1

RELATIONS BETWEEN THE TWO-PORT PARAMETERS

	Open circuit	Short circuit	Cascade	Hybrid	Inverse hybrid
$z_{11}(s)$	—	y_{22}/Δ_y	A/C	Δ_h/h_{22}	$1/g_{11}$
$z_{12}(s)$	—	$-y_{12}/\Delta_y$	$(AD - BC)/C$	h_{12}/h_{22}	$-g_{12}/g_{11}$
$z_{21}(s)$	—	$-y_{21}/\Delta_y$	$1/C$	$-h_{21}/h_{22}$	g_{21}/g_{11}
$z_{22}(s)$	—	y_{11}/Δ_y	D/C	$1/h_{22}$	Δ_g/g_{11}
$y_{11}(s)$	z_{22}/Δ_z	—	D/B	$1/h_{11}$	Δ_g/g_{22}
$y_{12}(s)$	$-z_{12}/\Delta_z$	—	$(BC - AD)/B$	$-h_{12}/h_{11}$	g_{12}/g_{22}
$y_{21}(s)$	$-z_{21}/\Delta_z$	—	$-1/B$	h_{21}/h_{11}	$-g_{21}/g_{22}$
$y_{22}(s)$	z_{11}/Δ_z	—	A/B	Δ_h/h_{11}	$1/g_{22}$
$A(s)$	z_{11}/z_{21}	$-y_{22}/y_{21}$	—	$-\Delta_h/h_{21}$	$1/g_{21}$
$B(s)$	Δ_z/z_{21}	$-1/y_{21}$	—	$-h_{11}/h_{21}$	g_{22}/g_{21}
$C(s)$	$1/z_{21}$	$-\Delta_y/y_{21}$	—	$-h_{22}/h_{21}$	g_{11}/g_{21}
$D(s)$	z_{22}/z_{21}	$-y_{11}/y_{21}$	—	$-1/h_{21}$	Δ_g/g_{21}
$h_{11}(s)$	Δ_z/z_{22}	$1/y_{11}$	B/D	—	g_{22}/Δ_g
$h_{12}(s)$	z_{12}/z_{22}	$-y_{12}/y_{11}$	$(AD - BC)/D$	—	$-g_{12}/\Delta_g$
$h_{21}(s)$	$-z_{21}/z_{22}$	y_{21}/y_{11}	$-1/D$	—	$-g_{21}/\Delta_g$
$h_{22}(s)$	$1/z_{22}$	Δ_y/y_{11}	C/D	—	g_{11}/Δ_g
$g_{11}(s)$	$1/z_{11}$	Δ_y/y_{22}	C/A	h_{22}/Δ_h	—
$g_{12}(s)$	$-z_{12}/z_{11}$	y_{12}/y_{22}	$(BC - AD)/A$	$-h_{12}/\Delta_h$	—
$g_{21}(s)$	z_{21}/z_{11}	$-y_{21}/y_{22}$	$1/A$	$-h_{21}/\Delta_h$	—
$g_{22}(s)$	Δ_z/z_{11}	$1/y_{22}$	B/A	h_{11}/Δ_h	—

$$\Delta_z = z_{11}z_{22} - z_{12}z_{21}$$
$$\Delta_y = y_{11}y_{22} - y_{12}y_{21}$$
$$\Delta_h = h_{11}h_{22} - h_{12}h_{21}$$
$$\Delta_g = g_{11}g_{22} - g_{12}g_{21}$$
$$\Delta_z = 1/\Delta_y$$
$$\Delta_h = 1/\Delta_g$$

For RLC networks:
$$z_{12} = z_{21}$$
$$y_{12} = y_{21}$$
$$h_{12} = -h_{21}$$
$$g_{12} = -g_{21}$$
$$AD - BC = 1$$

so that

$$\begin{bmatrix} V_1(s) \\ V_2(s) \end{bmatrix} = -\begin{bmatrix} 1 & -h_{12} \\ 0 & -h_{22} \end{bmatrix}^{-1} \begin{bmatrix} -h_{11} & 0 \\ -h_{21} & 1 \end{bmatrix} \begin{bmatrix} I_1(s) \\ I_2(s) \end{bmatrix}$$

$$= \frac{1}{h_{22}} \begin{bmatrix} h_{11}h_{22} - h_{12}h_{21} & h_{12} \\ -h_{21} & 1 \end{bmatrix} \begin{bmatrix} I_1(s) \\ I_2(s) \end{bmatrix}, \tag{4.120}$$

and the open-circuit parameter matrix is related to the hybrid parameter matrix by

$$\begin{bmatrix} z_{11}(s) & z_{12}(s) \\ z_{21}(s) & z_{22}(s) \end{bmatrix} = \frac{1}{h_{22}} \begin{bmatrix} h_{11}h_{22} - h_{12}h_{21} & h_{12} \\ -h_{21} & 1 \end{bmatrix}. \tag{4.121}$$

It is not difficult to find all the relations between the various parameters; the results are given in Table 4.1.

TABLE 4.2

RELATIONS BETWEEN TRANSFER FUNCTIONS AND NETWORK PARAMETERS

	Open circuit	Short circuit	Cascade	Hybrid	Inverse hybrid
$T_{12}(s)$	z_{21}/z_{11}	$-y_{21}/y_{22}$	$1/A$	$-h_{21}/\Delta_h$	g_{21}
$Z_{12}(s)$	z_{21}	$-y_{21}/\Delta_y$	$1/C$	$-h_{21}/h_{22}$	g_{21}/g_{11}
$Y_{12}(s)$	$-z_{21}/\Delta_z$	y_{21}	$-1/B$	h_{21}/h_{11}	$-g_{21}/g_{22}$
$K_{12}(s)$	$-z_{21}/z_{22}$	y_{21}/y_{11}	$-1/D$	h_{21}	$-g_{21}/\Delta_g$

Let us suppose that the output of a given two-port is open-circuited; that is, no connections are made on the output side. This will ensure that the output current $I_2(s)$ is zero. Under these conditions, the second equation of (4.115) becomes

$$V_2(s) = g_{21}(s)V_1(s), \qquad I_2(s) = 0, \tag{4.122}$$

or

$$g_{21}(s) = \left.\frac{V_2(s)}{V_1(s)}\right|_{I_2(s)=0} \tag{4.123}$$

Thus, $g_{21}(s)$ is the ratio of the output voltage to the input voltage when the output is open-circuited. This function is called the *open-circuit voltage-transfer function*, and is designated by $T_{12}(s)$. From Table 4.1, we have

$$T_{12}(s) = g_{21}(s) = \frac{-h_{21}(s)}{\Delta_h} = \frac{1}{A(s)} = \frac{-y_{21}(s)}{y_{22}(s)} = \frac{z_{21}(s)}{z_{11}(s)}. \tag{4.124}$$

Other transfer functions of interest are the *open-circuit transfer impedance* $Z_{12}(s)$, the *short-circuit transfer admittance* $Y_{12}(s)$, and the *short-circuit current-transfer function* $K_{12}(s)$. These are respectively defined by

$$Z_{12}(s) = \left.\frac{V_2(s)}{I_1(s)}\right|_{I_2(s)=0} \tag{4.125}$$

$$Y_{12}(s) = \left.\frac{I_2(s)}{V_1(s)}\right|_{V_2(s)=0} \tag{4.126}$$

$$K_{12}(s) = \left.\frac{I_2(s)}{I_1(s)}\right|_{V_2(s)=0} \tag{4.127}$$

Of course, $Z_{12}(s)$, $Y_{12}(s)$, and $K_{12}(s)$ can easily be expressed in terms of the various parameters of Eqs. (4.112), (4.113), (4.114), (4.115), and (4.116); the relations are tabulated in Table 4.2.

Since the various transfer functions are obtained by setting appropriate variables in the terminal equations equal to zero, the information about the transfer functions is contained in the terminal equations.

Another important conclusion is that, because all the two-port parameters are rational functions of s, any transfer function $G(s)$ will also be rational. That is,

$$G(s) = \frac{P(s)}{Q(s)}, \qquad (4.128)$$

where $P(s)$ and $Q(s)$ are polynomials in s.

To summarize this section, we have seen that when four-terminal networks are connected into a system only at two pairs of terminals, there is a considerable simplification obtainable through the use of a two-port representation. This involves only a two-element separated terminal graph and a pair of terminal equations. We have also shown that there is no difficulty involved in the transformations between any of the six possible forms that these equations may take, and have indicated the relations between various transfer functions and the several sets of network parameters.

4.9. INTERCONNECTIONS OF TWO-PORTS

Two-ports are frequently connected in various ways, and it is the purpose of this section to develop a few simple results which facilitate the analysis of the resulting networks. However, it must be remembered that some connections of two-ports may cause loading effects across pairs of terminals other than the input and output pairs. In such cases we cannot use the results which we shall obtain in this section, but must use the four-terminal representations of the networks in question.

The four most important methods of interconnection are: (a) cascade, (b) parallel, (c) series, and (d) series-parallel. The series-parallel connection is often called the "feedback" connection. We shall investigate each of these forms in turn.

Consider first, then, the cascade connection of two two-ports N_1, N_2, as illustrated in Fig. 4.43(a). The terminal graphs for N_1, N_2 are given in Fig. 4.43(b),

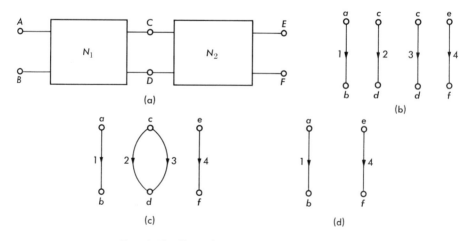

FIG. 4.43. Cascade connection of two-ports.

and the system graph resulting from their cascade connection is shown as Fig. 4.43(c). We shall find terminal equations for the overall network, corresponding to the terminal graph of Fig. 4.43(d).

If the terminal equations for N_1 and N_2 are given in terms of the cascade, or A, B, C, D, parameters, we have

$$\begin{bmatrix} V_1(s) \\ I_1(s) \end{bmatrix} = \begin{bmatrix} A_1(s) & B_1(s) \\ C_1(s) & D_1(s) \end{bmatrix} \begin{bmatrix} V_2(s) \\ -I_2(s) \end{bmatrix}, \tag{4.129}$$

$$\begin{bmatrix} V_3(s) \\ I_3(s) \end{bmatrix} = \begin{bmatrix} A_2(s) & B_2(s) \\ C_2(s) & D_2(s) \end{bmatrix} \begin{bmatrix} V_4(s) \\ -I_4(s) \end{bmatrix}. \tag{4.130}$$

Now, from Fig. 4.43(c), we have

$$\begin{bmatrix} V_2(s) \\ -I_2(s) \end{bmatrix} = \begin{bmatrix} V_3(s) \\ I_3(s) \end{bmatrix}, \tag{4.131}$$

so that, substituting (4.131) into (4.129), we get

$$\begin{bmatrix} V_1(s) \\ I_1(s) \end{bmatrix} = \begin{bmatrix} A_1(s) & B_1(s) \\ C_1(s) & D_1(s) \end{bmatrix} \begin{bmatrix} V_3(s) \\ I_3(s) \end{bmatrix}, \tag{4.132}$$

or, using (4.130),

$$\begin{bmatrix} V_1(s) \\ I_1(s) \end{bmatrix} = \begin{bmatrix} A_1(s) & B_1(s) \\ C_1(s) & D_1(s) \end{bmatrix} \begin{bmatrix} A_2(s) & B_2(s) \\ C_2(s) & D_2(s) \end{bmatrix} \begin{bmatrix} V_4(s) \\ -I_4(s) \end{bmatrix}, \tag{4.133}$$

so that the required terminal relations are

$$\begin{bmatrix} V_1(s) \\ I_1(s) \end{bmatrix} = \begin{bmatrix} A(s) & B(s) \\ C(s) & D(s) \end{bmatrix} \begin{bmatrix} V_4(s) \\ -I_4(s) \end{bmatrix}, \tag{4.134}$$

where

$$\begin{bmatrix} A(s) & B(s) \\ C(s) & D(s) \end{bmatrix} = \begin{bmatrix} A_1(s) & B_1(s) \\ C_1(s) & D_1(s) \end{bmatrix} \begin{bmatrix} A_2(s) & B_2(s) \\ C_2(s) & D_2(s) \end{bmatrix}. \tag{4.135}$$

Thus the A-B-C-D matrix for two two-ports connected in cascade is the product of the A-B-C-D matrices for the individual two-ports. Note that this simple result follows from the fact that the output current is assigned a negative sign in the cascade equations. This allows the very simple substitution of Eqs. (4.131).

EXAMPLE 4.11. In Example 4.7 we studied the network of Fig. 4.24. This was considered as three identical subnetworks connected in cascade; one of these subnetworks was illustrated in Fig. 4.27, and is shown here for convenience as Fig. 4.44(a). We obtained the terminal representation of the subnetwork as the terminal graph of Fig. 4.44(b), and the terminal equations

$$\begin{bmatrix} I_1(s) \\ I_2(s) \end{bmatrix} = \frac{sC}{\Delta} \begin{bmatrix} \Delta G_g/sC & 0 \\ y_m G_k & G_k y_p + G_L(G_k + g_m \mid g_p) \end{bmatrix} \begin{bmatrix} V_1(s) \\ V_2(s) \end{bmatrix}, \tag{4.78}$$

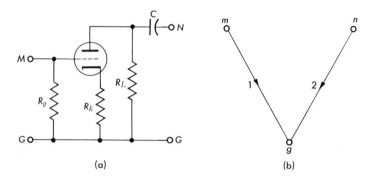

FIG. 4.44. A three-terminal subnetwork and its terminal graph.

where

$$\Delta = G_k g_p + (sC + G_L)(G_k + g_m + g_p). \tag{4.79}$$

Using Table 4.1, we transform these terminal equations into the cascade form, and obtain

$$\begin{bmatrix} V_1(s) \\ I_1(s) \end{bmatrix} = \begin{bmatrix} -(G_k g_p + G_L(G_k + g_m + g_p))/g_m G_k & -\Delta/sC g_m G_k \\ -G_g(G_k g_p + G_L(G_k + g_m + g_p))/g_m G_k & -G_g \Delta/sC g_m G_k \end{bmatrix} \begin{bmatrix} V_2(s) \\ -I_2(s) \end{bmatrix}, \tag{4.136}$$

or

$$\begin{bmatrix} V_1(s) \\ I_1(s) \end{bmatrix} = \frac{-1}{g_m G_k} \begin{bmatrix} N & P \\ N G_g & P G_g \end{bmatrix} \begin{bmatrix} V_2(s) \\ -I_2(s) \end{bmatrix}, \tag{4.137}$$

where

$$N = G_k g_p + G_L(G_k + g_m + g_p), \tag{4.138}$$

$$P = \frac{\Delta}{sC} = \frac{G_k g_p}{sC} + \left(1 + \frac{G_L}{sC}\right)(G_k + g_m + g_p). \tag{4.139}$$

The A-B-C-D matrix for the two-port representation of three networks identical to that of Fig. 4.44(a) is therefore

$$\begin{bmatrix} A & B \\ C & D \end{bmatrix} = \frac{-1}{(g_m G_k)^3} (N + P G_g)^2 \begin{bmatrix} N & P \\ N G_g & P G_g \end{bmatrix}. \tag{4.140}$$

Hence, we obtain, for the open-circuit voltage-transfer function,

$$T_{12}(s) = \frac{1}{A} = \frac{-(g_m G_k)^3}{(N + P G_g)^2 N}, \tag{4.141}$$

and we can easily show that this expression is just the coefficient of $E(s)$ in (4.75), which agrees with our previous analysis.

Let us now consider two two-ports, N_1, N_2, connected in parallel as shown in Fig. 4.45(a). The two-port terminal graphs of Fig. 4.45(b) are associated with N_1 and N_2, and we shall obtain a two-port representation of the overall network,

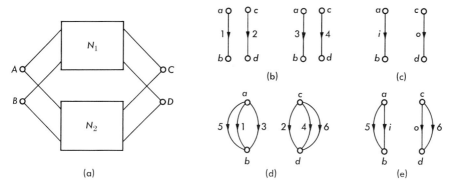

FIG. 4.45. Parallel connection of two-ports.

with the terminal graph of Fig. 4.45(c). We therefore apply two voltage drivers, and obtain the system graphs of Fig. 4.45(d) and (e). When the terminal equations for N_1 and N_2 are given in the short-circuit form, we have

$$\begin{bmatrix} I_1(s) \\ I_2(s) \end{bmatrix} = \begin{bmatrix} y_{11}^{(1)}(s) & y_{12}^{(1)}(s) \\ y_{21}^{(1)}(s) & y_{22}^{(1)}(s) \end{bmatrix} \begin{bmatrix} V_1(s) \\ V_2(s) \end{bmatrix}, \tag{4.142}$$

$$\begin{bmatrix} I_3(s) \\ I_4(s) \end{bmatrix} = \begin{bmatrix} y_{11}^{(2)}(s) & y_{12}^{(2)}(s) \\ y_{21}^{(2)}(s) & y_{22}^{(2)}(s) \end{bmatrix} \begin{bmatrix} V_3(s) \\ V_4(s) \end{bmatrix}. \tag{4.143}$$

Now, from the system graphs we obtain

$$\begin{bmatrix} I_i(s) \\ I_0(s) \end{bmatrix} = - \begin{bmatrix} I_5(s) \\ I_6(s) \end{bmatrix} = \begin{bmatrix} I_1(s) \\ I_2(s) \end{bmatrix} + \begin{bmatrix} I_3(s) \\ I_4(s) \end{bmatrix} \tag{4.144}$$

and

$$\begin{bmatrix} V_i(s) \\ V_0(s) \end{bmatrix} = \begin{bmatrix} V_5(s) \\ V_6(s) \end{bmatrix} = \begin{bmatrix} V_1(s) \\ V_2(s) \end{bmatrix} = \begin{bmatrix} V_3(s) \\ V_4(s) \end{bmatrix}. \tag{4.145}$$

Hence the terminal equations associated with the two-port graph of Fig. 4.45(c) are

$$\begin{bmatrix} I_i(s) \\ I_0(s) \end{bmatrix} = \begin{bmatrix} y_{11}(s) & y_{12}(s) \\ y_{21}(s) & y_{22}(s) \end{bmatrix} \begin{bmatrix} V_i(s) \\ V_0(s) \end{bmatrix}, \tag{4.146}$$

where

$$\begin{bmatrix} y_{11}(s) & y_{12}(s) \\ y_{21}(s) & y_{22}(s) \end{bmatrix} = \begin{bmatrix} y_{11}^{(1)}(s) & y_{12}^{(1)}(s) \\ y_{21}^{(1)}(s) & y_{22}^{(1)}(s) \end{bmatrix} + \begin{bmatrix} y_{11}^{(2)}(s) & y_{12}^{(2)}(s) \\ y_{21}^{(2)}(s) & y_{22}^{(2)}(s) \end{bmatrix}. \tag{4.147}$$

In short, when two-ports are connected in parallel, the short-circuit parameter matrix of the resulting two-port network is the sum of the short-circuit parameter matrices of the component two-ports.

EXAMPLE 4.12. In this example we shall find the two-port terminal equations for the network of Fig. 4.46(c). This is a parallel connection of the networks of Fig.

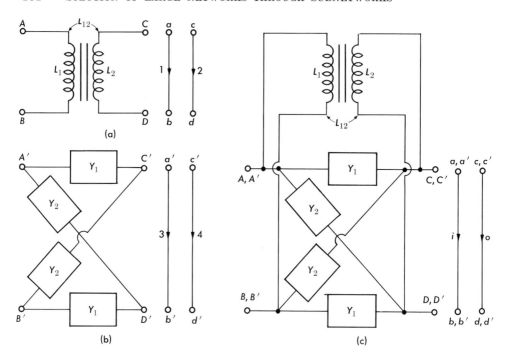

FIG. 4.46. Two two-ports and their parallel connection.

4.46(a) and (b). The short-circuit forms of the terminal equations for the two networks are given by

$$\begin{bmatrix} I_1(s) \\ I_2(s) \end{bmatrix} = \frac{1}{s(L_1L_2 - L_{12}^2)} \begin{bmatrix} L_2 & -L_{12} \\ -L_{12} & L_1 \end{bmatrix} \begin{bmatrix} V_1(s) \\ V_2(s) \end{bmatrix}, \tag{4.148}$$

$$\begin{bmatrix} I_3(s) \\ I_4(s) \end{bmatrix} = \tfrac{1}{2} \begin{bmatrix} Y_2 + Y_1 & Y_2 - Y_1 \\ Y_2 - Y_1 & Y_2 + Y_1 \end{bmatrix} \begin{bmatrix} V_3(s) \\ V_4(s) \end{bmatrix}. \tag{4.149}$$

Therefore, using Eqs. (4.147), we have

$$\begin{bmatrix} I_i(s) \\ I_0(s) \end{bmatrix} = \left\{ \tfrac{1}{2} \begin{bmatrix} Y_2 + Y_1 & Y_2 - Y_1 \\ Y_2 - Y_1 & Y_2 + Y_1 \end{bmatrix} + \frac{1}{s(L_1L_2 - L_{12}^2)} \begin{bmatrix} L_2 & -L_{12} \\ -L_{12} & L_1 \end{bmatrix} \right\} \begin{bmatrix} V_i(s) \\ V_0(s) \end{bmatrix} \tag{4.150}$$

$$= \frac{1}{2s(L_1L_2 - L_{12}^2)}$$

$$\times \begin{bmatrix} 2L_2 + (Y_2 + Y_1)(L_1L_2 - L_{12}^2)s & -2L_{12} + (Y_2 - Y_1)(L_1L_2 - L_{12}^2)s \\ -2L_{12} + (Y_2 - Y_1)(L_1L_2 - L_{12}^2)s & 2L_1 + (Y_2 + Y_1)(L_1L_2 - L_{12}^2)s \end{bmatrix}$$

$$\times \begin{bmatrix} V_i(s) \\ V_0(s) \end{bmatrix}. \tag{4.151}$$

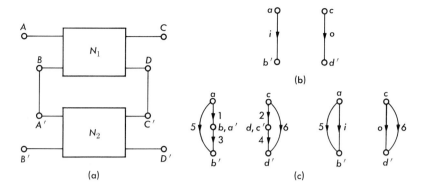

FIG. 4.47. Series connection of two-ports.

The third interconnection which we shall consider is the series connection of two two-ports, as illustrated in Fig. 4.47(a). We shall find the two-port representation of this assembly, with the terminal graph of Fig. 4.47(b). Accordingly, we apply two voltage drivers, and obtain the system graphs of Fig. 4.45(c). When the two-port terminal equations for N_1 and N_2 are given in the open-circuit form, we have

$$\begin{bmatrix} V_1(s) \\ V_2(s) \end{bmatrix} = \begin{bmatrix} z_{11}^{(1)}(s) & z_{12}^{(1)}(s) \\ z_{21}^{(1)}(s) & z_{22}^{(1)}(s) \end{bmatrix} \begin{bmatrix} I_1(s) \\ I_2(s) \end{bmatrix}, \tag{4.152}$$

$$\begin{bmatrix} V_3(s) \\ V_4(s) \end{bmatrix} = \begin{bmatrix} z_{11}^{(2)}(s) & z_{12}^{(2)}(s) \\ z_{21}^{(2)}(s) & z_{22}^{(2)}(s) \end{bmatrix} \begin{bmatrix} I_3(s) \\ I_4(s) \end{bmatrix}. \tag{4.153}$$

Also, from Fig. 4.47(c), we obtain the circuit and cut-set equations

$$\begin{bmatrix} V_i(s) \\ V_0(s) \end{bmatrix} = \begin{bmatrix} V_5(s) \\ V_6(s) \end{bmatrix} = \begin{bmatrix} V_1(s) \\ V_2(s) \end{bmatrix} + \begin{bmatrix} V_3(s) \\ V_4(s) \end{bmatrix}, \tag{4.154}$$

$$\begin{bmatrix} I_i(s) \\ I_0(s) \end{bmatrix} = - \begin{bmatrix} I_5(s) \\ I_6(s) \end{bmatrix} = \begin{bmatrix} I_1(s) \\ I_2(s) \end{bmatrix} = \begin{bmatrix} I_3(s) \\ I_4(s) \end{bmatrix}, \tag{4.155}$$

so that substituting (4.152), (4.153), and (4.155) successively into (4.154), we have

$$\begin{bmatrix} V_i(s) \\ V_0(s) \end{bmatrix} = \left\{ \begin{bmatrix} z_{11}^{(1)}(s) & z_{12}^{(1)}(s) \\ z_{21}^{(1)}(s) & z_{22}^{(1)}(s) \end{bmatrix} + \begin{bmatrix} z_{11}^{(2)}(s) & z_{12}^{(2)}(s) \\ z_{21}^{(2)}(s) & z_{22}^{(2)}(s) \end{bmatrix} \right\} \begin{bmatrix} I_i(s) \\ I_0(s) \end{bmatrix}, \tag{4.156}$$

which are the two-port terminal equations for the overall network. Thus the open-circuit parameter matrix for two two-ports connected in series is the sum of the individual open-circuit parameter matrices.

EXAMPLE 4.13. The "bridged T" network of Fig. 4.48(a) may be considered as a series connection of the two two-ports shown in Fig. 4.48(b) and (c). The open-circuit parameter matrix for the bridged T can therefore be calculated as the sum of the open-circuit parameter matrices of the two simpler networks. For the

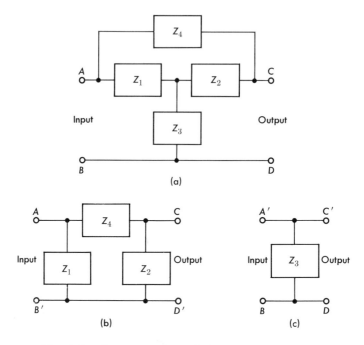

FIG. 4.48.   Two two-ports and their series connection.

network of Fig. 4.48(b), we have

$$
\begin{bmatrix} z_{11}^{(1)} & z_{12}^{(1)} \\ z_{21}^{(1)} & z_{22}^{(1)} \end{bmatrix} = \begin{bmatrix} \dfrac{Z_1(Z_2 + Z_4)}{Z_1 + Z_2 + Z_4} & \dfrac{Z_1 Z_2}{Z_1 + Z_2 + Z_4} \\ \dfrac{Z_1 Z_2}{Z_1 + Z_2 + Z_4} & \dfrac{Z_2(Z_1 + Z_4)}{Z_1 + Z_2 + Z_4} \end{bmatrix},
\tag{4.157}
$$

while for the network of Fig. 4.48(c), we obtain

$$
\begin{bmatrix} z_{11}^{(2)} & z_{12}^{(2)} \\ z_{21}^{(2)} & z_{22}^{(2)} \end{bmatrix} = \begin{bmatrix} Z_3 & Z_3 \\ Z_3 & Z_3 \end{bmatrix}.
\tag{4.158}
$$

Therefore, the required open-circuit parameters are

$$
z_{11} = \frac{Z_1(Z_2 + Z_4)}{Z_1 + Z_2 + Z_4} + Z_3, \qquad z_{22} = \frac{Z_2(Z_1 + Z_4)}{Z_1 + Z_2 + Z_4} + Z_3,
$$

$$
z_{21} = z_{12} = \frac{Z_1 Z_2}{Z_1 + Z_2 + Z_4} + Z_3.
\tag{4.159}
$$

The series-parallel or feedback connection of two-ports is the final configuration that we shall consider. Figure 4.49(a) shows two two-ports with their terminal representations, while Fig. 4.49(b) illustrates their interconnection and the corresponding two-port terminal graph. As can be seen from Fig. 4.49(b), the feedback

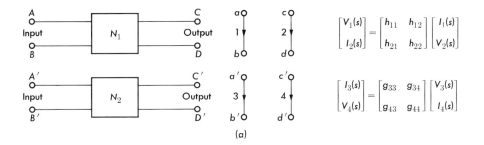

(a)

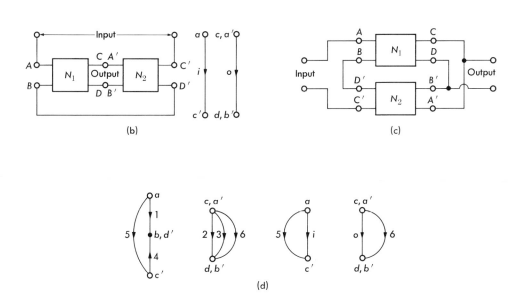

(b)   (c)

(d)

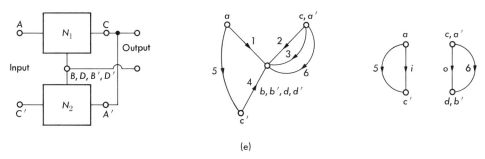

(e)

FIG. 4.49. Feedback connections. (a) Representations of two-ports. (b) Feedback connection of the networks of (a). (c) Feedback connection redrawn to show its series-parallel nature. (d) The system graphs. (e) The feedback connection when N_1 and N_2 are three-terminal networks.

connection consists of a cascade connection in which the output of N_1 is "fed back" into the input through N_2 and in which the input is taken across terminals A, C' rather than A, B. This, and the fact that the connection is effectively in series at the input and in parallel at the output, becomes even more apparent when Fig. 4.49(b) is redrawn as shown in Fig. 4.49(c). Figure 4.49(d) shows the system graphs that are required for obtaining the two-port representation of this network, and in Fig. 4.49(e) we have indicated the very slight alterations that are made when N_1 and N_2 are both three-terminal networks. The following derivation of the two-port representation is applicable for both cases.

In order to find the two-port equations associated with the terminal graph of Fig. 4.49(b), we first note, from the graphs of Fig. 4.49(d) or (e), that

$$\begin{bmatrix} V_i(s) \\ I_0(s) \end{bmatrix} = \begin{bmatrix} V_5(s) \\ -I_6(s) \end{bmatrix} = \begin{bmatrix} V_1(s) \\ I_2(s) \end{bmatrix} + \begin{bmatrix} -V_4(s) \\ I_3(s) \end{bmatrix} = \begin{bmatrix} V_1(s) \\ I_2(s) \end{bmatrix} + \begin{bmatrix} 0 & -1 \\ 1 & 0 \end{bmatrix} \begin{bmatrix} I_3(s) \\ V_4(s) \end{bmatrix}, \quad (4.160)$$

$$\begin{bmatrix} I_1(s) \\ V_2(s) \end{bmatrix} = \begin{bmatrix} -I_5(s) \\ V_6(s) \end{bmatrix} = \begin{bmatrix} I_i(s) \\ V_0(s) \end{bmatrix}, \quad (4.161)$$

$$\begin{bmatrix} V_3(s) \\ I_4(s) \end{bmatrix} = \begin{bmatrix} V_6(s) \\ I_5(s) \end{bmatrix} = \begin{bmatrix} V_0(s) \\ -I_i(s) \end{bmatrix} = \begin{bmatrix} 0 & 1 \\ -1 & 0 \end{bmatrix} \begin{bmatrix} I_i(s) \\ V_0(s) \end{bmatrix}. \quad (4.162)$$

Now, using the terminal equations of Fig. 4.49(a) in (4.160), we obtain

$$\begin{bmatrix} V_i(s) \\ I_0(s) \end{bmatrix} = \begin{bmatrix} h_{11} & h_{12} \\ h_{21} & h_{22} \end{bmatrix} \begin{bmatrix} I_1(s) \\ V_2(s) \end{bmatrix} + \begin{bmatrix} 0 & -1 \\ 1 & 0 \end{bmatrix} \begin{bmatrix} g_{33} & g_{34} \\ g_{43} & g_{44} \end{bmatrix} \begin{bmatrix} V_3(s) \\ I_4(s) \end{bmatrix}. \quad (4.163)$$

We substitute from (4.161) and (4.162) into (4.163):

$$\begin{bmatrix} V_i(s) \\ I_0(s) \end{bmatrix} = \begin{bmatrix} h_{11} & h_{12} \\ h_{21} & h_{22} \end{bmatrix} \begin{bmatrix} I_i(s) \\ V_0(s) \end{bmatrix} + \begin{bmatrix} 0 & -1 \\ 1 & 0 \end{bmatrix} \begin{bmatrix} g_{33} & g_{34} \\ g_{43} & g_{44} \end{bmatrix} \begin{bmatrix} 0 & 1 \\ -1 & 0 \end{bmatrix} \begin{bmatrix} I_i(s) \\ V_0(s) \end{bmatrix}. \quad (4.164)$$

Finally, upon performing the indicated matrix operations in (4.164), we obtain the terminal equations

$$\begin{bmatrix} V_i(s) \\ I_0(s) \end{bmatrix} = \begin{bmatrix} h_{11} + g_{44} & h_{12} - g_{43} \\ h_{21} - g_{34} & h_{22} + g_{33} \end{bmatrix} \begin{bmatrix} I_i(s) \\ V_0(s) \end{bmatrix}. \quad (4.165)$$

The feedback interconnection is of considerable importance in linear control theory, where the main interest is focused on the open-circuit voltage-transfer function $T_{i0}(s)$. From (4.165), we obtain

$$T_{i0}(s) = \frac{V_0}{V_i}\bigg|_{I_0=0} = \frac{-h_{21} + g_{34}}{(h_{11} + g_{44})(h_{22} + g_{33}) - (h_{21} - g_{34})(h_{12} - g_{43})}. \quad (4.166)$$

As it stands, Eq. (4.166) is of little value. Very frequently, however, the terminal equations for the two-ports N_1 and N_2 are such that $T_{i0}(s)$ takes on a much simpler form. Thus, when

$$h_{12} = g_{33} = g_{34} = g_{44} = 0, \quad (4.167)$$

we obtain

$$T_{i0}(s) = \frac{-h_{21}}{h_{11}h_{22} - h_{21}g_{43}} \qquad (4.168)$$

$$= \frac{-h_{21}/h_{11}h_{22}}{1 + g_{43}(-h_{21}/h_{11}h_{22})}. \qquad (4.169)$$

Now, under these circumstances, the open-circuit voltage-transfer functions for N_1 and N_2 are

$$\left.\frac{V_2}{V_1}\right|_{I_2=0} = T_{12}(s) = \frac{-h_{21}}{h_{11}h_{22}}, \qquad (4.170)$$

$$\left.\frac{V_4}{V_3}\right|_{I_4=0} = T_{34}(s) = g_{43}, \qquad (4.171)$$

so that the open-circuit voltage-transfer function of the overall network is related to the open-circuit transfer functions of N_1 and N_2 by the simple expression

$$T_{i0}(s) = \frac{T_{12}(s)}{1 + T_{12}(s)T_{34}(s)}. \qquad (4.172)$$

Equation (4.172) is frequently called the *feedback equation*.

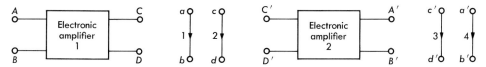

FIG. 4.50. Electronic amplifiers to be connected in the feedback connection.

EXAMPLE 4.14. The electronic amplifiers of Fig. 4.50 have terminal equations of the form

$$\begin{bmatrix} I_1(s) \\ V_2(s) \end{bmatrix} = \begin{bmatrix} Y_{11}(s) & 0 \\ -\mu_{21} & Z_{22}(s) \end{bmatrix} \begin{bmatrix} V_1(s) \\ I_2(s) \end{bmatrix}, \qquad (4.173)$$

$$\begin{bmatrix} I_3(s) \\ V_4(s) \end{bmatrix} = \begin{bmatrix} G_{33} & 0 \\ -\mu_{43} & R_{44} \end{bmatrix} \begin{bmatrix} V_3(s) \\ I_4(s) \end{bmatrix}. \qquad (4.174)$$

Here, G_{33} is the conductance of a resistor connected between the grid and cathode of a vacuum tube; since this resistor is usually of the order of 10^6 ohms, as a first approximation, it is reasonable to assume that $G_{33} = 0$. Also, when $I_4(s)$ is small, the product $R_{44}I_4(s)$ can be neglected. Thus, when the two amplifiers are connected as a feedback circuit, we can use Eq. (4.172) to obtain the open-circuit voltage-transfer function. In this case,

$$T_{12}(s) = -\mu_{21}, \qquad T_{34}(s) = -\mu_{43}, \qquad (4.175)$$

so that

$$T_{i0}(s) = \frac{-\mu_{21}}{1 + \mu_{21}\mu_{43}}. \qquad (4.176)$$

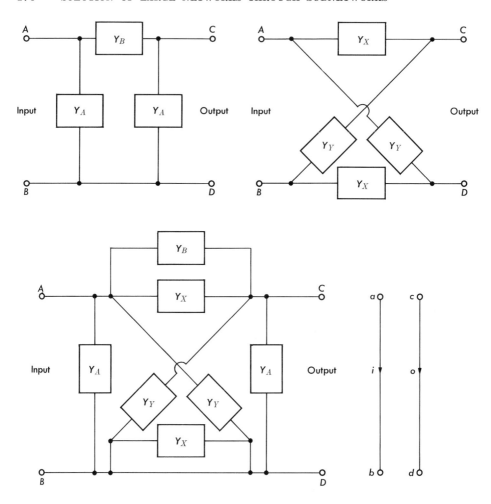

FIG. 4.51. A parallel connection for which it is *not* permissible to add the short-circuit parameter matrices of the two-port representations.

We have seen, in this section, that the two-port representations lead to very simple methods for obtaining the terminal equations and transfer functions for two-ports which are themselves made up of two-ports connected in cascade, series, parallel, or series-parallel. However, it cannot be overstressed that the two-port representations of the subnetworks are valid only for such interconnections where there is no effective loading, except at the input and output terminal pairs. Thus, they can be used only in these circumstances; whenever other loading conditions apply, the two-port representations are ineffective, and we must turn to a regular four-terminal representation. Nevertheless, except in the series connection, our results are always applicable for two-ports which have a common terminal between the input and output, and are thus three-terminal networks.

EXAMPLE 4.15. Figure 4.51 shows a symmetric lattice network, a symmetric π-network, and their parallel connection. It is seen that the parallel connection causes a short circuit across one of the components of the lattice; therefore we cannot add the short-circuit parameter matrices of the lattice and π-networks to obtain that of the combination.

For the lattice, we have

$$\begin{bmatrix} I_1(s) \\ I_2(s) \end{bmatrix} = \frac{1}{2}\begin{bmatrix} Y_y + Y_x & Y_y - Y_x \\ Y_y - Y_x & Y_y + Y_x \end{bmatrix}\begin{bmatrix} V_1(s) \\ V_2(s) \end{bmatrix},\tag{4.177}$$

and, for the π,

$$\begin{bmatrix} I_1(s) \\ I_2(s) \end{bmatrix} = \begin{bmatrix} Y_A + Y_B & -Y_B \\ -Y_B & Y_A + Y_B \end{bmatrix}\begin{bmatrix} V_1(s) \\ V_2(s) \end{bmatrix}.\tag{4.178}$$

Adding the parameter matrices, we obtain

$$\begin{bmatrix} I_i(s) \\ I_0(s) \end{bmatrix} = \begin{bmatrix} Y_A + Y_B + \frac{1}{2}(Y_y + Y_x) & \frac{1}{2}(Y_y - Y_x) - Y_B \\ \frac{1}{2}(Y_y - Y_x) - Y_B & Y_A + Y_B + \frac{1}{2}(Y_y + Y_x) \end{bmatrix}\begin{bmatrix} V_i(s) \\ V_0(s) \end{bmatrix},$$

a result which is *not* correct. In fact, the terminal equations are

$$\begin{bmatrix} I_i(s) \\ I_0(s) \end{bmatrix} = \begin{bmatrix} Y_A + Y_B + Y_x + Y_y & -(Y_B + Y_x) \\ -(Y_B + Y_x) & Y_A + Y_B + Y_x + Y_y \end{bmatrix}\begin{bmatrix} V_i(s) \\ V_0(s) \end{bmatrix}.\tag{4.179}$$

We leave the details as an exercise.

In summary, we have shown the use of the several sets of two-port parameters in four types of interconnection of two-ports. Also, we have emphasized that such simplifications will result only when the two-port representations are not invalidated by the interconnections. When such difficulties are encountered, we can always have recourse to the regular four-terminal representations.

4.10. EQUIVALENT NETWORKS

We have already seen that two-terminal subnetworks can be represented pictorially by either a voltage source in series with an impedance (the Thevenin equivalent), or a current source in parallel with an admittance (the Norton equivalent). These equivalent networks have the same terminal representations as the corresponding subnetworks. In a similar manner, we shall show that, for any two-port or three-terminal network, we can find an equivalent network whose components each have two terminals, and whose two-port representation is identical to that of the given two-port.

The main advantage of the use of such equivalent networks lies in the fact that every network may thereby be reduced to one whose components all have only two terminals; hence, the chord or branch equations can be written down by inspection. However, the system graph of our new network, with equivalent networks replacing all the three-terminal components and two-ports, invariably contains more elements or more vertices (or both) than the original system graph, so that the number of equations to be solved is increased. The equivalent networks, therefore, save us the labor of forming a matrix triple product only at the expense of the inversion of a larger matrix than necessary.

Another disadvantage lies in the fact that the equivalent network for a four-terminal component is only an equivalent two-port; it cannot be used when the component is arbitrarily connected into a larger system.

Finally, the currents and voltages associated with the components of equivalent networks cannot, in general, be measured. Terminal representations, on the other hand, lead to relations among the measurable variables of the system; nothing which cannot be measured ever appears in the network equations.

Nevertheless, network theory, especially in its application to vacuum-tube and transistor networks, was historically developed through the use of equivalent networks. They appear so frequently in the literature that it would be inappropriate for us to neglect them here.

Two n-terminal subnetworks N_1 and N_2 are said to be equivalent if there exists an n-terminal representation of N_1 which is also an n-terminal representation of N_2. This, of course, implies that the terminal equations for each subnetwork are identical for the same terminal graph, but it does not require identical internal construction of the two subnetworks.

Suppose that the terminal equations for a two-port network are given as

$$V_1(s) = z_{11}(s)I_1(s) + z_{12}(s)I_2(s), \tag{4.180}$$

$$V_2(s) = z_{21}(s)I_1(s) + z_{22}(s)I_2(s). \tag{4.181}$$

It is easy to see that these equations could readily represent the network of Fig. 4.52, which therefore is an equivalent of the given two-port.

This network contains four voltage drivers,

$$\begin{aligned} E_{11}(s) &= z_{11}(s)I_1(s), & E_{12}(s) &= z_{12}(s)I_2(s), \\ E_{21}(s) &= z_{21}(s)I_1(s), & E_{22}(s) &= z_{22}(s)I_2(s), \end{aligned} \tag{4.182}$$

which are dependent on the currents $I_1(s)$ and $I_2(s)$, and hence are called *dependent drivers*. In general, voltage or current drivers which are functions of other voltage or current variables in a network are called dependent drivers. Dependent drivers appear only in equivalent networks; they do not represent any physical device.

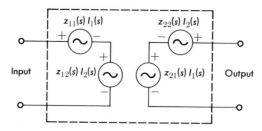

FIG. 4.52. A possible two-port equivalent network.

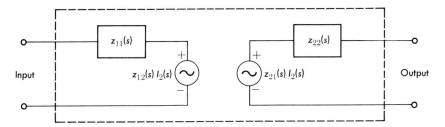

FIG. 4.53. General two-port equivalent network derived from the open-circuit parameters.

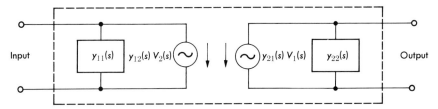

FIG. 4.54. General two-port equivalent network derived from the short-circuit parameters.

We can simplify the network of Fig. 4.52 by noting that the current through the driver $E_{11}(s) = z_{11}(s)I_1(s)$ is exactly $I_1(s)$. Therefore, we may replace this dependent driver with a two-terminal component whose impedance is $z_{11}(s)$. Similarly, the dependent driver $E_{22}(s) = z_{22}(s)I_2(s)$ may be replaced by a two-terminal component with impedance $z_{22}(s)$. This gives us the network of Fig. 4.53, which is a general two-port equivalent network.

In a very similar manner, we can derive a general two-port equivalent network based on the short-circuit form of the two-port equations. The result is shown in Fig. 4.54. This contains two dependent current drivers

$$I_{11}(s) = y_{12}(s)V_2(s), \qquad I_{22}(s) = y_{21}(s)V_1(s) \qquad (4.183)$$

which are in parallel respectively with two-terminal components having admittances $y_{11}(s)$ and $y_{22}(s)$.

Two other equivalent networks can be derived directly from the hybrid (h parameter) and inverse hybrid (g parameter) forms of the two-port equations. These are shown in Fig. 4.55.

EXAMPLE 4.16. Figure 4.56 shows a vacuum tube and the terminal graph used for the common cathode connection. The terminal equations corresponding to the terminal graph may be written in either of the forms

$$\begin{bmatrix} I_1(s) \\ V_2(s) \end{bmatrix} = \begin{bmatrix} 0 & 0 \\ -\mu & r_p \end{bmatrix} \begin{bmatrix} V_1(s) \\ I_2(s) \end{bmatrix}, \qquad (4.184)$$

$$\begin{bmatrix} I_1(s) \\ I_2(s) \end{bmatrix} = \begin{bmatrix} 0 & 0 \\ g_m & q_p \end{bmatrix} \begin{bmatrix} V_1(s) \\ V_2(s) \end{bmatrix}. \qquad (4.185)$$

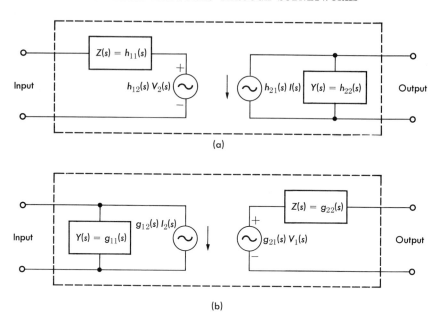

(a)

(b)

FIG. 4.55. Two more general equivalent networks. (a) General two-port equivalent network derived from the hybrid parameters. (b) General two-port equivalent network derived from the inverse hybrid parameters.

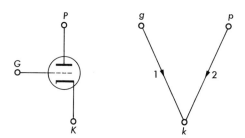

FIG. 4.56. Vacuum tube and terminal graph.

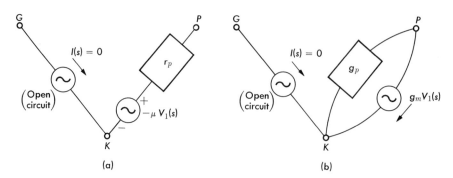

(a)   (b)

FIG. 4.57. Two equivalent networks for a vacuum tube.

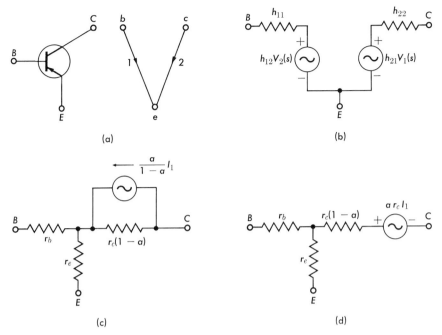

FIG. 4.58. A transistor and three equivalent networks.

Since (4.184) is in the inverse hybrid form, we may obtain an equivalent network similar to Fig. 4.55(b), with $g_{11}(s) = g_{12}(s) = 0$. This is shown in Fig. 4.57(a) and is called the Thevenin equivalent of the vacuum tube. Also, because (4.185) is in the short-circuit form, we obtain, in correspondence with Fig. 4.54, the equivalent network of Fig. 4.57(b). This is known as the Norton equivalent of the vacuum tube. The networks of Fig. 4.57 are frequently used in the analysis of electronic circuits, and with them we may write the branch and chord equations by inspection.

It might be expected, at first glance, that other equivalent networks could be used for vacuum tubes. However, the fact that the coefficient matrix of the terminal equations for the component cannot be inverted precludes this possibility. On the other hand, there are many possible equivalent networks for transistors. Three of the most frequently used of these networks are shown in Fig. 4.58(b), (c) and (d). When the transistor is represented as in Fig. 4.58(a), with the terminal equations

$$\begin{bmatrix} V_1(s) \\ I_2(s) \end{bmatrix} = \begin{bmatrix} h_{11} & h_{12} \\ h_{21} & h_{22} \end{bmatrix} \begin{bmatrix} I_1(s) \\ V_2(s) \end{bmatrix}, \tag{4.186}$$

it is a simple matter to verify that all three have the same terminal equations (corresponding to the same terminal graph), provided that

$$r_e = \frac{h_{12}}{h_{22}}, \qquad r_c = \frac{1 + h_{21}}{h_{22}}, \qquad r_b = \frac{\Delta_h - h_{12}}{h_{22}}, \qquad a = \frac{h_{12} + h_{21}}{1 + h_{21}}. \tag{4.187}$$

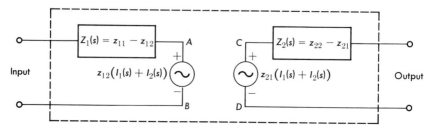

FIG. 4.59. Modification of the network of Fig. 4.53.

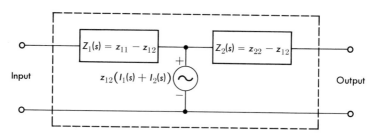

FIG. 4.60. Reduction of Fig. 4.59 for reciprocal networks.

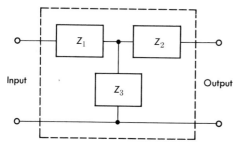

FIG. 4.61. T-equivalent for reciprocal
networks.

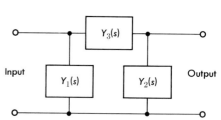

FIG. 4.62. π-equivalent for reciprocal networks.

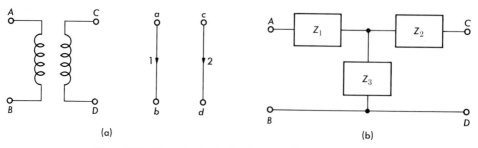

FIG. 4.63. T-equivalent of a two-winding transformer.

Let us now turn to the important special case of *reciprocal two-ports*. These are networks in which $z_{12}(s) = z_{21}(s)$, and $y_{12}(s) = y_{21}(s)$. Every RLC network is a reciprocal network. For such two-ports, we can simplify the equivalent networks of Figs. 4.53 and 4.54.

We first modify the equivalent network of Fig. 4.53 by redrawing it in the form of Fig. 4.59. In this network, remembering that $z_{12}(s) = z_{21}(s)$, we note that the voltage of the driver connected between A, B is identical to that of the driver between C, D. Therefore, since this will have no effect on the two-port representation, we may unite terminals A and C, and terminals B and D. We may then dispense with one of the two identical voltage drivers and obtain the network of Fig. 4.60. Here, however, we note that the current associated with the voltage driver is $I_1(s) + I_2(s)$, so that the driver may be replaced by a two terminal component whose impedance is $z_{12}(s)$. This yields Fig. 4.61, the T-*equivalent of a reciprocal two-port*. The impedances of the three arms of the T are

$$Z_1(s) = z_{11}(s) - z_{12}(s),$$

$$Z_2(s) = z_{22}(s) - z_{12}(s), \tag{4.188}$$

$$Z_3(s) = z_{12}(s).$$

Of course, we could have obtained the T-equivalent by direct comparison of the open-circuit parameters for the T-network with those of some general two-port. The only merit of the above method is that we are not required to know the result at the outset. We shall find another equivalent, the π-equivalent of a reciprocal two-port, by comparing the short-circuit parameters of the π-network of Fig. 4.62 with those of a general two-port. For this network, the short-circuit parameter matrix is

$$\begin{bmatrix} y_{11}(s) & y_{12}(s) \\ y_{21}(s) & y_{22}(s) \end{bmatrix} = \begin{bmatrix} Y_1(s) + Y_3(s) & -Y_3(s) \\ -Y_3(s) & Y_2(s) + Y_3(s) \end{bmatrix}. \tag{4.189}$$

Thus, if

$$Y_1(s) = y_{11}(s) - y_{12}(s) = y_{11}(s) - y_{21}(s),$$

$$Y_2(s) = y_{22}(s) - y_{12}(s) = y_{22}(s) - y_{21}(s), \tag{4.190}$$

$$Y_3(s) = -y_{12}(s) = -y_{21}(s),$$

the π-network is an equivalent for a reciprocal two-port. This network could equally well have been obtained by modifying Fig. 4.54 in a way similar to our development of the T-equivalent.

Several facts are worthy of mention in regard to the T- and π-equivalent networks. First, both networks are mathematical equivalents of two-port representations. This implies that the two-terminal components involved are not always physically realizable. Nevertheless, they are still useful insofar as they enable us to formulate the branch and chord equations by inspection. Another result is that the equivalent networks cannot be connected arbitrarily into a larger network; we can only load them at their input and output terminal pairs.

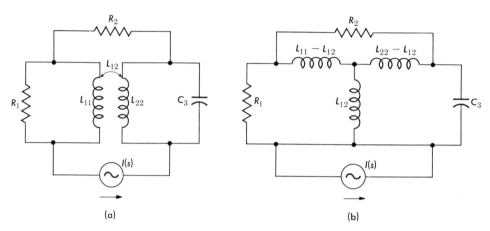

FIG. 4.64. A case in which equivalent networks cannot be used.

EXAMPLE 4.17. In this example, we shall find the T-equivalent of the two-winding transformer of Fig. 4.63(a) whose terminal equations are given by

$$\begin{bmatrix} V_1(s) \\ V_2(s) \end{bmatrix} = \begin{bmatrix} L_{11}s & L_{12}s \\ L_{12}s & L_{22}s \end{bmatrix} \begin{bmatrix} I_1(s) \\ I_2(s) \end{bmatrix}. \tag{4.191}$$

By direct comparison with Eqs. (4.191) and Fig. 4.63(b) we have

$$\begin{aligned} Z_1(s) &= (L_{11} - L_{12})s, \\ Z_2(s) &= (L_{22} - L_{12})s, \\ Z_3(s) &= L_{12}s. \end{aligned} \tag{4.192}$$

Since L_{12} may be negative, $Z_3(s)$ may represent a negative inductance, which is not physically realizable. Even if L_{12} is positive, either $L_{11} - L_{12}$ or $L_{22} - L_{12}$ may be negative, so that it is quite possible that the T-equivalent for a two-winding transformer contains nonrealizable elements.

We know that (4.191), together with the terminal graph of Fig. 4.63(a), can represent the transformer under any circumstances. However, consider Fig. 4.64. Part (a) of this figure shows a transformer connected to a simple system; part (b) is the same network with the transformer replaced by a T-equivalent. Here, the current driver is completely short-circuited, and so can have no effect on the rest of the network. Thus, the T-equivalent cannot be used for this network, a result of the fact that the transformer is not connected as a two-port.

The T- and π-network equivalences provide a simple result, known as the Δ-Y or T-π transformation. If we are given the three-terminal T-network of Fig. 4.65(a), its terminal equations, corresponding to the graph of Fig. 4.65(b), are

$$\begin{bmatrix} V_1(s) \\ V_2(s) \end{bmatrix} = \begin{bmatrix} Z_A(s) + Z_C(s) & Z_C(s) \\ Z_C(s) & Z_B(s) + Z_C(s) \end{bmatrix} \begin{bmatrix} I_1(s) \\ I_2(s) \end{bmatrix}. \tag{4.193}$$

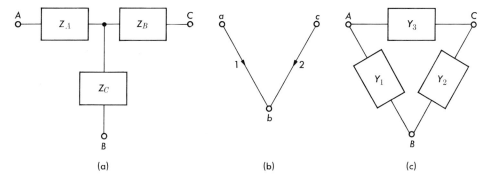

Fig. 4.65. A T- and a π-network which are to be made equivalent.

Now, this network has a π-equivalent such that, in Fig. 4.65(c),

$$\begin{bmatrix} y_{11}(s) & y_{12}(s) \\ y_{21}(s) & y_{22}(s) \end{bmatrix} = \begin{bmatrix} Y_1(s) + Y_3(s) & -Y_3(s) \\ -Y_3(s) & Y_2(s) + Y_3(s) \end{bmatrix}. \qquad (4.194)$$

From (4.193) we find that

$$\begin{bmatrix} y_{11}(s) & y_{12}(s) \\ y_{21}(s) & y_{22}(s) \end{bmatrix} = \begin{bmatrix} Z_A(s) + Z_C(s) & Z_C(s) \\ Z_C(s) & Z_B(s) + Z_C(s) \end{bmatrix}^{-1}$$

$$= \frac{1}{Z_C(s)Z_A(s) + Z_A(s)Z_B(s) + Z_B(s)Z_C(s)}$$

$$\times \begin{bmatrix} Z_B(s) + Z_C(s) & -Z_C(s) \\ -Z_C(s) & Z_A(s) + Z_C(s) \end{bmatrix}. \qquad (4.195)$$

Therefore,

$$Y_3(s) = \frac{Z_C(s)}{Z_C(s)Z_A(s) + Z_A(s)Z_B(s) + Z_B(s)Z_C(s)} = \frac{Y_A(s)\,Y_B(s)}{Y_A(s) + Y_B(s) + Y_C(s)}, \qquad (4.196)$$

$$Y_2(s) = \frac{Z_A(s)}{Z_C(s)Z_A(s) + Z_A(s)Z_B(s) + Z_B(s)Z_C(s)} = \frac{Y_B(s)\,Y_C(s)}{Y_A(s) + Y_B(s) + Y_C(s)}, \qquad (4.197)$$

$$Y_1(s) = \frac{Z_B(s)}{Z_C(s)Z_A(s) + Z_A(s)Z_B(s) + Z_B(s)Z_C(s)} = \frac{Y_C(s)\,Y_A(s)}{Y_A(s) + Y_B(s) + Y_C(s)}. \qquad (4.198)$$

We may similarly obtain

$$Z_A(s) = \frac{Z_1(s)Z_3(s)}{Z_1(s) + Z_2(s) + Z_3(s)}, \qquad (4.199)$$

$$Z_B(s) = \frac{Z_2(s)Z_3(s)}{Z_1(s) + Z_2(s) + Z_3(s)}, \qquad (4.200)$$

$$Z_C(s) = \frac{Z_1(s)Z_2(s)}{Z_1(s) + Z_2(s) + Z_3(s)}. \qquad (4.201)$$

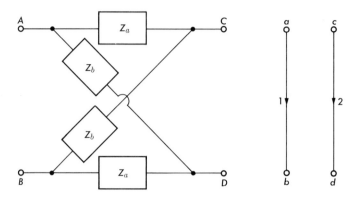

FIG. 4.66. A symmetrical lattice network.

Relations (4.196) through (4.201) give the complete conditions for equivalence between the T- and π-networks.

EXAMPLE 4.18. The terminal equations for the symmetric lattice network of Fig. 4.66 are easily obtained as

$$\begin{bmatrix} V_1(s) \\ V_2(s) \end{bmatrix} = \begin{bmatrix} \frac{1}{2}(Z_b + Z_a) & \frac{1}{2}(Z_b - Z_a) \\ \frac{1}{2}(Z_b - Z_a) & \frac{1}{2}(Z_b + Z_a) \end{bmatrix} \begin{bmatrix} I_1(s) \\ I_2(s) \end{bmatrix} \tag{4.202}$$

or

$$\begin{bmatrix} I_1(s) \\ I_2(s) \end{bmatrix} = \begin{bmatrix} \frac{1}{2}(Y_b + Y_a) & \frac{1}{2}(Y_b - Y_a) \\ \frac{1}{2}(Y_b - Y_a) & \frac{1}{2}(Y_b + Y_a) \end{bmatrix} \begin{bmatrix} V_1(s) \\ V_2(s) \end{bmatrix}. \tag{4.203}$$

Accordingly, by direct comparison between Eqs. (4.188) and (4.202) and between Eqs. (4.190) and (4.203), we may obtain the T- and π-equivalent networks for the symmetric lattice. In this case we have, for the T,

$$\begin{aligned} Z_1(s) &= z_{11}(s) - z_{12}(s) = Z_a, \\ Z_2(s) &= z_{22}(s) - z_{12}(s) = Z_a, \\ Z_3(s) &= z_{12}(s) = \tfrac{1}{2}(Z_b - Z_a), \end{aligned} \tag{4.204}$$

and for the π,

$$\begin{aligned} Y_1(s) &= y_{11}(s) - y_{12}(s) = Y_a, \\ Y_2(s) &= y_{22}(s) - y_{12}(s) = Y_a, \\ Y_3(s) &= -y_{12}(s) = \tfrac{1}{2}(Y_a - Y_b). \end{aligned} \tag{4.205}$$

To summarize, we have shown general methods for obtaining equivalent networks, and have illustrated the equivalents that are most frequently used in the analysis of vacuum-tube and transistor circuits. By examining equivalent reciprocal networks, we have obtained the Δ-Y network transformation; this device is often used to simplify networks under analysis. The equivalent networks contain only two-terminal components; their use allows us to formulate the network equations by inspection, so that, even though they result in a larger system graph, they may introduce some simplifications.

4.11. FREQUENCY RESPONSE AND RESONANCE

In the previous three sections, we developed the concepts of two-ports; we investigated the utility of equivalent networks, and established relationships between the two-port parameters and various transfer functions. In this section we shall study a method for quickly ascertaining the frequency characteristics of transfer functions. Such a procedure is often very effective, not only in evaluating the performance of proposed network designs, but also as a basis for comparing alternative designs. It is also very important in the study of linear control systems.

Consider a typical transfer function,

$$G(s) = \frac{F_2(s)}{F_1(s)}, \tag{4.206}$$

where $F_2(s)$, $F_1(s)$ are, respectively, the Laplace transforms of output and input variables (voltages or currents). When $f_1(t)$ and $f_2(t)$ are sinusoidal functions with angular frequency ω, we replace $F_1(s)$ and $F_2(s)$ by their corresponding phasors, and set $s = j\omega$ in (4.206). This yields

$$G(j\omega) = \frac{\overline{F}_2}{\overline{F}_1} = \frac{|\overline{F}_2|e^{j\phi_2}}{|\overline{F}_1|e^{j\phi_1}} = \left|\frac{\overline{F}_2}{\overline{F}_1}\right| e^{j(\phi_2-\phi_1)} \tag{4.207}$$

or

$$G(j\omega) = G(\omega)e^{j\phi(\omega)}, \tag{4.208}$$

where $G(\omega)$ is the ratio of the amplitude of the output sinusoid to that of the input sinusoid, and $\phi(\omega)$ is the difference in phase between the output and input. The frequency characteristics which we shall obtain are plots of $G(\omega)$ and $\phi(\omega)$ against frequency. They are called the *magnitude and phase characteristics*.

We know that every transfer function is a ratio of polynomials, so that

$$G(s) = \frac{P(s)}{Q(s)} = \frac{a_0 + a_1 s + \cdots + a_i s^i + \cdots + a_n s^n}{b_0 + b_1 s + \cdots + b_k s^k + \cdots + b_m s^m}. \tag{4.209}$$

When we factor the numerator and denominator of (4.209), we know that, since the coefficients a_i and b_k are all real, each factor is of one of the forms

(a) $(s + \omega_i)^{r_i} = \omega_i^{r_i}\left(1 + \dfrac{s}{\omega_i}\right)^{r_i}$ (ω_i real), \hfill (4.210)

(b) s^r, \hfill (4.211)

(c) $\big((s + a_k + jb_k)(s + a_k - jb_k)\big)^{r_k} = (s^2 + 2a_k s + a_k^2 + b_k^2)^{r_k}$ (a, b real)

$$= (a_k^2 + b_k^2)^{r_k}\left(1 + 2\,\frac{a_k}{a_k^2 + b_k^2}\,s + \frac{s^2}{a_k^2 + b_k^2}\right)^{r_k}$$

$$= \omega_k^{2r_k}\left(1 + 2\zeta_k\,\frac{s}{\omega_k} + \frac{s^2}{\omega_k^2}\right)^{r_k}, \tag{4.212}$$

where we have

$$\omega_k = \sqrt{a_k^2 + b_k^2}, \tag{4.213}$$

$$\zeta_k = \frac{a_k}{\omega_k}. \tag{4.214}$$

The constant ζ_k is called the *damping factor*.

If we lump together all the constants $\omega_i^{r_i}$, $\omega_k^{2r_k}$, we may write (4.209) in the factored form,

$$G(s) = K \frac{\Pi_i \left(1 + \frac{s}{\omega_i}\right)^{r_i} \Pi_p \left(1 + 2\zeta_p \frac{s}{\omega_p} + \frac{s^2}{\omega_p^2}\right)^{r_p}}{s^r \Pi_k \left(1 + \frac{s}{\omega_k}\right)^{r_k} \Pi_q \left(1 + 2\zeta_q \frac{s}{\omega_q} + \frac{s^2}{\omega_q^2}\right)^{r_q}}, \tag{4.215}$$

or, setting $s = j\omega$:

$$G(j\omega) = K \frac{\Pi_i \left(1 + j\frac{\omega}{\omega_i}\right)^{r_i} \Pi_p \left(1 - \frac{\omega^2}{\omega_p^2} + 2j\zeta_p \frac{\omega}{\omega_p}\right)^{r_p}}{(j\omega)^r \Pi_k \left(1 + j\frac{\omega}{\omega_k}\right)^{r_k} \Pi_q \left(1 - \frac{\omega^2}{\omega_q^2} + 2j\zeta_q \frac{\omega}{\omega_q}\right)^{r_q}}. \tag{4.216}$$

Of course, in (4.215) and (4.216), we may assume that there are no factors common to the numerator and denominator, since they may all be cancelled.

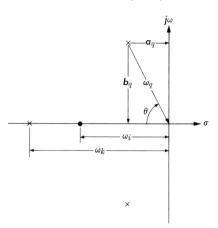

FIG. 4.67. Pole zero plot for a typical transfer function.

It is worth while noting that, when the points $s = -\omega_i$, $s = -a_q \pm jb_q$ are plotted in the complex plane, the numbers ω_i, ω_q are the distances of these points from the origin, and that $\zeta_q = a_q/\omega_q$ is the cosine of the angle between the negative real axis and the radius of point $-a_q + jb_q$. These facts are illustrated in Fig. 4.67. We shall observe that the locations of these points have profound effects on the form of the magnitude and phase characteristics.

We now examine the magnitude and phase functions in more detail. From (4.216), we have

$$\phi(\omega) = \sum_i r_i \arg\left(1 + j\frac{\omega}{\omega_i}\right) + \sum_p r_p \arg\left(1 - \frac{\omega^2}{\omega_p^2} + 2j\zeta_p \frac{\omega}{\omega_p}\right)$$

$$-r \arg j\omega - \sum_k r_k \arg\left(1 + j\frac{\omega}{\omega_k}\right) - \sum_q r_q \arg\left(1 - \frac{\omega^2}{\omega_q^2} + j2\zeta_q \frac{\omega}{\omega_q}\right) \qquad (4.217)$$

or

$$\phi(\omega) = \sum_i r_i \tan^{-1}\frac{\omega}{\omega_i} + \sum_p r_p \tan^{-1}\frac{2\zeta_p\omega/\omega_p}{1 - \omega^2/\omega_p^2} - \frac{r\pi}{2}$$

$$- \sum_k r_k \tan^{-1}\frac{\omega}{\omega_k} - \sum_q r_q \tan^{-1}\frac{2\zeta_q\omega/\omega_q}{1 - \omega^2/\omega_q^2}. \qquad (4.218)$$

Thus $\phi(\omega)$ is the sum of the arguments of all factors in the numerator less the sum of the arguments of all denominator factors. We can simply obtain the phase characteristics for each term and add all the results, point by point. On the other hand,

$$G(\omega) = K \frac{\prod_i \left|1 + j\frac{\omega}{\omega_i}\right|^{r_i} \prod_p \left|1 - \frac{\omega^2}{\omega_p^2} + j2\zeta_p \frac{\omega}{\omega_p}\right|^{r_p}}{|j\omega|^r \prod_k \left|1 + j\frac{\omega}{\omega_k}\right|^{r_k} \prod_q \left|1 - \frac{\omega^2}{\omega_q^2} + j2\zeta_q \frac{\omega}{\omega_q}\right|^{r_q}}. \qquad (4.219)$$

We cannot treat this as it stands on the same term-by-term basis. However, when we take the logarithm of (4.219), we obtain

$$\log G(\omega) = \log K + \sum_i r_i \log\left|1 + j\frac{\omega}{\omega_i}\right| + \sum_p r_p \log\left|1 - \frac{\omega^2}{\omega_p^2} + j2\zeta_p \frac{\omega}{\omega_p}\right|$$

$$-r \log|j\omega| - \sum_k r_k \log\left|1 + j\frac{\omega}{\omega_k}\right| - \sum_q r_q \log\left|1 - \frac{\omega^2}{\omega_q^2} + j2\zeta_q \frac{\omega}{\omega_q}\right|. \qquad (4.220)$$

It is standard practice to take 10 as the base of the logarithms in (4.220), and to multiply both sides of the equation by 20. The result, $20 \log_{10} G(\omega)$ is the magnitude in decibels (db). Following this custom, we have

$$20 \log_{10} G(\omega)$$
$$= 20 \log_{10} K + \sum_i 20r_i \log_{10}\left|1 + j\frac{\omega}{\omega_i}\right| + \sum_p 20r_p \log_{10}\left|1 - \frac{\omega^2}{\omega_p^2} \ 2j\zeta_p \frac{\omega}{\omega_p}\right|$$

$$- 20r \log_{10}|j\omega| - \sum_k 20r_k \log_{10}\left|1 + j\frac{\omega}{\omega_k}\right| - \sum_q 20r_q \log_{10}\left|1 - \frac{\omega^2}{\omega_q^2} + 2j\zeta_q \frac{\omega}{\omega_q}\right|. \qquad (4.221)$$

Using (4.217) and (4.221), we obtain both the magnitude characteristic (in db) and the phase characteristic by dealing with one term at a time and adding the results for each term.

Since it might be somewhat confusing to deal with all possible cases simultaneously, we will first treat the case in which (4.215) and (4.216) contain only simple linear factors.

Case 1. Factors of the form $(1 + j(\omega/\omega_i))^{r_i}$. First note that if

$$G(j\omega) = K \frac{\Pi_i \, (1 + j(\omega/\omega_i))^{r_i}}{\Pi_k \, (1 + j(\omega/\omega_k))^{r_k}},$$

the constant K does not affect the phase characteristic, but merely adds to the magnitude characteristic (in db) a constant, $20 \log_{10} K$, for all frequencies.

Consider a simple transfer function,

$$G_i(j\omega) = \left(1 + j \, \frac{\omega}{\omega_i}\right)^{r_i}. \tag{4.222}$$

We have

$$\phi_i(\omega) = r_i \arg \left(1 + j \, \frac{\omega}{\omega_i}\right) = r_i \tan^{-1} \frac{\omega}{\omega_i}, \tag{4.223}$$

and

$$20 \log_{10} G_i(\omega) = 20 r_i \log_{10} \left|1 + j \, \frac{\omega}{\omega_i}\right|. \tag{4.224}$$

In order to plot these functions against frequency, we examine two regions, namely $\omega/\omega_i \ll 1$, and $\omega/\omega_i \gg 1$. In the low-frequency region ($\omega/\omega_i \ll 1$), we have

$$1 + j \, \frac{\omega}{\omega_i} \approx 1, \tag{4.225}$$

so that

$$\phi_i(\omega) \approx r_i \arg 1 = 0 \tag{4.226}$$

and

$$20 \log_{10} G_i(\omega) \approx 20 r_i \log_{10} 1 = 0. \tag{4.227}$$

Similarly, in the high-frequency region, we obtain

$$1 + j \, \frac{\omega}{\omega_i} \approx j \, \frac{\omega}{\omega_i}, \tag{4.228}$$

so that

$$\phi_i(\omega) \approx r_i \arg j \, \frac{\omega}{\omega_i} = r_i \, \frac{\pi}{2} \tag{4.229}$$

and

$$20 \log_{10} G_i(\omega) \approx 20 r_i \log_{10} \frac{\omega}{\omega_i} = 20 r_i \, (\log_{10} \omega - \log_{10} \omega_i). \tag{4.230}$$

Equations (4.226) and (4.229) are the equations of the low- and high-frequency asymptotes to the phase characteristic, while (4.227) and (4.230) represent the asymptotes to the magnitude characteristic. When we plot these on a logarithmic frequency scale, we see that (4.230) represents a straight line whose slope is $20r_i$ db/decade. The intersection of this asymptote with the low-frequency asymptote is at the point for which

$$20r_i \log_{10} \omega = 20r_i \log_{10} \omega_i \quad \text{or} \quad \omega = \omega_i. \quad (4.231)$$

This frequency is called the *corner*, or *break* frequency.

The actual characteristics closely approximate the asymptotes for $\omega \ll \omega_i$ and $\omega \gg \omega_i$. The approximation is at its worst when $\omega = \omega_i$. At this point,

$$\phi_i(\omega_i) = \arg\left(1 + j\frac{\omega_i}{\omega_i}\right)^{r_i} = r_i \arg(1 + j) = r_i \frac{\pi}{4} \quad (4.232)$$

and

$$20 \log_{10} G_i(\omega_i) = 20 \log_{10}\left|1 + j\frac{\omega_i}{\omega_i}\right|^{r_i} = 10r_i \log_{10} 2 \approx 3r_i. \quad (4.233)$$

Hence the greatest deviation from the asymptotes for the magnitude plot is approximately $3r_i$ db, and the phase characteristic lies midway between the asymptotes at the break frequency. These results are shown in Fig. 4.68. The deviation from the asymptotic approximation for a few other frequencies is tabulated in Table 4.3.

Of course, the results are entirely similar for the transfer function

$$G_k(j\omega) = \frac{1}{\left(1 + j\dfrac{\omega}{\omega_k}\right)^{r_k}},$$

the corresponding plots being mirror images about the zero-db and zero-argument

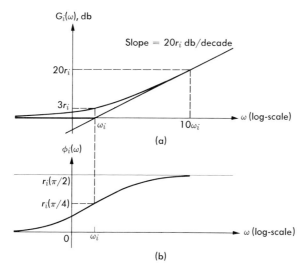

(a)

(b)

Fig. 4.08. Magnitude and phase characteristics for $G_i(j\omega) = [1 + j(\omega/\omega_i)]^{r_i}$.

TABLE 4.3
CORRECTION FACTORS FOR THE ASYMPTOTIC PLOTS

$\dfrac{\omega}{\omega_i}$	Asymptotic value of $20 \log_{10}\left\vert 1 + j\,\dfrac{\omega}{\omega_i}\right\vert$	Actual value of $20 \log_{10}\left\vert 1 + j\,\dfrac{\omega}{\omega_i}\right\vert$	Error in decibels (db)	$\operatorname{Arg}\left(1 + j\,\dfrac{\omega}{\omega_i}\right)$ (rad)
0.1	0	0.04	0.04	0.032π
0.125	0	0.07	0.07	0.039π
0.25	0	0.26	0.26	0.078π
0.5	0	0.97	0.97	0.15π
1	0	3.01	3.01	0.25π
2	6	7.00	1.0	0.35π
4	12	12.3	0.3	0.41π
8	18	18.1	0.1	0.46π
10	20	20.0	0.0	0.47π

axes of those in Fig. 4.68. For more complicated transfer functions involving only these simple factors, we treat each factor in turn and add point by point.

EXAMPLE 4.19. We shall obtain the magnitude and phase characteristics for the transfer function

$$G(s) = \frac{s + 1}{s^2 + 4s + 4} = \frac{1}{4}\,\frac{(1 + s)}{(1 + s/2)^2}. \tag{4.234}$$

Setting $s = j\omega$, we obtain

$$20 \log_{10} G(\omega) = -20 \log_{10} 4 + 20 \log_{10}|(1 + j\omega)| - 40 \log_{10}\left\vert\left(1 + \frac{j\omega}{2}\right)\right\vert, \tag{4.235}$$

$$\phi(\omega) = \arg \tfrac{1}{4} + \arg(1 + j\omega) - 2 \arg\left(1 + \frac{j\omega}{2}\right). \tag{4.236}$$

To obtain the required characteristics, we merely draw the magnitude and phase plots for each term, and add, point by point. All the steps are illustrated in Fig. 4.69; it should be noted that the asymptotic approximation for the overall magnitude plot can easily be drawn directly from the transfer function, since we need to know only the break frequencies and multiplicities of the numerator and denominator factors.

Case 2. A factor s^r. In addition to the simple factor of Case 1, there may be a term s^r in either the numerator or the denominator of a transfer function. We merely add the effects of this factor to the previously obtained results. For definiteness, let us assume that it is in the denominator, and consider a transfer function

$$G_0(j\omega) = \frac{1}{(j\omega)^r}. \tag{4.237}$$

We have

$$20 \log_{10} G_0(\omega) = -20r \log_{10}|j\omega| = -20r \log_{10} \omega, \tag{4.238}$$

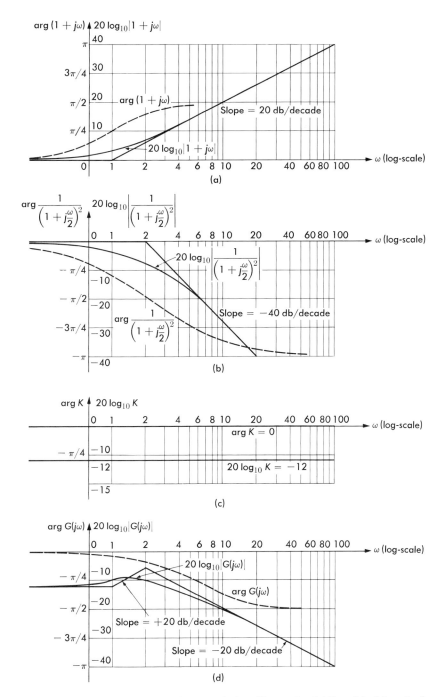

Fig. 4.69. Magnitude and phase characteristics (Example 4.19). (a) Magnitude and phase for numerator term $(1 + j\omega)$. (b) Magnitude and phase for denominator term $1/[1 + (j\omega/2)]^2$. (c) Magnitude and phase for constant term $K - \frac{1}{4}$. (d) Magnitude and phase characteristics for $G(j\omega) = \frac{1}{4}(1 + j\omega)/[1 + j(\omega/2)]^2$.

which, with ω plotted on a logarithmic scale, represents a straight line passing through the zero-db axis at the point $\omega = 1$, with a slope of $-20r$ db/decade. As to the phase, it is given by

$$\phi(\omega) = \arg (j\omega)^{-r} = -r(\pi/2). \tag{4.239}$$

Of course, the corresponding results for a numerator factor s^r are again mirror images about the zero-db and zero-argument axes of those for the denominator factor.

EXAMPLE 4.20. Here we shall investigate the magnitude and phase characteristics of the transfer function

$$G(s) = \frac{(s+2)^4}{16s^2} = \frac{(1+s/2)^4}{s^2}. \tag{4.240}$$

Again, we draw the magnitude and phase plots for each term, and add, point by point. The steps are shown in Fig. 4.70.

Case 3. Complex factors of the form $(1 - \omega^2/\omega_p^2 + 2j\zeta_p\omega/\omega_p)^{r_p}$. We must finally consider the effects of the complex factors. To do this, we shall study the transfer function

$$G_p(j\omega) = \left(1 - \frac{\omega^2}{\omega_p^2} + 2j\zeta_p\frac{\omega}{\omega_p}\right)^{r_p}. \tag{4.241}$$

We can write

$$20 \log_{10} G_p(\omega) = 20r_p \log_{10} \left|1 - \frac{\omega^2}{\omega_p^2} + j2\zeta_p\frac{\omega}{\omega_p}\right| \tag{4.242}$$

$$= 10r_p \log_{10} \left[\left(1 - \frac{\omega^2}{\omega_p^2}\right)^2 + 4\zeta_p^2\frac{\omega^2}{\omega_p^2}\right]. \tag{4.243}$$

Now, for $\omega \ll \omega_p$,

$$20 \log_{10} G_p(\omega) \approx 10r_p \log_{10} 1 = 0, \tag{4.244}$$

and, for $\omega \gg \omega_p$,

$$20 \log_{10} G_p(\omega) \approx 10r_p \log_{10} \left(\frac{\omega}{\omega_p}\right)^4 = 40r_p (\log_{10} \omega - \log_{10} \omega_p). \tag{4.245}$$

Equations (4.244) and (4.245) establish the low- and high-frequency asymptotes for factors of this nature; they are respectively the zero-db line and a straight line which cuts the zero-db line at the point $\log \omega = \log \omega_p$, and which has a slope of $40r_p$ db/decade. The actual magnitude characteristic depends on the value of ζ_p. When $\zeta_p = 1$, (4.241) reduces to

$$G_p(j\omega) = \left(1 - \frac{\omega^2}{\omega_p^2} + 2j\frac{\omega}{\omega_p}\right)^{r_p} = \left(1 + j\frac{\omega}{\omega_p}\right)^{2r_p}, \tag{4.246}$$

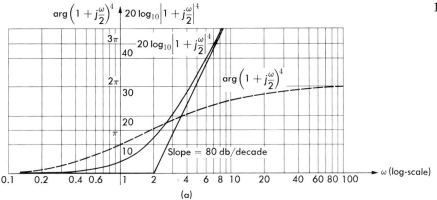

(a)

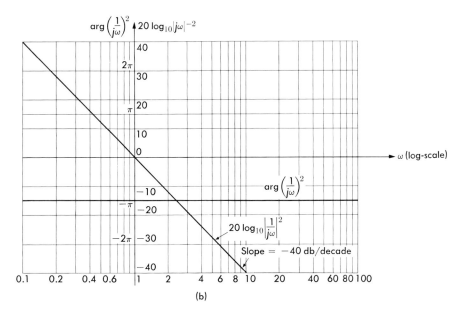

(b)

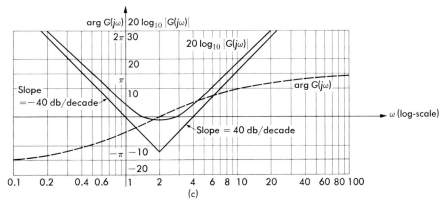

(c)

Fig. 4.70. Magnitude and phase characteristics (Example 4.20). (a) Magnitude and phase for numerator term $[1 + j(w/2)]^4$. (b) Magnitude and phase for denominator term $1/(j\omega)^2$. (c) Magnitude and phase for $G(j\omega) = [1 + j(\omega/2)]^4/(j\omega)^2$.

so that there are no complex factors. On the other hand, for $\zeta_p = 0$,

$$G_p(j\omega) = 1 - \frac{\omega^2}{\omega_p^2} \qquad (4.247)$$

and

$$20 \log_{10} G_p(\omega) = 20 \log_{10} \left| 1 - \frac{\omega^2}{\omega_p^2} \right|, \qquad (4.248)$$

which increases without bound as ω approaches ω_p. Thus, when $\zeta_p = 0$, there is a third asymptote, which is vertical, and cuts the zero-db line at $\omega = \omega_p$.

Of course, we can expect these simple results since $\zeta_p = 1$ implies that the zeros lie on the real axis, while $\zeta_p = 0$ implies that they are on the imaginary axis (see Fig. 4.67).

When $0 < \zeta_p < 1$, we have

$$20 \log_{10} G_p(\omega_p) = 10 r_p \log_{10} 4\zeta_p^2 \qquad (4.249)$$

$$= 20 r_p \log_{10} 2 + 20 r_p \log_{10} \zeta_p$$

$$\approx 20 r_p \log_{10} \zeta_p + 6 r_p, \qquad (4.250)$$

and we see that the actual magnitude at the intersection of the asymptotes depends on ζ_p. For instance, when $\zeta_p = \frac{1}{2}$,

$$20 \log_{10} G_p(\omega) = r_p(6 + 20 \log_{10} \tfrac{1}{2}) = 0, \qquad (4.251)$$

and the magnitude characteristic passes through the intersection point. For $\zeta_p < \frac{1}{2}$, $20 \log_{10} G_p(\omega_p) < 0$, whereas when $\zeta_p > \frac{1}{2}$, $20 \log_{10} G_p(\omega_p) > 0$. A family of typical magnitude characteristics is shown in Fig. 4.71(a) for the case $r_p = 1$.

For the phase characteristic, we note that

$$\phi(\omega) = \arg\left(1 - \frac{\omega^2}{\omega_p^2} + 2j\zeta_p \frac{\omega}{\omega_p} \right) \qquad (4.252)$$

$$= \tan^{-1} \frac{2\zeta_p \omega/\omega_p}{1 - \omega^2/\omega_p^2} = \tan^{-1} \frac{2\zeta_p \omega \omega_p}{\omega_p^2 - \omega^2}. \qquad (4.253)$$

A family of typical phase characteristics is shown in Fig. 4.71(b).

In order to plot the magnitude and phase characteristics for transfer functions containing complex factors, we follow the same procedures as used in Examples 4.19 and 4.20. It is a simple matter to determine the actual characteristics, which depend on the damping factors associated with the various complex factors.

To complete our discussion of frequency response, we shall investigate a simple example, which serves to introduce the concept of resonance.

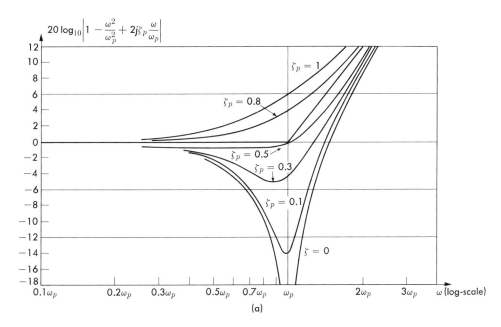

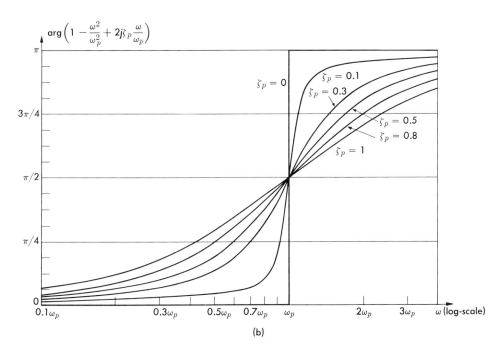

FIG. 4.71. Magnitude and phase characteristics for complex factors.   (a) Magnitude characteristics for $G(j\omega) = 1 - \omega^2/\omega_p^2 + 2j\zeta_p(\omega/\omega_p)$.   (b) Phase characteristics for $G(j\omega) = 1 - \omega^2/\omega_p^2 + 2j(\omega/\omega_p)$.

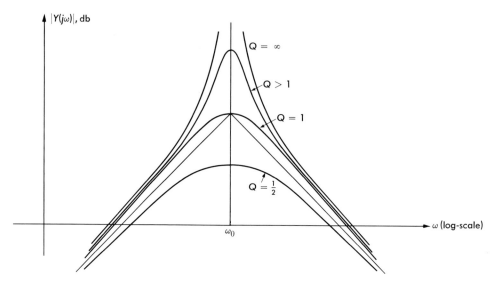

FIG. 4.72. Magnitude characteristic for Example 4.21.

EXAMPLE 4.21. The driving-point admittance of a simple series RLC network is

$$Y(j\omega) = \frac{1}{R + j(\omega L - 1/\omega C)} \tag{4.254}$$

$$= \frac{j\omega C}{1 - \omega^2 LC + j\omega RC} \tag{4.255}$$

$$= \frac{j\omega C}{1 - \omega^2/\omega_0^2 + 2j\zeta\omega/\omega_0} \tag{4.256}$$

$$= \frac{j\omega C}{1 - \omega^2/\omega_0^2 + j\omega/Q_0\omega_0} \tag{4.257}$$

$$= \frac{1/R}{1 + jQ_0(\omega/\omega_0 - \omega_0/\omega)}, \tag{4.258}$$

where

$$\omega_0 = 1/\sqrt{LC}, \tag{4.259}$$

$$\zeta = (R/2)\sqrt{C/L} = 1/2Q_0, \tag{4.260}$$

$$Q = \omega L/R = 1/\omega RC, \tag{4.261}$$

$$Q_0 = \omega_0 L/R = 1/\omega_0 RC = (1/R)\sqrt{L/C}. \tag{4.262}$$

The magnitude characteristic for $Y(j\omega)$ may take any one of the forms shown in Fig. 4.72, depending on the magnitude of ζ or Q_0.

Furthermore, note that when $\omega = \omega_0$, $Y(j\omega)$ is a real number. Whenever a transfer function takes on a purely real value, the system which it represents is said to be in *resonance*. The frequency for which resonance occurs is called the *natural* or *resonant* frequency of the system. There may, of course, be many different natural frequencies for a given network, with a more complicated transfer function.

The maximum value of $Y(j\omega)$ occurs at $\omega = \omega_0$, and is given by

$$Y(j\omega_0) = Y(j\omega)_{\max} = 1/R = Q_0/\omega_0 L. \tag{4.263}$$

Sometimes it is found that the effective inductance and resistance of a network vary with frequency. However, they often do so in such a way that Q remains constant over a wide frequency range, and

$$Q = Q_0. \tag{4.264}$$

Since the maximum value of the transfer function is proportional to Q_0 or Q, this number is known as the *quality factor* of a series RLC network. In general, Q is the ratio of stored energy to dissipated energy in a system.

Let us now consider the frequencies at which

$$|Y(j\omega)| = \frac{1}{\sqrt{2}}|Y(j\omega_0)|. \tag{4.265}$$

Let these frequencies be ω_1 and ω_2, such that $\omega_1 < \omega_0 < \omega_2$. Due to the symmetry of the magnitude characteristic, we have

$$\log \omega_2 - \log \omega_0 = \log \omega_0 - \log \omega_1$$

or

$$\log \omega_1 \omega_2 = \log \omega_0^2,$$

or

$$\omega_1 \omega_2 = \omega_0^2. \tag{4.266}$$

Now,

$$Y(j\omega_1) = \frac{1/R}{1 + jQ(\omega_1/\omega_0 - \omega_0/\omega_1)} \tag{4.267}$$

$$= \frac{1/R}{1 + jQ((\omega_1^2 - \omega_0^2)/\omega_1\omega_0)}, \tag{4.268}$$

and using (4.266), we find that (4.268) becomes

$$Y(j\omega_1) = \frac{\omega_0/R}{\omega_0 - jQ\Delta_\omega}, \tag{4.269}$$

where $\Delta_\omega = \omega_2 - \omega_1$ is called the *bandwidth* of the network. Now,

$$|Y(j\omega_1)|^2 = \frac{\omega_0^2}{R^2} \frac{1}{\omega_0^2 + Q^2\Delta_\omega^2} = \frac{1}{2}|Y(j\omega_0)|^2 = \frac{1}{2R^2}, \tag{4.270}$$

so that
$$2\omega_0^2 = \omega_0^2 + Q^2 \Delta_\omega^2,$$

or

$$Q = \frac{\omega_0}{\Delta_\omega}. \tag{4.271}$$

That is, the quality factor is the ratio of the resonant frequency to the bandwidth. As Q increases, the bandwidth decreases.

We have chosen as the bandwidth the difference between the frequencies at which the magnitude is $1/\sqrt{2}$ times its maximum value. Of course, any other choice would have given slightly different results; we choose these particular frequencies because, as can easily be verified, they correspond to frequencies at which the power associated with the circuit is half the maximum value. Hence, the bandwidth we have defined is often called the *half-power bandwidth*, and the frequencies ω_1 and ω_2 are called the *half-power frequencies*.

In conclusion, we have seen that it is a simple matter to obtain asymptotic approximations to the magnitude characteristic. The magnitude and phase characteristics can be plotted quite easily and accurately with the aid of Table 4.3 and Fig. 4.71. Because of the facility with which these plots can be obtained, they represent a very real aid in the evaluation of network designs. Our final example served to introduce a brief discussion of the concept of resonance.

4.12. SUMMARY

This chapter has been devoted to the special techniques that can be applied in the analysis of networks for which the direct methods of the previous chapters may be too cumbersome for easy calculation. The underlying principle is that of the terminal representation of subnetworks, which allowed us to analyze networks in simple stages. We then found that two-port representations, which are special cases of terminal representations, give even greater simplifications when they are applicable. We also introduced the subject of equivalent networks, and found that their use allows us to write the branch and chord equations for networks containing multiterminal components by inspection. This method is not, however, without its defects, owing to the increased complexity of the system graphs which result when equivalent networks are used.

In addition, we investigated some of the properties of transfer functions, and their relationships to the two-port parameters. This study led us naturally to the problem of plotting frequency-response curves, and of resonance.

PROBLEMS

4.1. Figure 4.73 shows a subnetwork which is to be connected to a larger network only at terminals A and B. Find a two-terminal representation of this subnetwork, corresponding to the indicated terminal graph.

4.2. Assume that the subnetwork of Fig. 4.73 is to be connected to a larger network at terminals A, B, C, and D. Find a suitable four-terminal representation.

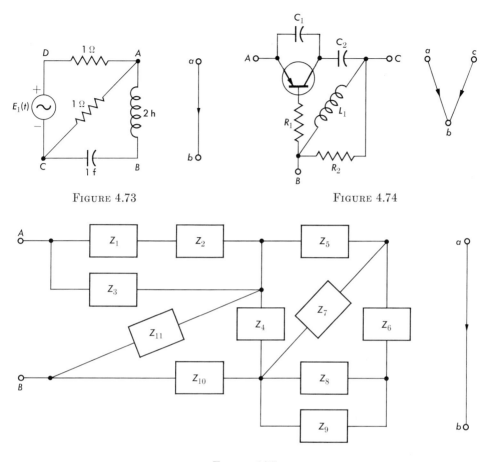

FIGURE 4.73

FIGURE 4.74

FIGURE 4.75

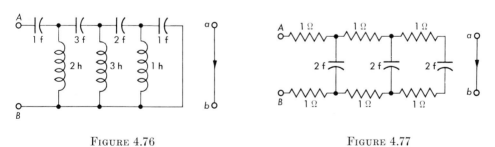

FIGURE 4.76

FIGURE 4.77

4.3. Find a three-terminal representation in the open-circuit form of the network of Fig. 4.74, corresponding to the indicated terminal graph.

4.4. Find a two-terminal representation of the "series-parallel" network of Fig. 4.75.

4.5. Find a two-terminal representation of the "ladder network" of Fig. 4.76.

4.6. Find a two-terminal representation of the network of Fig. 4.77.

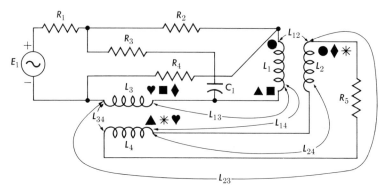

FIGURE 4.78

4.7. Write the chord equations for the network of Fig. 4.78. For the indicated magnetic polarity markings and your chosen terminal graph, which of the mutual inductance terms will be positive, and which negative?

4.8. Show symbolically that the short-circuit form of the terminal equations for an n-terminal representation results from the application of $n - 1$ voltage drivers to the given network in one-to-one correspondence with the n-terminal graph.

4.9. Derive Eqs. (4.56) using the branch technique.

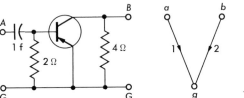

FIGURE 4.79

4.10. (a) Find a three-terminal representation of the network of Fig. 4.79, corresponding to the indicated terminal graph.

(b) Four subnetworks, identical to that shown in Fig. 4.79, are connected with a voltage driver, as illustrated in Fig. 4.80. If the transistor parameters are: $h_{11} = 4$, $h_{12} = 3$, $h_{21} = 2$, $h_{22} = 0$, calculate the steady-state voltage developed between terminals B_4, G_4.

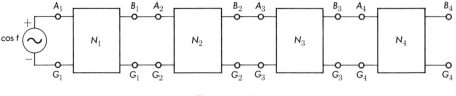

FIGURE 4.80

4.11. Use tree transformations to find terminal representations of the network of Fig. 4.79, corresponding to each of the terminal graphs of Fig. 4.81.

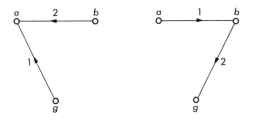

FIGURE 4.81

4.12. Find a four-terminal representation of the network of Fig. 4.82(a), corresponding to the terminal graph of Fig. 4.82(b). Use tree transformations to find terminal representations corresponding to the terminal graphs of Fig. 4.82(c), (d), and (e).

4.13. The network of Fig. 4.82(a) is to be connected as a two-port. The input terminals are A and C, while B and D are the output terminals. Find a two-port representation in the open-circuit form. Hence, find the short-circuit, hybrid, and A, B, C, D parameters.

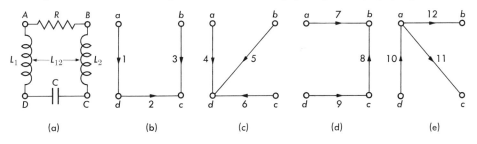

FIGURE 4.82

4.14. Find the open-circuit voltage-transfer function, the open-circuit transfer impedance, the short-circuit transfer admittance, and the short-circuit current-transfer function of the network of Fig. 4.79.

4.15. Two identical two-ports of the form of Fig. 4.40(a) are to be connected in cascade. Find the A, B, C, D parameters of the resulting two-port.

4.16. Find a T- and a π-equivalent for the network of Fig. 4.83.

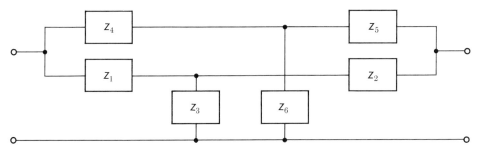

FIGURE 4.83

4.17. Repeat Problem 4.15 assuming that the networks are connected in series and assuming that the networks are connected in series-parallel.

4.18. Two identical networks of the form of Fig. 4.44(a) are connected in parallel, and the combination is connected in cascade with a third identical network. Find the open-circuit voltage-transfer function of the overall two-port.

4.19. Sketch the magnitude and phase characteristics of the transfer function

$$T_{12}(s) = \frac{2(s+1)(s+3)}{s(s+2)(s+4)}.$$

4.20. Find the open-circuit transfer impedance for the network of Fig. 4.84. Sketch the frequency-response magnitude characteristic.

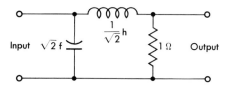

Input $\sqrt{2}$ f $\frac{1}{\sqrt{2}}$ h   1 Ω   Output

FIGURE 4.84

4.21. Sketch the magnitude and phase characteristics for the transfer function

$$T_{12} = 10 \frac{(s+\frac{1}{2})^2(s+1)(s^2+2s+4)}{s(s+3)(s^2+s+1)(s^2+16)}.$$

Chapter 5

STATE EQUATIONS
FOR ELECTRIC NETWORKS

In Chapter 2 we studied various methods for the formulation of network equations, and we subsequently showed in Chapters 3 and 4 that these methods were well suited for the use of analytical techniques in the solution of network problems. However, it is to be expected that in some networks the sheer size of the matrices involved will render these analytical methods inoperable; we must then turn to computer techniques. We are ultimately interested in time-domain solutions to network problems, and Laplace transform techniques are not generally conducive to numerical computations because of the inordinately long procedure involved. Therefore, it is our purpose here to investigate the form of the network equations which, among other things, is most suitable for computer solutions. The time-domain formulation, incidentally, lends further insight into network problems.

5.1. INTRODUCTION TO STATE EQUATIONS

Most numerical methods for the solution of sets of ordinary differential equations require that they be written in the *normal, standard,* or *canonical* form:

$$\frac{dx_i}{dt} = f_i(x_1, x_2, \ldots, x_n, h_1, h_2, \ldots, h_m, t), \tag{5.1}$$

where $i = 1, 2, \ldots, n$, x_i are the unknown variables of the system, and h_j are a set of m specified functions of time, t. Sets of equations of this type are also ideally suited to analog computation, since there is exactly one integrating network required for each equation.

The canonical form of sets of differential equations first appeared in the late eighteenth and early nineteenth centuries with the development of the Lagrangian and Hamiltonian formulation of classical mechanics. Later in the nineteenth century, the properties of the solutions of such equations were studied by Cauchy, who pointed out that, if all x_i are given at some time t_0, the equations completely specify all the variables at any later time $t > t_0$. If, for instance, the variables x_i represent the positions and velocities of a set of particles, and the functions h_j

represent a set of specified constraints on their motion, Eqs. (5.1) will specify all the positions and velocities at any future instant when all the positions and velocities are known at a given instant. Since, in classical mechanics, particles are characterized only by their positions and velocities, these variables describe the *complete state of the system.* Hence, when Eqs. (5.1) represent a physical system they are referred to as its *state equations.* Similarly, the variables x_i are called the *state variables.* In general, there are many possible different sets of state equations for a given system, and depending upon the chosen equations, the corresponding state variables may, or may not, be directly measurable.

The concept of state is readily extendable from particle mechanics to many other systems, and the state model has frequently been used as the starting point for theoretical studies in a variety of different fields, such as multivariable control systems, nonlinear mechanics, and the stability of nonlinear systems. Furthermore, state techniques need not be restricted to systems described by differential equations; they may also be used in the analysis and design of sequential machines, of switching networks, and of sampled data systems. Indeed, the present trend in system theory is toward an intensified study of time-domain models through the notion of "state."

It is desirable for most investigations that the state variables should involve, so far as is possible, only *directly measurable quantities.* In later sections of this chapter we shall illustrate systematic methods for finding sets of state equations for any linear electric network. The state variables will be some of the voltages and currents associated with the networks, and hence will all be directly measurable.

When we are dealing with linear systems, the state equations (5.1) may be written in the form

$$\frac{d}{dt}\begin{bmatrix} x_1 \\ x_2 \\ \vdots \\ x_n \end{bmatrix} = \begin{bmatrix} a_{11} & a_{12} & \cdots & a_{1n} \\ a_{21} & a_{22} & \cdots & a_{2n} \\ \vdots & \vdots & & \vdots \\ a_{n1} & a_{n2} & \cdots & a_{nn} \end{bmatrix} \begin{bmatrix} x_1 \\ x_2 \\ \vdots \\ x_n \end{bmatrix} + \begin{bmatrix} h_1(t) \\ h_2(t) \\ \vdots \\ h_n(t) \end{bmatrix}, \tag{5.2}$$

or, more concisely,

$$\frac{d}{dt}[X] = [A][X] + [H], \tag{5.3}$$

and it is, of course, equations of the form of (5.3) that we shall obtain. The column matrix $[X]$ is called the *state vector* of the system.

5.2. STATE EQUATIONS FROM TRANSFER FUNCTIONS

Before embarking upon a general formulation procedure for the state equations, we shall in this section derive a method for obtaining sets of state equations for electric networks from their transfer functions. Until very recently this was the most widely used technique, particularly in conjunction with control systems; we shall see that it has certain inherent disadvantages.

For definiteness, let us consider a transfer impedance:

$$Z_{12}(s) = \frac{V_2(s)}{I_1(s)} = \frac{a_m s^m + a_{m-1} s^{m-1} + \cdots + a_1 s + a_0}{b_n s^n + b_{n-1} s^{n-1} + \cdots + b_1 s + b_0}. \tag{5.4}$$

In (5.4) it is to be remembered that $V_2(s)$ is the output quantity, whereas $I_1(s)$ is the Laplace transform of an input specified variable. In order to find $V_2(s)$ from (5.4) by ordinary analytical methods, we would multiply both sides by $I_1(s)$ and find the inverse Laplace transform. Instead of doing this, let us rewrite the given expression as

$$(b_n s^n + b_{n-1} s^{n-1} + \cdots + b_1 s + b_0) V_2(s) = (a_m s^m + a_{m-1} s^{m-1} + \cdots + a_1 s + a_0) I_1(s). \tag{5.5}$$

Here, since the constants $a_1, a_2, \ldots, a_m$ are all known, the right-hand side is a sum of specified functions, while on the left-hand side we have a polynomial in s multiplying the Laplace transform of the unknown quantity $v_2(t)$.

Now disregarding initial conditions, we have

$$\mathcal{L} \frac{d^i}{dt^i} v_2(t) = s^i V_2(s), \qquad i = 0, 1, 2, \ldots, n, \tag{5.6}$$

so that we may regard (5.5) as the Laplace transform of the equation

$$b_n \frac{d^n}{dt^n} v_2(t) + b_{n-1} \frac{d^{n-1}}{dt^{n-1}} v_2(t) + \cdots + b_1 \frac{d}{dt} v_2(t) + b_0 v_2(t)$$

$$= a_m \frac{d^m}{dt^m} i_1(t) + a_{m-1} \frac{d^{m-1}}{dt^{m-1}} i_1(t) + \cdots + a_1 \frac{d}{dt} i_1(t) + a_0 i_1(t). \tag{5.7}$$

Dividing both sides of (5.7) by b_n, we obtain

$$\frac{d^n}{dt^n} v_2(t) + \frac{b_{n-1}}{b_n} \frac{d^{n-1}}{dt^{n-1}} v_2(t) + \cdots + \frac{b_1}{b_n} \frac{d}{dt} v_2(t) + \frac{b_0}{b_n} v_2(t)$$

$$= \frac{a_m}{b_n} \frac{d^m}{dt^m} i_1(t) + \frac{a_{m-1}}{b_n} \frac{d^{m-1}}{dt^{m-1}} i_1(t) + \cdots + \frac{a_1}{b_n} \frac{d}{dt} i_1(t) + \frac{a_0}{b_n} i_1(t). \tag{5.8}$$

Since the derivatives of specified functions are themselves regarded as specified functions, we write

$$f(t) = \frac{a_m}{b_n} \frac{d^m}{dt^m} i_1(t) + \frac{a_{m-1}}{b_n} \frac{d^{m-1}}{dt^{m-1}} i_1(t) + \cdots + \frac{a_1}{b_n} \frac{d}{dt} i_1(t) + \frac{a_0}{b_n} i_1(t), \tag{5.9}$$

and (5.8) becomes

$$\frac{d^n}{dt^n} v_2(t) + \frac{b_{n-1}}{b_n} \frac{d^{n-1}}{dt^{n-1}} v_2(t) + \cdots + \frac{b_1}{b_n} \frac{d}{dt} v_2(t) + \frac{b_0}{b_n} v_2(t) = f(t). \tag{5.10}$$

To rewrite (5.10) in the state equation form, we define new variables as follows:

$$v_2^{(1)}(t) = \frac{d}{dt} v_2(t),$$

$$v_2^{(2)}(t) = \frac{d^2}{dt^2} v_2(t) = \frac{d}{dt} v_2^{(1)}(t),$$

$$\vdots$$

$$v_2^{(i)}(t) = \frac{d^i}{dt^i} v_2(t) = \frac{d}{dt} v_2^{(i-1)}(t),$$ \qquad (5.11)

$$\vdots$$

$$v_2^{(n-1)}(t) = \frac{d^{(n-1)}}{dt^{(n-1)}} v_2(t) = \frac{d}{dt} v_2^{(n-2)}(t).$$

This is, we define $n - 1$ new variables as the first $n - 1$ derivatives of $v_2(t)$. Now, using (5.11) in (5.10), we obtain

$$\frac{d}{dt} v_2^{(n-1)}(t) = -\frac{b_{n-1}}{b_n} v_2^{(n-1)}(t) - \frac{b_{n-2}}{b_n} v_2^{(n-2)}(t) - \cdots - \frac{b_1}{b_n} v_2^{(1)}(t) - \frac{b_0}{b_n} v_2(t) + f(t),$$

$$(5.12)$$

and the combination of (5.12) with all the equations of (5.11) finally yields

$$\frac{d}{dt}
\begin{bmatrix}
v_2(t) \\
v_2^{(1)}(t) \\
\vdots \\
v_2^{(n-3)}(t) \\
v_2^{(n-2)}(t) \\
v_2^{(n-1)}(t)
\end{bmatrix}
=
\begin{bmatrix}
0 & 1 & 0 & \cdots & 0 & 0 \\
0 & 0 & 1 & \cdots & 0 & 0 \\
\vdots & \vdots & \vdots & & \vdots & \vdots \\
0 & 0 & 0 & \cdots & 1 & 0 \\
0 & 0 & 0 & \cdots & 0 & 1 \\
-\frac{b_0}{b_n} & -\frac{b_1}{b_n} & -\frac{b_2}{b_n} & \cdots & -\frac{b_{n-2}}{b_n} & -\frac{b_{n-1}}{b_n}
\end{bmatrix}
\begin{bmatrix}
v_2(t) \\
v_2^{(1)}(t) \\
\vdots \\
v_2^{(n-3)}(t) \\
v_2^{(n-2)}(t) \\
v_2^{(n-1)}(t)
\end{bmatrix}
+
\begin{bmatrix}
0 \\
0 \\
\vdots \\
0 \\
0 \\
f(t)
\end{bmatrix},$$

$$(5.13)$$

which are the required state equations.

EXAMPLE 5.1. In this example we shall obtain a set of state equations for a two-port network whose open-circuit voltage-transfer function is given by

$$\frac{E_0(s)}{E_i(s)} = \frac{s^2 + 1}{s^3 + s^2 + 4s + 6}. \qquad (5.14)$$

From (5.14) we obtain

$$(s^3 + s^2 + 4s + 6)E_0(s) = (s^2 + 1)E_i(s), \qquad (5.15)$$

or

$$\frac{d^3}{dt^3} e_0(t) + \frac{d^2}{dt^2} e_0(t) + 4 \frac{d}{dt} e_0(t) + 6e_0(t) = \frac{d^2}{dt^2} e_i(t) + e_i(t) = f(t). \qquad (5.16)$$

Now, defining

$$e_0^{(1)}(t) = \frac{d}{dt}\, e_0(t), \qquad e_0^{(2)}(t) = \frac{d}{dt}\, e_0^{(1)}(t), \tag{5.17}$$

we obtain

$$\frac{d}{dt}\, e_0^{(2)}(t) = f(t) - 6e_0(t) - 4e_0^{(1)}(t) - e_0^{(2)}(t), \tag{5.18}$$

so that the state equations are

$$\frac{d}{dt}\begin{bmatrix} e_0(t) \\ e_0^{(1)}(t) \\ e_0^{(2)}(t) \end{bmatrix} = \begin{bmatrix} 0 & 1 & 0 \\ 0 & 0 & 1 \\ -6 & -4 & -1 \end{bmatrix}\begin{bmatrix} e_0(t) \\ e_0^{(1)}(t) \\ e_0^{(2)}(t) \end{bmatrix} + \begin{bmatrix} 0 \\ 0 \\ f(t) \end{bmatrix}. \tag{5.19}$$

It can be seen by the above development and example that sets of state equations can readily be obtained from transfer functions. However, the state variables consist of just one measurable quantity and some of its derivatives. This is frequently disadvantageous because it may be awkward to specify in the solution the initial values of the derivatives. Moreover, this method for obtaining the state equations cannot be extended to nonlinear situations, where the state model is most useful. This is because we cannot define transfer functions for nonlinear systems. Finally, in forming the transfer functions from which a set of state equations for a given system might be obtained, all the information about the topology is lost; by preserving this, much may be gained for tackling problems in such fields as time-domain network synthesis. Because of all these difficulties, another more direct method for formulating state equations is essential. We shall discuss such a method in the following sections.

5.3. STATE EQUATIONS FOR *RLC* NETWORKS

We begin our discussion of the direct formulation of the state equations with the simplest case, the *RLC* networks. In this procedure we shall retain some information about the interconnection of the components of the networks in question; in particular, we shall arrange that the state variables be some of the branch voltages and chord currents with respect to a chosen formulation forest.

Our first concern, then, is the choice of the formulation forest. Of course, we must take into account the topological restrictions mentioned in Section 2.2; that is, voltage drivers must be consigned to the forest, and current drivers to the coforest. In Section 2.2 we also remarked on the desirability of placing elements corresponding to capacitors in the forest, and elements corresponding to inductors in the coforest; in the formulation of the state equations such a procedure is *highly advantageous*, owing to the fact that we can thereby be sure that the derivatives of some branch voltages and some chord currents occur in the terminal equations. We therefore select the formulation forest as follows:

(1) Elements corresponding to voltage drivers are consigned to the forest.

(2) As many elements corresponding to capacitors as possible are consigned to the forest.

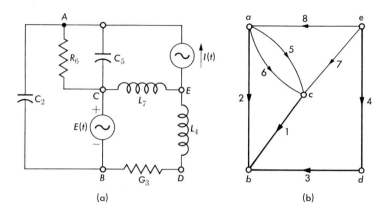

FIG. 5.1. Network and graph for Example 5.2.

(3) Elements corresponding to current drivers are consigned to the coforest.

(4) As many elements corresponding to inductors as possible are consigned to the coforest.

(5) It is of no consequence whether elements corresponding to resistances are consigned to the forest or coforest.

Because the terminal equations for capacitors and inductors are of the form

$$C \frac{dv}{dt} = i(t), \tag{5.20}$$

$$L \frac{di}{dt} = v(t), \tag{5.21}$$

it is clear that this choice of formulation forest not only satisfies the restrictions of Section 2.2, but also guarantees that the derivatives of as many branch voltages and chord currents as possible appear in the terminal equations, while on the other hand, the terminal equations contain as few derivatives of chord voltages and branch currents as possible.

Having decided on the method by which we shall choose our formulation forest, we are now in a position to introduce the technique for formulating the state equations. This we shall do by means of an example.

EXAMPLE 5.2. We shall find a set of state equations for the network of Fig. 5.1(a). The corresponding system graph is shown in Fig. 5.1(b).

Our first step is the choice of the formulation tree. This must contain element 1, which corresponds to the voltage driver, but it must not contain element 8, corresponding to the current driver. The second consideration is the set of elements corresponding to capacitances, that is, elements 2 and 5. We cannot consign both of these to the tree, so we arbitrarily relegate one of them, element 5, to the cotree. Finally, we must choose two elements from numbers 3, 4, and 7 to be consigned to the tree, and we do this in such a way as to include as few inductors as possible. One such possible choice is that element 7 be left in the cotree, while elements 3 and 4 are consigned to the tree. Thus the choice for the tree is elements 1, 2, 3, and 4, while elements 5, 6, **7**, and 8 form the cotree.

The second step in our formulation procedure consists in writing the terminal equations as follows:

$$\frac{d}{dt}\begin{bmatrix} C_2 & 0 \\ 0 & L_7 \end{bmatrix}\begin{bmatrix} v_2(t) \\ i_7(t) \end{bmatrix} = \begin{bmatrix} i_2(t) \\ v_7(t) \end{bmatrix}, \tag{5.22}$$

$$\frac{d}{dt}\begin{bmatrix} L_4 & 0 \\ 0 & C_5 \end{bmatrix}\begin{bmatrix} i_4(t) \\ v_5(t) \end{bmatrix} = \begin{bmatrix} v_4(t) \\ i_5(t) \end{bmatrix}, \tag{5.23}$$

$$\begin{bmatrix} G_3 & 0 \\ 0 & R_6 \end{bmatrix}\begin{bmatrix} v_3(t) \\ i_6(t) \end{bmatrix} = \begin{bmatrix} i_3(t) \\ v_6(t) \end{bmatrix}, \tag{5.24}$$

$$\begin{bmatrix} v_1(t) \\ i_8(t) \end{bmatrix} = \begin{bmatrix} E(t) \\ I(t) \end{bmatrix}. \tag{5.25}$$

Here we have arranged the equations in four groups,
(1) the branch capacitances and chord inductances;
(2) the chord capacitances and branch inductances;
(3) the resistive elements;
(4) the voltage and current drivers.

Note also that we have written the equations for the resistive elements so that it will be easy to substitute for the branch current and chord voltage involved. That is, we have written the equations to show the branch current $i_3(t)$ and the chord voltage $v_6(t)$ explicitly in terms of a branch voltage and a chord current.

As our next step, we write the fundamental circuit and cut-set equations in a convenient manner for substitution into the terminal equations. Thus

$$\begin{bmatrix} i_2(t) \\ v_7(t) \end{bmatrix} = \begin{bmatrix} 0 & -1 \\ 1 & 0 \end{bmatrix}\begin{bmatrix} v_4(t) \\ i_5(t) \end{bmatrix} + \begin{bmatrix} 0 & -1 \\ 1 & 0 \end{bmatrix}\begin{bmatrix} v_3(t) \\ i_6(t) \end{bmatrix} + \begin{bmatrix} 0 & 1 \\ -1 & 0 \end{bmatrix}\begin{bmatrix} v_1(t) \\ i_8(t) \end{bmatrix}, \tag{5.26}$$

$$\begin{bmatrix} i_4(t) \\ v_5(t) \end{bmatrix} = \begin{bmatrix} 0 & -1 \\ 1 & 0 \end{bmatrix}\begin{bmatrix} v_2(t) \\ i_7(t) \end{bmatrix} + \begin{bmatrix} 0 & -1 \\ -1 & 0 \end{bmatrix}\begin{bmatrix} v_1(t) \\ i_8(t) \end{bmatrix}, \tag{5.27}$$

$$\begin{bmatrix} i_3(t) \\ v_6(t) \end{bmatrix} = \begin{bmatrix} 0 & -1 \\ 1 & 0 \end{bmatrix}\begin{bmatrix} v_2(t) \\ i_7(t) \end{bmatrix} + \begin{bmatrix} 0 & -1 \\ -1 & 0 \end{bmatrix}\begin{bmatrix} v_1(t) \\ i_8(t) \end{bmatrix}. \tag{5.28}$$

The substitution of (5.26), (5.27), and (5.28) into (5.22), (5.23), and (5.24) eliminates all the branch currents and chord voltages. This operation is the fourth step in the formulation procedure, and it yields

$$\frac{d}{dt}\begin{bmatrix} C_2 & 0 \\ 0 & L_7 \end{bmatrix}\begin{bmatrix} v_2(t) \\ i_7(t) \end{bmatrix} = \begin{bmatrix} 0 & -1 \\ 1 & 0 \end{bmatrix}\begin{bmatrix} v_4(t) \\ i_5(t) \end{bmatrix} + \begin{bmatrix} 0 & -1 \\ 1 & 0 \end{bmatrix}\begin{bmatrix} v_3(t) \\ i_6(t) \end{bmatrix} + \begin{bmatrix} 0 & 1 \\ -1 & 0 \end{bmatrix}\begin{bmatrix} v_1(t) \\ i_8(t) \end{bmatrix},$$

$$\tag{5.29}$$

$$\frac{d}{dt}\begin{bmatrix} L_4 & 0 \\ 0 & C_5 \end{bmatrix}\begin{bmatrix} 0 & -1 \\ 1 & 0 \end{bmatrix}\begin{bmatrix} v_2(t) \\ i_7(t) \end{bmatrix} + \frac{d}{dt}\begin{bmatrix} L_4 & 0 \\ 0 & C_5 \end{bmatrix}\begin{bmatrix} 0 & -1 \\ -1 & 0 \end{bmatrix}\begin{bmatrix} v_1(t) \\ i_8(t) \end{bmatrix} = \begin{bmatrix} v_4(t) \\ i_5(t) \end{bmatrix}, \tag{5.30}$$

$$\begin{bmatrix} G_3 & 0 \\ 0 & R_6 \end{bmatrix}\begin{bmatrix} v_3(t) \\ i_6(t) \end{bmatrix} = \begin{bmatrix} 0 & -1 \\ 1 & 0 \end{bmatrix}\begin{bmatrix} v_2(t) \\ i_7(t) \end{bmatrix} + \begin{bmatrix} 0 & -1 \\ -1 & 0 \end{bmatrix}\begin{bmatrix} v_1(t) \\ i_8(t) \end{bmatrix}. \tag{5.31}$$

In (5.29), (5.30), and (5.31) the only nonspecified variables whose first derivatives do not appear are $v_3(t)$, $i_6(t)$, $v_4(t)$, and $i_5(t)$. Our next step consists in their elimination. We eliminate $v_3(t)$ and $i_6(t)$ by solving (5.31) and substituting for these variables into (5.29). The procedure is as follows. From (5.31)

$$
\begin{bmatrix} v_3(t) \\ i_6(t) \end{bmatrix} = \begin{bmatrix} 0 & -R_3 \\ G_6 & 0 \end{bmatrix} \begin{bmatrix} v_2(t) \\ i_7(t) \end{bmatrix} + \begin{bmatrix} 0 & -R_3 \\ -G_6 & 0 \end{bmatrix} \begin{bmatrix} v_1(t) \\ i_8(t) \end{bmatrix},
\tag{5.32}
$$

and substituting (5.32) into (5.29), we have

$$
\frac{d}{dt} \begin{bmatrix} C_2 & 0 \\ 0 & L_7 \end{bmatrix} \begin{bmatrix} v_2(t) \\ i_7(t) \end{bmatrix} = \begin{bmatrix} 0 & -1 \\ 1 & 0 \end{bmatrix} \begin{bmatrix} v_4(t) \\ i_5(t) \end{bmatrix} + \begin{bmatrix} -G_6 & 0 \\ 0 & -R_3 \end{bmatrix} \begin{bmatrix} v_2(t) \\ i_7(t) \end{bmatrix} + \begin{bmatrix} G_6 & 1 \\ -1 & -R_3 \end{bmatrix} \begin{bmatrix} v_1(t) \\ i_8(t) \end{bmatrix}.
\tag{5.33}
$$

To eliminate $v_4(t)$ and $i_5(t)$, we merely substitute (5.30) into (5.33), and obtain

$$
\frac{d}{dt} \begin{bmatrix} C_2 + C_5 & 0 \\ 0 & L_4 + L_7 \end{bmatrix} \begin{bmatrix} v_2(t) \\ i_7(t) \end{bmatrix}
$$
$$
= \begin{bmatrix} -G_6 & 0 \\ 0 & -R_3 \end{bmatrix} \begin{bmatrix} v_2(t) \\ i_7(t) \end{bmatrix} + \begin{bmatrix} G_6 & 1 \\ -1 & -R_3 \end{bmatrix} \begin{bmatrix} v_1(t) \\ i_8(t) \end{bmatrix} + \frac{d}{dt} \begin{bmatrix} C_5 & 0 \\ 0 & -L_4 \end{bmatrix} \begin{bmatrix} v_1(t) \\ i_8(t) \end{bmatrix}.
\tag{5.34}
$$

We finally obtain the state equations from (5.34) by substituting for $v_1(t)$ and $i_8(t)$ from (5.25). This gives

$$
\frac{d}{dt} \begin{bmatrix} v_2(t) \\ i_7(t) \end{bmatrix} = \begin{bmatrix} \dfrac{-G_6}{C_2 + C_5} & 0 \\ 0 & \dfrac{-R_3}{L_4 + L_7} \end{bmatrix} \begin{bmatrix} v_2(t) \\ i_7(t) \end{bmatrix}
$$
$$
+ \begin{bmatrix} \dfrac{G_6}{C_2 + C_5} & \dfrac{1}{C_2 + C_5} \\ \dfrac{-1}{L_4 + L_7} & \dfrac{-R_3}{L_4 + L_7} \end{bmatrix} \begin{bmatrix} E(t) \\ I(t) \end{bmatrix} + \frac{d}{dt} \begin{bmatrix} \dfrac{C_5}{C_2 + C_5} & 0 \\ 0 & \dfrac{-L_4}{L_4 + L_7} \end{bmatrix} \begin{bmatrix} E(t) \\ I(t) \end{bmatrix}
\tag{5.35}
$$

which are the required state equations. When there are no chord capacitances or branch inductances, it can be shown that the derivative term in the drivers does not appear.

Note that Eqs. (5.35) do not suffer from the disadvantages associated with those that could be obtained through transfer functions. The state variables are directly measurable, and we have retained some topological information about the network involved. Furthermore, the state equations have been obtained by a direct method.

At this point we could enter into a detailed symbolic derivation to justify our formulation technique for every *RLC* network. However, this would involve a somewhat cumbersome set of manipulations, and it is more convenient to summarize the salient features of our method.

We obtain the state equations for RLC networks through the following steps:

(1) The formulation forest is selected to include as many elements corresponding to capacitances and to exclude as many elements corresponding to inductances as possible.

(2) The terminal equations are arranged in four groups, containing:
   (a) the branch capacitances and chord inductances;
   (b) the chord capacitances and branch inductances;
   (c) the resistive elements;
   (d) the voltage and current drivers.

(3) The fundamental circuit and cut-set equations are written in three sets in a suitable form for substitution into (a), (b), and (c) above.

(4) The nonspecified branch currents and chord voltages are eliminated by substitution of the circuit and cut-set equations into the terminal equations.

(5) The nonspecified variables whose first time derivatives do not occur in the equations resulting from Step 4 are eliminated.

(6) The specified functions for the voltage and current drivers are inserted into the result of Step 5, and the resulting equations rearranged into the canonical form.

It is not difficult to prove that the above six steps will always produce the state equations, and as we mentioned, the state variables are directly measurable, and some topological information is retained.

5.4. SOME TOPOLOGICAL CONSIDERATIONS FOR NETWORKS WITH MULTITERMINAL COMPONENTS

The formulation of the state equations for RLC networks was fairly simple because of the form of the terminal equations that were involved; all the coefficient matrices were diagonal with constant coefficients. In the case of networks containing multiterminal components, however, the terminal equations do not have diagonal coefficient matrices, so that we find that it is not convenient to split the terminal equations into four groups for the purpose of formulation. Instead, we shall classify the elements of the system graph according to the form of the associated terminal equations. This will allow us to select the formulation forest in such a way that, as in the case of RLC networks, as many time derivatives of branch voltages and chord currents as possible appear in the terminal equations. In our selection, we must, of course, take into account all the topological restrictions mentioned in Sections 2.2 and 2.10.

Corresponding to element m of a system graph, there are two variables $v_m(t)$ and $i_m(t)$. The element classifications are made by examining which time derivatives of these variables occur in any of the terminal equations. We shall deal only with first derivatives here, although our method is readily extendable to take into account networks containing components whose terminal equations have derivatives of higher order.

If there exists at least one terminal equation in which dv_m/dt occurs, element m is called a *first-order V element*. Similarly, if di_m/dt occurs in at least one terminal equation, element m is called a *first-order I element*. It may be that an element is both a first-order V element and a first-order I element. In this case we call it a *first-order VI element*.

If neither dv_m/dt nor di_m/dt occur in any terminal relations, and if element m does not correspond to either a voltage driver or a current driver, we call element m an *algebraic element*.

For example, elements corresponding to capacitances are first-order V elements, elements corresponding to inductances are first-order I elements, and elements corresponding to resistances are algebraic elements.

There is one other case which we must take into account because of the topological restrictions which it implies. If a multiterminal component has terminal equations which can be written in the form

$$
\begin{bmatrix} H_{111} \dfrac{d}{dt} + H_{110} & 0 \\[2ex] 0 & H_{221} \dfrac{d}{dt} + H_{220} \end{bmatrix} \begin{bmatrix} V_1 \\ I_2 \end{bmatrix}
$$

$$
= \begin{bmatrix} 0 & K_{121} \dfrac{d}{dt} + K_{120} \\[2ex] K_{211} \dfrac{d}{dt} + K_{210} & 0 \end{bmatrix} \begin{bmatrix} I_1 \\ V_2 \end{bmatrix} + \begin{bmatrix} F_1(t) \\ F_2(t) \end{bmatrix}, \qquad (5.36)
$$

where $H_{111}, H_{221}, H_{110}, H_{220}, K_{121}, K_{120}, K_{211}, K_{210}$ are constant matrices; $F_1(t)$, $F_2(t)$ are column matrices of specified functions; and V_1, V_2, I_1, I_2 are column matrices of the voltages and currents corresponding to the elements of the terminal graph of the component, we must arrange that either the elements corresponding to V_1 and I_1 or the elements corresponding to V_2 and I_2 should be consigned to the forest, but not both. This is because Eqs. (5.36) express V_1 in terms of V_2 and I_1 in terms of I_2, and we must avoid doubly specifying any voltages or currents, as may occur when these equations are used in conjunction with the fundamental circuit and cut-set equations. Ideal transformers are simple examples of components whose terminal equations have the form of (5.36).

It is noteworthy that Eqs. (5.36) include as special cases all the voltage and current drivers. This occurs when some of the H_{ijk} and K_{ijk} are zero. Since the topological restrictions on elements whose equations have this form are very similar to those regarding the locations of the voltage and current drivers, we shall classify elements corresponding to components with terminal equations of the form of (5.36) as *generalized drivers*. For the purpose of selecting the formulation forest, we shall separate all the generalized drivers from the other first-order and algebraic elements.

EXAMPLE 5.3.   Figure 5.2 shows a simple network and its system graph. The terminal equations for the various components are as follows:

(a) ideal transformer, $\begin{bmatrix} v_2(t) \\ i_9(t) \end{bmatrix} = \begin{bmatrix} 0 & n_{92} \\ -n_{92} & 0 \end{bmatrix} \begin{bmatrix} i_2(t) \\ v_9(t) \end{bmatrix},$ (5.37)

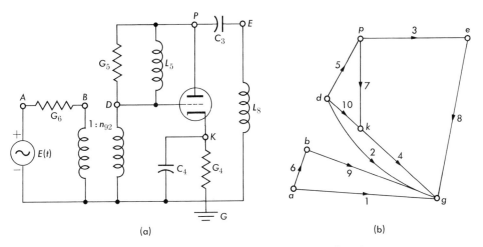

Fɪɢ. 5.2. Network and graph for Example 5.3.

(b) voltage driver, $\qquad$ $v_1(t) = E(t),$ $\hfill$ (5.38)

(c) vacuum tube, $\qquad$ $\begin{bmatrix} i_{10}(t) \\ i_7(t) \end{bmatrix} = \begin{bmatrix} 0 & 0 \\ g_m & g_p \end{bmatrix} \begin{bmatrix} v_{10}(t) \\ v_7(t) \end{bmatrix},$ $\hfill$ (5.39)

(d) cathode network, $\qquad$ $i_4(t) = \left(G_4 + C_4 \dfrac{d}{dt} \right) v_4(t),$ $\hfill$ (5.40)

(e) feedback network, $\qquad$ $L_5 \dfrac{di_5(t)}{dt} = \left(1 + G_5 L_5 \dfrac{d}{dt} \right) v_5(t),$ $\hfill$ (5.41)

(f) "coupling capacitance," $\qquad$ $C_3 \dfrac{dv_3(t)}{dt} = i_3(t),$ $\hfill$ (5.42)

(g) "load inductance," $\qquad$ $L_8 \dfrac{di_8(t)}{dt} = v_8(t),$ $\hfill$ (5.43)

(h) "source admittance," $\qquad$ $i_6(t) = G_6 v_6(t).$ $\hfill$ (5.44)

Accordingly, we may classify the elements of the system graph as

element 1: voltage driver $\qquad\qquad$ element 2: generalized voltage driver
element 3: first-order V element $\qquad$ element 4: first-order V element
element 5: first-order VI element $\qquad$ element 6: algebraic element
element 7: algebraic element $\qquad\qquad$ element 8: first-order I element
element 9: generalized current driver $\quad$ element 10: current driver

Two things are noteworthy here. The first is that we have classified the elements corresponding to the ideal transformer as generalized voltage and current drivers. This is to indicate that we intend to choose the formulation tree to include element 2, and exclude element 9. We could have made the opposite choice had we so desired. Secondly, we have classified element 10 as a current driver, even though it is an element of the terminal graph of the vacuum tube. This classification arises because the only terminal equation in which $i_{10}(t)$ occurs is

$$i_{10}(t) = 0. \tag{5.45}$$

This is the equation associated with a current driver whose specified function is identically zero.

The above classification forms the basis of the selection procedure for the formulation forest. This selection is made through the use of a set of subgraphs of the system graph. We shall now define these subgraphs.

Let G be the system graph for a given network. We define subgraphs G_1, G_2, G_3, G_4, G_5, and G_6 according to the classification of the elements. Thus, G_1 is the subgraph containing all the voltage drivers and all the generalized voltage drivers, and no other elements. To be certain that a complete solution exists, this subgraph must contain no circuits, and we shall henceforth assume that this is so.

The subgraph G_2 contains all the elements of G_1, and all the first-order V elements. We would prefer that this subgraph also should contain no circuits, for if it does, there may be trouble when initial conditions are arbitrarily specified. This is, of course, analogous to the situation which arises when there are circuits of capacitances in the RLC case.

The subgraph G_3 contains all the elements of G_2, and all the first-order VI elements; G_4 is the subgraph which contains all the elements of G_3 and all the algebraic elements; G_5 is the subgraph which contains all the elements of G_4 and all the first-order I elements; lastly, G_6 is the subgraph which contains all the elements of G_5, all the generalized current drivers, and all the current drivers. It can be seen that G_6 contains all the elements of the system graph, so that we can write

$$G_6 = G, \tag{5.46}$$

and any forest of G_6 is a forest of G.

We now let T be the required forest, and T_i be forests of G_i ($i = 1, 2, 3, 4, 5, 6$). We choose T_2 so that it contains T_1, T_3 so that it contains T_2, T_4 so that it contains T_3, T_5 so that it contains T_4, and T_6 so that it contains T_5. Thus we have, symbolically,

$$G_1 \subset G_2 \subset G_3 \subset G_4 \subset G_5 \subset G_6 = G,$$
$$T_1 \subset T_2 \subset T_3 \subset T_4 \subset T_5 \subset T_6,$$

where the expression $G_1 \subset G_2$ is read as: G_2 contains G_1, etc.

We see that T_6 is a forest of G_6, and therefore of G; this is the required forest, and we have

$$T_6 = T. \tag{5.47}$$

Note also that

$$G_1 = T_1. \tag{5.48}$$

Similarly, because all the generalized current drivers and all the current drivers must be in the coforest, we must have

$$T_5 = T_6. \tag{5.49}$$

In addition, we would prefer that all the first-order I elements should be in the coforest. In such a case, which is equivalent in RLC networks to the situation in which all the inductors are restricted to the coforest, we would have

$$T_4 = T_5 = T_6 = T.$$

EXAMPLE 5.4. For the network of Fig. 5.2, the subgraphs G_i are (see Example 5.3):

$$G_1 = \text{elements } 1, 2,$$
$$G_2 = \text{elements } 1, 2, 3, 4,$$
$$G_3 = \text{elements } 1, 2, 3, 4, 5,$$
$$G_4 = \text{elements } 1, 2, 3, 4, 5, 6, 7,$$
$$G_5 = \text{elements } 1, 2, 3, 4, 5, 6, 7, 8,$$
$$G_6 = G = \text{elements } 1, 2, 3, 4, 5, 6, 7, 8, 9, 10.$$

Also, the forests T_i are

$$T_1 = \text{elements } 1, 2,$$
$$T_2 = \text{elements } 1, 2, 3, 4,$$
$$T_3 = \text{elements } 1, 2, 3, 4, 5,$$
$$T_4 = T_5 = T_6 = T = \text{elements } 1, 2, 3, 4, 5, 6.$$

These subgraphs are illustrated in Fig. 5.3, in which the forests are shown as heavy lines.

It is to be observed that our selection of the formulation forest fulfills all the topological requirements, and as we desire, it forces as many derivatives of voltages to correspond to branches and as many derivatives of currents to correspond to chords as possible. Of course, in our example, $G_2 = T_2$ and $T_4 = T_5 = T_6 = T$ since there are no circuits of first-order V elements or cut sets of first-order I elements. This situation allows arbitrary specification of the initial conditions, with a complete solution at all times.

Our selection procedure is so systematic that it is eminently suitable for programming on a digital computer.

5.5. STATE EQUATIONS FOR NETWORKS WITH MULTITERMINAL COMPONENTS

In Section 5.4 we established a systematic method for choosing the formulation forest for the state equations associated with networks containing multiterminal components. In this section we shall introduce a procedure for formulating state equations, based on this selection. We shall do this by continuing our example.

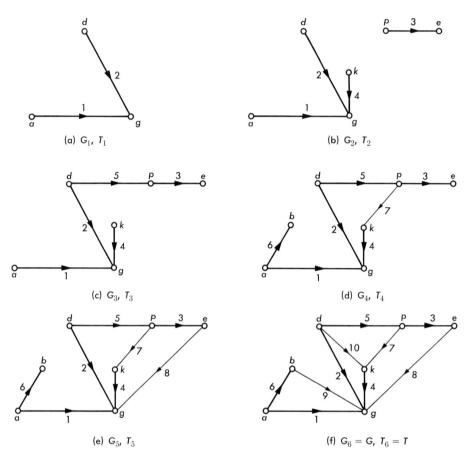

FIG. 5.3. Selection of the formulation forest for the network of Example 5.3.

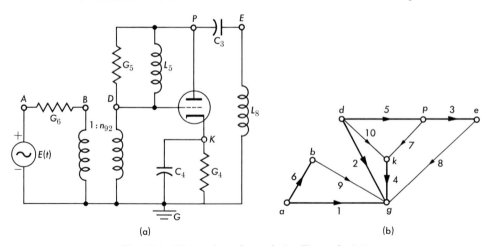

FIG. 5.4. Network and graph for Example 5.5.

EXAMPLE 5.5. Figure 5.4 shows the same network and system graph as that of Fig. 5.2. For this network we classified the elements (Example 5.4) as follows.

Element	Classification	Element	Classification
1	Voltage driver	6, 7	Algebraic elements
2	Generalized voltage driver	8	First-order I element
3, 4	First-order V elements	9	Generalized current driver
5	First-order VI element	10	Current driver

We also selected the formulation tree to include elements 1, 2, 3, 4, 5, and 6. The formulation procedure for the state equations is initiated by writing the terminal equations (Eqs. 5.37 through 5.44) in one group as follows:

$$v_1(t) = E(t), \qquad v_2(t) = n_{92}v_9(t),$$

$$C_3 \frac{dv_3(t)}{dt} = i_3(t), \qquad C_4 \frac{dv_4(t)}{dt} + G_4v_4(t) = i_4(t),$$

$$G_5L_5 \frac{dv_5(t)}{dt} + v_5(t) = L_5 \frac{di_5(t)}{dt}, \qquad G_6v_6(t) = i_6(t), \qquad (5.50)$$

$$i_7(t) = g_pv_7(t) + g_mv_{10}(t), \qquad L_8 \frac{di_8(t)}{dt} = v_8(t),$$

$$i_9(t) = -n_{92}i_2(t), \qquad i_{10}(t) = 0.$$

Here we have placed the branch voltages and chord currents on the left-hand side of the equations, and have ordered the variables according to the classification of the corresponding elements, placing the forest variables first, and the coforest variables last. In general, the ordering is as follows:

(1) voltage drivers,
(3) branch first-order V elements,
(5) branch algebraic elements,
(7) chord first-order V elements,
(9) chord algebraic elements,
(11) generalized current drivers,

(2) generalized voltage drivers,
(4) branch first-order VI elements,
(6) branch first-order I elements,
(8) chord first-order VI elements,
(10) chord first-order I elements,
(12) current drivers.

The next step in the formulation procedure consists in writing the fundamental circuit and cut-set equations together for substitution into (5.50). This gives

$$i_1(t) = -i_9(t), \qquad i_2(t) = -i_7(t) - i_8(t) - i_{10}(t),$$
$$i_3(t) = i_8(t), \qquad i_4(t) = i_7(t) + i_{10}(t),$$
$$i_5(t) = i_7(t) + i_8(t), \qquad i_6(t) = i_9(t), \qquad (5.51)$$
$$v_7(t) = v_2(t) - v_4(t) - v_5(t), \qquad v_8(t) = v_2(t) - v_3(t) - v_5(t),$$
$$v_9(t) = v_1(t) - v_6(t), \qquad v_{10}(t) = v_2(t) - v_4(t).$$

We now substitute (5.51) into the right hand side of (5.50). This eliminates the branch currents and chord voltages to yield

$$v_1(t) = E(t), \qquad v_2(t) = n_{92}v_1(t) - n_{92}v_6(t),$$

$$C_3 \frac{dv_3(t)}{dt} = i_8(t),$$

$$C_4 \frac{dv_4(t)}{dt} + G_4 v_4(t) = i_7(t) + i_{10}(t),$$

$$G_5 L_5 \frac{dv_5(t)}{dt} + v_5(t) = L_5 \frac{di_7(t)}{dt} + L_5 \frac{di_8(t)}{dt},$$

$$G_6 v_6(t) = i_9(t),$$

$$i_7(t) = (g_m + g_p)v_2(t) - (g_m + g_p)v_4(t) - g_p v_5(t),$$

$$L_8 \frac{di_8(t)}{dt} = v_2(t) - v_3(t) - v_5(t),$$

$$i_9(t) = n_{92}i_7(t) + n_{92}i_8(t) + n_{92}i_{10}(t),$$

$$i_{10}(t) = 0.$$

(5.52)

We separate the algebraic terms from the derivative terms by moving the former to the right-hand side of the equations and the latter to the left-hand side. This gives

$$0 = -v_1(t) + E(t), \qquad 0 = n_{92}v_1(t) - v_2(t) - n_{92}v_6(t),$$

$$C_3 \frac{dv_3(t)}{dt} = i_8(t), \qquad C_4 \frac{dv_4(t)}{dt} = -G_4 v_4(t) + i_7(t) + i_{10}(t),$$

$$G_5 L_5 \frac{dv_5}{dt} - L_5 \frac{di_8(t)}{dt} - L_5 \frac{di_7(t)}{dt} = -v_5(t),$$

$$0 = -G_6 v_6(t) + i_9(t),$$

$$0 = (g_m + g_p)v_2(t) - (g_m + g_p)v_4(t) - g_p v_5(t) - i_7(t),$$

$$L_8 \frac{di_8(t)}{dt} = v_2(t) - v_3(t) - v_5(t),$$

$$0 = n_{92}i_7(t) + n_{92}i_8(t) - i_9(t) + n_{92}i_{10}(t),$$

$$0 = i_{10}(t).$$

(5.53)

For convenience, we divide Eqs. (5.53) into four sets. They are:
(a) those equations which contain derivatives of the variables corresponding to first-order elements,

$$C_3 \frac{dv_3(t)}{dt} = i_8(t),$$

$$C_4 \frac{dv_4(t)}{dt} = -G_4 v_4(t) + i_7(t) + i_{10}(t),$$

$$G_5 L_5 \frac{dv_5(t)}{dt} - L_5 \frac{di_8(t)}{dt} - L_5 \frac{di_7(t)}{dt} = -v_5(t),$$

$$L_8 \frac{di_8(t)}{dt} = -v_3(t) - v_5(t) + v_2(t);$$

(5.54)

(b) those equations which specify the voltage and current drivers,

$$0 = -v_1(t) + E(t), \qquad 0 = i_{10}(t); \tag{5.55}$$

(c) a set of equations which can be solved for all the variables which appear *only* algebraically in (5.53), namely $v_2(t)$, $v_6(t)$, and $i_9(t)$,

$$
\begin{aligned}
0 &= n_{92}v_1(t) - v_2(t) - n_{92}v_6(t), \\
0 &= -G_6v_6(t) + i_9(t), \\
0 &= n_{92}i_8(t) + n_{92}i_7(t) + n_{92}i_{10}(t) - i_9(t);
\end{aligned} \tag{5.56}
$$

(d) the remaining equation(s),

$$0 = -(g_m + g_p)v_4(t) - g_pv_5(t) - i_7(t) + (g_m + g_p)v_2(t). \tag{5.57}$$

From this point on the procedure is conceptually simple, but algebraically messy. We first eliminate $v_2(t)$, $v_6(t)$, and $i_9(t)$ by solving Eqs. (5.56) for these variables, and substituting the results into Eqs. (5.54) and (5.57). Next, we solve Eq. (5.57) for $i_7(t)$, which is then eliminated from Eqs. (5.54). We use Eqs. (5.55) to eliminate $v_1(t)$ and $i_{10}(t)$. We are then left with four equations containing the specified functions, and the state variables $v_3(t)$, $v_4(t)$, $v_5(t)$, and $i_8(t)$, together with their derivatives. These final equations, when rearranged into the canonical form, are the state equations.

In order to follow this procedure without obscuring the steps with unduly large algebraic coefficients in the equations, we now assume that the various parameters have the following simple numerical values:

$$
\begin{aligned}
C_3 &= 3, & C_4 &= 4, & G_4 &= 4, & G_5 &= \tfrac{1}{5}, & G_6 &= 10, \\
L_5 &= 5, & L_8 &= 8, & g_m &= 1, & g_p &= 3, & n_{92} &= 2.
\end{aligned}
$$

Under these conditions, Eqs. (5.54) become

$$3\,\frac{dv_3(t)}{dt} = i_8(t),$$

$$4\,\frac{dv_4(t)}{dt} = -4v_4(t) + i_7(t) + i_{10}(t),$$

$$\frac{dv_5(t)}{dt} - 5\,\frac{di_8(t)}{dt} - 5\,\frac{di_7(t)}{dt} = -v_5(t), \tag{5.58}$$

$$8\,\frac{di_8(t)}{dt} = -v_3(t) - v_5(t) + v_2(t);$$

Eqs. (5.56) become

$$
\begin{aligned}
0 &= 2v_1(t) - v_2(t) - 2v_6(t), \\
0 &= -10v_6(t) + i_9(t), \\
0 &= 2i_8(t) + 2i_7(t) + 2i_{10}(t) - i_9(t),
\end{aligned} \tag{5.59}
$$

and Eq. (5.57) becomes

$$0 = -4v_4(t) - 3v_5(t) - i_7(t) + 4v_2(t). \tag{5.60}$$

Solving (5.59) for $v_2(t)$, $v_6(t)$, and $i_9(t)$, we obtain

$$\begin{aligned}
v_2(t) &= -\tfrac{2}{5}i_8(t) - \tfrac{2}{5}i_7(t) + 2v_1(t) - \tfrac{2}{5}i_{10}(t), \\
v_6(t) &= \tfrac{1}{5}i_8(t) + \tfrac{1}{5}i_7(t) + \tfrac{1}{5}i_{10}(t), \\
i_9(t) &= 2i_8(t) + 2i_7(t) + 2i_{10}(t).
\end{aligned} \tag{5.61}$$

We substitute (5.61) into (5.58) and (5.60), and find that

$$3\frac{dv_3(t)}{dt} = i_8(t),$$

$$4\frac{dv_4(t)}{dt} = -4v_4(t) + i_7(t) + i_{10}(t), \tag{5.62}$$

$$\frac{dv_5(t)}{dt} - 5\frac{di_8(t)}{dt} - 5\frac{di_7(t)}{dt} = -v_5(t),$$

$$8\frac{di_8(t)}{dt} = -v_3(t) - v_5(t) - \tfrac{2}{5}i_8(t) - \tfrac{2}{5}i_7(t) + 2v_1(t) - \tfrac{2}{5}i_{10}(t),$$

and

$$i_7(t) = -\tfrac{20}{13}v_4(t) - \tfrac{15}{13}v_5(t) - \tfrac{8}{13}i_8(t) + \tfrac{40}{13}v_1(t) - \tfrac{8}{13}i_{10}(t). \tag{5.63}$$

We next substitute (5.63) into (5.62) and eliminate $i_7(t)$. Thus,

$$3\frac{dv_3(t)}{dt} = i_8(t),$$

$$4\frac{dv_4(t)}{dt} = -\tfrac{72}{13}v_4(t) - \tfrac{15}{13}v_5(t) - \tfrac{8}{13}i_8(t) + \tfrac{40}{13}v_1(t) + \tfrac{5}{13}i_{10}(t),$$

$$\tfrac{100}{13}\frac{dv_4(t)}{dt} + \tfrac{88}{13}\frac{dv_5(t)}{dt} - \tfrac{25}{13}\frac{di_8(t)}{dt} = -v_5(t) + \tfrac{200}{13}\frac{dv_1(t)}{dt} - \tfrac{40}{13}\frac{di_{10}(t)}{dt}, \tag{5.64}$$

$$8\frac{di_8(t)}{dt} = -v_3(t) + \tfrac{8}{13}v_4(t) - \tfrac{7}{13}v_5(t) - \tfrac{2}{13}i_8(t) + \tfrac{10}{13}v_1(t) - \tfrac{2}{13}i_{10}(t).$$

We use (5.55) to eliminate $v_1(t)$ and $i_{10}(t)$:

$$3\frac{dv_3(t)}{dt} = i_8(t),$$

$$52\frac{dv_4(t)}{dt} = -72v_4(t) - 15v_5(t) - 8i_8(t) + 40E(t), \tag{5.65}$$

$$100\frac{dv_4(t)}{dt} + 88\frac{dv_5(t)}{dt} - 25\frac{di_8(t)}{dt} = -13v_5(t) + 200\frac{dE(t)}{dt},$$

$$104\frac{di_8(t)}{dt} = -13v_3(t) + 8v_4(t) - 7v_5(t) - 2i_8(t) + 10E(t).$$

We finally solve (5.65) for the derivatives of $v_3(t)$, $v_4(t)$, $v_5(t)$, and $i_8(t)$, and obtain the state equations

$$\frac{dv_3(t)}{dt} = 0.333i_8(t),$$

$$\frac{dv_4(t)}{dt} = -1.385v_4(t) - 0.288v_5(t) - 0.154i_8(t) + 0.769E(t),$$

$$\frac{dv_5(t)}{dt} = -0.355v_3(t) + 1.595v_4(t) + 0.163v_5(t) \qquad (5.66)$$

$$+ \, 0.169i_8(t) + \left(0.847 + 2.283\,\frac{d}{dt}\right)E(t),$$

$$\frac{di_8(t)}{dt} = -0.125v_3(t) + 0.0762v_4(t) - 0.0674v_5(t)$$

$$-0.0193i_8(t) + 0.0962E(t).$$

Although the manipulations involved in obtaining the state equations may seem somewhat complicated, they are conceptually very simple. *The method is very similar to the formulation of the branch-chord equations (Section 2.10) in that the fundamental circuit and cut-set equations are substituted into the terminal equations.* In this case, however, we continue by eliminating all the algebraic relations from the branch-chord equations. Furthermore, as soon as the forest is picked by the method of Section 5.4, we immediately know which will be the state variables; they are merely the voltages corresponding to branch first-order V elements (or first-order VI elements), and the currents corresponding to chord first-order I elements (or first-order VI elements). Thus the remaining manipulation is only an effort to eliminate the other variables. Frequently, in small systems, this can be done rapidly using an intuitive, *ad hoc* ordering of the steps of the procedure.

The symbolic development of our technique, using matrix methods, is too cumbersome for inclusion here. Therefore, we merely summarize the steps in the procedure, as follows:

(1) The elements of the system graph are classified according to the method of Section 5.4.
(2) The formulation forest is selected by the method of Section 5.4.
(3) The terminal equations for the various components are written in one matrix expression, so that the derivative terms are separated from the algebraic terms, and the variables in the column matrices are ordered in correspondence with the classifications of the elements.
(4) The fundamental circuit and cut-set equations are written in a form suitable for substitution into the terminal equations.
(5) The fundamental circuit and cut-set equations are substituted into the terminal equations.
(6) The algebraic relations are eliminated from the result of Step 5. This is best done by dividing the equations into groups and substituting one group into another.

(7) In the equations resulting from Step 6, there remain variables which do not correspond to first-order elements. These are eliminated by substituting some of the equations into the remainder.

(8) The equations resulting from Step 7 are rearranged into the canonical form. They are the state equations.

We are always assured that the various eliminations of variables are possible, owing to the fact that the equations resulting from Step 5 are merely the branch-chord equations formulated in the time domain. Hence they form a linearly in-dependent set. The last step (Step 8) involves a matrix inverse which must exist if we are to find a set of state equations.

It is well to point out the similarity between state equation formulation methods for *RLC* networks and for networks containing multiterminal components. In both cases the formulation forest is picked according to the same principles; indeed, although we did not do so, the systematic method of Section 5.4 may very suitably be used to pick the forest in the *RLC* case. In both cases the fundamental circuit and cut-set equations are substituted into the terminal equations. However, in the *RLC* case, it is convenient to divide the terminal equations into four groups for ease of elimination of the various unwanted variables at a later stage, while in the multiterminal case, it is not. Nevertheless, once the circuit and cut-set equations have been used in the terminal equations, the result can be divided into groups, and the remainder of the formulation technique is entirely similar in both situations. Various variables and equations are eliminated, until only the state equations remain.

5.6. MORE ON STATE EQUATION FORMULATION

In the previous sections we introduced the principles of a direct method for formu-lating the state equations for electric networks. Although it can be shown that our technique can be applied to any network whose component terminal relations are either algebraic or first-order differential equations, it may at first sight be ques-tionable whether or not the method could easily be utilized for very large net-works. For instance, in Example 5.5 we were required to handle a group of ten equations when formulating the state equations for a relatively small network. Therefore, it is important that we point out that it was to illustrate the details of the method rather than to solve the network problem in the most efficient way that we proceeded as we did.

How, then, can we obtain the state equations from the network without dealing with as many simultaneous equations as there are elements in the system graph? The answer to this question lies in the application of the terminal representation technique to subnetworks of the given network. When we are interested in a state equation model for a given network, we know that we must eliminate all the algebraic equations associated with the network. Suppose we partially solve the network in stages by obtaining terminal representations of subnetworks, all of whose components have algebraic terminal equations. When this is done, and wherever this is feasible, the terminal equations for the subnetworks will be less in number than the original terminal equations, and will also be algebraic. We thereby reduce the number of equations before starting on the general formulation procedure. If we include some first-order elements in the subnetworks, the terminal relations for the subnetworks will be differential equations, but again there will be fewer equations than there were associated with the original network.

Hence we can do two things. We may follow the method outlined in the previous sections after reducing the number of algebraic equations involved in the network by picking subnetworks whose components all have algebraic terminal relations. If, on the other hand, we do not find it convenient to choose such subnetworks, we may include components with first-order terminal equations. This will in general require us to extend the formulation technique to take into account higher-order differential equations among the terminal relationships.

We illustrate the first alternative with the following example.

EXAMPLE 5.6.   Consider the simple network of Fig. 5.5(a). Its system graph, shown in Fig. 5.5(b), contains thirteen elements, so that by applying our formulation technique directly, we would be required to work with thirteen simultaneous equations. However, we may avoid this by recognizing the two subnetworks enclosed in the dashed lines [Fig. 5.5(a)]. By finding terminal representations of these subnetworks, we may reduce the given network to that of Fig. 5.6(a). The corresponding system graph is shown in Fig. 5.6(b), and we see here that the number of elements that remain is reduced to seven. The terminal equations for the subnetworks may easily be obtained by applying the methods of Chapter 4; and, corresponding to the graph of Fig. 5.6(b), the terminal equations are

$$C_1 \frac{dv_1(t)}{dt} = i_1(t), \tag{5.67}$$

$$\begin{bmatrix} v_4(t) \\ v_2(t) \end{bmatrix} = \begin{bmatrix} 0 & 0 \\ 0 & -r_p - (\mu + 1)R_k \end{bmatrix} \begin{bmatrix} i_4(t) \\ i_2(t) \end{bmatrix} + \begin{bmatrix} 1 \\ -\mu \end{bmatrix} [E(t)], \tag{5.68}$$

$$L_3 \frac{di_3(t)}{dt} = v_3(t), \tag{5.69}$$

$$\frac{d}{dt} \begin{bmatrix} L_{55} & L_{56} \\ L_{56} & L_{66} \end{bmatrix} \begin{bmatrix} i_5(t) \\ i_6(t) \end{bmatrix} = \begin{bmatrix} v_5(t) \\ v_6(t) \end{bmatrix}, \tag{5.70}$$

$$i_7(t) = 0. \tag{5.71}$$

Hence, we classify the elements of the system graph as

Element	Classification
1	First-order V element
2	Algebraic element
3, 5, 6	First-order I element
4	Voltage driver
7	Current driver

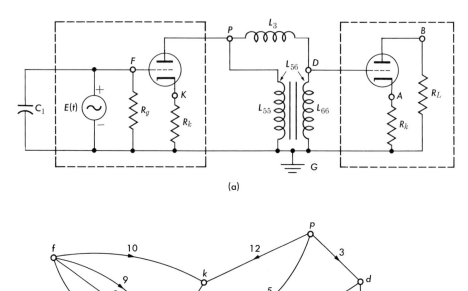

(a)

(b)

FIG. 5.5. Network and graph for Example 5.6.

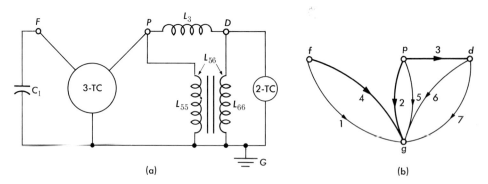

(a)   (b)

FIG. 5.6. Reduction of the network of Fig. 5.5 obtained through the terminal representation of subnetworks.

The formulation tree is picked by the method of Section 5.4, and includes elements 2, 3, and 4 as shown in Fig. 5.6. We can now follow the method outlined at the end of Section 5.5, and write the terminal equations in one matrix expression, which takes the form

$$
\frac{d}{dt}
\begin{bmatrix}
0 & 0 & 0 & 0 & 0 & 0 & 0 \\
0 & 0 & 0 & 0 & 0 & 0 & 0 \\
0 & 0 & 0 & 0 & 0 & 0 & 0 \\
0 & 0 & 0 & 0 & 0 & 0 & 0 \\
0 & 0 & 0 & 0 & L_{55} & L_{56} & 0 \\
0 & 0 & 0 & 0 & L_{56} & L_{66} & 0 \\
0 & 0 & 0 & 0 & 0 & 0 & 0
\end{bmatrix}
\begin{bmatrix}
v_4(t) \\ v_2(t) \\ v_3(t) \\ i_1(t) \\ i_5(t) \\ i_6(t) \\ i_7(t)
\end{bmatrix}
+
\begin{bmatrix}
1 & 0 & 0 & 0 & 0 & 0 & 0 \\
0 & 1 & 0 & 0 & 0 & 0 & 0 \\
0 & 0 & 1 & 0 & 0 & 0 & 0 \\
0 & 0 & 0 & 1 & 0 & 0 & 0 \\
0 & 0 & 0 & 0 & 0 & 0 & 0 \\
0 & 0 & 0 & 0 & 0 & 0 & 0 \\
0 & 0 & 0 & 0 & 0 & 0 & 1
\end{bmatrix}
\begin{bmatrix}
v_4(t) \\ v_2(t) \\ v_3(t) \\ i_1(t) \\ i_5(t) \\ i_6(t) \\ i_7(t)
\end{bmatrix}
$$

$$
= \frac{d}{dt}
\begin{bmatrix}
0 & 0 & 0 & 0 & 0 & 0 & 0 \\
0 & 0 & 0 & 0 & 0 & 0 & 0 \\
0 & 0 & L_3 & 0 & 0 & 0 & 0 \\
0 & 0 & 0 & C_1 & 0 & 0 & 0 \\
0 & 0 & 0 & 0 & 0 & 0 & 0 \\
0 & 0 & 0 & 0 & 0 & 0 & 0 \\
0 & 0 & 0 & 0 & 0 & 0 & 0
\end{bmatrix}
\begin{bmatrix}
i_4(t) \\ i_2(t) \\ i_3(t) \\ v_1(t) \\ v_5(t) \\ v_6(t) \\ v_7(t)
\end{bmatrix}
$$

$$
+
\begin{bmatrix}
0 & 0 & 0 & 0 & 0 & 0 & 0 \\
0 & -R & 0 & 0 & 0 & 0 & 0 \\
0 & 0 & 0 & 0 & 0 & 0 & 0 \\
0 & 0 & 0 & 0 & 0 & 0 & 0 \\
0 & 0 & 0 & 0 & 1 & 0 & 0 \\
0 & 0 & 0 & 0 & 0 & 1 & 0 \\
0 & 0 & 0 & 0 & 0 & 0 & 0
\end{bmatrix}
\begin{bmatrix}
i_4(t) \\ i_2(t) \\ i_3(t) \\ v_1(t) \\ v_5(t) \\ v_6(t) \\ v_7(t)
\end{bmatrix}
+
\begin{bmatrix}
E(t) \\ -\mu E(t) \\ 0 \\ 0 \\ 0 \\ 0 \\ 0
\end{bmatrix},
\qquad (5.72)
$$

where

$$
R = r_p + (\mu + 1) R_k. \qquad (5.73)
$$

The substitution of the cut-set and circuit equations into (5.72) yields, after some rearrangement,

$$
\frac{d}{dt}
\begin{bmatrix}
L_{55} & L_{56} & 0 & 0 \\
L_{56} & L_{66} & 0 & 0 \\
0 & 0 & 0 & 0 \\
0 & 0 & 0 & 0 \\
0 & 0 & 0 & 0 \\
0 & -L_3 & 0 & -L_3 \\
0 & 0 & -C_1 & 0
\end{bmatrix}
\begin{bmatrix}
i_5(t) \\ i_6(t) \\ v_4(t) \\ i_7(t)
\end{bmatrix}
$$

$$
=
\begin{bmatrix}
0 & 0 & 0 & 0 & 1 & 0 & 0 \\
0 & 0 & 0 & 0 & 1 & -1 & 0 \\
0 & 0 & -1 & 0 & 0 & 0 & 0 \\
0 & 0 & 0 & 1 & 0 & 0 & 0 \\
R & R & 0 & R & -1 & 0 & 0 \\
0 & 0 & 0 & 0 & 0 & -1 & 0 \\
0 & 0 & 0 & 0 & 0 & 0 & 1
\end{bmatrix}
\begin{bmatrix}
i_5(t) \\ i_6(t) \\ v_4(t) \\ i_7(t) \\ v_2(t) \\ v_3(t) \\ i_1(t)
\end{bmatrix}
+
\begin{bmatrix}
0 \\ 0 \\ E(t) \\ 0 \\ -\mu E(t) \\ 0 \\ 0
\end{bmatrix}. \qquad (5.74)
$$

We split Eqs. (5.74) into groups as follows:

$$\frac{d}{dt}\begin{bmatrix} L_{55} & L_{56} \\ L_{56} & L_{66} \end{bmatrix}\begin{bmatrix} i_5(t) \\ i_6(t) \end{bmatrix} = \begin{bmatrix} 1 & 0 & 0 \\ 1 & -1 & 0 \end{bmatrix}\begin{bmatrix} v_2(t) \\ v_3(t) \\ i_1(t) \end{bmatrix},\tag{5.75}$$

$$\begin{bmatrix} 0 \\ 0 \end{bmatrix} = \begin{bmatrix} -1 & 0 \\ 0 & 1 \end{bmatrix}\begin{bmatrix} v_4(t) \\ i_7(t) \end{bmatrix} + \begin{bmatrix} E(t) \\ 0 \end{bmatrix},\tag{5.76}$$

$$\frac{d}{dt}\begin{bmatrix} 0 & 0 \\ 0 & -L_3 \\ 0 & 0 \end{bmatrix}\begin{bmatrix} i_5(t) \\ i_6(t) \end{bmatrix} + \frac{d}{dt}\begin{bmatrix} 0 & 0 \\ 0 & -L_3 \\ -C_1 & 0 \end{bmatrix}\begin{bmatrix} v_4(t) \\ i_7(t) \end{bmatrix} = \begin{bmatrix} R & R \\ 0 & 0 \\ 0 & 0 \end{bmatrix}\begin{bmatrix} i_5(t) \\ i_6(t) \end{bmatrix} + \begin{bmatrix} 0 & R \\ 0 & 0 \\ 0 & 0 \end{bmatrix}\begin{bmatrix} v_4(t) \\ i_7(t) \end{bmatrix}$$
$$+ \begin{bmatrix} -\mu E(t) \\ 0 \\ 0 \end{bmatrix} + \begin{bmatrix} -1 & 0 & 0 \\ 0 & -1 & 0 \\ 0 & 0 & -1 \end{bmatrix}\begin{bmatrix} v_2(t) \\ v_3(t) \\ i_1(t) \end{bmatrix}.\tag{5.77}$$

The state equations are obtained by solving (5.77) for $v_2(t)$, $v_3(t)$, and $i_1(t)$, and substituting the result into (5.75). This gives

$$\frac{d}{dt}\begin{bmatrix} L_{55} & L_{56} \\ L_{56} & L_{66} \end{bmatrix}\begin{bmatrix} i_5(t) \\ i_6(t) \end{bmatrix} = \frac{d}{dt}\begin{bmatrix} 0 & 0 \\ 0 & -L_3 \end{bmatrix}\begin{bmatrix} i_5(t) \\ i_6(t) \end{bmatrix} + \frac{d}{dt}\begin{bmatrix} 0 & 0 \\ 0 & -L_3 \end{bmatrix}\begin{bmatrix} v_4(t) \\ i_7(t) \end{bmatrix}$$
$$+ \begin{bmatrix} R & R \\ R & R \end{bmatrix}\begin{bmatrix} i_5(t) \\ i_6(t) \end{bmatrix} + \begin{bmatrix} 0 & R \\ 0 & R \end{bmatrix}\begin{bmatrix} v_4(t) \\ i_7(t) \end{bmatrix} + \begin{bmatrix} -\mu E(t) \\ -\mu E(t) \end{bmatrix},\tag{5.78}$$

or

$$\frac{d}{dt}\begin{bmatrix} L_{55} & L_{56} \\ L_{56} & L_{66} + L_3 \end{bmatrix}\begin{bmatrix} i_5(t) \\ i_6(t) \end{bmatrix} = \begin{bmatrix} R & R \\ R & R \end{bmatrix}\begin{bmatrix} i_5(t) \\ i_6(t) \end{bmatrix} + \frac{d}{dt}\begin{bmatrix} 0 \\ -L_3 i_7(t) \end{bmatrix} + \begin{bmatrix} R i_7(t) \\ R i_7(t) \end{bmatrix} + \begin{bmatrix} -\mu E(t) \\ -\mu E(t) \end{bmatrix},\tag{5.79}$$

which, because of (5.76), becomes

$$\frac{d}{dt}\begin{bmatrix} i_5(t) \\ i_6(t) \end{bmatrix} = \begin{bmatrix} L_{55} & L_{56} \\ L_{56} & L_{66} + L_3 \end{bmatrix}^{-1}\left\{ \begin{bmatrix} R & R \\ R & R \end{bmatrix}\begin{bmatrix} i_5(t) \\ i_6(t) \end{bmatrix} + \begin{bmatrix} -\mu E(t) \\ -\mu E(t) \end{bmatrix}\right\}.\tag{5.80}$$

Note that in this example we were able to reduce the number of equations which it was necessary to handle from 13 to 7, a considerable saving. Should we wish to go much further, it is necessary, as we stated before, to extend our formulation technique.

It is beyond the scope of this book to provide a detailed study of a direct method for finding the state equations associated with a given network when its components have terminal equations of higher order than the first. We shall content ourselves with a brief description of an extension of our technique of the previous sections.

Clearly, the element classification which we introduced in Section 5.4 is insufficient to take into account high derivatives in the terminal equations. To extend this classification, we examine the derivatives of the various voltages and currents, and find, for a given element, the highest derivative. If this is the nth derivative of a voltage, (current), the corresponding element is called an nth order

V element (nth order I element). Of course, a given element could be both an nth order V element and an nth order I element; such an element is classified as an nth order VI element.

Having extended the classification of the elements, we must make a corresponding extension of the technique for choosing the formulation forest. We wish to place as many of the V elements in the forest as possible, and as many of the I elements in the coforest as possible, giving preference to the higher-order elements in each case; it is of no concern to us whether or not the VI elements are placed in the forest. Therefore, we define subgraphs in a manner similar to that of Section 5.4: the first includes the voltage drivers only; the second includes the first subgraph, and the highest-order V elements, say nth order; the third includes the second together with the $(n - 1)$th-order V elements, etc. Finally, the last subgraph includes all the elements of the next to last, and the current drivers. Thus, we have

$$G_1 \subset G_2 \subset \cdots \subset G_N = G. \tag{5.81}$$

We choose forests of the G_i such that

$$T_1 \subset T_2 \subset \cdots \subset T_N = T, \tag{5.82}$$

and T is the required forest.

The formulation of the state equations follows the same technique as given in Section 5.5. The terminal equations are written in a matrix expression, in which the various derivative terms are separated, and the variables are arranged so that substitution of the circuit and cut-set equations is simple. The branch currents and chord voltages are eliminated by this substitution, and in the resulting equations the various algebraic relations are substituted into the differential equations. As a result of these operations, the network equations are reduced to a set of linear differential equations whose variables are some of the state variables. Using a technique similar to that of Section 5.2, we finally obtain the canonical form by defining new variables equal to the several derivatives of higher order than the first that may appear.

It should be noted that the state variables obtained in this manner are not all directly measurable. They consist of a subset of the branch voltages and chord currents, and some of their time derivatives. Thus, by using the terminal representations of subnetworks of a given network, we lose topological information. This, of course, is no accident. The original three sets of equations (cut-set, fundamental circuit, and terminal), contain all the information about the network and its topology. Should any of these equations be eliminated in a partial solution of the network, some of this information must be lost. In particular, we can have no knowledge of the internal structure of a subnetwork when only its terminal representation is known. Hence the formulation technique of Section 5.5 retains the maximum amount of topological information consistent with using a state equation model for a given network. Nonetheless, when we do not require all the topological information, a considerable saving in calculation may be obtained through the use of the terminal-representation technique.

5.7. TIME-VARYING AND NONLINEAR COMPONENTS

The state equation model for a given system is of considerable importance when
the system in question contains components whose associated terminal equations
are either
(a) linear differential or algebraic equations with time-varying coefficients;
(b) nonlinear differential or algebraic equations.
One reason for this is that complete solutions for such networks are not easily
found by analytical methods, so that it becomes necessary to use numerical computations. Another is that it is appropriate to study the stability of such networks
through Lyapunov's methods, which require that systems be characterized by
their state equations.

Although we have concerned ourselves only with simple networks whose components have terminal relations which are linear algebraic or differential equations
with constant coefficients, it is reasonable to point out briefly how our methods
might be extended to include the more complex situations. Let us therefore first
turn our attention to time-varying coefficients.

Suppose, for instance, that the network of Example 5.5 is replaced by one whose
component terminal equations are similar to those of the original network (Eqs.
5.50), but such that the nonzero coefficients are all replaced by functions of time.
This has no effect on the substitution of the cut-set and fundamental circuit equations; nor does it alter the manner in which we split the equations into four groups
and eliminate the algebraic relations. It is only when we reduce the equations to
the form [analogous to Eqs. (5.65)]

$$\frac{d}{dt}[A(t)][X(t)] = [B(t)][X(t)] + [F(t)], \tag{5.83}$$

that any change can occur. In Example 5.5 we solved Eqs. (5.65) for the derivatives of the state variables and obtained the state equations; here we must proceed
as follows:

$$\frac{d}{dt}[A(t)][X(t)] = \left\{\frac{d}{dt}[A(t)]\right\}[X(t)] + [A(t)]\frac{d}{dt}[X(t)], \tag{5.84}$$

so that, from (5.83) and (5.84),

$$\left\{\frac{d}{dt}[A(t)]\right\}[X(t)] + [A(t)]\frac{d}{dt}[X(t)] = [B(t)][X(t)] + [F(t)], \tag{5.85}$$

or

$$[A(t)]\frac{d}{dt}[X(t)] = \left\{[B(t)] - \frac{d}{dt}[A(t)]\right\}[X(t)] + [F(t)], \tag{5.86}$$

and

$$\frac{d}{dt}[X(t)] = [A(t)]^{-1}\left\{[B(t)] - \frac{d}{dt}[A(t)]\right\}[X(t)] + [A(t)]^{-1}[F(t)]. \tag{5.87}$$

Thus we merely have to differentiate the left-hand side of (5.83) before inverting the coefficient matrix. We use the ordinary rule for the differentiation of a product, and note that the derivative of a matrix is the matrix of the derivatives of its entries.

Hence no real difficulty is encountered in the *formulation* of the state equations when time-varying coefficients are encountered in the component terminal relations. The following simple example will illustrate the procedure.

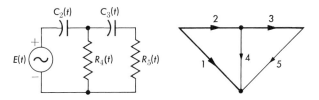

Fig. 5.7. A time-varying network.

EXAMPLE 5.7. Consider the simple network and graph of Fig. 5.7. In this network, let us assume that

$$C_2(t) = C_{2m} \sin \omega t, \qquad C_3(t) = C_{3m}e^{-\lambda t},$$
$$R_4(t) = R_{4m} \cos 2\omega t, \qquad R_5(t) = R_{5m}e^{-\sigma t}. \tag{5.88}$$

To formulate the state equations, we proceed by the method of Section 5.3, and write the terminal equations,

$$v_1(t) = E(t), \tag{5.89}$$

$$\frac{d}{dt}\begin{bmatrix} C_{2m} \sin \omega t & 0 \\ 0 & C_{3m}e^{-\lambda t} \end{bmatrix}\begin{bmatrix} v_2(t) \\ v_3(t) \end{bmatrix} = \begin{bmatrix} i_2(t) \\ i_3(t) \end{bmatrix}, \tag{5.90}$$

$$\begin{bmatrix} R_{4m} \cos 2\omega t & 0 \\ 0 & R_{5m}e^{-\sigma t} \end{bmatrix}\begin{bmatrix} i_4(t) \\ i_5(t) \end{bmatrix} = \begin{bmatrix} v_4(t) \\ v_5(t) \end{bmatrix}. \tag{5.91}$$

The cut-set equations are

$$\begin{bmatrix} i_2(t) \\ i_3(t) \end{bmatrix} = \begin{bmatrix} 1 & 1 \\ 0 & 1 \end{bmatrix}\begin{bmatrix} i_4(t) \\ i_5(t) \end{bmatrix}, \tag{5.92}$$

and the fundamental circuit equations,

$$\begin{bmatrix} v_4(t) \\ v_5(t) \end{bmatrix} = \begin{bmatrix} -1 & 0 \\ -1 & -1 \end{bmatrix}\begin{bmatrix} v_2(t) \\ v_3(t) \end{bmatrix} + \begin{bmatrix} 1 \\ 1 \end{bmatrix}[v_1(t)]. \tag{5.93}$$

Substituting the cut-set equations into (5.90), we obtain

$$\frac{d}{dt}\begin{bmatrix} C_{2m} \sin \omega t & 0 \\ 0 & C_{3m}e^{-\lambda t} \end{bmatrix}\begin{bmatrix} v_2(t) \\ v_3(t) \end{bmatrix} = \begin{bmatrix} 1 & 1 \\ 0 & 1 \end{bmatrix}\begin{bmatrix} i_4(t) \\ i_5(t) \end{bmatrix}, \tag{5.94}$$

and substituting the fundamental circuit equations into (5.91),

$$\begin{bmatrix} R_{4m}\cos 2\omega t & 0 \\ 0 & R_{5m}e^{-\sigma t} \end{bmatrix}\begin{bmatrix} i_4(t) \\ i_5(t) \end{bmatrix} = \begin{bmatrix} -1 & 0 \\ -1 & -1 \end{bmatrix}\begin{bmatrix} v_2(t) \\ v_3(t) \end{bmatrix} + \begin{bmatrix} 1 \\ 1 \end{bmatrix}[v_1(t)]. \qquad (5.95)$$

We solve (5.95) for $i_4(t)$ and $i_5(t)$, and obtain

$$\begin{bmatrix} i_4(t) \\ i_5(t) \end{bmatrix} = \begin{bmatrix} -1/R_{4m}\cos 2\omega t & 0 \\ -1/R_{5m}e^{-\sigma t} & -1/R_{5m}e^{-\sigma t} \end{bmatrix}\begin{bmatrix} v_2(t) \\ v_3(t) \end{bmatrix} + \begin{bmatrix} 1/R_{4m}\cos 2\omega t \\ 1/R_{5m}e^{-\sigma t} \end{bmatrix}[v_1(t)].$$

$$(5.96)$$

Next, we substitute (5.96) into (5.94). This gives

$$\frac{d}{dt}\begin{bmatrix} C_{2m}\sin \omega t & 0 \\ 0 & C_{3m}e^{-\lambda t} \end{bmatrix}\begin{bmatrix} v_2(t) \\ v_3(t) \end{bmatrix} = \begin{bmatrix} 1 & 1 \\ 0 & 1 \end{bmatrix}\begin{bmatrix} -1/R_{4m}\cos 2\omega t & 0 \\ -1/R_{5m}e^{-\sigma t} & -1/R_{5m}e^{-\sigma t} \end{bmatrix}\begin{bmatrix} v_2(t) \\ v_3(t) \end{bmatrix}$$

$$+ \begin{bmatrix} 1 & 1 \\ 0 & 1 \end{bmatrix}\begin{bmatrix} 1/R_{4m}\cos 2\omega t \\ 1/R_{5m}e^{-\sigma t} \end{bmatrix}[v_1(t)], \qquad (5.97)$$

or

$$\frac{d}{dt}\begin{bmatrix} C_{2m}\sin \omega t & 0 \\ 0 & C_{3m}e^{-\lambda t} \end{bmatrix}\begin{bmatrix} v_2(t) \\ v_3(t) \end{bmatrix} = \begin{bmatrix} -1/R_{4m}\cos 2\omega t - 1/R_{5m}e^{-\sigma t} & -1/R_{5m}e^{-\sigma t} \\ -1/R_{5m}e^{-\sigma t} & -1/R_{5m}e^{-\sigma t} \end{bmatrix}$$

$$\times \begin{bmatrix} v_2(t) \\ v_3(t) \end{bmatrix} + \begin{bmatrix} 1/R_{4m}\cos 2\omega t + 1/R_{5m}e^{-\sigma t} \\ 1/R_{5m}e^{-\sigma t} \end{bmatrix}[v_1(t)]. \qquad (5.98)$$

Now, we differentiate the left-hand side of (5.98), and obtain

$$\begin{bmatrix} C_{2m}\omega \cos \omega t & 0 \\ 0 & -C_{3m}\lambda e^{-\lambda t} \end{bmatrix}\begin{bmatrix} v_2(t) \\ v_3(t) \end{bmatrix} + \begin{bmatrix} C_{2m}\sin \omega t & 0 \\ 0 & C_{3m}e^{-\lambda t} \end{bmatrix}\frac{d}{dt}\begin{bmatrix} v_2(t) \\ v_3(t) \end{bmatrix}$$

$$= \begin{bmatrix} -1/R_{4m}\cos 2\omega t - 1/R_{5m}e^{-\sigma t} & -1/R_{5m}e^{-\sigma t} \\ -1/R_{5m}e^{-\sigma t} & -1/R_{5m}e^{-\sigma t} \end{bmatrix}\begin{bmatrix} v_2(t) \\ v_3(t) \end{bmatrix}$$

$$+ \begin{bmatrix} 1/R_{4m}\cos 2\omega t + 1/R_{5m}e^{-\sigma t} \\ 1/R_{5m}e^{-\sigma t} \end{bmatrix}[v_1(t)]. \qquad (5.99)$$

We rearrange (5.99), by combining the first term on the left with the first term on the right. This yields

$$\begin{bmatrix} C_{2m}\sin \omega t & 0 \\ 0 & C_{3m}e^{-\lambda t} \end{bmatrix}\frac{d}{dt}\begin{bmatrix} v_2(t) \\ v_3(t) \end{bmatrix}$$

$$= \begin{bmatrix} -1/R_{4m}\cos 2\omega t - 1/R_{5m}e^{-\sigma t} - C_{2m}\omega \cos \omega t & -1/R_{5m}e^{-\sigma t} \\ -1/R_{5m}e^{-\sigma t} & C_{3m}\lambda e^{-\lambda t} - 1/R_{5m}e^{-\sigma t} \end{bmatrix}\begin{bmatrix} v_2(t) \\ v_3(t) \end{bmatrix}$$

$$+ \begin{bmatrix} 1/R_{4m}\cos 2\omega t + 1/R_{5m}e^{-\sigma t} \\ 1/R_{5m}e^{-\sigma t} \end{bmatrix}[v_1(t)]. \qquad (5.100)$$

We finally obtain the state equations by inverting the coefficient matrix on the left of (5.100), and substituting for $v_1(t)$ from (5.89). The result is

$$\frac{d}{dt}\begin{bmatrix} v_2(t) \\ v_3(t) \end{bmatrix}$$

$$= \begin{bmatrix} (1/C_{2m} \sin \omega t)(-1/R_{4m} \cos 2\omega t - 1/R_{5m}e^{-\sigma t} - C_{2m}\omega \cos \omega t) & -1/C_{2m}R_{5m}e^{-\sigma t} \sin \omega t \\ -1/C_{3m}R_{5m}e^{-(\sigma+\lambda)t} & \lambda - 1/C_{3m}R_{5m}e^{-(\sigma+\lambda)t} \end{bmatrix}$$

$$\times \begin{bmatrix} v_2(t) \\ v_3(t) \end{bmatrix} + \begin{bmatrix} (1/C_{2m} \sin \omega t)(1/R_{4m} \cos 2\omega t + 1/R_{5m}e^{-\sigma t}) \\ 1/C_{3m}R_{5m}e^{-(\sigma+\lambda)t} \end{bmatrix} [E(t)]. \qquad (5.101)$$

As expected, the only difference in the procedure from the time-invariant case is the differentiation of the coefficient matrix of the state variables in Eqs. (5.98). Clearly, time-invariant networks are merely special cases of time-varying ones; the differentiation involved with constant coefficients is trivial.

When nonlinear components are encountered, the situation is much more complicated. It is not always clear whether or not there exists a solution for a set of nonlinear equations, and even if one does exist, there is seldom any analytical method for finding it. Matrix methods cannot be used to handle sets of nonlinear equations.

Nevertheless, we can always eliminate the chord voltages and branch currents from a set of nonlinear terminal equations; this can be done by simple substitution because the cut-set and fundamental circuit equations are linear.

Let us assume that the terminal equations of a given nonlinear network are, at worst, first-order differential equations. We can still classify the elements according to our method of Section 5.4. If there are no first-order VI elements, and if we can locate all the first-order V elements in the forest, and all the first-order I elements in the coforest, the situation is considerably simplified. If we assume in addition that the differential terminal relations can be written explicitly in the derivatives of the first-order elements, we can proceed to eliminate all the branch currents and chord voltages through the cut-set and circuit equations. This simplification will result in a set of equations which express the derivatives of the voltages of the branch first-order V elements and the derivatives of the currents of the chord first-order I elements in terms of all the branch voltages and chord currents.

Now, if the algebraic terminal relations can be written to show the voltages of the branch algebraic elements and the currents of the chord algebraic elements explicitly in terms of the remaining variables, we can substitute them into the differential equations and obtain the state equations.

This method requires that the equations can be written in rather special forms; unfortunately, we cannot give a reasonable criterion for deciding whether or not it is possible to write the equations in the required configuration. That is, no tractable set of necessary and sufficient conditions for the existence of sets of state equations for nonlinear networks has yet been formulated.

5.8. ANALYTICAL SOLUTION OF THE STATE EQUATIONS

The previous sections of this chapter were devoted to the formulation of sets of state equations characterizing electric networks. For the remainder of the chapter we shall consider different techniques for their solution. Accordingly, in this section we shall briefly introduce a method with which we can obtain, at least in principle, analytical solutions of the state equations for linear networks. This direct time-domain method will also be very useful in our discussion of a numerical technique in the next section.

For simplicity, let us first consider a network characterized by one state equation,

$$\frac{dx(t)}{dt} = ax(t) + f(t). \tag{5.102}$$

We can easily solve this equation by rearranging it to read

$$\frac{dx(t)}{dt} - ax(t) = f(t), \tag{5.103}$$

and multiplying both sides by the *integrating factor* e^{-at}. This gives

$$e^{-at}\frac{dx(t)}{dt} - ae^{-at}x(t) = e^{-at}f(t), \tag{5.104}$$

or

$$\frac{d}{dt}\left(x(t)e^{-at}\right) = e^{-at}f(t). \tag{5.105}$$

Hence,

$$\int_{t_0}^{t} \frac{d}{d\tau}\left(x(\tau)e^{-a\tau}\right)d\tau = \int_{t_0}^{t} e^{-a\tau}f(\tau)\,d\tau, \tag{5.106}$$

and the solution is

$$x(t)e^{-a(t)} - x(t_0)e^{-at_0} = \int_{t_0}^{t} e^{-a\tau}f(\tau)\,d\tau, \tag{5.107}$$

or

$$x(t) = e^{a(t-t_0)}x(t_0) + e^{at}\int_{t_0}^{t} e^{-a\tau}f(\tau)\,d\tau. \tag{5.108}$$

The solution of the set of state equations

$$\frac{d}{dt}[X(t)] = [A][X(t)] + [F(t)] \tag{5.109}$$

can be written by drawing an analogy between (5.109) and (5.102). This solution is

$$[X(t)] = [e^{(t-t_0)[A]}][X(t_0)] + [e^{t[A]}]\int_{t_0}^{t} [e^{-\tau[A]}][F(\tau)]\,d\tau. \tag{5.110}$$

It is easy to verify that (5.110) is the solution of (5.109), provided that we define exponentiation of a square matrix by

$$[e^{t[A]}] = [U] + \frac{t}{1!}[A] + \frac{t^2}{2!}[A]^2 + \frac{t^3}{3!}[A]^3 + \cdots \tag{5.111}$$

$$= [U] + \sum_{i=1}^{\infty} \frac{t^i}{i!}[A]^i \tag{5.112}$$

and

$$[e^{-t[A]}] = [e^{t[A]}]^{-1} = [U] + \sum_{i=1}^{\infty} \frac{(-1)^i t^i}{i!}[A]^i. \tag{5.113}$$

The integral of a matrix is also required in (5.110). This is defined as the matrix whose entries are the integrals of those of the original matrix.

Incidentally, one simple way of finding the exponential matrix in (5.110) is through the Laplace transform. This is because the solution obtained by the Laplace transform method must, of course, be identical to that obtained by the time-domain method. Consider the homogeneous equations

$$\frac{d}{dt}[X(t)] = [A][X(t)]. \tag{5.114}$$

The Laplace transform equations are

$$s[X(s)] = [A][X(s)] + [X(0+)], \tag{5.115}$$

where $[X(0+)]$ are the initial conditions of the state vector $[X(t)]$.

The solution of (5.115) is given by

$$[sU - A][X(s)] = [X(0+)], \tag{5.116}$$

or

$$[X(s)] = [sU - A]^{-1}[X(0+)]. \tag{5.117}$$

The time solution $[X(t)]$ is obtained by taking the inverse Laplace transform of (5.117), that is,

$$[X(t)] = \mathcal{L}^{-1}[X(s)] = \mathcal{L}^{-1}[sU - A]^{-1}[X(0+)]. \tag{5.118}$$

Comparing (5.118) with the homogeneous part of the solution in (5.110) at $t_0 = 0$, we find

$$[e^{t[A]}] = \mathcal{L}^{-1}[sU - A]^{-1}. \tag{5.119}$$

The above relation is introduced just for the sake of establishing the correspondence between the Laplace transform solution and the time-domain solution in the linear case. There is, of course, no need to appeal to Laplace transform techniques for the computation of $[e^{t[A]}]$.

A direct method for calculating $[e^{t[A]}]$ which is widely in vogue in mathematical literature is through *functions of matrices*. These methods are very elegant and lend further insight into linear analysis. However, we shall not dwell on them, for our primary aim is to give a numerical procedure which is suitable for digital computation. In the following section, we shall use the solution of (5.109) as the starting point for a numerical solution of the state equations.

5.9. A NUMERICAL METHOD FOR SOLVING THE STATE EQUATIONS*

It is unlikely that the analytical solution of the state equations presented in Section 5.8 would ever be particularly useful in itself for large systems. However, in this section we shall introduce a numerical technique for evaluating the solution (Eqs. 5.110).

Direct numerical integration of the state equations is entirely possible; however, when the specified functions involved are of a simple nature, such as exponentials, sinusoids, or step functions, the use of the analytical solution as the basis for a numerical technique can prove to be more economical. Furthermore, when the coefficient matrix of the state equations has few zero entries, the method which we shall present is decidedly advantageous. It is also very convenient when various different sets of driving functions are to be applied to a given network.

To simplify our technique, let us assume that the solution starts at time zero, so that it is given by

$$[X(t)] = [e^{t[A]}][X(0)] + [e^{t[A]}] \int_0^t [e^{-\tau[A]}][F(\tau)] \, d\tau. \tag{5.120}$$

In order to obtain a recursion for calculating successive values of the solution $[X(0)]$, $[X(h)]$, $[X(2h)]$, etc., we examine $[X(t + h)]$. From (5.120) we find this to be

$$[X(t+h)] = [e^{(t+h)[A]}][X(0)] + [e^{(t+h)[A]}] \int_0^{t+h} [e^{-\tau[A]}][F(\tau)] \, d\tau \tag{5.121}$$

$$= [e^{h[A]}]\{[e^{t[A]}][X(0)] + [e^{t[A]}] \int_0^t [e^{-\tau[A]}][F(\tau)] \, d\tau\}$$

$$+ [e^{(t+h)[A]}] \int_t^{t+h} [e^{-\tau[A]}][F(\tau)] \, d\tau \tag{5.122}$$

$$= [e^{h[A]}]\{[X(t)] + [e^{t[A]}] \int_t^{t+h} [e^{-\tau[A]}][F(\tau)] \, d\tau\} \cdot \tag{5.123}$$

In (5.123) we make the change of variable $\xi = \tau - t$, and obtain

$$[X(t+h)] = [e^{h[A]}]\{[X(t)] + [e^{t[A]}] \int_0^h [e^{-(\xi+t)[A]}][F(\xi+t)] \, d\xi\} \tag{5.124}$$

$$= [e^{h[A]}]\{[X(t)] + \int_0^h [e^{-\xi[A]}][F(\xi+t)] \, d\xi\}, \tag{5.125}$$

which is an effective recursion relation.

---

* The method to be presented here was suggested by J. D. Lawson, Department of Mathematics, University of Waterloo, Waterloo, Ontario, Canada.

To obtain a numerical solution for the state equations using (5.125), we must deal with two problems. We must be able to compute the exponential function of a matrix, and we need an accurate numerical quadrature (integration) formula. One of the more sophisticated Gaussian quadrature formulas, the Lobatto quadrature, is very suitable for this purpose. The well-known Simpson's rule is a special case of the Lobatto formula, and to maintain a simple procedure, we shall use it for our solution. The required formula is

$$\int_0^h [G(t)]\, dt = \frac{h}{6}[G(0)] + \frac{2h}{3}\left[G\left(\frac{h}{2}\right)\right] + \frac{h}{6}[G(h)] - \frac{h^5}{2880}[G^{(4)}(\theta)], \qquad (5.126)$$

where $0 \leq \theta \leq h$, and the superscript $^{(4)}$ indicates the fourth derivative.

We apply (5.126) to the integral in (5.125), so that our solution becomes

$$[X(t+h)] = [e^{h[A]}][X(t)] + \frac{h}{6}[e^{h[A]}][F(t)]$$

$$+ \frac{2h}{3}[e^{(h/2)[A]}]\left[F\left(t+\frac{h}{2}\right)\right] + \frac{h}{6}[F(t+h)] + [E(h)], \quad (5.127)$$

where the error $[E(h)]$ is given by

$$[E(h)] = -\frac{h^5}{2880}[e^{h[A]}]\frac{d^4}{d\xi^4}\{[e^{-\xi[A]}][F(\xi+t)]\}\Big|_{\xi=\theta}. \qquad (5.128)$$

It is necessary to estimate the error term in order to pick an economical value for h in our calculation. In general, this is not an easy problem since we know nothing about either θ or the fourth-derivative term in (5.128). The simplest method for checking whether or not a chosen value for h is reasonable consists in recalculating some of the results with a new value of h and making a comparison. Nevertheless, we should have some criterion for our original choice. Let us therefore consider the case in which there is only one state equation, so that $[A]$ and $[F(t)]$ become the scalars a and $f(t)$. If, in this case, $f(t) = b_i \sin(\omega_i t + \phi_i)$ or $f(t) = b_i e^{\omega_i t}$, we find, by actual differentiation, that the error is

$$|E(h)| \leq \frac{h^5}{2880} e^{ah}|b_i|(a+|\omega_i|)^4. \qquad (5.129)$$

We extend this result by analogy to the set of state equations. In doing so we make the assumption that e^{ah} may be replaced by $e^{\rho([A])h}$, where $\rho([A])$ is the magnitude of the largest eigenvalue of $[A]$, or the *spectral radius* of $[A]$. Thus, when the driving functions, or entries in $[F(t)]$, are all either sinusoidal or exponential functions, a reasonable estimate for largest entry in $[E(h)]$ is

$$E \approx \frac{h^5}{2880} e^{\rho([A])h}B[\rho([A])+\Omega]^4, \qquad (5.130)$$

where B, Ω, are the largest $|b_i|$ and $|\omega_i|$ occurring in $[F(t)]$.

When other functions are entries in $[F(t)]$, other means of estimating the error must be found. Also, a further restriction on h is necessary if $[F(t)]$ is only sectionally continuous. The intervals between discontinuities must then be integral multiples of h. Nevertheless, (5.130) can be used to provide a choice for h. Let E be the maximum allowable error; we pick h such that

$$h = 2^{-l} \leq \left\{ \frac{2880E}{B\{\rho([A]) + \Omega\}^4} \right\}^{1/5}, \qquad (5.131)$$

where l is an integer. Here we have neglected the factor $e^{h\rho([A])}$. However, we expect that $h\rho([A])$ will be a small fraction, so that $e^{h\rho([A])}$ is approximately unity. When the driving functions are not simple sinusoids, we can replace Ω by the angular frequency of the highest significant term of their Fourier series.

Let us now turn to the problem of estimating $[e^{h[A]}]$ and $[e^{(h/2)[A]}]$. Clearly,

$$[e^{h[A]}] = [e^{(h/2)[A]}]^2,$$

so that we need only find one exponential function of a matrix, and square it. In order to find this function, we shall use the exponential series. However, it may take a very large number of terms before the error involved in truncating the series becomes small. For instance, in the case of scalars, we find that the eighth term in the series for e^8 is $8^7/7!$, or approximately 420. On the other hand, the eighth term in the series for $e^{1/8}$ is $1/8^7 7!$, or approximately 10^{-10}. This suggests that the first seven terms in the exponential series for $e^{1/8}$ provide a good approximation, from which we could calculate e^8. Thus, since

$$e^8 = (e^{1/8})^{2^6},$$

having computed $e^{1/8}$ from the series, we can obtain e^8 by simply squaring six times. Of course, the relative error is increased by this calculation, but the exponent involved here is much larger than those which we should expect in our calculations.

The above argument suggests that we might calculate e^a by the following procedure:

(a) Find m such that $a/2^m \leq \frac{1}{8} \leq a/2^{m-1}$.

(b) Compute $e^{a/2^m} \approx \sum_{i=0}^{6} 1/i! \, (a/2^m)^i$.

(c) Since $e^a = (e^{a/2^m})^{2^m}$, square the result of (b), m times.

It can be shown that this procedure gives a relative error of less than 10^{-8} for all $a \leq 8$, neglecting round-off errors, while for larger values of a we would require more terms than seven in the truncated series. This is because the relative error is roughly proportional to 2^m.

We shall not enter into a lengthy justification of our next step, which is the extension, by analogy, of the above algorithm, to provide a means for computing the exponential function of a matrix. Suffice it to say that the spectral radius of the matrix can be used to provide a reasonable estimate of the errors involved.

The following algorithm is therefore suggested for finding $[e^{[B]}]$.

(1) Estimate $\rho([B])$.

(2) Compute m such that $\rho([B])/2^m \leq 0.125 \leq \rho([B])/2^{m-1}$.

(3) Define $[\overline{B}] = (1/2^m)[B]$.

(4) Compute $[e^{[\overline{B}]}] = \sum_{i=0}^{6} (1/i!)[\overline{B}]^i$.

(5) $[e^{[B]}] = [e^{[\overline{B}]}]^{2^m}$.

One problem still remains; we must estimate the spectral radius of the coefficient matrix in the state equations. A very crude upper bound on this is

$$r([A]) = \min\left\{\max_j\left(\sum_{i=1}^{n}|a_{ij}|\right), \max_i\left(\sum_{j=1}^{n}|a_{ij}|\right)\right\} > \rho([A]), \qquad (5.132)$$

where n is the order of $[A]$. That is, to estimate the spectral radius, we may first obtain the magnitudes of each of the entries in $[A]$, then find the largest of the sums of the entries in each row, and the largest of the sums of the entries in each column; the spectral radius is less than the smaller of these two sums.

A better estimate of $\rho([A])$ can be obtained from

$$\rho([A]) \leq \rho([A][A]')^{1/2}, \qquad (5.133)$$

and since $[A][A]'$ is symmetrical, its eigenvalues are real. To find $\rho([A][A]')$, we can use the well-known power method*, which proceeds as follows:

(a) Let $[M_1]$ be a column vector (n rows) whose components are all unity, and let B be a symmetrical matrix.

(b) Compute $[B][M_1] = \lambda_1[M_2]$, $[B][M_2] = \lambda_2[M_3]$, etc., in which λ_i is the largest component of $[B][M_i]$.

In general, the sequence in (b) converges to give the largest eigenvalue of $[B]$, say λ. Therefore we obtain $\rho([B]) = \lambda$, and when $[B] = [A][A]'$,

$$\rho([A]) \leq \sqrt{\lambda}. \qquad (5.134)$$

We conclude this section with a brief step-by-step outline of the overall procedure.

Solution of $(d/dt)[X(t)] = [A][X(t)] + [F(t)]$, *given* $[X(0)]$. The solution is given by the recursion formula,

$$[X(t+h)] = [e^{h[A]}][X(t)] + \frac{h}{6}[E^{h[A]}][F(t)] + \frac{2h}{3}[e^{(h/2)[A]}]\left[F\left(t+\frac{h}{2}\right)\right] + \frac{h}{6}[F(t+h)]. \qquad (5.135)$$

A. *Selection of* h

(1) Estimate $\rho([A])$, using the power method.

(2) Compute

$$h_1 = \left\{\frac{2880E}{B(\rho([A]) + \Omega)^4}\right\}^{1/5},$$

---

* See, for instance, R. G. Stanton, *Numerical Methods for Science and Engineering.* Englewood Cliffs, N. J.: Prentice-Hall, 1961.

where E is the maximum allowable error in each step of the solution, B is the maximum magnitude of the largest component of $[F(t)]$ over the range of integration, and Ω is the largest significant angular frequency in $[F(t)]$.

(3) Find l such that $2^{-l} \leq h_1 \leq 2^{-(l-1)}$.

(4) Select $h = 2^{-l}$.

B. *Calculation of* $[e^{(h/2)[A]}]$, $[e^{h[A]}]$

(1) Compute m such that $h\rho([A])/2^m \leq \frac{1}{8} < h\rho([A])/2^{m-1}$.

(2) Define $[\overline{A}] = h/2^m[A]$.   (3) Compute $[e^{[\overline{A}]}] = \sum_{i=0}^{6} [\overline{A}]^i/i!$.

(4) Compute $[e^{(h/2)[A]}] = [e^{[\overline{A}]}]^{2^{m-1}}$.   (5) Compute $[e^{h[A]}] = [e^{(h/2)[A]}]^2$.

C. *Calculation of the solution*

(1) Set $j = 0$.   (2) Compute $(h/6)[F(jh)]$.

(3) Compute $(h/6)[F(jh)] + [X(jh)]$.

(4) Compute $[e^{h[A]}][X(jh)] + (h/6)[F(jh)]$.

(5) Compute $[F((2jh + h)/2)]$.

(6) Compute $(2h/3)[e^{(h/2)[A]}][F((2jh + h)/2)]$.

(7) Compute $[e^{h[A]}]\{[X(jh)] + (h/6)[F(jh)]\} + (2h/3)[e^{(h/2)[A]}][F((2jh + h)/2)]$.

(8) Compute $(h/6)[F(jh + h)]$.

(9) $[X(jh + h)] = [e^{h[A]}]\{[X(jh)] + (h/6)[F(jh)]\}$
$\qquad\qquad + (2h/3)[e^{(h/2)[A]}][F((2jh + h)/2)] + (h/6)[F(jh + h)]$.

(10) Add 1 to j.

(11) Repeat Steps 2 through 11.

Since the estimate for h may be very conservative, we could improve this calculation by comparing some of the initial numerical results for two values of h, say h_1 and $h_2 = 2h_1$. If the difference between these results is less than the maximum error E, the solution could be continued with the larger value of h, or we could again double h, and compare. A procedure of this sort would greatly speed up the calculations, owing to the fact that fewer points would need to be calculated for a given interval.

The calculation of the exponential matrices requires $m + 7$ matrix multiplications, or $(m + 7)n^3$ multiplications. However, this is only done once for a given network and integration step size h. Thus the response of a given network could easily be ascertained by our technique, for several sets of driving functions; far less computation time would be required than that taken by a direct method for numerically integrating the state equations for each set of driving functions.

5.10. ANALOG COMPUTER SOLUTIONS FOR THE STATE EQUATIONS

We have mentioned that not only are the state equations amenable to numerical solution, but also they are in a very suitable form for solution by means of analog computation. In this section we shall indicate how analog computer wiring dia-

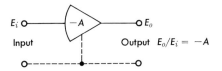

FIG. 5.8. Operational amplifier schematic representation.

grams (or programs) can be obtained for typical sets of state equations. We shall limit our discussion to the solution of linear equations.

The basic operations of an electronic analog computer are: (a) integration, (b) multiplication by a constant, (c) addition, (d) inversion (change of sign). These operations are performed by simple networks which include a very high-gain dc-amplifier, whose open-circuit voltage-transfer function is given by $E_0/E_i = -A$. These amplifiers, called *operational amplifiers*, are usually three-terminal devices which are represented for the purpose of analog computation by the diagram of Fig. 5.8. The common terminal between the input and output is shown dashed in this figure, because it is usually omitted when analog computer wiring diagrams are drawn.

We first consider integration; it is very simple, and we leave it as an exercise to show that when A is very large, the output voltage of the three terminal network of Fig. 5.9(a) is related to the input voltage by

$$e_0(t) = -K \int_0^t e_i(t)\, dt + e_0(0), \qquad (5.136)$$

where $K = 1/RC$. Thus, this circuit accomplishes the operation of integration; it is usually represented on an analog computer diagram by the symbol of Fig. 5.9(b). The constant K in (5.136) can be altered at will by simply changing the numerical value of either the resistance or the capacitance of Fig. 5.9(a).

Now, let us turn to the multiplication of a variable by a constant; we may show, and again we leave it as an exercise, that when A is very large, the network of

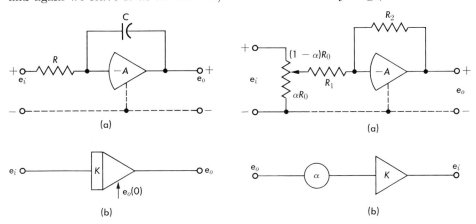

FIG. 5.9. Integrating network

FIG. 5.10. Multiplication by a constant.

Fig. 5.10(a) gives

$$e_0 = -\alpha K e_i \qquad (5.137)$$

where $K = R_2/R_1$ and $0 \leq \alpha \leq 1$. This circuit, which thus allows us to multiply a voltage by any real negative constant, is usually represented diagramatically by the symbol of Fig. 5.10(b). Note that when $\alpha = 1$ and $R_2 = R_1$, Eq. (5.137) reduces to

$$e_0 = -e_i, \qquad (5.138)$$

so that the sign of any voltage may be changed at will. The symbol for sign inversion is shown in Fig. 5.11.

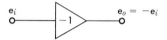

FIG. 5.11. Sign inversion.

Summation of a number of variables, each of which is to be multiplied by an appropriate constant, is achieved by applying several voltages in parallel to the input of an operational amplifier, as shown in Fig. 5.12(a). The output voltage of this network is given by

$$e_0(t) = -\alpha_1 K_1 e_1(t) - \alpha_2 K_2 e_2(t) - \cdots - \alpha_n K_n e_n(t), \qquad (5.139)$$

where

$$K_i = R/R_i, \ 0 \leq \alpha_i \leq 1, \qquad i = 1, 2, \ldots, n.$$

The corresponding symbol for analog computer diagrams is shown in Fig. 5.12(b).

Similarly, we obtain summation and integration of a number of variables by the use of the network of Fig. 5.13(a). For this network

$$e_0(t) = -\int \{K_1 e_1(t) + K_2 e_2(t) + \cdots + K_n e_n(t)\} \, dt + e_0(0), \qquad (5.140)$$

where

$$K_i = 1/R_i C, \qquad i = 1, 2, \ldots, n.$$

The analog computer symbol for this network is shown in Fig. 5.13(b).

Operational amplifiers are used in conjunction with special devices in analog computers to produce many other functions; many analog computers include networks which will, for example, multiply two variables, produce the square or square root of a given variable, find the logarithm of a given variable, or find the exponential function of a variable. These networks usually find their application in the solution of nonlinear problems, or the simulation of nonlinear systems; since we are restricting our discussion to linear systems, we shall not investigate them here.

Having introduced the symbolism of analog computer schematic diagrams, we are now in a position to obtain suitable diagrams to correspond with sets of state equations. We shall do this by illustrating the procedure with a simple example.

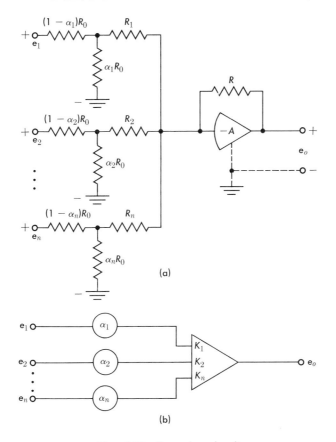

FIG. 5.12. Summing circuit.

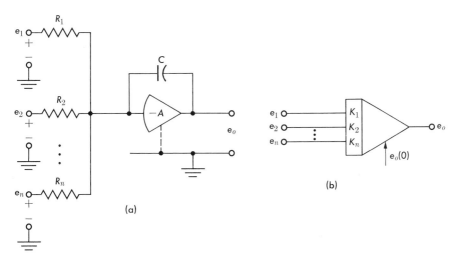

FIG. 5.13. Summing integrator.

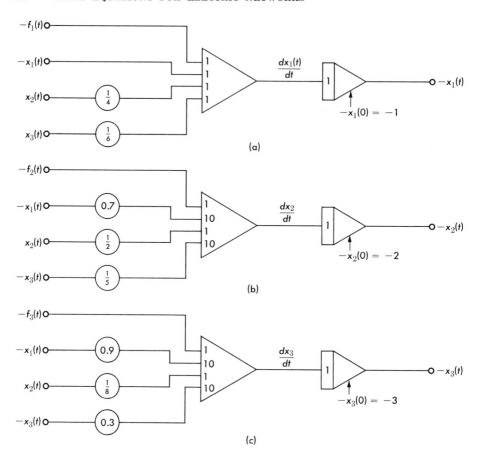

FIG. 5.14. Preliminary analog diagrams for Example 5.8.

EXAMPLE 5.8. In this example we shall find an analog computer diagram corresponding to the equations

$$\frac{d}{dt}\begin{bmatrix} x_1(t) \\ x_2(t) \\ x_3(t) \end{bmatrix} = \begin{bmatrix} 1 & -\frac{1}{4} & -\frac{1}{6} \\ 7 & -\frac{1}{2} & 2 \\ 9 & -\frac{1}{8} & 3 \end{bmatrix} \begin{bmatrix} x_1(t) \\ x_2(t) \\ x_3(t) \end{bmatrix} + \begin{bmatrix} f_1(t) \\ f_2(t) \\ f_3(t) \end{bmatrix}$$

(5.141)

given that

$$\begin{bmatrix} x_1(0) \\ x_2(0) \\ x_3(0) \end{bmatrix} = \begin{bmatrix} 1 \\ 2 \\ 3 \end{bmatrix}.$$

(5.142)

To do this we associate *machine variables* with the variables of the state equations. These are voltages equal to $x_1(t)$, $x_2(t)$, $x_3(t)$, $f_1(t)$, $f_2(t)$, and $f_3(t)$. Now, in correspondence with the first equation of (5.141), we can draw the schematic diagram

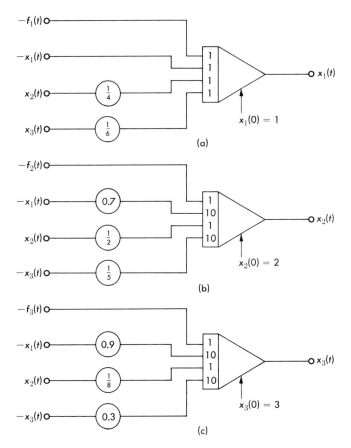

FIG. 5.15. Modification of Fig. 5.14.

of Fig. 5.14(a). This is merely a picture of the statements,

$$-\frac{dx_1(t)}{dt} = x_1(t) - \tfrac{1}{4}x_2(t) - \tfrac{1}{6}x_3(t) + f_1(t), \qquad (5.143)$$

and

$$x_1(t) = \int \frac{dx_1(t)}{dt}\, dt + 1. \qquad (5.144)$$

Figure 5.14(b) and (c) similarly represent the second and third equations of (5.141).

The first noticeable fact about the schematic diagrams of Fig. 5.14 is that each one uses both a summing network and an integrator. We could well combine these operations by using summing integrator networks; and when this is done, we obtain the three diagrams of Fig. 5.15. We note that in this case there is one fewer sign inversion than there was in Fig. 5.14.

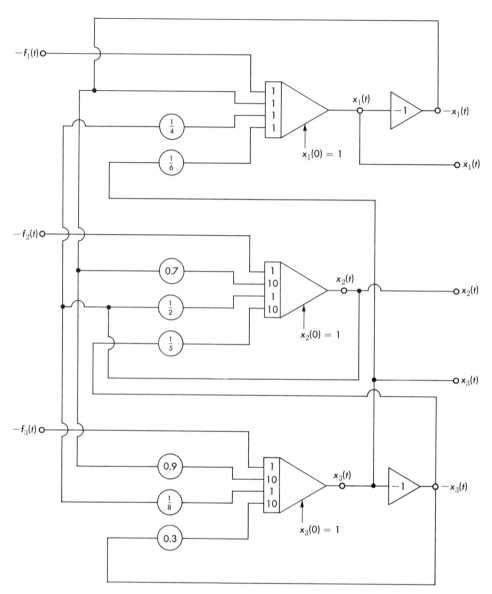

FIG. 5.16. Analog computer diagram for Example 5.8.

Note that the outputs of the three integrators in Fig. 5.15 are just the variables $x_1(t)$, $x_2(t)$, $x_3(t)$. These variables are required at the input of each integrator (sometimes with reversed sign), so that we merely join the diagrams together by feeding their outputs to the appropriate input terminals. In some cases we require a sign inversion network. The result of this operation is shown in Fig. 5.16, which is the required analog computer diagram. The state variables can all be measured as soon as we supply the machine with the required inputs, $-f_1(t)$, $-f_2(t)$, $-f_3(t)$.

Of course, the driving functions of a given network can take any form; to supply them as the inputs for an analog computer program, we can either generate them separately on the computer or use an electronic function generator.

The general method for drawing analog computer diagrams directly from the state equations follows exactly the procedure of our example; with very little practice the diagram can be drawn in one step. We need only note that

(a) The number of summing integrator networks required is exactly the same as the number of state variables.

(b) The output of the ith summing integrator network is the state variable x_i.

(c) The input to the ith summing integrator network corresponds to the negative of the right-hand side of the ith state equation; the input signals are obtained from the outputs of the several summing integrators (using sign inversion networks where necessary), and from a signal source whose output is $-f_i(t)$.

As a result of the above observations, we find the number of operational amplifiers required is less than or equal to twice the number of state variables, while the number of coefficient-setting potentiometers is no greater than the square of the number of state variables.

Practical problems often arise in programming analog computers due to the physical limitations of the operational amplifiers. We cannot apply any voltage whatever to their inputs. For example, in most vacuum-tube analog computers the magnitude of any voltage should not exceed 100 v, and this is reduced to 10 v for some transistorized computers. Also, if the voltages are too small, accuracy is lost because of inherent noise problems. In addition, we cannot compute functions with high-frequency components because of the limited bandwidth of the amplifiers, or with very low frequency characteristics because of amplifier drift. Hence it is frequently necessary to adjust the magnitude and time scale of the computer variables. We shall not pursue this subject any further since it is not our intention to enter into a discussion of the details of analog computer operation; most books on analog computers contain detailed accounts of scaling techniques.

To summarize this section we need merely state that we have observed that the solution of the state equations is very simple using analog computation; the size of the system which can be handled is limited by the number of operational amplifiers and coefficient potentiometers on a given computer.

5.11. SUMMARY

In this chapter we have introduced a direct method for the formulation of the state equations for electric networks. While our treatment was very brief, it should be evident that our method leads, through a series of straightforward steps, to sets of state equations which include the maximum possible number of *directly measurable* state variables. This form of the state equations is the most convenient for many applications; for instance, in a solution by either numerical or analog methods, we directly find some of the variables which can be measured in a given network.

We discussed analytical solutions of the state equations for linear networks in order to obtain a numerical technique for their solution. The method which we introduced is very effective when the same network is to be analyzed under the action of different sets of driving functions or with different initial conditions. Although we used a simple integration formula, which decreases the efficiency of the method, the computing time for our technique compares favorably with direct numerical integration of the state equations.

Finally, we discussed a technique for associating an analog computer wiring diagram with a given set of state equations. It was seen that this method is very simple, and the diagram can usually be drawn directly by inspection of the state equations.

A further problem remains; if a given network problem is too large for a reasonably short analytical solution, we may use either an analog or a digital computer. How do we choose between the two techniques? The answer to this question depends on the problem at hand. If we wish to obtain a very precise knowledge of the response of a given network we only use a digital machine. This can easily give results whose accuracy is better than one part in 10^8. On the other hand, an analog computer can solve sets of differential equations much faster than a digital computer. However, very few analog machines can achieve accuracy as great as one part in 10^4. Nevertheless, because of our ability to adjust the parameters of a system at will, the analog computer is highly effective for checking proposed designs, and for optimizing proposed system parameters.

One final word. We have not discussed the procedure involved in deriving state models of large networks through the state models of their subnetworks. This would entail retaining the set of algebraic equations that we finally eliminated in deriving the state equations, for otherwise it is not possible to characterize the subnetworks completely for the purpose of interconnection. For this reason the first-order differential equations along with the algebraic relations are frequently referred to as the complete state model. This subject is discussed in detail elsewhere,* and our treatment provides all the necessary background for comprehending this development. Furthermore, we already provided a method for reducing the complexity of the derivation of state models for large networks in Section 5.6, where we made use of the concept of terminal representations to reduce the number of algebraic equations before proceeding to the state model.

PROBLEMS

5.1. Given the transfer function

$$\frac{V_2(s)}{V_1(s)} = \frac{5s^3 + 6s^2 + 3s + 2}{s^4 + 4s^3 + 3s^2 + 2s + 1}$$

for a system, find a set of state equations for the same system.

---

* H. E. Koenig, Y. Tokad, and H. K. Kesavan, *Analysis of Discrete Physical Systems.* New York: McGraw-Hill, in press.

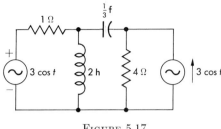

FIGURE 5.17

5.2. Formulate a set of state equations for the network of Fig. 5.17.

5.3. Formulate a set of state equations for the network of Fig. 5.18.

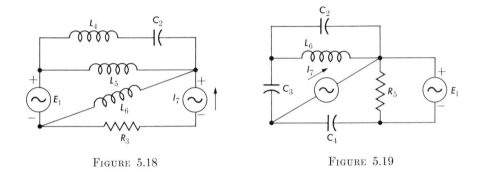

FIGURE 5.18   FIGURE 5.19

5.4. Formulate a set of state equations for the network of Fig. 5.19.

5.5. Formulate a set of state equations for the network of Fig. 5.20. The transformer is ideal.

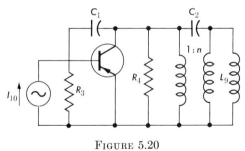

FIGURE 5.20

5.6. Draw an analog computer diagram for the solution of the equations of Problem 5.8.

5.7. Assume that the capacitance in Fig. 5.17 varies sinusoidally with time. Formulate the state equations for the network.

5.8. Use the method of Section 5.8 to find a solution of the equations

$$\frac{d}{dt}\begin{bmatrix} x_1(t) \\ x_2(t) \end{bmatrix} = \begin{bmatrix} 1 & 2 \\ 4 & 5 \end{bmatrix}\begin{bmatrix} x_1(t) \\ x_2(t) \end{bmatrix} + \begin{bmatrix} 3 \\ 2 \end{bmatrix}.$$

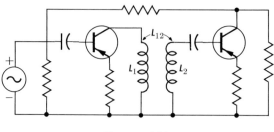

FIGURE 5.21

5.9. Write a computer program to solve sets of state equations, following the algorithm given in Section 5.9.

5.10. Formulate a set of state equations for the network of Fig. 5.21. Use terminal representations of subnetworks.

5.11. Show that the output voltages of the networks of Fig. 5.9, 5.10, 5.12, and 5.13 are given by Eqs. (5.136), (5.137), (5.139), and (5.140), respectively.

Chapter 6

ANALYSIS OF OTHER LINEAR PHYSICAL SYSTEMS

In the first five chapters we introduced and explained some of the techniques and underlying theories connected with the analysis of linear electric networks. Our basic point of view has been that the variables with whose interrelations we have been concerned all arise as direct results of measurements. In this final chapter we shall attempt to show how we can apply identical methods in the analysis of mechanical and hydraulic systems.

6.1. INTRODUCTION

Our analysis of electric networks is based on the following facts.
(1) For every pair of terminals of a given electric component, we can make oriented measurements of two variables; a current and a voltage.
(2) The current measurement is made by a meter *in series* with the pair of terminals.
(3) The voltage measurement is made by a meter *in parallel* with, or across, the pair of terminals.
(4) We associate a terminal graph with a chosen pair of orientations of the current and voltage measurements.
(5) For a given component, the current and voltage variables are related by algebraic or differential equations (or both).
(6) A system graph is associated with a given network; this is merely the union of the terminal graphs of the network components.
(7) The current and voltage variables of the system graph satisfy the vertex and circuit postulates, respectively.

In order to apply all our techniques to other systems, we need only find pairs of variables which can be measured in the same way as are current and voltage and which also satisfy the corresponding vertex and circuit postulates. Variables which satisfy the vertex postulate are called *through variables*, while those which satisfy the circuit postulate are called *across variables*. For given components, these variables are related by algebraic or differential equations.

An across variable is measured by a device placed between (or across) a given pair of terminals, while a through variable is measured with a meter placed in series with the terminal pair. By a terminal pair, we mean, in general, two points, areas, or regions with which we associate a pair of through and across measurements.

As a first step in the analysis procedure, we associate terminal graphs with the components of a given system; each oriented element corresponds to a pair of oriented measurements (through and across) and we denote across variables in general by the letter X, and through variables by the letter Y. Electric current is, of course, an example of a through variable, while voltage is an example of an across variable.

6.2. THROUGH AND ACROSS VARIABLES OF MECHANICAL SYSTEMS

In the study of mechanical systems, we can define all the concepts and variables which arise in terms of *displacements*, and *forces* or *torques*. In general, the motion of rigid bodies involves both *translation* and *rotation*. At present, however, we shall consider only components in which there is translation with no rotation, or rotation with no translation. This does not mean that our methods cannot be used in the more complex case; we intend only to introduce the fundamental concepts of our discipline, which would be obscured were we to treat the more complicated situations at the outset.

If we wish to measure the displacement of one point with respect to another, we need first to define a set of coordinate axes with appropriate calibrated scales. In general, the axes may be curved in any way whatever, and the calibrations of the scales need not even be linear. Nevertheless, it is convenient for our purposes to use a *right-hand cartesian* set of axes with similar linearly calibrated scales on each axis, as illustrated in Fig. 6.1.

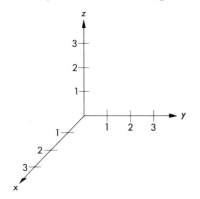

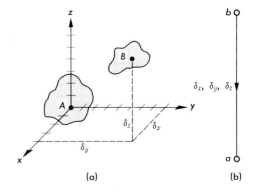

FIG. 6.1.   A right-hand cartesian set of axes.

FIG. 6.2. Displacement measurement. (a) Measurement of displacement of B with respect to A. (b) Corresponding terminal graph.

The displacement of one point, B, with respect to another point, A, is measured by means of a right-hand cartesian set of linearly calibrated axes whose origin is fixed at A, as shown in Fig. 6.2(a). The three coordinates of the point B, δ_x, δ_y, δ_z, with respect to this set of axes are an effective measure of the displacement B with respect to A. To obtain the displacement of A with respect to B, we shift the origin of the axes (without rotation) to B, and obtain the coordinates of A. These will be equal in magnitude but opposite in sign to those obtained in measuring the displacement of B with respect to A. Thus, *displacement is a two-point oriented measurement*. We can indicate in which way the measurement is to be made by means of a terminal graph. The measurement of the displacement of B with respect to A is implied by an oriented line segment between corresponding vertices b and a, such that the orientation is from b to a. If we wish to measure the displacement of A with respect to B, the orientation of the line segment is reversed. Thus the terminal graph indicates the orientation of a displacement measurement between A and B. Such a terminal graph is illustrated in Fig. 6.2(b).

Displacement measurements are made by means of calibrated scales placed between, or across, two points or terminals, A and B. Thus *displacement is an across variable*. It is, furthermore, easy to verify experimentally that displacement measurements satisfy the circuit postulate, provided only that the orientations and scales of each set of coordinate axes involved are identical. Since displacement measurements are always made between two points, all such measurements between rigid bodies are made between fixed points or terminals in each body, such as those shown in Fig. 6.2(a).

The intuitive concept of a force is something pushing or pulling at a point. However, the instrument used to measure a force must be connected at two points, and the result of the measurement depends on the orientation of the instrument. Force can be measured by means of a displacement of one end of a standard spring with respect to the other, using a scale directly calibrated in units of force (newtons). The scale is attached to one end of the spring, and the pointer is attached to the other, the whole instrument being placed in series with the terminals of the mechanical component, as shown in Fig. 6.3(a) or (b). Terminal graphs representing force measurements are also shown in the figure. Note that the orientation of the terminal graph is directly related to the mode of connection of pointer and scale on the force meter; the orientation is from the vertex associated with the pointer, and toward the vertex associated with the scale. In Fig. 6.3 it is also important to note that both force meters have the same scale orientation; that this is essential whenever several forces are to be measured becomes obvious when it is realized that force measurements are effected by means of displacement measurements,

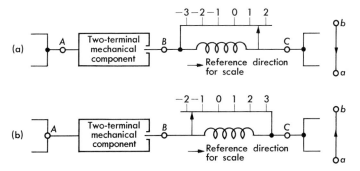

FIG. 6.3. Force measurements and corresponding terminal graphs.

and similarly oriented axes must be used in order that the terminal graph may have a unique meaning.

A positive force is one which causes or is caused by an extension of the two-terminal mechanical component of Fig. 6.3(a), while this same force would be regarded as a negative one if the representation of Fig. 6.3(b) were used. This naturally agrees with the fact that compression and tension do not in themselves have any polarity; unique characterizations, of forces are obtained as soon as reference directions are defined, and measurement polarities are established. Although there are many possible ways of doing this, our method is convenient for further development.

Force is clearly a two-point oriented measurement, and it can be shown, either through experiment or by d'Alembert's principle, that forces satisfy the vertex postulate. Therefore, *force is a through variable*. Although we have discussed only a one-dimensional measurement, we could just as well have described a three-dimensional case. We would merely apply three force meters whose scale orientations correspond to a right-hand cartesian set of axes, and obtain three components, f_x, f_y, f_z, of the total force. Together the measurements would be described by a single terminal graph.

In the electrical case, we found it convenient to connect all our pairs of volt-meters and ammeters in such a way as to be able to use a single terminal graph for the measurement of both voltage and current. In the same way, for translational mechanical measurements, it is convenient to arrange the measurements of displacements and forces so that a single terminal graph will indicate the orientations of both measurements. For the one-dimensional case, such a single reference system is illustrated in Fig. 6.4. Of course, a similar situation would exist for measurements in three dimensions.

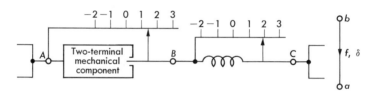

FIG. 6.4. One-dimensional force and displacement measurements.

We now turn our attention to measurements of rotational displacement and torques. The rotational displacement of a body may be characterized by a combination of rotations about three orthogonal axes; unfortunately, the numerical values of these rotations are not mutually independent; they depend on the sequence in which they occur. For this reason we shall limit our discussion to rotations about only one axis.

The rotational displacement between two terminals is measured with a linearly calibrated circular scale. Usually, the scale is calibrated so that the direction of increasing scale corresponds to the direction in which a right-hand screw rotates when it advances in the direction of the axis of rotation, but whatever convention

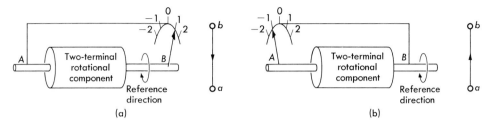

FIG. 6.5. Rotational displacement measurements and terminal graphs.

is chosen, it is important that we use it consistently for every measurement in a given system. The measurement of rotational displacement is illustrated in Fig. 6.5(a) and (b), and it is evident that *rotational displacement is an across variable*. In Fig. 6.5(a) the measurement is of the rotational displacement of terminal B with respect to terminal A, while in Fig. 6.5(b) the role of the two terminals is reversed; this fact is reflected in the terminal graphs shown in the figure. Of course, the reference direction for the measurement scales is identical in both cases. Clearly also, rotational displacement satisfies the circuit postulate.

Just as forces are measured by means of standard springs, torques are measured by means of standard torsional springs. The rotational displacement of one terminal of the standard torsional spring with respect to the other provides a measure of the torque involved. Although intuitively a torque is applied at a single point, its measurement requires two points. Indeed, torque measurement is conceptually very similar to the measurement of forces; by an analogous discussion we would be led to the conclusion that torque is a two-point oriented variable which satisfies the vertex postulate. Therefore, *torque is a through variable*. Its measurement is illustrated in Fig. 6.6 for a two-terminal component. Note that the orientation of the terminal graph corresponding to torque measurement is from the vertex associated with the pointer and toward the vertex associated with the scale; moreover, for uniqueness it is necessary also to define a reference direction for torque measurements.

It is convenient to connect torque and rotational displacement meters so that a single terminal graph can be used to indicate the polarity of both kinds of measurement. This, of course, requires that the same reference direction be used for both rotational displacement and torque. Such measurements are illustrated in Fig. 6.7.

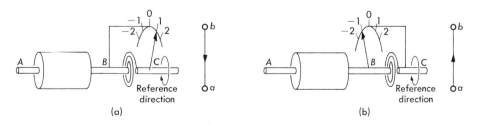

FIG. 6.6 Torque measurement.

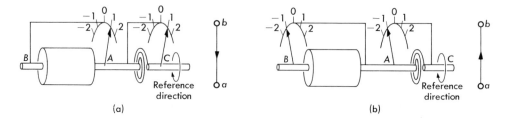

FIG. 6.7. Combined measurement of torque and rotational displacement.

The measuring instruments which we have used in our discussions of force and torque are somewhat impractical. For example, it may be difficult, if not impossible, to insert a torsional spring between two shafts in order to make a torque measurement. However, the instruments we employed very aptly illustrate the through and across natures of the measurements involved; for practical measurements we would, of course, use other devices, such as strain gauges cemented to the mechanical components. Electro-mechanical transducers provide an effective means of obtaining mechanical measurements.

It should also be noted that translational power is defined as the product of force and the derivative of translational displacement, and rotational power is defined as the product of torque and the derivative of rotational displacement. These definitions are of immense significance in the analysis of mixed systems. In fact, it will be of little value to select through and across variables (the terms through and across variables include their derivatives and integrals) whose product does not correspond to the power of the system.

We have discussed in this section the through and across measurements associated with mechanical systems. For translational components these are, respectively, force and displacement, while for rotational systems they are torque and rotational displacement.

6.3. THROUGH AND ACROSS VARIABLES OF HYDRAULIC SYSTEMS

We can define all the variables and concepts which are associated with hydraulic systems in terms of measurements of *pressure difference* and *fluid flow*. A pressure difference, or differential pressure, is measured by placing a pressure meter across a pair of terminals of a hydraulic component, as shown in Fig. 6.8(a). In this figure the marked terminal of the pressure meter is connected to terminal B, indicating that the pressure of terminal B with respect to that of terminal A is being measured. This information is portrayed by the terminal graph of Fig. 6.8(b), where the line segment is oriented from vertex b to vertex a. Should a measurement of the pressure at terminal A with respect to that at terminal B be made, the marked terminal of the meter would be connected to terminal A, the terminal graph would be oriented from vertex a to vertex b, and the meter indication would be opposite in sign but equal in magnitude to that associated with

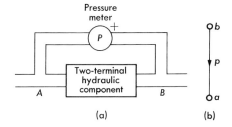

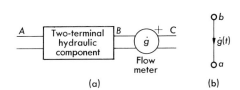

FIG. 6.8.   Pressure   measurement. (a)   FIG. 6.9.   Fluid flow measurement.   (a)
Measurement of differential pressure. (b)   Schematic diagram of flow measurement.
Corresponding terminal graph.   (b) Corresponding terminal graph.

Fig. 6.8(a).   Thus *differential pressure* is a two-point oriented measurement;
furthermore, it is evident that the corresponding variable satisfies the circuit
postulate, and is the *across variable for hydraulic systems*. A typical pressure meter
consists of a diaphragm separating regions of differing pressures, with an appropriate dial linkage.

Measurement of fluid flow through a hydraulic component is performed by a
flowmeter connected effectively in series with the terminals of the component, as
shown in Fig. 6.9(a).   In this diagram the marked terminal of the flow meter
indicates that there will be a positive reading if the fluid flow through the component is from terminal B to terminal A. The terminal graph of Fig. 6.9(b) is used
to record this information.   If the meter orientation is reversed, the meter indication will reverse in sign for the same flow, demonstrating that fluid flow is a
two-point oriented measurement.   It is also clear that the variable representing
fluid flow satisfies the vertex postulate.   Thus *fluid flow is a through variable*.   A
typical flow meter might consist of a turbine whose angular velocity is proportional
to the fluid flow.

Just as in the electrical and mechanical cases, we use a single terminal graph to
indicate the orientations of both a pressure and a flow measurement.   The correspondence between the orientations and the graph is shown in Fig. 6.10.

In this section we have discussed the fact that differential pressure p and fluid
flow $\dot{g}$ are the across and through variables for hydraulic systems.   Table 6.1 serves

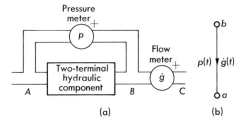

FIG. 6.10.   The terminal graph for pressure and flow measurements.   (a) Pressure and
flow measurements. (b) Corresponding terminal graph.

TABLE 6.1
THROUGH AND ACROSS VARIABLES

Type of system	Through variable		Across variable	
	Name	Symbol	Name	Symbol
General		$x(t)$		$y(t)$
Electrical	Current	$i(t)$	Voltage	$v(t)$
Mechanical translational	Force	$f(t)$	Displacement	$\delta(t)$
Mechanical rotational	Torque	$T(t)$	Rotational displacement	$\phi(t)$
Hydraulic	Fluid flow	$\dot{g}(t)$	Differential pressure	$p(t)$

to gather together all the various variables for the several types of systems which we have mentioned, while Fig. 6.11 shows the one-to-one correspondence between a pair of oriented measurements on a general two-terminal component and its terminal graph.

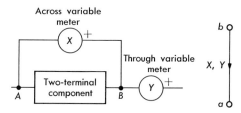

FIG. 6.11. Through and across measurements on a general two-terminal component and its terminal graph. (a) Symbolic measurement of through and across variables. (b) Corresponding terminal graph.

6.4. TYPICAL MECHANICAL AND HYDRAULIC COMPONENTS

We did not discuss the physical principles of the components used in electrical systems. Similarly, we shall avoid discussion of the physics connected with mechanical and hydraulic devices. We shall merely tabulate the schematic diagrams, terminal graphs, and associated terminal equations for some typical components, and limit our discussion to those few cases in which there may be a possibility of misinterpretation. It should be clearly understood, however, that we have proceeded to the mathematical model of each of the components from its physical characteristics and that these have not been discussed here for the sake of brevity.

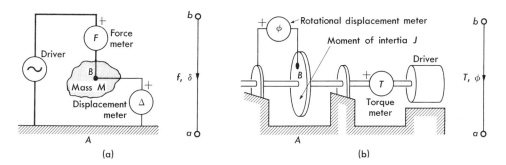

FIG. 6.12.   Mass and inertial components.   (a) Mass as a two-terminal component. (b) Inertia as a two-terminal component.

A rigid body which has finite mass or inertia has only one terminal, which is some point fixed with respect to the body.   However, measurements of force or torque and displacement associated with such a body require two terminals.   In fact, to provide meaning for such measurements, we require a reference point, such as the earth, or the frame of the mechanical system under study.   Thus bodies with mass or inertia are regarded as two-terminal components, one terminal being associated with the body and the other at a fixed reference.   The measurements that are required are illustrated in Fig. 6.12.

A hydraulic reservoir which is open to the atmosphere is another two-terminal component which could be misunderstood.   The terminals of such a device are the atmospheric region and the inlet pipe.   Pressure and flow measurements defining the terminal graph for this component are shown in Fig. 6.13.

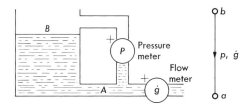

FIG. 6.13.   Open hydraulic reservoir as a two-terminal component.

As to other components, typical schematics, terminal graphs and corresponding terminal equations are listed in Table 6.2.   It should be emphasized that this table is by no means exhaustive; the terminal equations may take other forms than those shown in the table.   For instance, we may choose to regard velocity, $\dot{\delta}(t)$, as the across variable in a particular problem; in this case the terminal equation, say for a mass, becomes

$$f(t) = M \frac{d}{dt} \dot{\delta}(t). \tag{6.1}$$

TABLE 6.2
Typical Mechanical and Hydraulic Components

Name	Schematic	Terminal graph	Terminal equations — t-domain	Terminal equations — s-domain
Damper (translational)			$f(t) = B \dfrac{d}{dt} \delta(t)$	$F(s) = Bs\,\Delta(s) - B\,\delta(0+)$ $\Delta(s) = \dfrac{1}{Bs} F(s) + \dfrac{1}{s}\,\delta(0+)$
Spring (translational)			$f(t) = K\,\delta(t)$	$F(s) = K\,\Delta(s)$
Mass			$f(t) = M \dfrac{d^2}{dt^2} \delta(t)$	$F(s) = Ms^2\,\Delta(s) - Ms\,\delta(0+) - M\,\dot{\delta}(0+)$ $\Delta(s) = \dfrac{1}{Ms^2} F(s) + \dfrac{1}{s}\,\delta(0+) + \dfrac{1}{s^2}\,\dot{\delta}(0+)$
Damper (rotational)			$T(t) = B \dfrac{d}{dt} \phi(t)$	$T(s) = Bs\,\Phi(s) - B\,\phi(0+)$ $\Phi(s) = \dfrac{1}{Bs} T(s) + \dfrac{1}{s}\,\phi(0+)$
Spring (rotational or shaft)			$T(t) = K\,\phi(t)$	$T(s) = K\,\Phi(s)$
Inertial component			$T(t) = J \dfrac{d^2}{dt^2} \phi(t)$	$T(s) = Js^2\,\Phi(s) - Js\,\phi(0+) - J\,\dot{\phi}(0+)$ $\Phi(s) = \dfrac{1}{Js^2} T(s) + \dfrac{1}{s}\,\phi(0+) + \dfrac{1}{s^2}\,\dot{\phi}(0+)$
Hydraulic resistance			$p(t) = R\dot{g}(t)$	$P(s) = R\dot{g}(s)$
Reservoir			$\dot{g}(t) = C \dfrac{d}{dt} p(t)$	$\dot{g}(s) = CsP(s) - Cp(0+)$ $P(s) = \dfrac{1}{Cs} \dot{g}(s) + \dfrac{1}{s}\,p(0+)$
Force driver			$f(t)$ specified	$F(s)$ specified
Displacement driver			$\delta(t)$ specified	$\Delta(s)$ specified

Component	Diagram	Network graph	Time domain	Transform domain
Torque driver			$T(t)$ specified	$T(s)$ specified
Rotational displacement driver			$\phi(t)$ specified	$\Phi(s)$ specified
Pressure driver			$p(t)$ specified	$P(s)$ specified
Flow driver			$\dot{g}(t)$ specified	$\dot{g}(s)$ specified
Lever (small displacement)			$\begin{bmatrix} f_1(t) \\ \delta_2(t) \end{bmatrix} = \begin{bmatrix} B_1\dfrac{d}{dt}+M_1\dfrac{d^2}{dt^2} & \dfrac{l_2}{l_1} \\ -\dfrac{l_2}{l_1} & 0 \end{bmatrix}\begin{bmatrix} \delta_1(t) \\ f_2(t) \end{bmatrix}$	$\begin{bmatrix} F_1(s) \\ \Delta_2(s) \end{bmatrix} = \begin{bmatrix} B_1 s+M_1 s^2 & \dfrac{l_2}{l_1} \\ -\dfrac{l_2}{l_1} & 0 \end{bmatrix}\begin{bmatrix} \Delta_1(s) \\ F_2(s) \end{bmatrix}$ Neglecting initial conditions
Gear train (N = No. of teeth)			$\begin{bmatrix} T_1(t) \\ \phi_2(t) \end{bmatrix} = \begin{bmatrix} B_1\dfrac{d}{dt}+J_1\dfrac{d^2}{dt^2} & \dfrac{N_1}{N_2} \\ -\dfrac{N_1}{N_2} & 0 \end{bmatrix}\begin{bmatrix} \phi_2(t) \\ T_2(t) \end{bmatrix}$	$\begin{bmatrix} T_1(s) \\ \Phi_2(s) \end{bmatrix} = \begin{bmatrix} B_1 s+J_1 s^2 & \dfrac{N_1}{N_2} \\ -\dfrac{N_1}{N_2} & 0 \end{bmatrix}\begin{bmatrix} \Phi_1(s) \\ T_2(s) \end{bmatrix}$ Neglecting initial conditions
Three-terminal reservoir (inertial effects included)			$\begin{bmatrix} P_1(t) \\ \dot{g}_2(t) \end{bmatrix} = \begin{bmatrix} 2R_{12}-\dfrac{R_{12}^2}{C_1}\dfrac{d}{dt} & 1-\dfrac{R_{12}}{C_1}\dfrac{d}{dt} \\ \dfrac{R_{12}}{C_1}\dfrac{d}{dt}-1 & \dfrac{1}{C_1}\dfrac{d}{dt} \end{bmatrix}\begin{bmatrix} \dot{g}_1(t) \\ P_2(t) \end{bmatrix}$	$\begin{bmatrix} P_1(s) \\ \dot{g}_2(s) \end{bmatrix} = \begin{bmatrix} 2R_{12}-\dfrac{R_{12}^2}{C_1}s & 1-\dfrac{R_{12}}{C_1}s \\ \dfrac{R_{12}}{C_1}s-1 & \dfrac{s}{C_1} \end{bmatrix}\begin{bmatrix} \dot{g}_1(s) \\ P_2(s) \end{bmatrix}$ Neglecting initial conditions

Of course, we are always at liberty to make this choice of across variable, since, as we have already mentioned, the derivatives of across variables are themselves across variables. Likewise, the derivatives of through variables are also through variables.

6.5. MIXED SYSTEMS

Our method of analysis through terminal representations is not limited to purely electrical, purely mechanical, or purely hydraulic systems. Other types of systems, such as magnetic or pneumatic systems, can be analyzed using the same techniques. In addition, we may analyze mixed systems in which mechanical, electrical, or

TABLE 6.3

TYPICAL TRANSDUCERS

Name	Schematic	Terminal graph	Terminal equations
Potentiometer (displacement to voltage transducer)			$\begin{bmatrix} f_1(t) \\ v_2(t) \end{bmatrix} = \begin{bmatrix} B\frac{d}{dt} + M\frac{d^2}{dt^2} & 0 \\ \dfrac{E}{\delta_m} & \dfrac{R}{\delta_m}\delta_1(t) \end{bmatrix} \begin{bmatrix} \delta_1(t) \\ i_2(t) \end{bmatrix}$ $\delta_1(t) \le \delta_m$
Rack and gear (rotational-translational transducer)			$\begin{bmatrix} T_1(t) \\ \delta_2(t) \end{bmatrix} = \begin{bmatrix} B_1\frac{d}{dt} + J\frac{d^2}{dt^2} & -r \\ r & 0 \end{bmatrix} \begin{bmatrix} \phi_1(t) \\ f_2(t) \end{bmatrix}$ $r = $ radius of pinion
Take-up spool			$\begin{bmatrix} \delta_1(t) \\ T_2(t) \end{bmatrix} = \begin{bmatrix} r & 0 \\ B\frac{d}{dt} + J\frac{d^2}{dt^2} & -r \end{bmatrix} \begin{bmatrix} \phi_2(t) \\ f_1(t) \end{bmatrix}$ $r = $ radius of spool
Tachometer (rotational velocity to voltage transducer) (permanent-magnet dc-generator)			$\begin{bmatrix} T_1(t) \\ v_2(t) \end{bmatrix} = \begin{bmatrix} -k & B\frac{d}{dt} + J\frac{d^2}{dt^2} \\ R + L\frac{d}{dt} & k\frac{d}{dt} \end{bmatrix} \begin{bmatrix} i_2(t) \\ \phi_1(t) \end{bmatrix}$
Commutating machine			$v_1(t) = \left(R_1 + L_1\frac{d}{dt}\right)i_1(t)$ $v_2(t) = A_{af}\frac{d\phi_3(t)}{dt}i_1(t) + \left(R_2 + L_2\frac{d}{dt}\right)i_2(t)$ $T_3(t) = -A_{a}i_2(t)i_1(t) + \left(B\frac{d}{dt} + J\frac{d^2}{dt^2}\right)\phi_3(t)$
Hydraulic piston			$\begin{bmatrix} \dot{g}_1(t) \\ f_2(t) \end{bmatrix} = \begin{bmatrix} -k_{21}\frac{d}{dt} & 0 \\ k_2 + B_2\frac{d}{dt} + M_2\frac{d^2}{dt^2} & k_{21} \end{bmatrix} \begin{bmatrix} \delta_2(t) \\ p_1(t) \end{bmatrix}$ $k_{21} = $ cross-sectional area of piston

TABLE 6.4
LINEAR MODELS OF COMMUTATING MACHINES

Name	Schematic	Terminal graph	Terminal equations
Electromechanical transducer (motor)			$$\begin{bmatrix} v_2(t) \\ T_3(t) \end{bmatrix} = \begin{bmatrix} K_m \dfrac{d}{dt} & R_2 + L_2 \dfrac{d}{dt} \\ B \dfrac{d}{dt} + J \dfrac{d^2}{dt^2} & -K_m \end{bmatrix} \begin{bmatrix} \phi_3(t) \\ i_2(t) \end{bmatrix}$$ where $K_m = A_{af} i_1(t) = \text{const}$
Rotating amplifier (generator)			$$\begin{bmatrix} v_1(t) \\ v_2(t) \end{bmatrix} = \begin{bmatrix} R_1 + L_1 \dfrac{d}{dt} & 0 \\ K_g & R_2 + L_2 \dfrac{d}{dt} \end{bmatrix} \begin{bmatrix} i_1(t) \\ i_2(t) \end{bmatrix}$$ where $K_g = A_{af} \dfrac{d\phi_3(t)}{dt} = \text{const}$
Electromechanical amplifier			$$\begin{bmatrix} v_1(t) \\ T_3(t) \end{bmatrix} = \begin{bmatrix} R_1 + L_1 \dfrac{d}{dt} & 0 \\ -K_e & B \dfrac{d}{dt} + J \dfrac{d^2}{dt^2} \end{bmatrix} \begin{bmatrix} i_1(t) \\ \phi_3(t) \end{bmatrix}$$ where $K_e = A_{af} i_2(t) = \text{const}$

hydraulic components, etc., may occur together. The main property of such systems is that they contain components which have terminal pairs at which different types of measurements are made. Thus, at one pair of terminals we may make electrical measurements, at another we may make mechanical measurements, and at yet another we may make hydraulic measurements.

Components which have this characteristic are called *transducers*, and almost invariably their terminal representations have separated terminal graphs similar to those encountered in our discussion of coupled coils (Section 4.4). The terminal representations of some typical transducers are listed in Table 6.3, and we shall not enter into any further discussion of the details of their properties, or the derivation of their relationships.

It should be noted that some of the terminal equations listed in Table 6.3 are nonlinear. In particular, the commutating machine deserves further comment. The terminal equations are nonlinear, but such machines are usually operated in one of three ways: either the field current $i_1(t)$, or $d\phi_3(t)/dt$, or $i_2(t)$ (Table 6.3) is held constant. The result in each case is a set of linear terminal equations, and the corresponding terminal representations are shown in Table 6.4.

6.6. SOME TYPICAL SYSTEM GRAPHS

In the previous sections of this chapter we briefly introduced the terminal representations of mechanical and hydraulic components. In this section we shall illustrate the system graphs associated with some typical systems; we shall also write the corresponding fundamental circuit and cut-set equations.

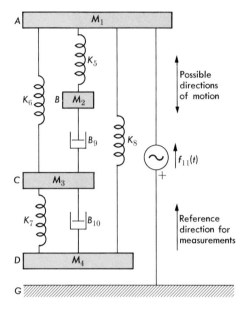

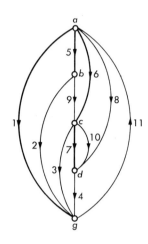

FIG. 6.14. A mass-spring-damper system.

FIG. 6.15.   The system graph associated with the system of Fig. 6.14.

EXAMPLE 6.1 (*A mass-spring-damper system*).   Figure 6.14 shows a mass-spring-damper system driven by a force driver.   It contains four masses, four springs, and two dampers, all of which are assumed to be constrained so that motion can occur in only one direction.   To draw the system graph for this assembly, we first note that the terminals of each of the springs and dampers are fixed to the masses, and that the measurements associated with each mass are made between terminals fixed on the masses and the reference point G.   The system graph is shown in Fig. 6.15.   We have numbered the elements of this graph in correspondence with

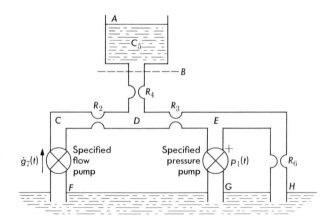

FIG. 6.16.   A hydraulic system.

the subscripts identifying the masses, spring constants, etc., in Fig. 6.14. Thus, elements 1, 2, 3, 4 are associated with masses M_1, M_2, M_3, M_4, elements 5, 6, 7 and 8 are associated with the springs, elements 9 and 10 with the dampers, and element 11 with the force driver.

In Fig. 6.15 we have shown a possible formulation tree with heavy lines. Corresponding to this tree the fundamental circuit and cut-set equations are

$$
\begin{bmatrix} \delta_2(t) \\ \delta_3(t) \\ \delta_4(t) \\ \delta_8(t) \\ \delta_9(t) \\ \delta_{10}(t) \\ \delta_{11}(t) \end{bmatrix} =
\begin{bmatrix} 1 & -1 & 0 & 0 \\ 1 & 0 & -1 & 0 \\ 1 & 0 & -1 & -1 \\ 0 & 0 & 1 & 1 \\ 0 & -1 & 1 & 0 \\ 0 & 0 & 0 & 1 \\ -1 & 0 & 0 & 0 \end{bmatrix}
\begin{bmatrix} \delta_1(t) \\ \delta_5(t) \\ \delta_6(t) \\ \delta_7(t) \end{bmatrix}
\quad \text{(circuit equations)},
$$

(6.2)

$$
\begin{bmatrix} f_1(t) \\ f_5(t) \\ f_6(t) \\ f_7(t) \end{bmatrix} =
\begin{bmatrix} -1 & -1 & -1 & 0 & 0 & 0 & 1 \\ 1 & 0 & 0 & 0 & 1 & 0 & 0 \\ 0 & 1 & 1 & -1 & -1 & 0 & 0 \\ 0 & 0 & 1 & -1 & 0 & -1 & 0 \end{bmatrix}
\begin{bmatrix} f_2(t) \\ f_3(t) \\ f_4(t) \\ f_8(t) \\ f_9(t) \\ f_{10}(t) \\ f_{11}(t) \end{bmatrix}
\quad \text{(cut-set equations)}.
$$

(6.3)

EXAMPLE 6.2 (*A system of two-terminal hydraulic components*). Figure 6.16 is the schematic diagram of a hydraulic system containing four hydraulic resistances, two pumps, and a reservoir. In this system terminals A, F, G, and H are all at atmospheric pressure, and they are all represented by the same vertex in the associated system graph (Fig. 6.17). Elements 2, 3, 4, and 6 are associated with the measurements made on the corresponding sections of the pipe, element 5 is associated with the reservoir, element 1 is associated with the pressure driver, and finally, element 7 is associated with the flow driver. The system graph is formed by combining all the elements in correspondence with the interconnection of their associated components.

The fundamental circuit and cut-set equations corresponding to a possible formulation tree (shown by heavy lines) in the graph of Fig. 6.17 are

$$
\begin{bmatrix} p_5(t) \\ p_6(t) \\ p_7(t) \end{bmatrix} =
\begin{bmatrix} -1 & 0 & -1 & -1 \\ -1 & 0 & 0 & 0 \\ -1 & -1 & -1 & 0 \end{bmatrix}
\begin{bmatrix} p_1(t) \\ p_2(t) \\ p_3(t) \\ p_4(t) \end{bmatrix}
$$

(6.4)

(circuit equations),

$$
\begin{bmatrix} \dot{g}_1(t) \\ \dot{g}_2(t) \\ \dot{g}_3(t) \\ \dot{g}_4(t) \end{bmatrix} =
\begin{bmatrix} 1 & 1 & 1 \\ 0 & 0 & 1 \\ 1 & 0 & 1 \\ 1 & 0 & 0 \end{bmatrix}
\begin{bmatrix} \dot{g}_5(t) \\ \dot{g}_6(t) \\ \dot{g}_7(t) \end{bmatrix}
$$

(6.5)

(cut-set equations).

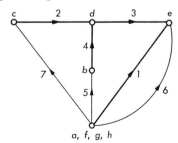

FIG. 6.17. The system graph associated with the system of Fig. 6.16.

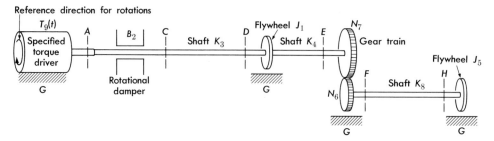

FIG. 6.18. A rotational mechanical system.

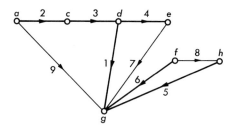

FIG. 6.19. The system graph associated with Fig. 6.18.

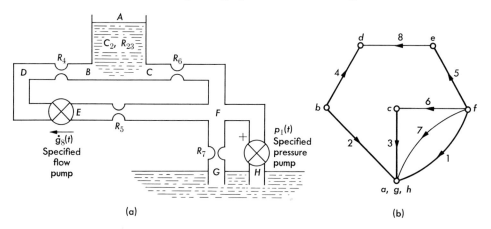

FIG. 6.20. A hydraulic system. (a) Schematic. (b) System graph.

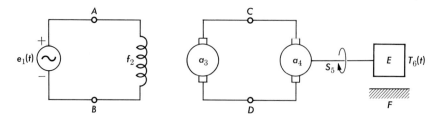

FIG. 6.21. Schematic of a simple electromechanical system.

EXAMPLE 6.3 (*A rotational mechanical system*). A simple rotational system containing a rotational damper, three shafts (rotational springs), two flywheels, and a gear train is illustrated in Fig. 6.18. In drawing the system graph associated with this system we merely unite the terminal graphs (Table 6.2) for the various components; the result is shown in Fig. 6.19. The fundamental circuit and cut-set equations corresponding to the formulation tree shown by heavy lines in Fig. 6.19 are

$$
\begin{bmatrix} \phi_7(t) \\ \phi_8(t) \\ \phi_9(t) \end{bmatrix} = \begin{bmatrix} 1 & 0 & 0 & -1 & 0 & 0 \\ 0 & 0 & 0 & 0 & -1 & 1 \\ 1 & 1 & 1 & 0 & 0 & 0 \end{bmatrix} \begin{bmatrix} \phi_1(t) \\ \phi_2(t) \\ \phi_3(t) \\ \phi_4(t) \\ \phi_5(t) \\ \phi_6(t) \end{bmatrix} \quad \text{(circuit equations)}, \quad (6.6)
$$

$$
\begin{bmatrix} T_1(t) \\ T_2(t) \\ T_3(t) \\ T_4(t) \\ T_5(t) \\ T_6(t) \end{bmatrix} = \begin{bmatrix} -1 & 0 & -1 \\ 0 & 0 & -1 \\ 0 & 0 & -1 \\ 1 & 0 & 0 \\ 0 & 1 & 0 \\ 0 & -1 & 0 \end{bmatrix} \begin{bmatrix} T_7(t) \\ T_8(t) \\ T_9(t) \end{bmatrix} \quad \text{(cut-set equations)}. \quad (6.7)
$$

EXAMPLE 6.4 (*A hydraulic system*). A schematic diagram and the associated system graph of a hydraulic system containing a "three-terminal reservoir" are shown in Fig. 6.20. The fundamental circuit and cut-set equations for the indicated formulation tree are

$$
\begin{bmatrix} p_6(t) \\ p_7(t) \\ p_8(t) \end{bmatrix} = \begin{bmatrix} 1 & 0 & -1 & 0 & 0 \\ 1 & 0 & 0 & 0 & 0 \\ 1 & -1 & 0 & 1 & -1 \end{bmatrix} \begin{bmatrix} p_1(t) \\ p_2(t) \\ p_3(t) \\ p_4(t) \\ p_5(t) \end{bmatrix} \quad \text{(circuit equations)}, \quad (6.8)
$$

$$
\begin{bmatrix} \dot{g}_1(t) \\ \dot{g}_2(t) \\ \dot{g}_3(t) \\ \dot{g}_4(t) \\ \dot{g}_5(t) \end{bmatrix} = \begin{bmatrix} -1 & -1 & -1 \\ 0 & 0 & 1 \\ 1 & 0 & 0 \\ 0 & 0 & -1 \\ 0 & 0 & 1 \end{bmatrix} \begin{bmatrix} \dot{g}_6(t) \\ \dot{g}_7(t) \\ \dot{g}_8(t) \end{bmatrix} \quad \text{(cut-set equations)}. \quad (6.9)
$$

EXAMPLE 6.5 (*An electromechanical system*). Figure 6.21 shows a simple system consisting of a rotating amplifier, a dc-motor, a voltage driver, and a specified torque load. The corresponding system graph is shown in Fig. 6.22, with a suitable formulation forest indicated by heavy lines. The fundamental circuit and cut-set

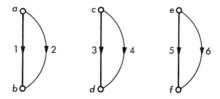

FIG. 6.22. System graph associated with Fig. 6.21.

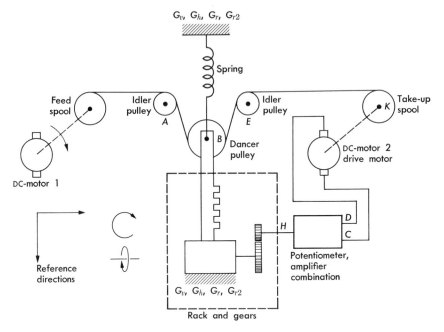

FIG. 6.23. Schematic of tension regulator.

equations with respect to this formulation forest are

$$
\begin{bmatrix} v_2(t) \\ v_4(t) \\ \phi_6(t) \end{bmatrix} = \begin{bmatrix} 1 & 0 & 0 \\ 0 & 1 & 0 \\ 0 & 0 & 1 \end{bmatrix} \begin{bmatrix} v_1(t) \\ v_3(t) \\ \phi_5(t) \end{bmatrix} \quad \text{(circuit equations)}, \tag{6.10}
$$

$$
\begin{bmatrix} i_1(t) \\ i_3(t) \\ T_5(t) \end{bmatrix} = \begin{bmatrix} -1 & 0 & 0 \\ 0 & -1 & 0 \\ 0 & 0 & -1 \end{bmatrix} \begin{bmatrix} i_2(t) \\ i_4(t) \\ T_6(t) \end{bmatrix} \quad \text{(cut-set equations)}. \tag{6.11}
$$

EXAMPLE 6.6 (*A typical control system*). Figure 6.23 is the schematic diagram of
an electromechanical system for controlling the tension of, say, the output of a
paper manufacturing process. The terminal representations for the various components are illustrated in Fig. 6.24. The system graph is obtained by uniting all the
terminal graphs of Fig. 6.24 in one-to-one correspondence with the interconnections
of the components (Fig. 6.23). The result is shown in Fig. 6.25. A possible formulation forest consists of elements 2, 3, 5, 7, 8, and 10. With respect to this forest,
the fundamental circuit equations are

$$
\begin{bmatrix} \Delta_1 \\ \Delta_6 \\ \Delta_9 \\ \Delta_{13} \\ V_{11} \\ \Phi_4 \\ \Phi_{12} \end{bmatrix} = \begin{bmatrix} 1 & 0 & 0 & 0 & 0 & 0 \\ 0 & 0 & 1 & 0 & 0 & 0 \\ 0 & 1 & 0 & 0 & 0 & 0 \\ 0 & 0 & 1 & 0 & 0 & 0 \\ 0 & 0 & 0 & 1 & 0 & 0 \\ 0 & 0 & 0 & 0 & 1 & 0 \\ 0 & 0 & 0 & 0 & 0 & 1 \end{bmatrix} \begin{bmatrix} \Delta_{10} \\ \Delta_2 \\ \Delta_3 \\ V_5 \\ \Phi_7 \\ \Phi_8 \end{bmatrix}. \tag{6.12}
$$

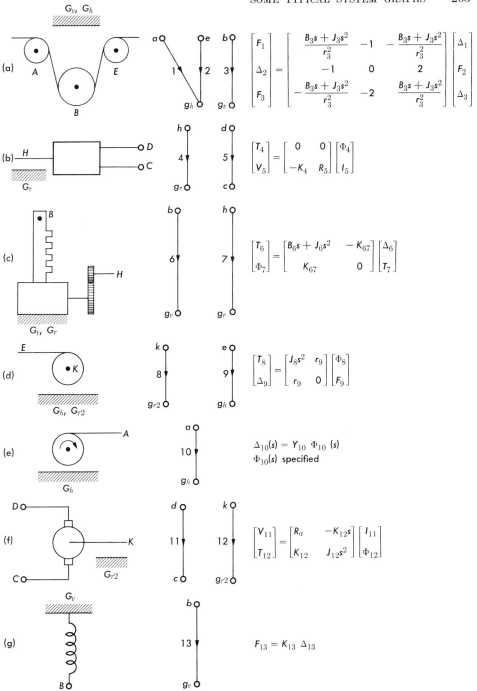

FIG. 6.24. Terminal representations (s domain) for components of the system of Fig. 6.23. (a) Dancer pulley and idler pulley combination. (b) Potentiometer, amplifier combination. (c) Rack and gears. (d) Take-up spool. (e) Feed spool. (f) Drive motor. (g) Spring.

The cut-set equations are

$$
\begin{bmatrix} F_{10} \\ F_2 \\ F_3 \\ I_5 \\ T_7 \\ T_8 \end{bmatrix} = \begin{bmatrix} -1 & 0 & 0 & 0 & 0 & 0 & 0 \\ 0 & 0 & -1 & 0 & 0 & 0 & 0 \\ 0 & -1 & 0 & -1 & 0 & 0 & 0 \\ 0 & 0 & 0 & 0 & -1 & 0 & 0 \\ 0 & 0 & 0 & 0 & 0 & -1 & 0 \\ 0 & 0 & 0 & 0 & 0 & 0 & -1 \end{bmatrix} \begin{bmatrix} F_1 \\ F_6 \\ F_9 \\ F_{13} \\ I_{11} \\ T_4 \\ T_{12} \end{bmatrix} .
\tag{6.13}
$$

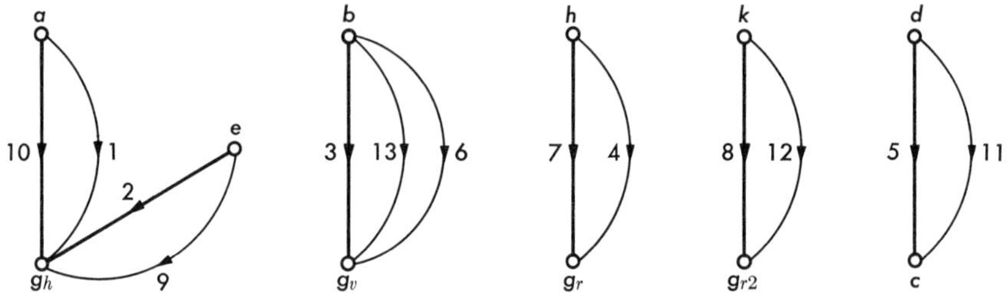

Fig. 6.25. System graph for tension regulator system.

6.7. BRANCH AND CHORD FORMULATION FOR TYPICAL SYSTEMS

The methods for formulating systems of equations for analyzing nonelectrical systems using terminal graphs are exactly the same as those which we used in the electrical case. Instead of voltage and current as the across and through variables, we may have displacement and force, or angular displacement and torque, etc. The criteria for the application of the various techniques, branch, chord, or branch-chord, are entirely similar to the electrical case. Thus, to formulate the chord equations, it must be possible to write all the terminal equations explicitly in the *across* variables, while in formulating the branch equations the terminal equations must first be written explicitly in the *through* variables.

Because of this direct correspondence between the electrical and non-electrical cases, we shall not discuss the formulation procedures in detail; we shall limit ourselves to two examples.

EXAMPLE 6.7 (*Formulation of the branch equations for a mass-spring-damper system*). The terminal equations for the mass-spring-damper system of Example 6.1 (Figs. 6.14 and 6.15) in the Laplace domain may easily be written as

$$
\begin{bmatrix} F_1(s) \\ F_5(s) \\ F_6(s) \\ F_7(s) \\ F_2(s) \\ F_3(s) \\ F_4(s) \\ F_8(s) \\ F_9(s) \\ F_{10}(s) \end{bmatrix} = \begin{bmatrix} M_1 s^2 & 0 & 0 & 0 & 0 & 0 & 0 & 0 & 0 & 0 \\ 0 & K_5 & 0 & 0 & 0 & 0 & 0 & 0 & 0 & 0 \\ 0 & 0 & K_6 & 0 & 0 & 0 & 0 & 0 & 0 & 0 \\ 0 & 0 & 0 & K_7 & 0 & 0 & 0 & 0 & 0 & 0 \\ 0 & 0 & 0 & 0 & M_2 s^2 & 0 & 0 & 0 & 0 & 0 \\ 0 & 0 & 0 & 0 & 0 & M_3 s^2 & 0 & 0 & 0 & 0 \\ 0 & 0 & 0 & 0 & 0 & 0 & M_4 s^2 & 0 & 0 & 0 \\ 0 & 0 & 0 & 0 & 0 & 0 & 0 & K_8 & 0 & 0 \\ 0 & 0 & 0 & 0 & 0 & 0 & 0 & 0 & B_9 s & 0 \\ 0 & 0 & 0 & 0 & 0 & 0 & 0 & 0 & 0 & B_{10} s \end{bmatrix} \begin{bmatrix} \Delta_1(s) \\ \Delta_5(s) \\ \Delta_6(s) \\ \Delta_7(s) \\ \Delta_2(s) \\ \Delta_3(s) \\ \Delta_4(s) \\ \Delta_8(s) \\ \Delta_9(s) \\ \Delta_{10}(s) \end{bmatrix} - \begin{bmatrix} M_1(s\,\delta_1(0+) + \delta_1'(0+)) \\ 0 \\ 0 \\ 0 \\ M_2(s\,\delta_2(0+) + \delta_2'(0+)) \\ M_3(s\,\delta_3(0+) + \delta_3'(0+)) \\ M_4(s\,\delta_4(0+) + \delta_4'(0+)) \\ 0 \\ B_9\,\delta_9(0+) \\ B_{10}\,\delta_{10}(0+) \end{bmatrix}
$$

$$\tag{6.14}$$

The cut-set equations (6.3) are rewritten in the form

$$
\begin{bmatrix}
1 & 0 & 0 & 0 & 1 & 1 & 1 & 0 & 0 & 0 \\
0 & 1 & 0 & 0 & -1 & 0 & 0 & 0 & -1 & 0 \\
0 & 0 & 1 & 0 & 0 & -1 & -1 & 1 & 1 & 0 \\
0 & 0 & 0 & 1 & 0 & 0 & -1 & 1 & 0 & 1
\end{bmatrix}
\begin{bmatrix}
F_1(s) \\ F_5(s) \\ F_6(s) \\ F_7(s) \\ F_2(s) \\ F_3(s) \\ F_4(s) \\ F_8(s) \\ F_9(s) \\ F_{10}(s)
\end{bmatrix}
+
\begin{bmatrix}
-1 \\ 0 \\ 0 \\ 0
\end{bmatrix}
[F_{11}(s)] =
\begin{bmatrix}
0 \\ 0 \\ 0 \\ 0
\end{bmatrix}.
$$

(6.15)

Substituting (6.14) into (6.15), we obtain

$$
\begin{bmatrix}
1 & 0 & 0 & 0 & 1 & 1 & 1 & 0 & 0 & 0 \\
0 & 1 & 0 & 0 & -1 & 0 & 0 & 0 & -1 & 0 \\
0 & 0 & 1 & 0 & 0 & -1 & -1 & 1 & 1 & 0 \\
0 & 0 & 0 & 1 & 0 & 0 & -1 & 1 & 0 & 1
\end{bmatrix}
$$

$$
\times
\begin{bmatrix}
M_1 s^2 & 0 & 0 & 0 & 0 & 0 & 0 & 0 & 0 & 0 \\
0 & K_5 & 0 & 0 & 0 & 0 & 0 & 0 & 0 & 0 \\
0 & 0 & K_6 & 0 & 0 & 0 & 0 & 0 & 0 & 0 \\
0 & 0 & 0 & K_7 & 0 & 0 & 0 & 0 & 0 & 0 \\
0 & 0 & 0 & 0 & M_2 s^2 & 0 & 0 & 0 & 0 & 0 \\
0 & 0 & 0 & 0 & 0 & M_3 s^2 & 0 & 0 & 0 & 0 \\
0 & 0 & 0 & 0 & 0 & 0 & M_4 s^2 & 0 & 0 & 0 \\
0 & 0 & 0 & 0 & 0 & 0 & 0 & K_8 & 0 & 0 \\
0 & 0 & 0 & 0 & 0 & 0 & 0 & 0 & B_9 s & 0 \\
0 & 0 & 0 & 0 & 0 & 0 & 0 & 0 & 0 & B_{10} s
\end{bmatrix}
\begin{bmatrix}
\Delta_1(s) \\ \Delta_5(s) \\ \Delta_6(s) \\ \Delta_7(s) \\ \Delta_2(s) \\ \Delta_3(s) \\ \Delta_4(s) \\ \Delta_8(s) \\ \Delta_9(s) \\ \Delta_{10}(s)
\end{bmatrix}
$$

$$
=
\begin{bmatrix}
s\big(M_1\,\delta_1(0+) + M_2\,\delta_2(0+) + M_3\,\delta_3(0+) + M_4\,\delta_4(0+)\big) + M_1\,\delta_1'(0+) + M_2\,\delta_2'(0+) + M_3\,\delta_3'(0+) + M_4\,\delta_4'(0+) \\
-M_2\big(s\,\delta_2(0+) + \delta_2'(0+)\big) - B_9\,\delta_9(0+) \\
-s\big(M_3\,\delta_3(0+) + M_4\,\delta_4(0+)\big) - M_3\,\delta_3'(0+) - M_4\,\delta_4'(0+) + B_9\,\delta_9(0+) \\
-M_4 s\,\delta_4(0+) - M_4\,\delta_4'(0+) + B_{10}\,\delta_{10}(0+)
\end{bmatrix}
$$

$$
+
\begin{bmatrix}
1 \\ 0 \\ 0 \\ 0
\end{bmatrix}
[F_{11}(s)].
$$

(6.16)

The fundamental circuit equations are written in the form

$$
\begin{bmatrix}
\Delta_1(s) \\ \Delta_5(s) \\ \Delta_6(s) \\ \Delta_7(s) \\ \Delta_2(s) \\ \Delta_3(s) \\ \Delta_4(s) \\ \Delta_8(s) \\ \Delta_9(s) \\ \Delta_{10}(s)
\end{bmatrix}
=
\begin{bmatrix}
1 & 0 & 0 & 0 \\
0 & 1 & 0 & 0 \\
0 & 0 & 1 & 0 \\
0 & 0 & 0 & 1 \\
1 & -1 & 0 & 0 \\
1 & 0 & -1 & 0 \\
1 & 0 & -1 & -1 \\
0 & 0 & 1 & 1 \\
0 & -1 & 1 & 0 \\
0 & 0 & 0 & 1
\end{bmatrix}
\begin{bmatrix}
\Delta_1(s) \\ \Delta_5(s) \\ \Delta_6(s) \\ \Delta_7(s)
\end{bmatrix}.
$$

(6.17)

The substitution of (6.17) into (6.16) gives the branch equations. They include a matrix triple product of the form $[M][W][M]'$, which is easily calculated. The result is

$$
\begin{bmatrix}
(M_1 + M_2 + M_3 + M_4)s^2 & -M_2s^2 & -(M_3 + M_4)s^2 & -M_4s^2 \\
-M_2s^2 & K_5 + B_9s + M_2s^2 & -B_9s & 0 \\
-(M_3 + M_4)s^2 & -B_9s & K_6 + K_8 + B_9s + (M_3 + M_4)s^2 & K_8 + M_4s^2 \\
-M_4s^2 & 0 & K_8 + M_4s^2 & K_7 + K_8 + B_{10}s + M_4s^2
\end{bmatrix}
\begin{bmatrix}
\Delta_1(s) \\
\Delta_5(s) \\
\Delta_6(s) \\
\Delta_7(s)
\end{bmatrix}
$$

$$
=
\begin{bmatrix}
s\big(M_1\,\delta_1(0+) + M_2\,\delta_2(0+) + M_3\,\delta_3(0+) + M_4\,\delta_4(0+)\big) + M_1\,\dot\delta_1(0+) + M_2\,\dot\delta_2(0+) + M_3\,\dot\delta_3(0+) + M_4\,\dot\delta_4(0+) \\
-M_2\big(s\,\delta_2(0+) + \dot\delta_2(0+)\big) - B_9\,\delta_9(0+) \\
-s\big(M_3\,\delta_3(0+) + M_4\,\delta_4(0+)\big) - M_3\,\dot\delta_3(0+) - M_4\,\dot\delta_4(0+) + B_9\,\delta_9(0+) \\
-M_4s\,\delta_4(0+) - M_4\,\dot\delta_4(0+) + B_{10}\,\delta_{10}(0+)
\end{bmatrix}
$$

$$
+ \begin{bmatrix} 1 \\ 0 \\ 0 \\ 0 \end{bmatrix} [F_{11}(s)]. \tag{6.18}
$$

Of course, these equations could have been written by inspection, following a rule entirely similar to Rule 2.1.

EXAMPLE 6.8 (*Formulation of the chord equations for a hydraulic system*). In this example we shall write the chord equations for the hydraulic system of Example 6.2.

The terminal equations for the system may easily be written in the form

$$
\begin{bmatrix}
P_2(s) \\
P_3(s) \\
P_4(s) \\
P_5(s) \\
P_6(s)
\end{bmatrix}
=
\begin{bmatrix}
R_2 & 0 & 0 & 0 & 0 \\
0 & R_3 & 0 & 0 & 0 \\
0 & 0 & R_4 & 0 & 0 \\
0 & 0 & 0 & \dfrac{1}{C_5 s} & 0 \\
0 & 0 & 0 & 0 & R_6
\end{bmatrix}
\begin{bmatrix}
\dot g_2(s) \\
\dot g_3(s) \\
\dot g_4(s) \\
\dot g_5(s) \\
\dot g_6(s)
\end{bmatrix}
+
\begin{bmatrix}
0 \\
0 \\
0 \\
\dfrac{1}{s}\,p_5(0+) \\
0
\end{bmatrix},
\tag{6.19}
$$

and when the fundamental circuit equations (6.4) are written in the form

$$
\begin{bmatrix} 1 \\ 1 \\ 1 \end{bmatrix} [P_1(s)] +
\begin{bmatrix}
0 & 1 & 1 & 1 & 0 \\
0 & 0 & 0 & 0 & 1 \\
1 & 1 & 0 & 0 & 0
\end{bmatrix}
\begin{bmatrix}
P_2(s) \\
P_3(s) \\
P_4(s) \\
P_5(s) \\
P_6(s)
\end{bmatrix}
+
\begin{bmatrix} 0 \\ 0 \\ 1 \end{bmatrix} [P_7(s)] =
\begin{bmatrix} 0 \\ 0 \\ 0 \end{bmatrix},
\tag{6.20}
$$

the chord equations may easily be obtained as

$$
\begin{bmatrix} 1 \\ 1 \\ 1 \end{bmatrix} [P_1(s)] +
\begin{bmatrix}
R_3 + R_4 + \dfrac{1}{C_5 s} & 0 & R_3 \\
0 & R_6 & 0 \\
R_3 & 0 & R_2 + R_3
\end{bmatrix}
\begin{bmatrix}
\dot g_5(s) \\
\dot g_6(s) \\
\dot g_7(s)
\end{bmatrix}
$$

$$
+ \begin{bmatrix} 0 \\ 0 \\ 1 \end{bmatrix} [P_7(s)] +
\begin{bmatrix}
\dfrac{1}{s}\,p_5(0+) \\
0 \\
0
\end{bmatrix}
=
\begin{bmatrix} 0 \\ 0 \\ 0 \end{bmatrix}.
\tag{6.21}
$$

These equations may, of course, be written from the system graph, using Rule 2.2.

6.8. FORMULATION OF THE STATE EQUATIONS

We have already mentioned that there is no difference in the formulation procedures for the branch, chord, or branch-chord equations associated with various
types of systems, except in the names of the through and across variables. This
is also true in the formulation of the state equations; our treatment in Chapter 5
could easily have been in terms of general through and across variables, which
could represent electrical, mechanical, or hydraulic measurements, depending on
the system in question. We shall therefore once again refrain from a detailed
discussion, and limit ourselves to two examples followed by a general summary of
the formulation procedures.

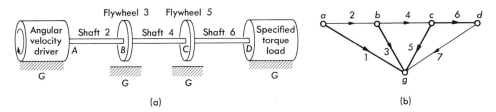

Fig. 6.26. Schematic and system graph for a rotating assembly.

EXAMPLE 6.9 (*A simple rotating assembly*). In this example we shall find a set of
state equations for the simple rotating assembly of Fig. 6.26(a). The method we
used in Chapter 5 cannot be directly applied here, because the flywheels are characterized by second-order differential equations of the form

$$T(t) = J \frac{d^2}{dt^2} \phi(t). \tag{6.22}$$

However, we can treat these as first-order components if we consider the angular
velocity $\dot{\phi}(t)$ rather than the angular displacement $\phi(t)$ as our across variable.
A similar situation would also arise in translational mechanical systems, in which
we would use velocity $\dot{\delta}(t)$ instead of displacement $\delta(t)$ for the across variable.
When we make this choice of across variable, the terminal equations for the system
of Fig. 6.26 may be written as

$$\begin{bmatrix} \dot{\phi}_1(t) \\ T_7(t) \end{bmatrix} \text{ specified,}$$

$$\frac{d}{dt} \begin{bmatrix} \dot{\phi}_3(t) \\ \dot{\phi}_5(t) \\ T_2(t) \\ T_4(t) \end{bmatrix} = \begin{bmatrix} 1/J_3 & 0 & 0 & 0 \\ 0 & 1/J_5 & 0 & 0 \\ 0 & 0 & K_2 & 0 \\ 0 & 0 & 0 & K_4 \end{bmatrix} \begin{bmatrix} T_3(t) \\ T_5(t) \\ \dot{\phi}_2(t) \\ \dot{\phi}_4(t) \end{bmatrix}, \tag{6.23}$$

$$\frac{d}{dt} T_6(t) = K_6 \dot{\phi}_6(t). \tag{6.24}$$

It can be readily seen that the selection of the formulation tree by the method of Section 5.3 yields that part of Fig. 6.26(b) shown by heavy lines. The fundamental circuit and cut-set equations with respect to this tree are written down for substitution into (6.23) and (6.24). The results are

$$
\begin{bmatrix} T_3(t) \\ T_5(t) \\ \dot{\phi}_2(t) \\ \dot{\phi}_4(t) \end{bmatrix} = \begin{bmatrix} 0 & 0 & 1 & -1 \\ 0 & 0 & 0 & 1 \\ -1 & 0 & 0 & 0 \\ 1 & -1 & 0 & 0 \end{bmatrix} \begin{bmatrix} \dot{\phi}_3(t) \\ \dot{\phi}_5(t) \\ T_2(t) \\ T_4(t) \end{bmatrix} + \begin{bmatrix} 0 \\ 0 \\ 0 \\ 0 \end{bmatrix} [\dot{\phi}_6(t)] + \begin{bmatrix} 0 & 0 \\ 0 & -1 \\ 1 & 0 \\ 0 & 0 \end{bmatrix} \begin{bmatrix} \dot{\phi}_1(t) \\ T_7(t) \end{bmatrix},
$$

$$ (6.25) $$

$$
[T_6(t)] = \begin{bmatrix} 0 & 0 & 0 & 0 \end{bmatrix} \begin{bmatrix} \dot{\phi}_3(t) \\ \dot{\phi}_5(t) \\ T_2(t) \\ T_4(t) \end{bmatrix} + [0] [\dot{\phi}_6(t)] + \begin{bmatrix} 0 & 1 \end{bmatrix} \begin{bmatrix} \dot{\phi}_1(t) \\ T_7(t) \end{bmatrix}. \qquad (6.26)
$$

We proceed by the method of Section 5.3, and substitute (6.25) and (6.26) into (6.23) and (6.24). This gives,

$$
\frac{d}{dt} \begin{bmatrix} \dot{\phi}_3(t) \\ \dot{\phi}_5(t) \\ T_2(t) \\ T_4(t) \end{bmatrix} = \begin{bmatrix} 1/J_3 & 0 & 0 & 0 \\ 0 & 1/J_5 & 0 & 0 \\ 0 & 0 & K_2 & 0 \\ 0 & 0 & 0 & K_4 \end{bmatrix} \begin{bmatrix} 0 & 0 & 1 & -1 \\ 0 & 0 & 0 & 1 \\ -1 & 0 & 0 & 0 \\ 1 & -1 & 0 & 0 \end{bmatrix} \begin{bmatrix} \dot{\phi}_3(t) \\ \dot{\phi}_5(t) \\ T_2(t) \\ T_4(t) \end{bmatrix}
$$

$$
+ \begin{bmatrix} 1/J_3 & 0 & 0 & 0 \\ 0 & 1/J_5 & 0 & 0 \\ 0 & 0 & K_2 & 0 \\ 0 & 0 & 0 & K_4 \end{bmatrix} \begin{bmatrix} 0 \\ 0 \\ 0 \\ 0 \end{bmatrix} [\dot{\phi}_6(t)] + \begin{bmatrix} 1/J_3 & 0 & 0 & 0 \\ 0 & 1/J_5 & 0 & 0 \\ 0 & 0 & K_2 & 0 \\ 0 & 0 & 0 & K_4 \end{bmatrix} \begin{bmatrix} 0 & 0 \\ 0 & -1 \\ 1 & 0 \\ 0 & 0 \end{bmatrix} \begin{bmatrix} \dot{\phi}_1(t) \\ T_7(t) \end{bmatrix}
$$

$$ (6.27) $$

and

$$
\frac{d}{dt} T_7(t) = K_6 \dot{\phi}_6(t). \qquad (6.28)
$$

Simplifying (6.27), we obtain

$$
\frac{d}{dt} \begin{bmatrix} \dot{\phi}_3(t) \\ \dot{\phi}_5(t) \\ T_2(t) \\ T_4(t) \end{bmatrix} = \begin{bmatrix} 0 & 0 & 1/J_3 & -1/J_3 \\ 0 & 0 & 0 & 1/J_5 \\ -K_2 & 0 & 0 & 0 \\ K_4 & -K_4 & 0 & 0 \end{bmatrix} \begin{bmatrix} \dot{\phi}_3(t) \\ \dot{\phi}_5(t) \\ T_2(t) \\ T_4(t) \end{bmatrix}
$$

$$
+ \begin{bmatrix} 0 \\ 0 \\ 0 \\ 0 \end{bmatrix} [\dot{\phi}_6(t)] + \begin{bmatrix} 0 & 0 \\ 0 & -1/J_5 \\ K_2 & 0 \\ 0 & 0 \end{bmatrix} \begin{bmatrix} \dot{\phi}_1(t) \\ T_7(t) \end{bmatrix}. \qquad (6.29)
$$

Normally, at this point, we would substitute (6.28) into (6.29) to eliminate $\dot{\phi}_6(t)$. However, since $\dot{\phi}_6(t)$ is multiplied by zero in every equation in (6.29), this step is unnecessary, so that (6.29) represents the state equations. These equations may

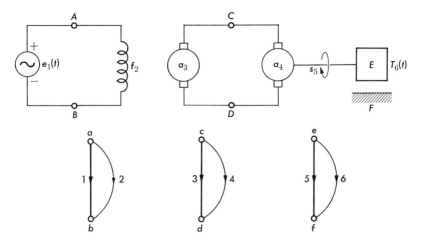

FIG. 6.27. Schematic and system graph of a simple electromechanical system.

be written more concisely as

$$\frac{d}{dt}\begin{bmatrix} \dot{\phi}_3(t) \\ \dot{\phi}_5(t) \\ T_2(t) \\ T_4(t) \end{bmatrix} = \begin{bmatrix} 0 & 0 & 1/J_3 & -1/J_3 \\ 0 & 0 & 0 & 1/J_5 \\ -K_2 & 0 & 0 & 0 \\ K_4 & -K_4 & 0 & 0 \end{bmatrix} \begin{bmatrix} \dot{\phi}_3(t) \\ \dot{\phi}_5(t) \\ T_2(t) \\ T_4(t) \end{bmatrix} + \begin{bmatrix} 0 \\ -T_7(t)/J_5 \\ K_2\dot{\phi}_1(t) \\ 0 \end{bmatrix}. \quad (6.30)$$

Note that if we wish to describe the angular displacements in our state model, we need only add two more equations:

$$\frac{d}{dt}\begin{bmatrix} \phi_3(t) \\ \phi_5(t) \end{bmatrix} = \begin{bmatrix} \dot{\phi}_3(t) \\ \dot{\phi}_5(t) \end{bmatrix}. \quad (6.31)$$

EXAMPLE 6.10 (*An electromechanical system*). In this example we shall find a set of state equations for the simple system of Example 6.5. For convenience, the schematic (Fig. 6.21) and system graph (Fig. 6.22) are shown again in Fig. 6.27.

In order to avoid second-order terminal equations, we shall again consider angular velocity $\dot{\phi}(t)$ as the across variable, so that the terminal equations for the various components take the form

$$\begin{bmatrix} v_1(t) \\ T_6(t) \end{bmatrix} = \begin{bmatrix} e_1(t) \\ T(t) \end{bmatrix} \quad \text{(specified)}, \quad (6.32)$$

$$\begin{bmatrix} v_2(t) \\ v_3(t) \end{bmatrix} = \begin{bmatrix} R_2 + L_2 \dfrac{d}{dt} & 0 \\ K_g & R_3 + L_3 \dfrac{d}{dt} \end{bmatrix} \begin{bmatrix} i_2(t) \\ i_3(t) \end{bmatrix}, \quad (6.33)$$

$$\begin{bmatrix} v_4(t) \\ T_5(t) \end{bmatrix} = \begin{bmatrix} R_4 + L_4 \dfrac{d}{dt} & K_m \\ -K_m & B + J \dfrac{d}{dt} \end{bmatrix} \begin{bmatrix} i_4(t) \\ \dot{\phi}_5(t) \end{bmatrix}. \quad (6.34)$$

We classify the elements of the system graph in a manner similar to that given in Section 5.4, the only difference being that since we are dealing with across and through variables other than voltage and current, we speak of first-order across, or first-order through elements, as the case may be. Thus we identify the elements as

(a) across driver: element 1,
(b) first-order across element: element 5,
(c) first-order through element: elements 2, 3, 4,
(d) through driver: element 6.

We next select the formulation forest, following the procedure of Section 5.4. One possible choice is that shown by heavy lines in Fig. 6.27. We now proceed by writing the terminal equations together as

$$
\frac{d}{dt}
\begin{bmatrix}
0 & 0 & 0 & 0 & 0 & 0 \\
0 & J & 0 & 0 & 0 & 0 \\
0 & 0 & 0 & 0 & 0 & 0 \\
0 & 0 & 0 & L_2 & 0 & 0 \\
0 & 0 & 0 & 0 & L_4 & 0 \\
0 & 0 & 0 & 0 & 0 & 0
\end{bmatrix}
\begin{bmatrix}
v_1(t) \\
\dot{\phi}_5(t) \\
v_3(t) \\
i_2(t) \\
i_4(t) \\
T_6(t)
\end{bmatrix}
+
\begin{bmatrix}
1 & 0 & 0 & 0 & 0 & 0 \\
0 & B & 0 & 0 & -K_m & 0 \\
0 & 0 & 1 & -K_g & 0 & 0 \\
0 & 0 & 0 & R_2 & 0 & 0 \\
0 & K_m & 0 & 0 & R_4 & 0 \\
0 & 0 & 0 & 0 & 0 & 1
\end{bmatrix}
\begin{bmatrix}
v_1(t) \\
\dot{\phi}_5(t) \\
v_3(t) \\
i_2(t) \\
i_4(t) \\
T_6(t)
\end{bmatrix}
$$

$$
= \frac{d}{dt}
\begin{bmatrix}
0 & 0 & 0 & 0 & 0 & 0 \\
0 & 0 & 0 & 0 & 0 & 0 \\
0 & 0 & L_3 & 0 & 0 & 0 \\
0 & 0 & 0 & 0 & 0 & 0 \\
0 & 0 & 0 & 0 & 0 & 0 \\
0 & 0 & 0 & 0 & 0 & 0
\end{bmatrix}
\begin{bmatrix}
i_1(t) \\
T_5(t) \\
i_3(t) \\
v_2(t) \\
v_4(t) \\
\dot{\phi}_6(t)
\end{bmatrix}
+
\begin{bmatrix}
0 & 0 & 0 & 0 & 0 & 0 \\
0 & 1 & 0 & 0 & 0 & 0 \\
0 & 0 & R_3 & 0 & 0 & 0 \\
0 & 0 & 0 & 1 & 0 & 0 \\
0 & 0 & 0 & 0 & 1 & 0 \\
0 & 0 & 0 & 0 & 0 & 0
\end{bmatrix}
\begin{bmatrix}
i_1(t) \\
T_5(t) \\
i_3(t) \\
v_2(t) \\
v_4(t) \\
\dot{\phi}_6(t)
\end{bmatrix}
+
\begin{bmatrix}
e_1(t) \\
0 \\
0 \\
0 \\
0 \\
T(t)
\end{bmatrix},
$$

$$(6.35)$$

or, more concisely,

$$
\frac{d}{dt}
\begin{bmatrix}
0 & 0 & 0 \\
J & 0 & 0 \\
0 & 0 & 0 \\
0 & L_2 & 0 \\
0 & 0 & L_4 \\
0 & 0 & 0
\end{bmatrix}
\begin{bmatrix}
\dot{\phi}_5(t) \\
i_2(t) \\
i_4(t)
\end{bmatrix}
+
\begin{bmatrix}
1 & 0 & 0 & 0 & 0 & 0 \\
0 & B & 0 & 0 & -K_m & 0 \\
0 & 0 & 1 & -K_g & 0 & 0 \\
0 & 0 & 0 & R_2 & 0 & 0 \\
0 & K_m & 0 & 0 & R_4 & 0 \\
0 & 0 & 0 & 0 & 0 & 1
\end{bmatrix}
\begin{bmatrix}
v_1(t) \\
\dot{\phi}_5(t) \\
v_3(t) \\
i_2(t) \\
i_4(t) \\
T_6(t)
\end{bmatrix}
$$

$$
= \frac{d}{dt}
\begin{bmatrix}
0 \\
0 \\
L_3 \\
0 \\
0 \\
0
\end{bmatrix}
[i_3(t)] +
\begin{bmatrix}
0 & 0 & 0 & 0 \\
1 & 0 & 0 & 0 \\
0 & R_3 & 0 & 0 \\
0 & 0 & 1 & 0 \\
0 & 0 & 0 & 1 \\
0 & 0 & 0 & 0
\end{bmatrix}
\begin{bmatrix}
T_5(t) \\
i_3(t) \\
v_2(t) \\
v_4(t)
\end{bmatrix}
+
\begin{bmatrix}
e_1(t) \\
0 \\
0 \\
0 \\
0 \\
T(t)
\end{bmatrix}.
$$

$$(6.36)$$

The fundamental circuit and cut-set equations (6.10) and (6.11) may be written together to give

$$
\begin{bmatrix}
T_5(t) \\
i_3(t) \\
v_2(t) \\
v_4(t)
\end{bmatrix}
=
\begin{bmatrix}
0 & 0 & 0 & 0 & 0 & -1 \\
0 & 0 & 0 & 0 & -1 & 0 \\
1 & 0 & 0 & 0 & 0 & 0 \\
0 & 0 & 1 & 0 & 0 & 0
\end{bmatrix}
\begin{bmatrix}
v_1(t) \\
\dot{\phi}_5(t) \\
v_3(t) \\
i_2(t) \\
i_4(t) \\
T_6(t)
\end{bmatrix},
$$

$$(6.37)$$

and substituting (6.37) into (6.36), we obtain

$$
\frac{d}{dt}
\begin{bmatrix}
0 & 0 & 0 \\
J & 0 & 0 \\
0 & 0 & 0 \\
0 & L_2 & 0 \\
0 & 0 & L_4 \\
0 & 0 & 0
\end{bmatrix}
\begin{bmatrix}
\dot{\phi}_5(t) \\
\dot{i}_2(t) \\
\dot{i}_4(t)
\end{bmatrix}
+
\begin{bmatrix}
1 & 0 & 0 & 0 & 0 & 0 \\
0 & B & 0 & 0 & -K_m & 0 \\
0 & 0 & 1 & -K_g & 0 & 0 \\
0 & 0 & 0 & R_2 & 0 & 0 \\
0 & K_m & 0 & 0 & R_4 & 0 \\
0 & 0 & 0 & 0 & 0 & 1
\end{bmatrix}
\begin{bmatrix}
v_1(t) \\
\dot{\phi}_5(t) \\
v_3(t) \\
i_2(t) \\
i_4(t) \\
T_6(t)
\end{bmatrix}
$$

$$
= \frac{d}{dt}
\begin{bmatrix}
0 \\
0 \\
L_3 \\
0 \\
0 \\
0
\end{bmatrix}
[0 \quad 0 \quad 0 \quad 0 \quad -1 \quad 0]
\begin{bmatrix}
v_1(t) \\
\dot{\phi}_5(t) \\
v_3(t) \\
i_2(t) \\
i_4(t) \\
T_6(t)
\end{bmatrix}
$$

$$
+
\begin{bmatrix}
0 & 0 & 0 & 0 \\
1 & 0 & 0 & 0 \\
0 & R_3 & 0 & 0 \\
0 & 0 & 1 & 0 \\
0 & 0 & 0 & 1 \\
0 & 0 & 0 & 0
\end{bmatrix}
\begin{bmatrix}
0 & 0 & 0 & 0 & 0 & -1 \\
0 & 0 & 0 & 0 & -1 & 0 \\
1 & 0 & 0 & 0 & 0 & 0 \\
0 & 0 & 1 & 0 & 0 & 0
\end{bmatrix}
\begin{bmatrix}
v_1(t) \\
\dot{\phi}_5(t) \\
v_3(t) \\
i_2(t) \\
i_4(t) \\
T_6(t)
\end{bmatrix}
+
\begin{bmatrix}
e_1(t) \\
0 \\
0 \\
0 \\
0 \\
T(t)
\end{bmatrix} .
$$

$$(6.38)$$

We perform the indicated operations in (6.38), and the result is

$$
\frac{d}{dt}
\begin{bmatrix}
0 & 0 & 0 \\
J & 0 & 0 \\
0 & 0 & 0 \\
0 & L_2 & 0 \\
0 & 0 & L_4 \\
0 & 0 & 0
\end{bmatrix}
\begin{bmatrix}
\dot{\phi}_5(t) \\
\dot{i}_2(t) \\
\dot{i}_4(t)
\end{bmatrix}
+
\begin{bmatrix}
1 & 0 & 0 & 0 & 0 & 0 \\
0 & B & 0 & 0 & -K_m & 0 \\
0 & 0 & 1 & -K_g & 0 & 0 \\
0 & 0 & 0 & R_2 & 0 & 0 \\
0 & K_m & 0 & 0 & R_4 & 0 \\
0 & 0 & 0 & 0 & 0 & 1
\end{bmatrix}
\begin{bmatrix}
v_1(t) \\
\dot{\phi}_5(t) \\
v_3(t) \\
i_2(t) \\
i_4(t) \\
T_6(t)
\end{bmatrix}
$$

$$
= \frac{d}{dt}
\begin{bmatrix}
0 \\
0 \\
-L_3 \\
0 \\
0 \\
0
\end{bmatrix}
[i_4(t)] +
\begin{bmatrix}
0 & 0 & 0 & 0 & 0 & 0 \\
0 & 0 & 0 & 0 & 0 & -1 \\
0 & 0 & 0 & 0 & -R_3 & 0 \\
1 & 0 & 0 & 0 & 0 & 0 \\
0 & 0 & 1 & 0 & 0 & 0 \\
0 & 0 & 0 & 0 & 0 & 0
\end{bmatrix}
\begin{bmatrix}
v_1(t) \\
\dot{\phi}_5(t) \\
v_3(t) \\
i_2(t) \\
i_4(t) \\
T_6(t)
\end{bmatrix}
+
\begin{bmatrix}
e_1(t) \\
0 \\
0 \\
0 \\
0 \\
T(t)
\end{bmatrix} .
$$

$$(6.39)$$

Next, we collect similar terms in (6.39), and obtain

$$
\frac{d}{dt}
\begin{bmatrix}
0 & 0 & 0 \\
J & 0 & 0 \\
0 & 0 & L_3 \\
0 & L_2 & 0 \\
0 & 0 & L_4 \\
0 & 0 & 0
\end{bmatrix}
\begin{bmatrix}
\dot{\phi}_5(t) \\
\dot{i}_2(t) \\
\dot{i}_4(t)
\end{bmatrix}
=
\begin{bmatrix}
-1 & 0 & 0 & 0 & 0 & 0 \\
0 & -B & 0 & 0 & K_m & -1 \\
0 & 0 & -1 & K_g & -R_3 & 0 \\
1 & 0 & 0 & -R_2 & 0 & 0 \\
0 & -K_m & 1 & 0 & -R_4 & 0 \\
0 & 0 & 0 & 0 & 0 & -1
\end{bmatrix}
\begin{bmatrix}
v_1(t) \\
\dot{\phi}_5(t) \\
v_3(t) \\
i_2(t) \\
i_4(t) \\
T_6(t)
\end{bmatrix}
+
\begin{bmatrix}
e_1(t) \\
0 \\
0 \\
0 \\
0 \\
T(t)
\end{bmatrix} .
$$

$$(6.40)$$

Equations (6.40) are split into three sets as follows:

$$\begin{bmatrix} v_1(t) \\ T_6(t) \end{bmatrix} = \begin{bmatrix} e_1(t) \\ T(t) \end{bmatrix}, \tag{6.32}$$

$$\frac{d}{dt}\begin{bmatrix} J & 0 & 0 \\ 0 & 0 & L_3 \\ 0 & L_2 & 0 \end{bmatrix}\begin{bmatrix} \dot{\phi}_5(t) \\ i_2(t) \\ i_4(t) \end{bmatrix} = \begin{bmatrix} -B & 0 & K_m \\ 0 & K_g & -R_3 \\ 0 & -R_2 & 0 \end{bmatrix}\begin{bmatrix} \dot{\phi}_5(t) \\ i_2(t) \\ i_4(t) \end{bmatrix}$$

$$+ \begin{bmatrix} 0 \\ -1 \\ 0 \end{bmatrix}[v_3(t)] + \begin{bmatrix} 0 & -1 \\ 0 & 0 \\ 1 & 0 \end{bmatrix}\begin{bmatrix} v_1(t) \\ T_6(t) \end{bmatrix}, \tag{6.41}$$

and

$$\frac{d}{dt}L_4 i_4(t) = v_3(t) + \begin{bmatrix} -K_m & 0 & -R_4 \end{bmatrix}\begin{bmatrix} \dot{\phi}_5(t) \\ i_2(t) \\ i_4(t) \end{bmatrix}. \tag{6.42}$$

We substitute (6.42) and (6.32) into (6.41), and obtain

$$\frac{d}{dt}\begin{bmatrix} J & 0 & 0 \\ 0 & 0 & L_3 \\ 0 & L_2 & 0 \end{bmatrix}\begin{bmatrix} \dot{\phi}_5(t) \\ i_2(t) \\ i_4(t) \end{bmatrix} = \begin{bmatrix} -B & 0 & K_m \\ 0 & K_g & -R_3 \\ 0 & -R_2 & 0 \end{bmatrix}\begin{bmatrix} \dot{\phi}_5(t) \\ i_2(t) \\ i_4(t) \end{bmatrix} + \begin{bmatrix} 0 & -1 \\ 0 & 0 \\ 1 & 0 \end{bmatrix}\begin{bmatrix} e_1(t) \\ T(t) \end{bmatrix}$$

$$+ \begin{bmatrix} 0 \\ -1 \\ 0 \end{bmatrix}\frac{d}{dt}L_4 i_4(t) + \begin{bmatrix} 0 \\ -1 \\ 0 \end{bmatrix}\begin{bmatrix} K_m & 0 & R_4 \end{bmatrix}\begin{bmatrix} \dot{\phi}_5(t) \\ i_2(t) \\ i_4(t) \end{bmatrix}. \tag{6.43}$$

We perform the indicated operations, and (6.43) is reduced to

$$\frac{d}{dt}\begin{bmatrix} J & 0 & 0 \\ 0 & 0 & L_3 + L_4 \\ 0 & L_2 & 0 \end{bmatrix}\begin{bmatrix} \dot{\phi}_5(t) \\ i_2(t) \\ i_4(t) \end{bmatrix} = \begin{bmatrix} -B & 0 & K_m \\ -K_m & K_g & -(R_3 + R_4) \\ 0 & -R_2 & 0 \end{bmatrix}\begin{bmatrix} \dot{\phi}_5(t) \\ i_2(t) \\ i_4(t) \end{bmatrix} + \begin{bmatrix} -T(t) \\ 0 \\ e_1(t) \end{bmatrix}, \tag{6.44}$$

or

$$\frac{d}{dt}\begin{bmatrix} \dot{\phi}_5(t) \\ i_2(t) \\ i_4(t) \end{bmatrix} = \begin{bmatrix} -\dfrac{B}{J} & 0 & \dfrac{K_m}{J} \\ 0 & -\dfrac{R_2}{L_2} & 0 \\ \dfrac{-K_m}{L_3 + L_4} & \dfrac{K_g}{L_3 + L_4} & \dfrac{-(R_3 + R_4)}{L_3 + L_4} \end{bmatrix}\begin{bmatrix} \dot{\phi}_5(t) \\ i_2(t) \\ i_4(t) \end{bmatrix} + \begin{bmatrix} -\dfrac{T(t)}{J} \\ \dfrac{e_1(t)}{L_2} \\ 0 \end{bmatrix}, \tag{6.45}$$

which are the state equations.

In this example we have somewhat laboriously followed the general procedure outlined in Section 5.5; in practice, the calculations could be considerably shortened. However, the examples of this section serve to illustrate the fact that there are no new difficulties encountered in the formulation of the state equations for non-electrical or mixed systems.

In order to stress the fact that we are not discussing electromechanical analogies, and also to facilitate a quick review, we conclude this section with a general summary of the formulation procedures. Of course, electrical systems are included as a special case. We shall limit ourselves to systems in which it is possible to choose the through and across variables so that the terminal relations are all algebraic or first-order differential equations.

Although systems of two-terminal components may be handled by the same techniques as those containing multiterminal components, the structure of their terminal equations leads to some simplifications. Therefore, we shall first list the procedure for the formulation of the state equations for these simpler systems.

State equations for systems containing only two-terminal components

(1) The elements of the system graph are classified, by the method of Section 5.4, as first-order across or first-order through elements, etc.
(2) The formulation forest is selected to include as many first-order across elements and to exclude as many first-order through elements as possible.
(3) The terminal equations are arranged in four groups, containing
    (a) the branch first-order across and chord first-order through elements;
    (b) the chord first-order across and branch first-order through elements;
    (c) the algebraic elements;
    (d) the through and across drivers.
(4) The fundamental circuit and cut-set equations are written in three sets in a suitable form for substitution into the terminal equations, (a), (b), and (c), above.
(5) The nonspecified branch through variables and chord across variables are eliminated by substitution of the circuit and cut-set equations into the terminal equations.
(6) The nonspecified variables whose first time derivatives do not occur in the equations resulting from Step 5 are eliminated.
(7) The specified functions for the through and across drivers are inserted into the result of Step 6, and the resulting equations rearranged into the canonical form. They are the state equations.

A glance through Example 6.9 will show that we followed exactly the above procedure. On the other hand, in Example 6.10 we encountered multiterminal components. Our method for such systems is summarized in the following.

State equations for systems containing multiterminal components

(1) The elements of the system graph are classified, by the method of Section 5.4, as first-order across or first-order through elements, etc.
(2) The formulation forest is selected by the method of Section 5.4.
(3) The various terminal equations are written together in one expression, the derivative terms are separated from the algebraic terms, and the variables are ordered as follows:
    (a) across drivers;
    (b) generalized across drivers;

     (c) branch first-order across elements;
     (d) branch first-order across-through elements;
     (e) branch algebraic elements;
     (f) branch first-order through elements;
     (g) chord first-order across elements;
     (h) chord first-order across-through elements;
     (i) chord algebraic elements;
     (j) chord first-order through elements;
     (k) generalized through drivers;
     (l) through drivers.

(4) The fundamental circuit and cut-set equations are written together in a form suitable for substitution into the terminal equations.

(5) The fundamental circuit and cut-set equations are substituted into the terminal equations.

(6) The algebraic relations are eliminated from the result of Step 5. This is best done by dividing the equations into groups and substituting from one group into another.

(7) In the equations resulting from Step 6, there remain variables which do not correspond to first-order elements. These are eliminated by substituting some of the equations into the remainder.

(8) The equations resulting from Step 7 are rearranged into the canonical form. They are the state equations.

6.9. CONCLUDING REMARKS

We have dealt with linear nonelectrical systems after a detailed discussion of electric networks. In doing this, we have seen that our treatment of electric networks is a special case of a general method which applies to any system whose components are characterized by linear differential or algebraic equations, and whose variables satisfy the vertex and circuit postulates. Of course, we could have applied ourselves to all these systems simultaneously throughout the previous chapters; we did not do so because it is our belief that it is better to learn about one situation first; when this is well understood, it becomes easier to comprehend a generalization.

Our method of presentation of mechanical and hydraulic systems is *not* to be construed as a discussion of analogies. In fact, the study of mechanical and hydraulic systems on the basis of system-graph concepts makes no appeal to a knowledge of electric network theory. Thus the formation of electro-mechanical analogies, etc., is shown to be a redundant step in the solution of a given problem.

Our method can nevertheless be used as a formal technique for finding an analogous electric network for a given nonelectrical physical system. Such a study may be well warranted in connection with the transducers involved in measurement techniques. Having obtained the system graph associated with a given system, we merely have to find an electric network with the same system graph, and whose system equations have the same mathematical form as those in the given system. This procedure, however, does not simplify an analytical or numerical solution in any way, since all our methods of Chapters 3, 4, and 5 can be applied directly.

The central concept of the mathematical model presented here is the notion of terminal representations. This concept, being directly linked to the physical characteristics of a component, provides a vital link between the physical world under purview and its corresponding mathematical models. Furthermore, it is comforting to note that we have proceeded to the mathematical model, one that fits the systems problem, only from a knowledge of the physical system and not vice versa.

In any unified approach to a large class of problems, it is difficult to bring specific results to a sharp focus. For instance, one would hardly expect to learn the detailed characteristics of a vacuum tube, a transistor, or an electro-mechanical transducer, from such a study as presented here. On the other hand, we believe that these details can be easily filled in once the fundamental systems discipline is comprehended.

PROBLEMS

6.1. Can you name any kind of measurement which does not require two "terminals"? Discuss your answer.

6.2. In the study of traffic systems, vehicle flow is an obvious through variable. Suggestions for an across variable include "propensity to travel" and "profit," both of which are difficult to measure. Discuss the practicality of these variables, and make your own suggestions for a suitable across variable which satisfies the circuit postulate.

6.3. Demonstrate to your own satisfaction, by actually rotating an object, that a series of rotations about three orthogonal axes, taken in two different orders, can lead to different overall rotational displacements.

6.4. Formulate the chord equations for the system of Fig. 6.14.

6.5. Formulate the branch equations for the system of Fig. 6.16.

6.6. Formulate both the branch and the chord equations for the systems of Fig. 6.18 and Fig. 6.20.

6.7. Formulate a set of system equations for the system of Fig. 6.23.

6.8. For the system of Fig. 6.26, find the angular displacement of one end of shaft 6 with respect to the other when

$$\dot{\phi}_1(t) = 10 \text{ rad/sec}, \quad T_7(t) = 7 \text{ n-m}, \quad J_3 = \tfrac{1}{3} \text{ n-m sec}^2/\text{rad},$$
$$J_5 = \tfrac{1}{5} \text{ n-m sec}^2/\text{rad}, \quad K_2 = 2 \text{ n-m/rad}, \quad K_4 = 4 \text{ n-m/rad},$$
$$K_6 = 6 \text{ n-m/rad}.$$

6.9. Formulate a set of state equations for the system of Fig. 6.18.

6.10. The classical methods of mechanics, using energy considerations, lead to state models for mechanical systems. Contrast, with an example, these methods with those explained in this text.

APPENDIXES

THE LAPLACE TRANSFORM

A.1. DEFINITION AND EXISTENCE OF THE LAPLACE TRANSFORM

If a function $f(t)$, defined for all positive values of the variable t, is multiplied by e^{-st} and integrated with respect to t from zero to infinity, a new function $F(s)$ of the parameter s is obtained. That is

$$F(s) = \int_0^\infty e^{-st} f(t) \, dt. \tag{A.1}$$

$F(s)$ is called the *Laplace transform* of $f(t)$, and we frequently write

$$F(s) = \mathcal{L} f(t), \tag{A.2}$$

or

$$f(t) = \mathcal{L}^{-1} F(s). \tag{A.3}$$

Since nothing has been said about the parameter s, it may be assumed to take on complex values, so that

$$s = \sigma + j\omega \tag{A.4}$$

where σ, ω are real.

EXAMPLE A.1. Let $f(t) = u(t)$, the unit step function, then

$$F(s) = \int_0^\infty e^{-st} u(t) \, dt = \int_0^\infty e^{-st} \, dt = \left[-\frac{1}{s} e^{-st} \right]_0^\infty,$$

so that for Re $(s) = \sigma > 0$,

$$\mathcal{L} u(t) = \frac{1}{s}. \tag{A.5}$$

EXAMPLE A.2. Let $f(t) = e^{\alpha t}$, $t > 0$, α a constant, then

$$F(s) = \int_0^\infty e^{-st} e^{\alpha t} \, dt = \int_0^\infty e^{-(s-\alpha)t} \, dt = \left[\frac{1}{\alpha - s} e^{-(s-\alpha)t} \right]_0^\infty,$$

so that for Re $(s - \alpha) > 0$,

$$\mathcal{L} e^{\alpha t} = \frac{1}{s - \alpha}.$$

279

Not all functions have Laplace transforms. It can be shown that a function $f(t)$ has a Laplace transform only if it is of exponential order. That is, the Laplace transform of $f(t)$ exists when $\lim_{t \to \infty} e^{-at} f(t)$ is finite for some real positive constant a. Furthermore, to guarantee the existence of the Laplace transform, $f(t)$ must be at least sectionally continuous for all $t \geq 0$.

EXAMPLE A.3. The function e^{t^2} is not of exponential order since

$$\lim_{t \to \infty} (e^{-at} e^{t^2}) = \lim_{t \to \infty} e^{t(t-a)} = \infty.$$

In the following, we shall deal only with functions which have Laplace transforms.

A.2. SOME SIMPLE PROPERTIES

In the process of finding Laplace transforms and inverse Laplace transforms, and in the solution of differential equations, the following simple theorems frequently offer considerable simplifications.

Theorem A.1.

$$\mathcal{L}\big(Af(t) + Bg(t)\big) = AF(s) + BG(s). \tag{A.6}$$

Proof

$$\mathcal{L}\big(Af(t) + Bg(t)\big) = \int_0^\infty \big(Af(t) + Bg(t)\big)e^{-st}\, dt$$

$$= A \int_0^\infty f(t)e^{-st}\, dt + B \int_0^\infty g(t)e^{-st}\, dt$$

$$= A\mathcal{L}f(t) + B\mathcal{L}g(t).$$

Theorem A.2.

$$\mathcal{L}\left(\frac{df(t)}{dt}\right) = sF(s) - f(0+), \tag{A.7}$$

where $f(0+)$ is the value of $f(t)$ as the origin is approached from the positive, or right-hand side.

Proof

$$\mathcal{L}\left(\frac{df(t)}{dt}\right) = \int_0^\infty \frac{df(t)}{dt} e^{-st}\, dt$$

$$= [f(t)e^{-st}]_0^\infty + s \int_0^\infty f(t)e^{-st}\, dt$$

$$= s\mathcal{L}f(t) - f(0+).$$

Theorem A.3.

$$\mathcal{L}\left(\frac{d^n f(t)}{dt^n}\right) = s^n F(s) - s^{n-1}f(0+) - s^{n-2}f'(0+) - \cdots - f^{(n-1)}(0+). \tag{A.8}$$

Proof. For $n = 1$, this reduces to Theorem A.2. Assume the theorem is true for $n = k$, and let $d^k f(t)/dt^k = g(t)$, then,

$$g'(t) = \frac{d^{k+1}f(t)}{dt^{k+1}},$$

$$\begin{aligned}
\mathcal{L}g'(t) &= s\mathcal{L}g(t) - g(0+) \\
&= s\left(s^k \mathcal{L}f(t) - s^{k-1}f(0+) - \cdots - f^{(k-1)}(0+)\right) - f^{(k)}(0+) \\
&= s^{k+1}\mathcal{L}f(t) - s^k f(0+) - \cdots - s f^{(k-1)}(0+) - f^{(k)}(0+).
\end{aligned}$$

Therefore, the proof follows immediately by mathematical induction.

Theorem A.4.

$$\mathcal{L}\left(\int_0^t f(x)\, dx\right) = \frac{1}{s}[F(s)]. \tag{A.9}$$

Proof

$$\begin{aligned}
\mathcal{L}\left(\int_0^t f(x)\, dx\right) &= \int_0^\infty e^{-st} \int_0^t f(x)\, dx\, dt \\
&= \left[-\frac{1}{s} e^{-st} \int_0^t f(x)\, dx\right]_0^\infty + \frac{1}{s}\int_0^\infty e^{-st}f(t)\, dt = \frac{1}{s}\mathcal{L}f(t).
\end{aligned}$$

Theorem A.5.

$$\mathcal{L}\left(\int f(t)\, dt\right) = \frac{1}{s}F(s) + \frac{1}{s}\int f(t)\, dt\bigg|_{t=0+}. \tag{A.10}$$

Proof

$$\begin{aligned}
\mathcal{L}\left(\int f(t)\, dt\right) &= \mathcal{L}\left(\int_0^t f(x)\, dx + \int f(t)\, dt\bigg|_{t=0+}\right) \\
&= \frac{1}{s}\mathcal{L}f(t) + \int f(t)\, dt\bigg|_{t=0+} \quad \mathcal{L}u(t) \\
&= \frac{1}{s}\mathcal{L}f(t) + \frac{1}{s}\int f(t)\, dt\bigg|_{t=0+}.
\end{aligned}$$

Theorems A.4 and A.5 may easily be extended to cover higher-order integrals. Thus we have

$$\mathcal{L}\left(\int_0^t \int_0^x f(\lambda)\, d\lambda\, dx\right) = \frac{1}{s^2}\mathcal{L}f(t), \tag{A.11}$$

$$\mathcal{L}\iint f(t)\, dt\, dt = \frac{1}{s^2}F(s) + \frac{1}{s^2}\int f(t)\, dt\bigg|_{t=0+} + \frac{1}{s}\iint f(t)\, dt\, dt\bigg|_{t=0+}. \tag{A.12}$$

If we denote $\int f(t)\,dt$ by $f^{(-1)}(t)$, formulas (A.10) and (A.12) become

$$\mathcal{L}f^{(-1)}(t) = \frac{1}{s}F(s) + \frac{1}{s}f^{(-1)}(0+),$$ (A.13)

$$\mathcal{L}f^{(-2)}(t) = \frac{1}{s^2}F(s) + \frac{1}{s^2}f^{(-1)}(0+) + \frac{1}{s}f^{(-2)}(0+).$$ (A.14)

Theorem A.6.

$$\mathcal{L}(tf(t)) = -F'(s).$$ (A.15)

Proof

$$F(s) = \int_0^\infty e^{-st}f(t)\,dt,$$

so that differentiating with respect to s, we obtain

$$F'(s) = \int_0^\infty -t\,e^{-st}f(t)\,dt = -\mathcal{L}tf(t).$$

Theorem A.6 is easily extended to give the following theorem.

Theorem A.7.

$$\mathcal{L}(t^n f(t)) = (-1)^n F^{(n)}(s).$$ (A.16)

Theorem A.8.

$$\mathcal{L}\left(\frac{1}{t}f(t)\right) = \int_s^\infty F(x)\,dx.$$ (A.17)

Proof

$$\int_s^\infty F(x)\,dx = \int_s^\infty \int_0^\infty e^{-xt}f(t)\,dt\,dx = \int_0^\infty f(t)\int_s^\infty e^{-xt}\,dx\,dt$$

$$= \int_0^\infty f(t)\left[\frac{-1}{t}e^{-xt}\right]_s^\infty dt = \int_0^\infty f(t)\cdot\frac{1}{t}e^{-st}\,dt = \mathcal{L}\left(\frac{1}{t}f(t)\right).$$

Theorem A.9.

$$\mathcal{L}(e^{at}f(t)) = F(s - a).$$ (A.18)

Proof

$$\mathcal{L}[e^{at}f(t)] = \int_0^\infty e^{-st}e^{at}f(t)\,dt = \int_0^\infty e^{-(s-a)t}f(t)\,dt = F(s - a).$$

Theorem A.10.

$$\mathcal{L}f(t - b) = e^{-bs}F(s),$$ (A.19)

where $f(t) = 0$ for $t < 0$.

Proof $\mathcal{L}f(t - b) = \int_0^\infty e^{-st}f(t - b)\,dt = \int_b^\infty e^{-st}f(t - b)\,dt$

$$= \int_0^\infty e^{-s(\tau+b)}f(\tau)\,d\tau = e^{-sb}\int_0^\infty e^{-s\tau}f(\tau)\,d\tau = e^{-sb}F(s).$$

Theorem A.11.

$$\mathcal{L}\frac{1}{c}f\left(\frac{t}{c}\right) = F(cs). \tag{A.20}$$

Proof

$$\mathcal{L}\frac{1}{c}f\left(\frac{t}{c}\right) = \int_0^\infty \frac{1}{c}f\left(\frac{t}{c}\right)e^{-st}\,dt = \int_0^\infty f(\tau)e^{-cs\tau}\,d\tau = F(cs).$$

If in (A.20) we replace c by $1/b$, we immediately obtain

$$\mathcal{L}f(bt) = (1/b)F(s/b). \tag{A.21}$$

Furthermore, combining the results of Theorems A.9 and A.11, we have

$$\mathcal{L}[(1/c)e^{bt/c}f(t/c)] = F(cs - b). \tag{A.22}$$

The calculation of Laplace transforms for periodic waveforms is simplified by the following theorem.

Theorem A.12. If $f(t + a) = f(t)$, then

$$\mathcal{L}f(t) = \frac{\int_0^a e^{-st}f(t)\,dt}{1 - e^{-as}}. \tag{A.23}$$

Proof

$$\mathcal{L}f(t) = \int_0^\infty f(t)e^{-st}\,dt = \sum_{n=0}^\infty \int_{na}^{(n+1)a} f(t)e^{-st}\,dt$$

$$= \sum_{n=0}^\infty \int_0^a f(\tau + na)e^{-s(\tau+na)}\,d\tau = \sum_{n=0}^\infty e^{-nas}\int_0^a f(\tau + na)e^{-s\tau}\,d\tau$$

$$= \sum_{n=0}^\infty e^{-nas}\int_0^a f(\tau)e^{-s\tau}\,d\tau = \int_0^a f(t)e^{-st}\,dt \sum_{n=0}^\infty e^{-nas}$$

$$= \frac{\int_0^a f(t)e^{-st}\,dt}{1 - e^{-as}}.$$

We can similarly prove the theorem following.

Theorem A.13. If $f(t + a) = -f(t)$, then

$$\mathcal{L}f(t) = \frac{\int_0^a f(t)e^{-st}\,dt}{1 + e^{-as}}. \tag{A.24}$$

TABLE A.1

		$f(t)$	$F(s)$
1	Definition	$f(t)$	$\int_0^\infty e^{-st}f(t)\ dt$
2	Theorem A.1	$Af(t) + Bg(t)$	$AF(s) + BG(s)$
3	Theorem A.2	$f'(t)$	$sF(s) - f(0+)$
4	Theorem A.3	$f^{(n)}(t)$	$s^nF(s) - s^{n-1}f(0+) - s^{n-2}f'(0+)$ $- \cdots - f^{(n-1)}(0+)$
5	Theorem A.4	$\int_0^t f(x)\ dx$	$(1/s)F(s)$
6	Theorem A.5	$\int f(t)\ dt = f^{(-1)}(t)$	$(1/s)F(s) + (1/s)f^{(-1)}(0+)$
7		$\int_0^t \int_0^x f(\lambda)\ d\lambda\ dx$	$(1/s^2)F(s)$
8		$f^{(-2)}(t)$	$(1/s^2)F(s) + (1/s^2)f^{(-1)}(0+) + (1/s)f^{(-2)}(0+)$
9	Theorem A.6	$tf(t)$	$-F'(s)$
10	Theorem A.7	$t^nf(t)$	$(-1)^nF^{(n)}(s)$
11	Theorem A.8	$(1/t)f(t)$	$\int_s^\infty F(x)\ dx$
12	Theorem A.9	$e^{at}f(t)$	$F(s - a)$
13	Theorem A.10	$f(t - b)$	$e^{-bs}F(s)$
14	Theorem A.11	$(1/c)f(t/c)$	$F(cs)$
15		$f(bt)$	$(1/b)F(s/b)$
16		$(1/c)e^{bt/c}f(t/c)$	$F(cs - b)$
17	Theorem A.12	$f(t + a) = f(t)$	$\dfrac{\int_0^a e^{-st}f(t)\ dt}{1 - e^{-as}}$
18	Theorem A.13	$f(t + a) = -f(t)$	$\dfrac{\int_0^a e^{-st}f(t)\ dt}{1 + e^{-as}}$

The results of the above theorems are summarized in Table A.1. We illustrate some of them in the following examples.

EXAMPLE A.4. Find $\mathcal{L}(\cos \omega t)$:

$$\cos \omega t = \tfrac{1}{2}e^{j\omega t} + \tfrac{1}{2}e^{-j\omega t},$$

$$\mathcal{L} \cos \omega t = \tfrac{1}{2}\mathcal{L}e^{j\omega t} + \tfrac{1}{2}\mathcal{L}e^{-j\omega t} \qquad \text{(Theorem A.1)}$$

$$= \frac{1}{2}\frac{1}{s - j\omega} + \frac{1}{2}\frac{1}{s + j\omega} \qquad \text{(from Example A.2),}$$

or

$$\mathcal{L} \cos \omega t = \frac{s}{s^2 + \omega^2}. \tag{A.25}$$

EXAMPLE A.5. Find $\mathcal{L}(\sin \omega t)$:

$$\sin \omega t = -\frac{1}{\omega}\frac{d}{dt}\cos \omega t,$$

$$\mathcal{L}\sin \omega t = -\frac{1}{\omega}\mathcal{L}\frac{d}{dt}\cos \omega t$$

$$= -\frac{1}{\omega}\left[s\left(\frac{s}{s^2+\omega^2}\right)-1\right] \quad \text{(Theorem A.2)}$$

$$= -\frac{1}{\omega}\left(\frac{s^2}{s^2+\omega^2}-1\right) = -\frac{1}{\omega}\left(\frac{-\omega^2}{s^2+\omega^2}\right),$$

or

$$\mathcal{L}\sin \omega t = \frac{\omega}{s^2+\omega^2}. \tag{A.26}$$

EXAMPLE A.6. From examples A.1 and A.2, we have

$$\mathcal{L}e^{at} = \frac{1}{s-a}, \qquad \mathcal{L}u(t) = \frac{1}{s},$$

so that

$$\mathcal{L}\frac{1}{a}(e^{at}-1) = \frac{1}{a}\left(\frac{1}{s-a}-\frac{1}{s}\right) = \frac{1}{s(s-a)}.$$

Now an alternative method for finding this transform is

$$\mathcal{L}\frac{1}{a}(e^{at}-1) = \mathcal{L}\int_0^t e^{a\tau}\,d\tau = \frac{1}{s}\mathcal{L}e^{at} = \frac{1}{s(s-a)} \quad \text{(Theorem A.4)}.$$

Similarly,

$$\mathcal{L}\frac{1}{a}\int_0^t (e^{a\tau}-1)\,d\tau = \mathcal{L}\left(\frac{1}{a^2}e^{at}-\frac{1}{a^2}-t\right) = \frac{1}{s^2(s-a)},$$

and

$$\mathcal{L}\left(\int_0^t\int_0^\tau\int_0^x e^{a\lambda}\,d\lambda\,dx\,d\tau\right) = \frac{1}{s^3(s-a)}.$$

EXAMPLE A.7. Find $\mathcal{L}^{-1}(1/(s-a)^2)$:

$$\frac{1}{(s-a)^2} = -\frac{d}{ds}\frac{1}{(s-a)} = -\frac{d}{ds}\mathcal{L}e^{at}$$

$$= \mathcal{L}t\,e^{at} \quad \text{(Theorem A.6)}. \tag{A.27}$$

EXAMPLE A.8. Find $\mathcal{L}(e^{-at}\cos \omega t)$ and $\mathcal{L}(e^{-at}\sin \omega t)$:

$$\mathcal{L}\cos \omega t = \frac{s}{s^2+\omega^2},$$

$$\mathcal{L}e^{-at}f(t) = F(s+a) \quad \text{(Theorem A.9)}.$$

Therefore,

$$\mathcal{L}(e^{-at}\cos \omega t) = \frac{(s+a)}{(s+a)^2 + \omega^2}. \tag{A.28}$$

Similarly,

$$\mathcal{L}e^{-at}\sin \omega t = \frac{\omega}{(s+a)^2 + \omega^2}. \tag{A.29}$$

EXAMPLE A.9. Find the Laplace transform of the function

$$f(t) = \begin{cases} 1 & 0 < t < 1, \\ -1 & 1 < t < \infty. \end{cases} \tag{A.30}$$

This function may be written as

$$f(t) = u(t) - 2u(t-1). \tag{A.31}$$

Therefore,

$$\mathcal{L}f(t) = \mathcal{L}u(t) - 2\mathcal{L}u(t-1) \qquad \text{(Theorem A.1)}$$

$$= \frac{1}{s} - \frac{2e^{-s}}{s} = \frac{1 - 2e^{-s}}{s}.$$

EXAMPLE A.10. Find the Laplace transform of the square wave described by

$$f(t) = \begin{cases} 1 & 0 < t < 1, \\ -1 & 1 < t < 2, \end{cases} \tag{A.32}$$

$$f(t+2) = f(t).$$

Using Theorem A.12, we have

$$\mathcal{L}f(t) = \frac{\int_0^2 e^{-st}f(t)\, dt}{1 - e^{-2s}}$$

$$= \frac{1}{1 - e^{-2s}} \left(\int_0^1 e^{-st}\, dt - \int_1^2 e^{-st}\, dt \right)$$

$$= \frac{1}{1 - e^{-2s}} \left(\frac{1}{s} [-e^{-st}]_0^1 + \frac{1}{s} [e^{-st}]_1^2 \right)$$

$$= \frac{1}{1 - e^{-2s}} \left(\frac{1}{s} (1 - e^{-s} + e^{-2s} - e^{-s}) \right)$$

$$= \frac{1}{s} \frac{(1 - e^{-s})^2}{1 - e^{-2s}} = \frac{1}{s} \frac{1 - e^{-s}}{1 + e^{-s}}. \tag{A.33}$$

Alternatively, this function can be described by

$$f(t) = 1, \qquad 0 < t < 1,$$

$$f(t+1) = -f(t). \tag{A.34}$$

We now use Theorem A.13 and obtain

$$\mathcal{L}f(t) = \frac{\int_0^1 e^{-st}f(t)\,dt}{1+e^{-s}} = \frac{1}{1+e^{-s}}\int_0^1 e^{-st}\,dt = \frac{1}{s}\frac{1-e^{-s}}{1+e^{-s}}. \tag{A.33}$$

A.3. THE CONVOLUTION THEOREM

A result which is often of theoretical value and which can aid in finding inverse Laplace transforms is embodied in the *convolution theorem*.

Theorem A.14. *(Convolution)*

$$\mathcal{L}^{-1}F_1(s)F_2(s) = \int_0^t f_1(t-\tau)f_2(\tau)\,d\tau, \tag{A.35}$$

where

$$F_1(s) = \mathcal{L}f_1(t), \qquad F_2(s) = \mathcal{L}f_2(t).$$

Proof

$$F_2(s) = \int_0^\infty e^{-st}f_2(t)\,dt,$$

$$F_1(s)F_2(s) = \int_0^\infty e^{-st}F_1(s)f_2(t)\,dt = \int_0^\infty e^{-s\tau}F_1(s)f_2(\tau)\,d\tau.$$

Now,

$$\mathcal{L}f_1(t-\tau) = \int_0^\infty e^{-st}f_1(t-\tau)\,dt = e^{-s\tau}F_1(s) \qquad \text{(Theorem A.10)}.$$

Therefore,

$$F_1(s)F_2(s) = \int_0^\infty f_2(\tau)\int_0^\infty e^{-st}f_1(t-\tau)\,dt\,d\tau$$

$$= \int_0^\infty e^{-st}\int_0^\infty f_1(t-\tau)f_2(\tau)\,d\tau\,dt.$$

But $f_1(t-\tau) = 0$ when $\tau > t$, so that

$$F_1(s)F_2(s) = \int_0^\infty e^{-st}\left(\int_0^t f_1(t-\tau)f_2(\tau)\,d\tau\right)dt$$

$$= \mathcal{L}\left(\int_0^t f_1(t-\tau)f_2(\tau)\,d\tau\right).$$

The expression $\int_0^t f_1(t-\tau)f_2(\tau)\,d\tau$ is called the convolution product of $f_1(t)$ with $f_2(t)$. This is frequently written as

$$\int_0^t f_1(t-\tau)f_2(\tau)\,d\tau = f_1(t) * f_2(t). \tag{A.36}$$

It is a simple matter to show that

$$f_1 * f_2 = f_2 * f_1.$$

EXAMPLE A.11. To illustrate the use of the convolution theorem, we shall find the function whose Laplace transform is

$$F(s) = \frac{1}{\sqrt{s}\,(s-1)}. \tag{A.37}$$

Let

$$F_1(s) = \frac{1}{\sqrt{s}}, \tag{A.38}$$

$$F_2(s) = \frac{1}{s-1}. \tag{A.39}$$

Now,

$$\int_0^\infty e^{-st}\frac{1}{\sqrt{\pi t}}\,dt = \int_0^\infty \frac{2\tau}{\pi}e^{-s\tau^2/\pi}\frac{d\tau}{\tau},$$

where $\sqrt{\pi t} = \tau$, or

$$\mathcal{L}\,\frac{1}{\sqrt{\pi t}} = \frac{2}{\pi}\int_0^\infty e^{-s\tau^2/\pi}\,d\tau = \frac{2}{\pi}\sqrt{\frac{\pi}{s}}\int_0^\infty e^{-x^2}\,dx = \frac{2}{\pi}\sqrt{\frac{\pi}{s}}\cdot\frac{\sqrt{\pi}}{2} = \frac{1}{\sqrt{s}}.$$

Therefore

$$F_1(s) = \mathcal{L}\,\frac{1}{\sqrt{\pi t}}. \tag{A.40}$$

Also

$$F_2(s) = \mathcal{L}e^t. \tag{A.41}$$

Therefore

$$F_1(s)F_2(s) = \mathcal{L}e^t * \frac{1}{\sqrt{\pi t}} = \mathcal{L}\int_0^t \frac{1}{\sqrt{\pi \tau}}e^{(t-\tau)}\,d\tau \tag{A.42}$$

$$= \mathcal{L}e^t\,\frac{2}{\sqrt{\pi}}\int_0^t e^{-\tau}\frac{d\tau}{2\sqrt{\tau}} = \mathcal{L}e^t\,\frac{2}{\sqrt{\pi}}\int_0^{\sqrt{t}} e^{-x^2}\,dx,$$

or

$$\mathcal{L}e^t(\text{erf}\,\sqrt{t}) = \frac{1}{(s-1)\sqrt{s}}, \tag{A.43}$$

where

$$\text{erf}\,x = \frac{2}{\sqrt{\pi}}\int_0^x e^{-r^2}\,dr. \tag{A.44}$$

A.4. INVERSE LAPLACE TRANSFORMS

The inverse Laplace transform of a function $F(s)$ is denoted by

$$\mathcal{L}^{-1}F(s) = f(t). \tag{A.3}$$

An obvious method for finding inverse Laplace transforms is by reading them from a table of Laplace transform pairs; we may use the convolution theorem and some of the theorems of Section A.2 to extend such a table. There are explicit formulas for $\mathcal{L}^{-1}F(s)$; however, since the most useful of these involves an integral in the complex plane, we shall not investigate them here. Suffice it to say that inverse Laplace transforms are essentially unique, so that we can use tables to find them.

A.5. INVERSE LAPLACE TRANSFORMS OF RATIONAL FUNCTIONS

Let us suppose that we wish to find the inverse Laplace transform of a function given by

$$F(s) = \frac{N(s)}{D(s)}, \tag{A.45}$$

where $N(s)$, $D(s)$ are polynomials in s with real coefficients, and the degree of $N(s)$ is less than that of $D(s)$. Then we can write

$$F(s) = \frac{KN(s)}{s^n + a_{n-1}s^{n-1} + \cdots + a_1 s + a_0}, \tag{A.46}$$

where K is a real constant, or

$$F(s) = \frac{KN(s)}{(s - s_1)(s - s_2) \cdots (s - s_n)}, \tag{A.47}$$

in which we have factored the denominator $D(s)$. If the $s_1, s_2, \ldots s_n$ are not distinct, (A.47) takes the form

$$F(s) = \frac{KN(s)}{(s - s_1)^{p_1}(s - s_2)^{p_2} \cdots (s - s_m)^{p_m}}, \tag{A.48}$$

where $p_1 + p_2 + \cdots + p_m = n$.

Now the right-hand side of (A.48) can be expanded in terms of partial fractions to give

$$F(s) = \sum_{i=1}^{m} \sum_{k=1}^{p_i} \frac{A_{i,k}}{(s - s_i)^k} \tag{A.49}$$

$$= \frac{A_{1,1}}{s - s_1} + \frac{A_{1,2}}{(s - s_1)^2} + \cdots + \frac{A_{1,p_1}}{(s - s_1)^{p_1}} + \frac{A_{2,1}}{s - s_2} + \frac{A_{2,2}}{(s - s_2)^2}$$

$$+ \cdots + \frac{A_{m,p_m}}{(s - s_m)^{p_m}},$$

so that, using example A.2 and Theorem A.3, we have

$$f(t) = \mathcal{L}^{-1}F(s) = \sum_{i=1}^{m}\sum_{k=1}^{p_i} A_{i,k}\frac{1}{(k-1)!}t^{k-1}e^{s_it}. \qquad (A.50)$$

We therefore only need find the constants $A_{i,k}$ in order to find the inverse Laplace transform of a rational function. Let us multiply each side of (A.49) by $(s - s_i)^{p_i}$. This gives

$$(s - s_i)^{p_i}F(s) = \frac{A_{1,1}(s - s_i)^{p_i}}{s - s_1} + \cdots + \frac{A_{1,p_1}(s - s_i)^{p_i}}{(s - s_1)^{p_1}} + \cdots + A_{i,1}(s - s_i)^{p_i-1}$$

$$+ A_{i,2}(s - s_i)^{p_i-2} + \cdots + A_{i,p_i-2}(s - s_i)^2 + A_{i,p_i-1}(s - s_i)$$

$$+ A_{i,p_i} + \cdots + \frac{A_{m,p_m}(s - s_i)^{p_i}}{(s - s_m)^{p_m}}. \qquad (A.51)$$

Now, in (A.51) let $s \to s_i$, so that we obtain

$$A_{i,p_i} = \lim_{s \to s_i}(s - s_i)^{p_i}F(s). \qquad (A.52)$$

Also, differentiating (A.51) with respect to s, we have

$$\frac{d}{ds}(s - s_i)^{p_i}F(s) = \frac{d}{ds}\left(\frac{A_{1,1}(s - s_i)^{p_i}}{s - s_1} + \cdots + \frac{A_{1,p_1}(s - s_i)^{p_i}}{(s - s_1)^{p_1}} + \cdots\right)$$

$$+ (p_i - 1)A_{i,1}(s - s_i)^{p_i-2} + (p_i - 2)A_{i,2}(s - s_i)^{p_i-3} + \cdots + 2A_{i,p_i-2}(s - s_i)$$

$$+ A_{i,p_i-1} + \frac{d}{ds}\left(\frac{A_{i+1,1}(s - s_i)^{p_i}}{s - s_{i+1}} + \cdots + \frac{A_{m,p_m}(s - s_i)^{p_i}}{(s - s_m)^{p_m}}\right), \qquad (A.53)$$

so that, letting $s \to s_i$, we obtain

$$A_{i,p_i-1} = \lim_{s \to s_i}\frac{d}{ds}\left((s - s_i)^{p_i}F(s)\right). \qquad (A.54)$$

Similarly, differentiating (A.53) with respect to s, we obtain

$$A_{i,p_i-2} = \frac{1}{2!}\lim_{s \to s_i}\frac{d^2}{ds^2}\left((s - s_i)^{p_i}F(s)\right), \qquad (A.55)$$

and repeating the process, we obtain for the general case

$$A_{i,p_i-k} = \frac{1}{k!}\lim_{s \to s_i}\frac{d^k}{ds^k}\left((s - s_i)^{p_i}F(s)\right). \qquad (A.56)$$

EXAMPLE A.12. Find

$$\mathcal{L}^{-1}\frac{s+1}{s(s+2)^3(s+3)}.$$

TABLE A.2

LAPLACE TRANSFORM PAIRS

	$f(t)$	$F(s)$
1	$u(t)$	$1/s$
2	t	$1/s^2$
3	$t^{n-1}/(n-1)!$	$1/s^n$
4	e^{at}	$1/(s-a)$
5	$t\,e^{at}$	$1/(s-a)^2$
6	$t^{n-1}e^{at}/(n-1)!$	$1/(s-a)^n$
7	$\cos at$	$s/(s^2+a^2)$
8	$\sin at$	$a/(s^2+a^2)$
9	$e^{-bt}\cos at$	$s+b/((s+b)^2+a^2)$
10	$e^{-bt}\sin at$	$a/((s+b)^2+a^2)$
11	$\cosh at$	$s/(s^2-a^2)$
12	$\sinh at$	$a/(s^2-a^2)$

We write

$$\frac{s+1}{s(s+2)^3(s+3)} = \frac{A_{11}}{s+2} + \frac{A_{12}}{(s+2)^2} + \frac{A_{13}}{(s+2)^3} + \frac{A_{21}}{s+3} + \frac{A_{31}}{s}. \quad (A.57)$$

Now, using (A.52), we obtain

$$A_{13} = \lim_{s\to-2}\left(\frac{(s+1)(s+2)^3}{s(s+2)^3(s+3)}\right) = \frac{s+1}{s(s+3)}\bigg|_{s=-2} = \frac{1}{2},$$

and using (A.56),

$$A_{12} = \frac{d}{ds}\frac{s+1}{s(s+3)}\bigg|_{s=-2} = \frac{-s^2-2s-3}{s^2(s+3)^2}\bigg|_{s=-2} = -\frac{3}{4},$$

$$A_{11} = \frac{1}{2}\frac{d^2}{ds^2}\frac{s+1}{s(s+3)}\bigg|_{s=-2} = \frac{5}{8}.$$

Also,

$$A_{21} = \lim_{s\to-3}\left(\frac{(s+1)(s+3)}{s(s+2)^3(s+3)}\right) = \frac{(s+1)}{s(s+2)^3}\bigg|_{s=-3} = -\frac{2}{3},$$

$$A_{31} = \lim_{s\to0}\left(\frac{s(s+1)}{s(s+2)^3(s+3)}\right) = \frac{(s+1)}{(0+2)^3(s+3)}\bigg|_{s=0} = \frac{1}{24},$$

so that

$$\frac{s+1}{s(s+2)^3(s+3)} = \frac{\frac{5}{8}}{s+2} - \frac{\frac{3}{4}}{(s+2)^2} + \frac{\frac{1}{2}}{(s+2)^3} - \frac{\frac{2}{3}}{s+3} + \frac{\frac{1}{24}}{s}, \qquad \text{(A.58)}$$

and

$$\mathcal{L}^{-1} \frac{s+1}{s(s+2)^3(s+3)} = (\tfrac{5}{8} - \tfrac{3}{4}t + \tfrac{1}{4}t^2)e^{-2t} - \tfrac{2}{3}e^{-3t} + \tfrac{1}{24}. \qquad \text{(A.59)}$$

Because we can use the partial-fraction expansions, it is unnecessary to obtain a large table of Laplace transform pairs when the Laplace transforms in question are rational. The transform pairs of Table A.2 and the operations indicated in Table A.1 provide more than sufficient information in such cases.

A.6. SOLUTION OF LINEAR DIFFERENTIAL EQUATIONS WITH CONSTANT COEFFICIENTS

One of the main uses of Laplace transforms lies in the solution of linear differential equations with constant coefficients. Consider the second-order equation

$$a\,\frac{d^2f(t)}{dt^2} + b\,\frac{df(t)}{dt} + cf(t) = g(t), \qquad \text{(A.60)}$$

where a, b, c are constants and $g(t)$ is a known function. Let us take the Laplace transform of both sides of this equation, and write $\mathcal{L}f(t) = F(s)$, $\mathcal{L}g(t) = G(s)$. We obtain

$$as^2F(s) - af'(0+) - asf(0+) + bsF(s) - bf(0+) + cF(s) = G(s), \qquad \text{(A.61)}$$

or

$$(as^2 + bs + c)F(s) = G(s) + af'(0+) + (as + b)f(0+), \qquad \text{(A.62)}$$

and

$$F(s) = \frac{G(s) + af'(0+) + (as + b)f(0+)}{as^2 + bs + c}, \qquad \text{(A.63)}$$

so that

$$f(t) = \mathcal{L}^{-1}\left(\frac{G(s) + af'(0+) + (as + b)f(0+)}{as^2 + bs + c}\right). \qquad \text{(A.64)}$$

Now if $G(s)$ is a rational function, we may use Table A.2 and the partial-fraction expansion to obtain $f(t)$. As expected, there are two arbitrary constants in the solution, and once these are specified the complete solution is obtained.

EXAMPLE A.13. Solve

$$\frac{d^2f(t)}{dt^2} + 4\,\frac{df(t)}{dt} + 3f(t) = e^{-2t}, \qquad \text{(A.65)}$$

where $f'(0+) = 1$, $f(0+) = -1$.

Solution. The Laplace transform of (A.65) is

$$(s^2 + 4s + 3)F(s) = \frac{1}{s+2} - 1 + s + 4, \tag{A.66}$$

or

$$(s + 3)(s + 1)F(s) = \frac{1}{s+2} + s + 3.$$

Therefore,

$$F(s) = \frac{1}{(s+1)(s+2)(s+3)} + \frac{1}{(s+1)};$$

that is,

$$F(s) = \frac{\frac{3}{2}}{s+1} + \frac{-1}{s+2} + \frac{\frac{1}{2}}{s+3},$$

so that

$$f(t) = \tfrac{3}{2}e^{-t} + \tfrac{1}{2}e^{-3t} - e^{-2t}. \tag{A.67}$$

EXAMPLE A.14. Solve

$$3f''(t) + 5f'(t) + 2f(t) = 4 \sin 2t, \tag{A.68}$$

where $f'(0+) = f(0+) = 0$.

Solution. The Laplace transform of (A.68) is

$$(3s^2 + 5s + 2)F(s) = \frac{8}{s^2 + 4},$$

or

$$F(s) = \frac{8}{(s^2 + 4)(3s^2 + 5s + 2)} = \frac{8}{(s^2 + 4)(3s + 2)(s + 1)}$$

$$= \frac{-\frac{8}{5}}{s+1} + \frac{\frac{9}{5}}{s + 2/3} + \frac{-1 + j/10}{s + 2j} + \frac{-1 - j/10}{s - 2j}$$

$$= \frac{-\frac{8}{5}}{s+1} + \frac{\frac{9}{5}}{s + 2/3} - \frac{s/5}{s^2 + 4} + \frac{\frac{2}{5}}{s^2 + 4},$$

so that

$$f(t) = -\tfrac{8}{5}e^{-t} + \tfrac{9}{5}e^{-2t/3} - \tfrac{1}{5}\cos 2t + \tfrac{1}{5}\sin 2t \tag{A.69}$$

EXAMPLE A.15. Solve

$$f''(t) - f(t) = \sinh t \tag{A.70}$$

where $f'(0+) = f(0+) = 1$.

Solution. The Laplace transform of (A.70) is

$$(s^2 - 1)F(s) = \frac{1}{s^2 - 1} + s + 1,$$

so that

$$F(s) = \frac{1}{(s^2-1)^2} + \frac{1}{s-1} = \frac{1}{(s-1)^2(s+1)^2} + \frac{1}{s-1}$$

$$= \frac{\frac{3}{4}}{s-1} + \frac{\frac{1}{4}}{(s-1)^2} + \frac{\frac{1}{4}}{(s+1)} + \frac{\frac{1}{4}}{(s+1)^2},$$

and

$$f(t) = \tfrac{3}{4}e^t + \tfrac{1}{4}e^{-t} + \tfrac{1}{4}t(e^t + e^{-t})$$

$$= \tfrac{1}{2}e^t + \tfrac{1}{2}(1+t)\cosh t. \tag{A.71}$$

FOURIER SERIES

B.1. ORTHOGONAL FUNCTIONS

Our object in this appendix is to find a representation of arbitrary functions defined in some time interval, in terms of either a series of sinusoidal functions or a series of exponentials. That is, we wish to express a given function in one of the forms

$$f(t) = \frac{a_0}{2} + \sum_{n=1}^{\infty} (a_n \cos n\omega t + b_n \sin n\omega t), \tag{B.1}$$

$$f(t) = \sum_{n=-\infty}^{\infty} c_n e^{jn\omega t}. \tag{B.2}$$

To do this, we first introduce the idea of a set of *orthogonal functions*. A set of functions $\{g_n(t)\}$ is said to be orthogonal in the interval $a < t < b$ if and only if

$$\int_a^b g_n(t)g_m(t) \, dt = 0 \qquad \text{for} \qquad n \neq m,$$

and $\tag{B.3}$

$$\int_a^b \left(g_n(t)\right)^2 dt \neq 0.$$

The set of functions is *orthonormal* if in addition,

$$\int_a^b \left(g_n(t)\right)^2 dt = 1. \tag{B.4}$$

If there is no function $h(t)$ which is orthogonal to every $g_n(t)$, the orthogonal set $\{g_n(t)\}$ is said to be complete. Let

$$S_m(t) = \sum_{n=1}^{m} a_n g_n(t) \qquad (a < t < b), \tag{B.5}$$

where a_n are constants yet to be determined. Then, if there exists a set of numbers $\{a_n\}$ such that

$$\lim_{m \to \infty} \int_a^b [f(t) - S_m(t)]^2 \, dt = 0, \tag{B.6}$$

295

the set of orthogonal functions $\{g_n(t)\}$ is said to be *closed*, and the series

$$\sum_{n=1}^{m} a_n g_n(t)$$

is said to converge to $f(t)$ *in the mean*.

B.2. THE GENERALIZED FOURIER SERIES

Let $\{g_n(t)\}$ be a complete, closed, orthonormal set of functions, and for some function $f(t)$, let us write

$$f(t) = a_1 g_1(t) + a_2 g_2(t) + \cdots + a_n g_n(t) + \cdots \qquad (a < t < b), \qquad \text{(B.7)}$$

or

$$f(t) = \sum_{n=1}^{\infty} a_n g_n(t) \qquad (a < t < b). \qquad \text{(B.8)}$$

Multiplying both sides of (B.8) by $g_m(t)$ and integrating between the limits a, b, we have

$$\int_a^b f(t) g_m(t) \, dt = \int_a^b \sum_{n=1}^{\infty} a_n g_n(t) g_m(t) \, dt$$

$$= \sum_{n=1}^{\infty} a_n \int_a^b g_n(t) g_m(t) \, dt. \qquad \text{(B.9)}$$

By (B.3), all the terms on the right-hand side of (B.9) are zero, except the term for which $n = m$. Since $\{g_n(t)\}$ is orthonormal, the integral in this term is equal to unity, so that (B.9) becomes

$$a_m = \int_a^b f(t) g_m(t) \, dt. \qquad \text{(B.10)}$$

Thus we are provided with a fairly simple method for finding series expansions in terms of sets of orthogonal functions, provided that the functions involved are bounded and integrable in the given interval, or *fundamental interval*.

There are many different sets of orthonormal functions $\{g_n(t)\}$, and the series expansion (B.7) is known as a *generalized Fourier series* of the function $f(t)$ with respect to the orthonormal set $\{g_n(t)\}$. Let us examine more closely the coefficients in this series. First, let

$$K_m(t) = c_1 g_1(t) + c_2 g_2(t) + \cdots + c_m g_m(t), \qquad \text{(B.11)}$$

in which we choose $c_1, c_2, \ldots, c_m$ such that

$$J = \int_a^b \left(f(t) - K_m(t) \right)^2 dt \qquad \text{(B.12)}$$

is as small as possible. Then,

$$J = \int_a^b \left(f(t) - c_1 g_1(t) - c_2 g_2(t) - \cdots - c_m g_m(t) \right)^2 dt$$

$$= \int_a^b \left(f(t) \right)^2 dt - 2 \int_a^b \left(c_1 f(t) g_1(t) \right) dt - \cdots$$

$$-2 \int_a^b \left(c_m f(t) g_m(t) \right) dt + \int_a^b c_1^2 \left(g_1(t) \right)^2 dt + \cdots$$

$$+ \int_a^b c_m^2 \left(g_m(t) \right)^2 dt - 2c_1 c_2 \int_a^b g_1(t) g_2(t) dt$$

$$-2c_1 c_3 \int_a^b g_1(t) g_3(t) dt - \cdots - 2c_{m-1} c_m \int_a^b g_{m-1}(t) g_m(t) dt. \qquad (B.13)$$

When we use (B.3), (B.4), and (B.10), in (B.13), we obtain

$$J = \int_a^b \left(f(t) \right)^2 dt - 2a_1 c_1 - 2a_2 c_2 - \cdots - 2a_m c_m + c_1^2 + c_2^2 + \cdots + c_m^2,$$

or

$$J = \int_a^b \left(f(t) \right)^2 dt - \sum_{n=1}^m a_n^2 + \sum_{n=1}^m (c_n - a_n)^2. \qquad (B.14)$$

Since J is always positive, it is clear that it is minimum when

$$c_n = a_n, \; n = 1, 2, \ldots, m.$$

Therefore,

$$J = \int_a^b \left(f(t) \right)^2 dt - \sum_{n=1}^m a_n^2 \geq 0,$$

or

$$\sum_{n=1}^m a_n^2 \leq \int_a^b \left(f(t) \right)^2 dt. \qquad (B.15)$$

Now, since the right-hand side of (B.15) is a positive number independent of m, we immediately conclude that

$$\lim_{n \to \infty} a_n = 0 \qquad (B.16)$$

or, the Fourier coefficients approach zero as n tends to infinity.

B.3. ORTHOGONAL SETS OF SINUSOIDAL FUNCTIONS

Since we wish to expand given functions in terms of sinusoids, it is necessary for us to show when such functions form orthogonal sets.

Consider first the functions

$$\left\{ \sin\left(\frac{n\pi t}{L}\right) \right\} \qquad (0 < t < L, \qquad n = 1, 2, \ldots).$$

We observe that

$$\int_0^L \sin\left(\frac{n\pi t}{L}\right) \sin\left(\frac{m\pi t}{L}\right) dt = 0, \qquad n \neq m, \tag{B.17}$$

and

$$\int_0^L \left(\sin\frac{n\pi t}{L}\right)^2 dt = \frac{L}{2}, \tag{B.18}$$

so that this set satisfies the conditions (B.3) and is an orthogonal set of functions. It is also easy to show that $\{\sqrt{2/L} \sin (n\pi t/L)\}$ is an orthonormal set of functions in the interval $0 < t < L$.

Similarly, the set of functions $\{\cos (n\pi t/L)\}$ $(0 < t < L, n = 0, 1, 2, \ldots)$ is orthogonal, and the corresponding orthonormal set is $\{1/\sqrt{L}, \sqrt{2/L} \cos (n\pi t/L)\}$ $(0 < t < L, n = 1, 2, \ldots)$.

Finally, let us examine the set

$$\left\{ \sin\frac{\pi t}{L}, \sin\frac{2\pi t}{L}, \ldots, 1, \cos\frac{\pi t}{L}, \cos\frac{2\pi t}{L}, \ldots \right\} \tag{B.19}$$

in the interval $-L < t < L$. That this set is orthogonal becomes obvious when we note that

$$\int_{-L}^L \cos\frac{m\pi t}{L} \cos\frac{n\pi t}{L} dt = 0 \qquad (m \neq n), \tag{B.20}$$

$$\int_{-L}^L \sin\frac{m\pi t}{L} \sin\frac{n\pi t}{L} dt = 0 \qquad (m \neq n), \tag{B.21}$$

$$\int_{-L}^L \cos\frac{m\pi t}{L} \sin\frac{n\pi t}{L} dt = 0 \qquad (\text{all } m, n), \tag{B.22}$$

$$\int_{-L}^L \left(\cos\frac{n\pi t}{L}\right)^2 dt = L, \tag{B.23}$$

$$\int_{-L}^L dt = 2L, \tag{B.24}$$

$$\int_{-L}^L \left(\sin\frac{n\pi t}{L}\right)^2 dt = L. \tag{B.25}$$

The corresponding orthonormal set is

$$\left\{\frac{1}{\sqrt{2L}}, \frac{1}{\sqrt{L}}\sin\frac{\pi t}{L}, \frac{1}{\sqrt{L}}\cos\frac{\pi t}{L}, \frac{1}{\sqrt{L}}\sin\frac{2\pi t}{L}, \frac{1}{\sqrt{L}}\cos\frac{2\pi t}{L}, \ldots\right\} \qquad (-L < t < L).$$

(B.26)

When we expand a given function $f(t)$ in a Fourier series using either the set (B.19) or (B.26), we obtain

$$f(t) = \frac{a_0}{2} + \sum_{n=1}^{\infty}\left(a_n\cos\frac{n\pi t}{L} + b_n\sin\frac{n\pi t}{L}\right) \qquad (-L < t < L). \qquad (B.27)$$

We call this the *Fourier trigonometrical series* and it may be written in the form of (B.1) by substituting

$$\omega = \pi/L. \qquad (B.28)$$

B.4. PERIODICITY OF THE SERIES EXPANSION

If a Fourier series expansion approximates a given function, it does so in the *fundamental interval* in which the given set of functions are orthogonal. However, in the case of sets of sinusoidal functions, the resulting Fourier series is periodic with period $2L$, or using (B.28), with period $2\pi/\omega$. Thus, if the function for which we find the expansion is also periodic with the same period, the Fourier series representation will be valid for the interval $-\infty < t < \infty$.

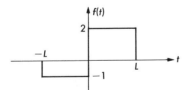

FIGURE B.1

EXAMPLE B.1. Let us calculate the Fourier trigonometrical series corresponding to the function, shown in Fig. B.1:

$$f(t) = \begin{cases} -1 & -L < t < 0, \\ 2 & 0 < t < L. \end{cases} \qquad (B.29)$$

Using (B.10), we calculate,

$$a_n = \frac{1}{L}\int_{-L}^{L}\cos\frac{n\pi t}{L}f(t)\,dt = \frac{1}{L}\int_{-L}^{0}-\cos\frac{n\pi t}{L}\,dt + \frac{1}{L}\int_{0}^{L}2\cos\frac{n\pi t}{L}\,dt, \qquad (B.30)$$

so that

$$a_n = \frac{-1}{n\pi}\sin\frac{n\pi t}{L}\Big|_{-L}^{0} + \frac{2}{n\pi}\sin\frac{n\pi t}{L}\Big|_{0}^{L} = \frac{-1}{n\pi}(\sin 0 + \sin n\pi) + \frac{2}{n\pi}(\sin n\pi - \sin 0),$$

or $\qquad a_n = 0,$ (B.31)

$$a_0 = \frac{1}{L}\int_{-L}^{L} f(t)\, dt = \frac{1}{L}\int_{-L}^{0} -dt + \frac{1}{2L}\int_{0}^{L} 2\, dt$$ (B.32)

$$= \frac{1}{L}\left(-t\bigg|_{-L}^{0} + 2t\bigg|_{0}^{L}\right) = \frac{1}{L}\left(-(0+L) + 2(L-0)\right),$$

or

$$\frac{a_0}{2} = \frac{1}{2},$$ (B.33)

$$b_n = \frac{1}{L}\int_{-L}^{L} \sin\frac{n\pi t}{L}\, f(t)\, dt = \frac{1}{L}\int_{-L}^{0} -\sin\frac{n\pi t}{L}\, dt + \frac{1}{L}\int_{0}^{L} 2\sin\frac{n\pi t}{L}\, dt$$ (B.34)

$$= \frac{1}{n\pi}\cos\frac{n\pi t}{L}\bigg|_{-L}^{0} - \frac{2}{n\pi}\cos\frac{n\pi t}{L}\bigg|_{0}^{L}$$

$$= \frac{1}{n\pi}\left(1 - \cos n\pi\right) - \frac{2}{n\pi}\left(\cos n\pi - 1\right) = \frac{3}{n\pi}\left(1 - \cos n\pi\right),$$

or

$$b_n = \begin{cases} 0 & \text{for } n \text{ even,} \\ \dfrac{6}{n\pi} & \text{for } n \text{ odd.} \end{cases}$$ (B.35)

Hence the Fourier series expansion becomes

$$f(t) = \frac{1}{2} + \frac{6}{\pi}\sum_{p=0}^{\infty} \frac{1}{2p+1}\sin\frac{(2p+1)\pi t}{L}.$$ (B.36)

This series may equally well be used to approximate the function

$$f(t) = \begin{cases} -1 & -L < t < 0, \\ 2 & 0 < t < L, \end{cases}$$ (B.37)

$$f(t + 2L) = f(t),$$

which is shown in Fig. B.2, since it is periodic with period $2L$. The periodic function in Fig. B.2 is a square wave with an average value of $\frac{1}{2}$ and "peak-to-peak"

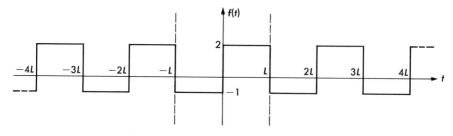

FIGURE B.2

value of 3 units. If we subtract the average value from this function, it becomes a symmetric square wave with amplitude of $\frac{3}{2}$. The Fourier expansion of this new function is

$$f(t) = \frac{6}{\pi} \sum_{m=0}^{\infty} \frac{1}{2m+1} \sin \frac{(2m+1)\pi t}{L}. \tag{B.38}$$

Note that this differs from (B.36) only in that the constant term is missing. Furthermore, the constant term is equal to the average value of the function. This is a natural consequence of the fact that the average value of any sinusoidal function is zero, and we have only altered the average of the function.

The remaining noteworthy fact about this expansion (B.38) is that only the sine terms occur; there are no cosine terms. We can explain this through the properties of *even* and *odd* functions.

B.5. EVEN AND ODD FUNCTIONS

A function which has the property that

$$f(t) = f(-t) \tag{B.39}$$

is called an *even function*, while a function for which

$$f(t) = -f(-t) \tag{B.40}$$

is an *odd function*. As examples of interest, $\sin kt$ is an odd function while $\cos kt$ is an even function. It is easy to establish the following:

(a) The sum or difference of *even* functions is *even*.
(b) The sum or difference of *odd* functions is *odd*.
(c) The product or quotient of *even* functions is *even*.
(d) The product or quotient of *odd* functions is *even*.
(e) The product or quotient of an even and an odd function is odd.
(f) The sum or difference of an even and odd function is neither even nor odd.

Thus, if we are to represent an even function by a Fourier series, the nonzero terms must be even functions so that only the cosine terms can appear. Similarly, only the sine terms can appear in the Fourier expansion of an odd function.

Not all functions are either even or odd; however, any function can be expressed as the sum of an even part and an odd part. Consider an arbitrary function $f(t)$. We can always write

$$f(t) = \tfrac{1}{2}(f(t) + f(-t)) + \tfrac{1}{2}(f(t) - f(-t)), \tag{B.41}$$

and it is easy to see that the first term on the right-hand side of (B.41) is even while the second term is odd.

We can therefore write the Fourier series for any function as the sum of the Fourier series for the even part, and the Fourier series for the odd part. The function of Example B.1 has for its even part the constant $\frac{1}{2}$, and its odd part is

$$f(t) = \begin{cases} \frac{3}{2} & 0 < t < L, \\ -\frac{3}{2} & -L < t < 0, \end{cases} \tag{B.42}$$

or the symmetric square wave with amplitude $\frac{3}{2}$.

B.6. THE FOURIER SINE AND COSINE SERIES

Let us suppose that we wish to expand a function defined in the interval $0 < t < L$ in terms of the orthonormal set $\{\sqrt{2/L} \sin (n\pi t/L)\}$. The series that we obtain will be

$$f(t) = \sum_{n=1}^{\infty} b_n \sin \frac{n\pi t}{L}, \tag{B.43}$$

in which

$$b_n = \frac{2}{L} \int_0^L f(t) \sin \frac{n\pi t}{L} dt. \tag{B.44}$$

Consider now the expansion of the odd function $f_1(t)$ defined by

$$\begin{aligned} f_1(t) &= f(t), \quad 0 < t < L, \\ f_1(-t) &= -f_1(t). \end{aligned} \tag{B.45}$$

The Fourier series expansion of this function in the range $-L < t < L$ is

$$f_1(t) = \sum_{n=1}^{\infty} b_{n1} \sin \frac{n\pi t}{L},$$

where

$$\begin{aligned} b_{n1} &= \frac{1}{L} \int_{-L}^{L} f_1(t) \sin \frac{n\pi t}{L} dt \\ &= \frac{1}{L} \int_{-L}^{0} f_1(t) \sin \frac{n\pi t}{L} dt + \frac{1}{L} \int_0^L f_1(t) \sin \frac{n\pi t}{L} dt, \end{aligned}$$

but $f_1(t) \sin (n\pi t/L)$ is an *even* function, so that

$$\frac{1}{L} \int_{-L}^{0} f_1(t) \sin \frac{n\pi t}{L} dt = \frac{1}{L} \int_0^L f_1(t) \sin \frac{n\pi t}{L} dt. \tag{B.46}$$

Therefore,

$$b_{n1} = \frac{2}{L} \int_0^L f_1(t) \sin \frac{n\pi t}{L} dt = \frac{2}{L} \int_0^L f(t) \sin \frac{n\pi t}{L} dt = b_n. \tag{B.47}$$

Thus the Fourier series in terms of the orthonormal set (B.26) for *odd* functions corresponds exactly to the Fourier series in terms of the orthonormal set

$$\{\sqrt{2/L}\ \sin\ (n\pi t/L)\}$$

in the range $0 < t < L$. This latter series is called the *Fourier sine series*.

In an exactly similar manner, we can show that the Fourier series in terms of the orthonormal set (B.26) for *even* functions corresponds exactly to the Fourier series in terms of the orthonormal set $\{\sqrt{2/L}\ \cos\ (n\pi t/L),\ \sqrt{1/L}\}$ in the range $0 < t < L$. This series is called the *Fourier cosine series*.

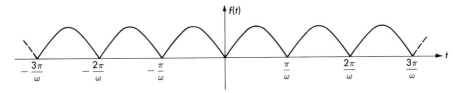

FIGURE B.3

B.7. EXAMPLES

EXAMPLE B.2. Let us find the Fourier series for the full-wave rectified sine wave shown in Fig. B.3. This function may be expressed as

$$f(t)\ =\ A\ \sin\ \omega t,\qquad 0 < t < \pi/\omega,$$
$$f(t \pm \pi/\omega)\ =\ f(t),\tag{B.48}$$

which is, of course, an even function. We can therefore use the Fourier cosine series to find

$$f(t)\ =\ \frac{a_0}{2} + \sum_{n=1}^{\infty} a_n \cos n\omega t.\tag{B.49}$$

Here,

$$a_n\ =\ \frac{2\omega}{\pi} \int_0^{\pi/\omega} f(t) \cos n\omega t\ dt,\tag{B.50}$$

so that

$$a_n\ =\ \frac{2\omega}{\pi} \int_0^{\pi/\omega} A \sin \omega t \cos n\omega t\ dt\tag{B.51}$$

$$=\ \frac{A\omega}{\pi} \int_0^{\pi/\omega} \big(\sin\ (n+1)\omega t - \sin\ (n-1)\omega t\big)\ dt$$

$$=\ \frac{A\omega}{\pi} \left(\frac{\cos\ (n-1)\omega t}{(n-1)\omega} - \frac{\cos\ (n+1)\omega t}{(n+1)\omega}\right)\bigg|_0^{\pi/\omega}\quad (n \neq 1)$$

$$=\ \frac{A}{\pi} \left(\frac{\cos\ (n-1)\pi}{n-1} - \frac{1}{n-1} - \frac{\cos\ (n+1)\pi}{n+1} + \frac{1}{n+1}\right)$$

$$=\ \frac{A}{\pi(n^2-1)} \big((n+1) \cos\ (n-1)\pi - (n-1) \cos\ (n+1)\pi - 2\big).$$

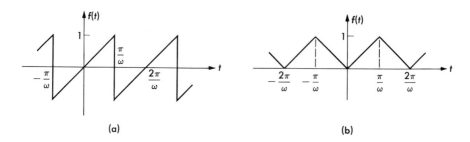

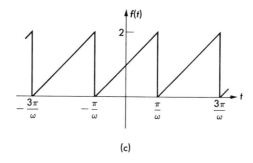

(c)

FIGURE B.4

Now, for $n = 0, 2, 4, 6, \ldots,$ $\cos(n-1)\pi = \cos(n+1)\pi = -1$, so that

$$a_{2m} = \frac{A}{\pi(4m^2 - 1)}\left(2m - 1 - 2m - 1 - 2\right) \qquad m = 0, 1, 2, \ldots,$$

$$= \frac{-4A}{\pi(4m^2 - 1)}; \tag{B.52}$$

also, for $n = 3, 5, 7, \ldots,$ $\cos(n-1)\pi = \cos(n+1)\pi = 1$, so that

$$a_{2m+1} = \frac{A}{\pi(4m^2 + 2m)}\left((2m+2) - 2m - 2\right) = 0.$$

Moreover, $a_1 = 0$. Therefore,

$$f(t) = \frac{2A}{\pi} + \sum_{m=1}^{\infty} \frac{-4A}{\pi(4m^2 - 1)} \cos 2m\omega t, \tag{B.53}$$

or

$$f(t) = A\left(\frac{2}{\pi} - \frac{4}{3\pi}\cos 2\omega t - \frac{4}{15\pi}\cos 4\omega t - \cdots\right). \tag{B.54}$$

EXAMPLE B.3. In this example we shall find Fourier series for the functions illustrated in Fig. B.4. The waveform of Fig. B.4(a) is an odd function, and can be described by

$$f(t) = (\omega/\pi)t, \qquad -\pi/\omega < t < \pi/\omega,$$
$$f(t + 2\pi/\omega) = f(t). \tag{B.55}$$

We may therefore use the Fourier sine series, and expand the function in the form

$$f(t) = \sum_{n=1}^{\infty} b_n \sin n\omega t, \tag{B.56}$$

where

$$b_n = \frac{2\omega}{\pi} \int_0^{\pi/\omega} \frac{\omega}{\pi} t \sin n\omega t \, dt$$

$$= \frac{2\omega^2}{\pi^2} \left\{ -\frac{1}{n\omega} t \cos n\omega t \Big|_0^{\pi/\omega} + \int_0^{\pi/\omega} \frac{1}{n\omega} \cos n\omega t \, dt \right\}$$

$$= \frac{2\omega^2}{\pi^2} \left(-\frac{\pi}{n\omega^2} \cos n\pi + \frac{1}{n^2\omega^2} (\sin n\omega t) \Big|_0^{\pi/\omega} \right)$$

$$= \frac{2\omega^2}{\pi^2} \left(-\frac{\pi}{n\omega^2} \cos n\pi + \frac{1}{n^2\omega^2} \sin n\pi \right)$$

$$= \frac{-2\omega^2}{\pi^2} \frac{\pi}{n\omega^2} \cos n\pi = \frac{-2}{n\pi} \cos n\pi,$$

or

$$b_n = \frac{-2}{n\pi} (-)^n = \frac{2}{n\pi} (-)^{n+1}, \tag{B.57}$$

so that

$$f(t) = \frac{2}{\pi} \sum_{n=1}^{\infty} \frac{(-)^{n+1}}{n} \sin n\omega t. \tag{B.58}$$

The waveform of Fig. B.4(b) is an even function, so that it may be described as

$$\begin{aligned} f(t) &= (\omega/\pi)t, \quad & 0 < t < \pi/\omega, \\ f(t) &= f(-t), \quad & f(t + 2\pi/\omega) = f(t). \end{aligned} \tag{B.59}$$

Here, we can use the Fourier cosine series, so that

$$f(t) = \frac{a_0}{2} + \sum_{n=1}^{\infty} a_n \cos n\omega t, \tag{B.60}$$

where

$$a_n = \frac{2\omega}{\pi} \int_0^{\pi/\omega} \frac{\omega t}{\pi} \cos n\omega t \, dt = \frac{2\omega^2}{\pi^2} \left(\frac{t}{n\omega} \sin n\omega t \Big|_0^{\pi/\omega} - \int_0^{\pi/\omega} \frac{1}{n\omega} \sin n\omega t \, dt \right)$$

$$= \frac{2\omega^2}{\pi^2} \left(\frac{1}{n^2\omega^2} \cos n\omega t \Big|_0^{\pi/\omega} \right) = \frac{2\omega^2}{\pi^2} \left(\frac{1}{n^2\omega^2} \cos n\pi - \frac{1}{n^2\omega^2} \right)$$

$$= \frac{2}{n^2\pi^2} ((-)^n - 1), \tag{B.61}$$

and if $n = 2m + 1$, $a_{2m+1} = -4/(2m + 1)^2\pi^2$, whereas if $n = 2m$, then $a_{2m} = 0$. Furthermore,

$$a_0 = \frac{2\omega}{\pi} \int_0^{\pi/\omega} \frac{\omega}{\pi} t \, dt = \frac{2\omega^2}{\pi^2} \left(\frac{t^2}{2}\right)\Big|_0^{\pi/\omega} = \frac{2\omega^2}{\pi^2} \cdot \frac{\pi^2}{2\omega^2} = 1. \qquad (B.62)$$

Therefore,

$$f(t) = \frac{1}{2} - \frac{4}{\pi^2} \sum_{m=0}^{\infty} \frac{1}{(2m + 1)^2} \cos (2m + 1)\omega t. \qquad (B.63)$$

Finally, the function of Fig. B.4(c) is the same as that of Fig. B.4(a), only displaced upward through 1 unit. Hence its Fourier series is

$$f(t) = 1 + \frac{2}{\pi} \sum_{n=1}^{\infty} \frac{(-)^{n+1}}{n} \sin n\omega t. \qquad (B.64)$$

B.8. THE EXPONENTIAL FOURIER SERIES

Let us examine the following set of functions,

$$\{e^{jn\pi t/L}\}, \qquad n = 0, \pm 1, \pm 2, \ldots, \qquad -L < t < L. \qquad (B.65)$$

For this set, we have

$$\int_{-L}^{L} e^{jn\pi t/L} e^{jm\pi t/L} \, dt = \int_{-L}^{L} e^{j(n+m)\pi t/L} \, dt$$

$$= \frac{L}{j\pi(n + m)} \left(e^{j(n+m)\pi t/L}\right)\Big|_{-L}^{L}$$

$$= \frac{L}{j\pi(n + m)} \left(e^{j(n+m)\pi} - e^{-j(n+m)\pi}\right)$$

$$= \frac{2L}{\pi(n + m)} \sin (n + m)\pi$$

$$= 0 \qquad (n \neq -m), \qquad (B.66)$$

and

$$\int_{-L}^{L} e^{jn\pi t/L} e^{-jn\pi t/L} \, dt = \int_{-L}^{L} dt = 2L. \qquad (B.67)$$

Thus, although this set of functions is not orthogonal in the sense of conditions (B.3), it satisfies very similar properties, namely

$$\int_{-L}^{L} f_m(t) f_n(t) \, dt = 0, \qquad n \neq -m,$$

$$\int_{-L}^{L} f_n(t) f_{-n}(t) \, dt \neq 0. \qquad (B.68)$$

We say that functions satisfying conditions (B.68) are orthogonal in the *Hermitian sense*, and if the second integral in (B.68) is equal to unity, they are *orthonormal in the Hermitian sense*. Hence the set of functions

$$\left\{\frac{1}{\sqrt{2L}}\, e^{jn\pi t/L}\right\}, \qquad n = 0, \pm1, \pm2, \ldots, \quad -L < t < L, \qquad (B.69)$$

is orthonormal in the Hermitian sense.

Let us expand a function in terms of this set (B.69). We write

$$f(t) = \sum_{n=-\infty}^{\infty} c_n e^{jn\pi t/L}, \qquad -L < t < L. \qquad (B.70)$$

Now, to calculate c_m, we note that

$$\int_{-L}^{L} f(t) e^{-jm\pi t/L}\, dt = \sum_{n=-\infty}^{\infty} c_n \int_{-L}^{L} e^{jn\pi t/L} e^{-jm\pi t/L}\, dt = 2Lc_m,$$

so that

$$c_m = \frac{1}{2L} \int_{-L}^{L} f(t) e^{-jm\pi t/L}\, dt, \qquad (B.71)$$

and

$$f(t) = \sum_{n=-\infty}^{\infty} e^{jn\pi t/L} \frac{1}{2L} \int_{-L}^{L} f(t) e^{-jn\pi t/L}\, dt. \qquad (B.72)$$

This series is called the *exponential Fourier series* for $f(t)$.

It is easy to see that the exponential Fourier series is exactly equivalent to the trigonometric series

$$f(t) = \frac{a_0}{2} + \sum_{n=1}^{\infty} \left(a_n \cos \frac{n\pi t}{L} + b_n \sin \frac{n\pi t}{L}\right). \qquad (B.27)$$

This is so because, if we write in (B.27)

$$\cos \frac{n\pi t}{L} = \frac{1}{2}(e^{jn\pi t/L} + e^{-jn\pi t/L}), \qquad \sin \frac{n\pi t}{L} = \frac{1}{2j}(e^{jn\pi t/L} - e^{-jn\pi t/L}), \qquad (B.73)$$

we obtain

$$f(t) = \frac{a_0}{2} + \frac{1}{2}\sum_{n=1}^{\infty}(a_n - jb_n)e^{jn\pi t/L} + (a_n + jb_n)e^{-jn\pi t/L}$$

$$= \frac{a_0}{2}e^0 + \sum_{n=1}^{\infty}\frac{a_n - jb_n}{2}e^{jn\pi t/L} + \sum_{n=-\infty}^{-1}\frac{a_{-n} + jb_{-n}}{2}e^{jn\pi t/L}$$

$$= \sum_{n=-\infty}^{\infty} c_n e^{jn\pi t/L}, \qquad (B.74)$$

where

$$c_n = \frac{a_n - jb_n}{2}, \quad n \geq 1; \quad c_0 = \frac{a_0}{2}; \quad c_n = \frac{a_{-n} + jb_{-n}}{2}, \quad n \leq -1.$$

EXAMPLE B.4. Here we shall calculate the exponential Fourier series for the symmetric square wave shown in Fig. B.5. This function may be represented analytically by

$$f(t) = \begin{cases} 1 & \text{for} \quad -L/2 < t < L/2, \\ -1 & \text{for} \quad -L < t < -L/2 \quad \text{and} \quad L/2 < t < L, \end{cases} \tag{B.75}$$
$$f(t + 2L) = f(t).$$

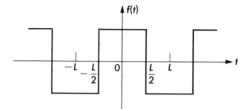

FIGURE B.5

The exponential Fourier series therefore is

$$f(t) = \sum_{n=-\infty}^{\infty} c_n e^{jn\pi t/L}, \tag{B.70}$$

where

$$c_n = \frac{1}{2L} \int_{-L}^{L} f(t) e^{-jn\pi t/L} \, dt$$

$$= \frac{1}{2L} \left(\int_{-L}^{-L/2} -e^{-jn\pi t/L} \, dt + \int_{-L/2}^{L/2} e^{-jn\pi t/L} \, dt + \int_{L/2}^{L} -e^{-jn\pi t/L} \, dt \right)$$

$$= \frac{1}{j2n\pi} (e^{-jn\pi t/L}) \Big|_{-L}^{-L/2} - \frac{1}{j2n\pi} (e^{-jn\pi t/L}) \Big|_{-L/2}^{L/2} + \frac{1}{j2n\pi} (e^{-jn\pi t/L}) \Big|_{L/2}^{L}$$

$$= \frac{1}{j2n\pi} (e^{jn\pi/2} - e^{jn\pi} - e^{-jn\pi/2} + e^{jn\pi/2} + e^{-jn\pi} - e^{-jn\pi/2})$$

$$= \frac{1}{j2n\pi} (2e^{jn\pi/2} - e^{jn\pi} - 2e^{-jn\pi/2} + e^{-jn\pi}), \quad (n \neq 0),$$

or

$$c_n = \frac{2}{n\pi} \sin \frac{n\pi}{2} - \frac{1}{n\pi} \sin n\pi. \tag{B.76}$$

Now,

$$\sin \frac{2m\pi}{2} = \sin m\pi = 0,$$

and

$$\sin \frac{(2m+1)\pi}{2} = \sin m\pi \cos \frac{\pi}{2} + \cos m\pi \sin \frac{\pi}{2} = \cos m\pi = (-1)^m,$$

so that

$$c_n = 0 \quad \text{for } n \text{ even,} \quad \text{and} \quad c_{2m+1} = \frac{2(-1)^m}{(2m+1)\pi}.$$

Also, $c_0 = 0$, so that

$$f(t) = \frac{2}{\pi} \sum_{m=-\infty}^{\infty} \frac{(-1)^m}{2m+1} e^{j(2m+1)\pi t/L}. \tag{B.77}$$

Appendix C

MATRICES

C.1. DEFINITION OF A MATRIX

A *matrix* is a rectangular array of numbers and is represented by

$$[A] = \begin{bmatrix} a_{11} & a_{12} & \cdots & a_{1n} \\ a_{21} & a_{22} & \cdots & a_{2n} \\ \vdots & \vdots & & \vdots \\ a_{m1} & a_{m2} & \cdots & a_{mn} \end{bmatrix}. \tag{C.1}$$

We shall denote matrices with pairs of brackets. Matrix $[A]$ in (C.1) has m rows and n columns. The typical entry in $[A]$ is denoted by a_{ij}, where the subscript i refers to the row and the subscript j refers to the column. The entries of $[A]$ are called *elements* and these may be either numbers or functions.

A matrix having m rows and n columns is called a matrix of *order* (m, n); when $m = n$, it is called a square matrix of order n. The elements $a_{11}, a_{22}, \ldots, a_{nn}$ of a square matrix constitute its main diagonal.

C.2. ADDITION AND SUBTRACTION

Two matrices are *equal* when the matrices are of the same order and when their corresponding elements are equal. For example, the matrices

$$[A] = \begin{bmatrix} a_{11} & a_{12} & a_{13} \\ a_{21} & a_{22} & a_{23} \end{bmatrix}_{(2,3)} \quad \text{and} \quad [B] = \begin{bmatrix} b_{11} & b_{12} & b_{13} \\ b_{21} & b_{22} & b_{23} \end{bmatrix}_{(2,3)} \tag{C.2}$$

are equal when $a_{ij} = b_{ij}$ for all i and j.

The *sum* of two matrices of order (m, n) is another matrix of the same order and is determined by adding their corresponding elements.

EXAMPLE C.1. When

$$[A] = \begin{bmatrix} 1 & 2 & 3 \\ 1 & 0 & -1 \end{bmatrix}_{(2,3)} \quad \text{and} \quad [B] = \begin{bmatrix} 0 & 1 & 2 \\ -1 & 1 & 2 \end{bmatrix}_{(2,3)}, \tag{C.3}$$

the matrix $[C]$ obtained by their addition is given by

$$[C] = [A] + [B] = \begin{bmatrix} 1 & 3 & 5 \\ 0 & 1 & 1 \end{bmatrix}_{(2,3)} \tag{C.4}$$

When two matrices are of the same order, they are said to be *conformable* for addition.

The negative of a matrix $[A]$ is obtained by multiplying every element of $[A]$ by -1.

Thus subtraction of two matrices of the same order is defined as

$$[A]_{(m,n)} - [B]_{(m,n)} = [A]_{(m,n)} + [-B]_{(m,n)} = [C]_{(m,n)}. \tag{C.5}$$

When every element of a matrix $[A]_{(m,n)}$ is zero, it is called a *zero matrix* of order (m, n); it is also called a *null matrix*.

Two matrices $[A]$ and $[B]$ of the same order obey the commutative law of addition

$$[A] + [B] = [B] + [A]. \tag{C.6}$$

Likewise, the associative law of addition is also valid:

$$[A] + [B + C] = [A + B] + [C]. \tag{C.7}$$

When a matrix $[A]$ is multiplied by a scalar α, the result is a new matrix whose elements are the elements of $[A]$ multiplied by α. For example,

$$2 \begin{bmatrix} 1 & 2 \\ 0 & 1 \end{bmatrix} = \begin{bmatrix} 2 & 4 \\ 0 & 2 \end{bmatrix}. \tag{C.8}$$

C.3. MULTIPLICATION OF MATRICES

In order to define the product

$$[A]_{(m,n)}[B]_{(n,p)} = [C]_{(m,p)}, \tag{C.9}$$

we introduce first the idea of premultiplication and postmultiplication. In (C.9), matrix $[B]$ postmultiplies $[A]$, or matrix $[A]$ premultiplies $[B]$. Two matrices are said to be conformable for multiplication if the number of columns of the premultiplying matrix is equal to the number of rows of the postmultiplying matrix; the order of the resulting product matrix is given by the number of rows of the premultiplying matrix and the number of columns of the postmultiplying matrix.

The rule for multiplication is best explained through an example.

EXAMPLE C.2. Compute the elements of $[C]$ when

$$\begin{bmatrix} a_{11} & a_{12} & a_{13} \\ a_{21} & a_{22} & a_{23} \end{bmatrix} \begin{bmatrix} b_{11} & b_{12} & b_{13} \\ b_{21} & b_{22} & b_{23} \\ b_{31} & b_{32} & b_{33} \end{bmatrix} = \begin{bmatrix} c_{11} & c_{12} & c_{13} \\ c_{21} & c_{22} & c_{23} \end{bmatrix}. \tag{C.10}$$

To compute c_{11}, we multiply the elements of the first row of $[A]$ by the corresponding elements of the first column of $[B]$ and form their sum. Thus,

$$c_{11} = a_{11}b_{11} + a_{12}b_{21} + a_{13}b_{31}. \tag{C.11}$$

Similarly,

$$
\begin{aligned}
c_{12} &= a_{11}b_{12} + a_{12}b_{22} + a_{13}b_{32}, \\
c_{13} &= a_{11}b_{13} + a_{12}b_{23} + a_{13}b_{33}, \\
c_{21} &= a_{21}b_{11} + a_{22}b_{21} + a_{23}b_{31}, \\
c_{22} &= a_{21}b_{12} + a_{22}b_{22} + a_{23}b_{32}, \\
c_{23} &= a_{21}b_{13} + a_{22}b_{23} + a_{23}b_{23}.
\end{aligned}
\tag{C.12}
$$

From the above rule for multiplication of two matrices, it is easy to see that, in general, $[A][B] \neq [B][A]$.

In example C.2, it is clear that the matrices $[B]$ and $[A]$ are not even conformable for the multiplication $[B][A]$.

Some other important properties of matrix multiplication are listed.

Property C.1.

(i) $[A][B] = [0]$ does not imply that either $[A]$ or $[B]$ is a zero matrix.

(ii) $[A][B] = [A][C]$ does not imply that $[B] = [C]$; the cancellation law does not hold.

The associative and distributive laws of multiplication are valid for matrices; when the matrices are conformable for multiplication,

$$[A][BC] = [AB][C] \qquad \text{(associative law of multiplication).} \tag{C.13}$$

Also, assuming conformability,

$$[A][B + C] = [AB] + [AC], \tag{C.14}$$
$$\text{(distributive laws of multiplication)}$$
$$[D + E][F] = [DF] + [EF]. \tag{C.15}$$

C.4. TRANSPOSE OF A MATRIX

The matrix obtained by interchanging the rows and columns of a matrix $[A]$ is called the tranpose of $[A]$ and is denoted by $[A]'$.

EXAMPLE C.3. If

$$
[A] = \begin{bmatrix} a_{11} & a_{12} & a_{13} \\ a_{21} & a_{22} & a_{23} \end{bmatrix},
\tag{C.16}
$$

then

$$
[A]' = \begin{bmatrix} a_{11} & a_{21} \\ a_{12} & a_{22} \\ a_{13} & a_{23} \end{bmatrix}.
\tag{C.17}
$$

Property C.2. If the transpose of $[A]$ and $[B]$ are denoted by $[A]'$ and $[B]'$ respectively, and if α is a scalar, then

$$\text{(i)} \qquad [A']' = [A], \tag{C.18}$$

$$\text{(ii)} \quad [A + B]' = [A]' + [B]', \tag{C.19}$$

and also   (iii) $[AB]' = [B]'[A]',$ (C.20)

                             (iv) $[\alpha A]' = \alpha[A]'.$ (C.21)

EXERCISE C.1. Verify the above four properties when

$$[A] = \begin{bmatrix} 2 & 3 & 1 \\ 0 & 2 & 1 \\ 1 & 1 & 1 \end{bmatrix}, \quad [B] = \begin{bmatrix} 1 & 1 & 1 \\ 0 & 1 & 2 \\ 1 & -1 & 1 \end{bmatrix}, \quad \text{and} \quad \alpha = 2. \quad (C.22)$$

If a square matrix $[A]$ is equal to its own transpose, it is called a *symmetric matrix*. An example of such a matrix is

$$[A] = \begin{bmatrix} a_{11} & a_{12} & a_{13} \\ a_{12} & a_{22} & a_{23} \\ a_{13} & a_{23} & a_{33} \end{bmatrix} = [A]'. \quad (C.23)$$

If a square matrix

$$[A] = [-A]', \quad (C.24)$$

then $[A]$ is called a *skew symmetric matrix*. An example of a skew symmetric matrix is

$$[A] = \begin{bmatrix} 0 & 2 \\ -2 & 0 \end{bmatrix}. \quad (C.25)$$

Note that the main diagonal elements of a skew symmetric matrix are zero.

When the elements of a matrix $[A]$ are replaced by their complex conjugates, the resulting matrix is called the *conjugate* of $[A]$ and is denoted by $[A^*]$.

EXAMPLE C.4. If

$$[A] = \begin{bmatrix} 1 & 1 & 1 \\ 1 & e^{j2\pi/3} & e^{-j2\pi/3} \\ 1 & e^{-j2\pi/3} & e^{j2\pi/3} \end{bmatrix}, \quad (C.26)$$

then

$$[A^*] = \begin{bmatrix} 1 & 1 & 1 \\ 1 & e^{-j2\pi/3} & e^{j2\pi/3} \\ 1 & e^{j2\pi/3} & e^{-j2\pi/3} \end{bmatrix}. \quad (C.27)$$

The matrix $[A]$ of this example is called the symmetric component matrix.

The square matrix,

$$[U]_n = \begin{bmatrix} 1 & 0 & 0 & \cdots & 0 \\ 0 & 1 & 0 & \cdots & 0 \\ 0 & 0 & 1 & \cdots & 0 \\ \vdots & \vdots & \vdots & & \vdots \\ 0 & 0 & 0 & \cdots & 1 \end{bmatrix}_{(n)}, \quad (C.28)$$

is called a *unit matrix* of order n; the main diagonal elements are equal to 1 and all the off-diagonal elements are zero. The role of the unit or identity matrix in matrix algebra is similar to the number 1 in ordinary algebra.

C.5. MATRIX PARTITIONING

Sometimes it is expedient to divide a matrix into rectangular blocks of elements. The submatrices thus obtained can be considered as elements, as for example, in the matrix

$$[A] = \begin{bmatrix} a_{11} & a_{12} & a_{13} & a_{14} \\ a_{21} & a_{22} & a_{23} & a_{24} \\ \hline a_{31} & a_{32} & a_{33} & a_{34} \end{bmatrix} = \begin{bmatrix} A_{11} & A_{12} \\ A_{21} & A_{22} \end{bmatrix}, \qquad \text{(C.29)}$$

where

$$[A_{11}] = \begin{bmatrix} a_{11} & a_{12} \\ a_{21} & a_{22} \end{bmatrix}, \qquad [A_{12}] = \begin{bmatrix} a_{13} & a_{14} \\ a_{23} & a_{24} \end{bmatrix}, \qquad [A_{21}] = [a_{31} \quad a_{32}],$$

and

$$[A_{22}] = [a_{33} \quad a_{34}]. \qquad \text{(C.30)}$$

The horizontal subdivision indicated in (C.29) is called a *row partitioning* and the vertical subdivision is called a *column partitioning*.

Property C.3. When the submatrices indicated below are conformable for the intended operations, we have,

$$\begin{bmatrix} A_{11} & A_{12} \\ A_{21} & A_{22} \end{bmatrix} + \begin{bmatrix} B_{11} & B_{12} \\ B_{21} & B_{22} \end{bmatrix} = \begin{bmatrix} A_{11} + B_{11} & A_{12} + B_{12} \\ A_{21} + B_{21} & A_{22} + B_{22} \end{bmatrix}, \qquad \text{(C.31)}$$

$$\begin{bmatrix} A_{11} & A_{12} & A_{13} \\ A_{21} & A_{22} & A_{23} \end{bmatrix} \begin{bmatrix} B_{11} & B_{12} \\ B_{21} & B_{22} \\ B_{31} & B_{32} \end{bmatrix}$$

$$= \begin{bmatrix} A_{11}B_{11} + A_{12}B_{21} + A_{13}B_{31} & A_{11}B_{12} + A_{12}B_{22} + A_{13}B_{32} \\ A_{21}B_{11} + A_{22}B_{21} + A_{23}B_{31} & A_{21}B_{12} + A_{22}B_{22} + A_{23}B_{32} \end{bmatrix}, \qquad \text{(C.32)}$$

$$\begin{bmatrix} A_{11} & A_{12} \\ A_{21} & A_{22} \end{bmatrix}' = \begin{bmatrix} A'_{11} & A'_{21} \\ A'_{12} & A'_{22} \end{bmatrix}. \qquad \text{(C.33)}$$

EXERCISE C.2. (a) Verify Eq. (C.31) when two matrices $[A]$ and $[B]$ are partitioned as

$$[A] = \begin{bmatrix} 1 & 2 & 3 \\ \hline 1 & 1 & 2 \\ 1 & 1 & 0 \end{bmatrix} \quad \text{and} \quad [B] = \begin{bmatrix} 0 & 1 & 0 \\ \hline 0 & -1 & 0 \\ 1 & 0 & 0 \end{bmatrix}. \qquad \text{(C.34)}$$

(b) Verify Eq. (C.32) when the two matrices $[A]$ and $[B]$ are given in the partitioned form,

$$[A] = \begin{bmatrix} 1 & 2 & 3 & 4 & 5 & 0 \\ \hline 0 & 1 & 0 & 1 & 0 & 1 \end{bmatrix} \quad \text{and} \quad [B] = \begin{bmatrix} 1 & 1 \\ 0 & 1 \\ \hline -1 & 0 \\ -2 & 1 \\ \hline 3 & 2 \\ 1 & 0 \end{bmatrix}. \qquad \text{(C.35)}$$

(c) Verify Eq. (C.33) for the matrix $[A]$ in (a).

C.6. THE DETERMINANT OF A SQUARE MATRIX

The *determinant* of a square matrix,

$$[A] = \begin{bmatrix} a_{11} & a_{12} & \cdots & a_{1n} \\ a_{21} & a_{22} & \cdots & a_{2n} \\ \vdots & \vdots & & \vdots \\ a_{n1} & a_{n2} & \cdots & a_{nn} \end{bmatrix},$$

is denoted by det A or $|A|$, and defined by

$$\det A = \sum \epsilon_{j_1 j_2 j_3 \ldots j_n} a_{1j_1} a_{2j_2} \ldots a_{nj_n}, \tag{C.36}$$

where

$$\epsilon_{j_1 j_2 \ldots j_n} = \pm 1. \tag{C.37}$$

according as the *permutation* $j_1 j_2 \cdots j_n$ of the integers $1, 2, \ldots, n$ is even or odd. A permutation of n integers is an ordering of the integers. It is even if the integers can be returned to their natural order by an even number of interchanges in position of pairs; it is odd otherwise. There are exactly $n!$ permutations of n integers, and the summation in (C.36) is carried over all $n!$ of the permutations.

EXAMPLE C.5

$$\det \begin{bmatrix} a_{11} & a_{12} \\ a_{21} & a_{22} \end{bmatrix} = \epsilon_{12} a_{11} a_{22} + \epsilon_{21} a_{12} a_{21} = a_{11} a_{22} - a_{12} a_{21}.$$

The row subscripts in (C.36) were maintained in natural order. The determinant can also be defined by

$$\det A = \sum \epsilon_{j_1 j_2 j_3 \ldots j_n} a_{j_1 1} a_{j_2 2} a_{j_3 3} \cdots a_{j_n n}, \tag{C.38}$$

where the column subscripts are in the natural order. The two definitions are equivalent.

The following properties of determinants are stated without proof.

Property C.4. Each term of the expansion of det A contains exactly one element from each row and one element from each column.

Property C.5. If any two rows or any two columns of $[A]$ are interchanged, the determinant of the resulting matrix is $-\det A$.

Property C.6. For every square matrix A, det $A = \det A'$.

The *cofactor* A_{ij} of an element a_{ij} of a square matrix $[A]$ is defined as $(-1)^{i+j}$ times the determinant of the square submatrix obtained by deleting the ith row and jth column of $[A]$. It may easily be shown that

$$\det A = a_{i1} A_{i1} + a_{i2} A_{i2} + \cdots + a_{in} A_{in}, \tag{C.39}$$

or, equivalently,

$$\det A = a_{1i}A_{1i} + a_{2i}A_{2i} + \cdots + a_{ni}A_{ni}. \tag{C.40}$$

Equation (C.39) is called the expansion of det A in terms of the elements of the ith row, and Eq. (C.40) is the expansion of det A in terms of the elements of the ith column.

EXAMPLE C.6

$$\det \begin{bmatrix} 1 & 2 & 3 \\ 1 & 1 & 4 \\ 1 & 0 & 3 \end{bmatrix} = 1 \det \begin{bmatrix} 1 & 4 \\ 0 & 3 \end{bmatrix} - 2 \det \begin{bmatrix} 1 & 4 \\ 1 & 3 \end{bmatrix} + 3 \det \begin{bmatrix} 1 & 1 \\ 1 & 0 \end{bmatrix}$$

$$= 1\ (3 - 0) - 2\ (3 - 4) + 3\ (0 - 1)$$

$$= 2.$$

We close this section by stating without proof a few more properties of the determinant of a square matrix, and illustrating their use in some examples.

Property C.7. If all the elements in any row or in any column of $[A]$ are zero,

$$\det A = 0.$$

Property C.8. If $[A]$ has two identical rows or two identical columns, det $A = 0$.

Property C.9. If any one row or any one column of $[A]$ is multiplied by a constant K, the determinant of the resulting matrix is K det A.

Property C.10. If any multiple of one row of $[A]$ is added to a different row, the determinant of the resulting matrix is det A. This property also applies to the columns.

EXAMPLE C.7

$$\det \begin{bmatrix} 0 & 1 & 2 \\ 0 & 3 & 4 \\ 0 & 4 & 5 \end{bmatrix} = 0 \qquad \text{(by Property C.6.4)}.$$

EXAMPLE C.8

$$\det \begin{bmatrix} 1 & 2 & 3 \\ 4 & 5 & 7 \\ 2 & 4 & 6 \end{bmatrix} = 2 \det \begin{bmatrix} 1 & 2 & 3 \\ 4 & 5 & 7 \\ 1 & 2 & 3 \end{bmatrix} \qquad \text{(by Property C.9)}$$

$$= 0 \qquad\qquad \text{(by Property C.8)}.$$

EXAMPLE C.9. We evaluate

$$\det \begin{bmatrix} 4 & 8 & 8 & 8 \\ 3 & 2 & 14 & 10 \\ 2 & 1 & 3 & -14 \\ 1 & 0 & 8 & 7 \end{bmatrix}$$

by repeated applications of Properties C.9 and C.10, as follows:

$$\det \begin{bmatrix} 4 & 8 & 8 & 8 \\ 3 & 2 & 14 & 10 \\ 2 & 1 & 3 & -14 \\ 1 & 0 & 8 & 7 \end{bmatrix} = 4 \det \begin{bmatrix} 1 & 2 & 2 & 2 \\ 3 & 2 & 14 & 10 \\ 2 & 1 & 3 & -14 \\ 1 & 0 & 8 & 7 \end{bmatrix}$$

$$= 4 \det \begin{bmatrix} 1 & 2 & 2 & 2 \\ 0 & -4 & 8 & 4 \\ 0 & -3 & -1 & -18 \\ 0 & -2 & 6 & 5 \end{bmatrix} = -16 \det \begin{bmatrix} 1 & 2 & 2 & 2 \\ 0 & 1 & -2 & -1 \\ 0 & -3 & -1 & -18 \\ 0 & -2 & 6 & 5 \end{bmatrix}$$

$$= -16 \det \begin{bmatrix} 1 & 2 & 2 & 2 \\ 0 & 1 & -2 & -1 \\ 0 & 0 & -7 & -21 \\ 0 & 0 & 2 & 3 \end{bmatrix} = 112 \det \begin{bmatrix} 1 & 2 & 2 & 2 \\ 0 & 1 & -2 & -1 \\ 0 & 0 & 1 & 3 \\ 0 & 0 & 2 & 3 \end{bmatrix}$$

$$= 112 \det \begin{bmatrix} 1 & 2 & 2 & 2 \\ 0 & 1 & -2 & -1 \\ 0 & 0 & 1 & 3 \\ 0 & 0 & 0 & -3 \end{bmatrix} = -336 \det \begin{bmatrix} 1 & 2 & 2 & 2 \\ 0 & 1 & -2 & -1 \\ 0 & 0 & 1 & 3 \\ 0 & 0 & 0 & 1 \end{bmatrix} = -336.$$

C.7. RANK AND ELEMENTARY TRANSFORMATIONS

A matrix is said to be of *rank r* if
(i) it has at least one square submatrix of order r whose determinant is nonzero, and
(ii) the determinants of all square submatrices of order greater than r are zero.

EXAMPLE C.10. The rank of the matrix

$$[A] = \begin{bmatrix} 1 & 2 & 3 \\ 4 & 5 & 6 \\ 7 & 8 & 9 \end{bmatrix}$$

is 2 since det $A = 0$, and there exists at least one submatrix of order 2 whose determinant is nonzero. For example

$$\det \begin{bmatrix} 1 & 2 \\ 4 & 5 \end{bmatrix} \neq 0.$$

The procedure for determining the rank of a matrix from its definition is extremely tedious; it can be greatly simplified by the concept of *elementary transformations*, which is comprised of the following three operations on a matrix:
(i) interchange of two rows (columns) of a matrix;
(ii) multiplication of a row (column) by a nonzero constant;
(iii) addition to any row (column) of any arbitrary multiple of another row (column).
We state the following theorem without proof.

Theorem C.1. Elementary transformations on a matrix do not alter its rank.

By means of the above theorem, we can define a procedure for determining the rank of a matrix. We shall illustrate the procedure for the matrix

$$[A] = \begin{bmatrix} 2 & 2 & 1 & -1 \\ 1 & 3 & 0 & 1 \\ 6 & 10 & 2 & 0 \end{bmatrix}. \tag{C.41}$$

(i) If the element a_{11} is not already equal to unity, we make it so either by an interchange of rows or by multiplying the first row by a suitable constant.

The (1, 1) entry of the matrix of (C.41) is 2. To make it equal to 1, we can either multiply the first row by $\frac{1}{2}$ or interchange rows one and two. The latter step will result in

$$\begin{bmatrix} 1 & 3 & 0 & 1 \\ 2 & 2 & 1 & -1 \\ 6 & 10 & 2 & 0 \end{bmatrix}. \tag{C.42}$$

(ii) We multiply the first row of the new matrix by appropriate constants so that when the first row is added to the remaining rows, we obtain zeros for the elements in the first column below the (1, 1) element.

When we multiply the first row of (C.42) by -2 and add it to the second row, and then again multiply the first row by -6 and add it to the third row, the resulting matrix is

$$\begin{bmatrix} 1 & 3 & 0 & 1 \\ 0 & -4 & 1 & -3 \\ 0 & -8 & 2 & -6 \end{bmatrix}. \tag{C.43}$$

(iii) We now proceed to repeat Steps (i) and (ii) operating on the (2, 2) element of the matrix resulting from Step (ii).

Multiply the second row of (C.43) by $-\frac{1}{4}$ to introduce 1 in the (2, 2) position:

$$\begin{bmatrix} 1 & 3 & 0 & 1 \\ 0 & 1 & -\frac{1}{4} & \frac{3}{4} \\ 0 & -8 & 2 & -6 \end{bmatrix}. \tag{C.44}$$

Multiply the second row by 8 and add it to the third row:

$$\begin{bmatrix} 1 & 3 & 0 & 1 \\ 0 & 1 & -\frac{1}{4} & \frac{3}{4} \\ 0 & 0 & 0 & 0 \end{bmatrix}. \tag{C.45}$$

(Note that this step does not replace the entries already zeroed out by nonzero terms.)

By inspection, the rank of (C.45) is 2 because

$$\det \begin{bmatrix} 1 & 3 \\ 0 & 1 \end{bmatrix} = 1.$$

The matrices in (C.41) through (C.45) are all "rank equivalent" matrices, and this equivalence is denoted by the symbol $\sim$. Thus,

$$\begin{bmatrix} 2 & 2 & 1 & -1 \\ 1 & 3 & 0 & 1 \\ 6 & 10 & 2 & 0 \end{bmatrix} \sim \begin{bmatrix} 1 & 3 & 0 & 1 \\ 2 & 2 & 1 & -1 \\ 6 & 10 & 2 & 0 \end{bmatrix} \sim \begin{bmatrix} 1 & 3 & 0 & 1 \\ 0 & -4 & 1 & -3 \\ 0 & -8 & 2 & -6 \end{bmatrix}$$

$$\sim \begin{bmatrix} 1 & 3 & 0 & 1 \\ 0 & 1 & -\frac{1}{4} & \frac{3}{4} \\ 0 & -8 & 2 & -6 \end{bmatrix} \sim \begin{bmatrix} 1 & 3 & 0 & 1 \\ 0 & 1 & -\frac{1}{4} & \frac{3}{4} \\ \hline 0 & 0 & 0 & 0 \end{bmatrix}.$$

EXAMPLE C.11. Determine the rank of the matrix

$$\begin{bmatrix} 1 & 3 & 0 & 1 & 4 \\ -1 & 2 & 1 & 1 & 2 \\ 5 & 1 & 2 & 3 & 1 \\ 2 & 1 & 0 & 1 & -1 \end{bmatrix},$$

by means of elementary row operations.

$$\begin{bmatrix} 1 & 3 & 0 & 1 & 4 \\ -1 & 2 & 1 & 1 & 2 \\ 5 & 1 & 2 & 3 & 1 \\ 2 & 1 & 0 & 1 & -1 \end{bmatrix} \sim \begin{bmatrix} 1 & 3 & 0 & 1 & 4 \\ 0 & 5 & 1 & 2 & 6 \\ 0 & -14 & 2 & -2 & -19 \\ 0 & -5 & 0 & -1 & -9 \end{bmatrix}$$

$$\sim \begin{bmatrix} 1 & 3 & 0 & 1 & 4 \\ 0 & 1 & \frac{1}{5} & \frac{2}{5} & \frac{6}{5} \\ 0 & -14 & 2 & -2 & -19 \\ 0 & -5 & 0 & -1 & -9 \end{bmatrix} \sim \begin{bmatrix} 1 & 3 & 0 & 1 & 4 \\ 0 & 1 & \frac{1}{5} & \frac{2}{5} & \frac{6}{5} \\ 0 & 0 & \frac{24}{5} & \frac{18}{5} & -\frac{7}{5} \\ 0 & 0 & 1 & 1 & -3 \end{bmatrix}$$

$$\sim \begin{bmatrix} 1 & 3 & 0 & 1 & 4 \\ 0 & 1 & \frac{1}{5} & \frac{2}{5} & \frac{6}{5} \\ 0 & 0 & 1 & \frac{3}{4} & -\frac{7}{24} \\ 0 & 0 & 1 & 1 & -3 \end{bmatrix} \sim \begin{bmatrix} 1 & 3 & 0 & 1 & 4 \\ 0 & 1 & \frac{1}{5} & \frac{2}{5} & \frac{6}{5} \\ 0 & 0 & 1 & \frac{3}{4} & -\frac{7}{24} \\ 0 & 0 & 0 & \frac{1}{4} & -\frac{65}{24} \end{bmatrix}$$

$$\sim \begin{bmatrix} 1 & 3 & 0 & 1 & 4 \\ 0 & 1 & \frac{1}{5} & \frac{2}{5} & \frac{6}{5} \\ 0 & 0 & 1 & \frac{3}{4} & -\frac{7}{24} \\ 0 & 0 & 0 & 1 & -\frac{65}{6} \end{bmatrix}. \tag{C.46}$$

The rank of the matrix is 4.

C.8. ADJOINT AND INVERSE

Let $[A]$ be a square matrix of order n and A_{ij} be the cofactor of a_{ij} in the determinant of $[A]$ (det A); then,

$$[A_1] = [A_{ij}]' = \begin{bmatrix} A_{11} & A_{21} & \cdots & A_{n1} \\ A_{12} & A_{22} & \cdots & A_{n2} \\ \vdots & & & \vdots \\ A_{1n} & A_{2n} & \cdots & A_{nn} \end{bmatrix}, \tag{C.47}$$

is called the *adjoint matrix* of $[A]$.

EXAMPLE C.12. If

$$[A] = \begin{bmatrix} 1 & 1 & 2 \\ 0 & 1 & 1 \\ 1 & 1 & -1 \end{bmatrix}, \tag{C.48}$$

then,

$$[A_{ij}] = \begin{bmatrix} -2 & 1 & -1 \\ 3 & -3 & 0 \\ -1 & -1 & 1 \end{bmatrix}, \tag{C.49}$$

and

$$[A_1] = [A_{ij}]' = \begin{bmatrix} -2 & 3 & -1 \\ 1 & -3 & -1 \\ -1 & 0 & 1 \end{bmatrix}. \tag{C.50}$$

If two square matrices $[A]$ and $[B]$ of order n satisfy the relation

$$[A][B] = [B][A] = [U]_{(n)}, \tag{C.51}$$

then matrix $[B]$ is called the *inverse* of $[A]$, and is denoted by

$$[B] = [A]^{-1}. \tag{C.52}$$

From the theory of determinants, we have the relation,

$$[A][A_1] = [A_1][A] = \det A [U]_{(n)}. \tag{C.53}$$

Comparing Eqs. (C.51) and (C.53), we have

$$[A]^{-1} = \frac{[A_1]}{\det A}. \tag{C.54}$$

EXAMPLE C.13. Calculate the inverse of

$$[A] = \begin{bmatrix} 1 & 1 & 2 \\ 0 & 1 & 1 \\ 1 & 1 & -1 \end{bmatrix}. \tag{C.48}$$

We have

$$[A_1] = \begin{bmatrix} -2 & 3 & -1 \\ 1 & -3 & -1 \\ -1 & 0 & 1 \end{bmatrix} \tag{C.50}$$

and

$$\det A = -3. \tag{C.55}$$

Therefore, the inverse of $[A]$ is given by

$$[A]^{-1} = \frac{1}{-3} \begin{bmatrix} -2 & 3 & -1 \\ 1 & -3 & -1 \\ -1 & 0 & 1 \end{bmatrix} = \begin{bmatrix} \frac{2}{3} & -1 & \frac{1}{3} \\ -\frac{1}{3} & 1 & \frac{1}{3} \\ \frac{1}{3} & 0 & -\frac{1}{3} \end{bmatrix}. \tag{C.56}$$

That the result is correct can be verified by

$$\begin{bmatrix} 1 & 1 & 2 \\ 0 & 1 & 1 \\ 1 & 1 & -1 \end{bmatrix} \begin{bmatrix} \frac{2}{3} & -1 & \frac{1}{3} \\ -\frac{1}{3} & 1 & \frac{1}{3} \\ \frac{1}{3} & 0 & -\frac{1}{3} \end{bmatrix} = \begin{bmatrix} \frac{2}{3} & -1 & \frac{1}{3} \\ -\frac{1}{3} & 1 & \frac{1}{3} \\ \frac{1}{3} & 0 & -\frac{1}{3} \end{bmatrix} \begin{bmatrix} 1 & 1 & 2 \\ 0 & 1 & 1 \\ 1 & 1 & -1 \end{bmatrix}$$

$$= \begin{bmatrix} 1 & 0 & 0 \\ 0 & 1 & 0 \\ 0 & 0 & 1 \end{bmatrix}. \tag{C.57}$$

For a matrix to have an inverse, it is essential that its determinant be nonzero. Matrices having inverses are called *nonsingular* matrices; otherwise, they are called *singular* matrices.

Property C.12.

(i) When the determinant of $[A]$ exists,

$$\det A^{-1} = \frac{1}{\det A}. \tag{C.58}$$

(ii) When $[A]^{-1}$ exists,

$$[A^{-1}]' = [A']^{-1}. \tag{C.59}$$

EXERCISE C.3. Verify the above properties when

$$[A] = \begin{bmatrix} 1 & 2 & 3 \\ 0 & 1 & 1 \\ 0 & 0 & -4 \end{bmatrix}. \tag{C.60}$$

C.9. SYSTEMS OF ALGEBRAIC EQUATIONS

The definition of matrix multiplication allows us to write a system of m non-homogeneous algebraic equations in n unknowns,

$$\begin{aligned} a_{11}x_1 + a_{12}x_2 + a_{13}x_3 + \cdots + a_{1n}x_n &= b_1, \\ a_{21}x_1 + a_{22}x_2 + a_{23}x_3 + \cdots + a_{2n}x_n &= b_2, \\ &\vdots \\ a_{m1}x_1 + a_{m2}x_2 + a_{m3}x_3 + \cdots + a_{mn}x_n &= b_m, \end{aligned} \tag{C.61}$$

in the matrix notation

$$\begin{bmatrix} a_{11} & a_{12} & a_{13} & \cdots & a_{1n} \\ a_{21} & a_{22} & a_{23} & \cdots & a_{2n} \\ \vdots & & & & \vdots \\ a_{m1} & a_{m2} & a_{m3} & \cdots & a_{mn} \end{bmatrix} \begin{bmatrix} x_1 \\ x_2 \\ \vdots \\ x_n \end{bmatrix} = \begin{bmatrix} b_1 \\ b_2 \\ \vdots \\ b_m \end{bmatrix}, \tag{C.62}$$

or symbolically,

$$[A][X] = [B]. \tag{C.63}$$

The matrix $[A]$ in Eq. (C.63) is called the *coefficient matrix*, and the matrix $[A\ B]$

is called the *augmented matrix;* the matrix $[X]$ with n rows and one column is called an *n-vector* or simply a column matrix; the column matrix $[B]$ has m rows.

When the matrix $[B] = [0]$, the equations are called *homogeneous.*

If a system of equations has at least one solution, it is said to be *consistent.*

Since $[X] = 0$ is always a solution of

$$[A][X] = [0], \tag{C.64}$$

a system of homogeneous equations is always consistent.

In most cases, the solution

$$[X] = [0] \tag{C.65}$$

is not very significant, and hence it is called a *trivial solution.* Mostly, we are interested in nontrivial solutions.

We state the following theorems on homogeneous equations without proof.

Theorem C.2. A system of m homogeneous equations in n unknowns has non-trivial solutions if and only if the rank of the coefficient matrix is less then the number of unknowns.

EXAMPLE C.14. Examine the following system of equations for nontrivial solutions:

$$\begin{bmatrix} 1 & 1 & 2 \\ 0 & 1 & 1 \\ 1 & 1 & -1 \end{bmatrix} \begin{bmatrix} x_1 \\ x_2 \\ x_3 \end{bmatrix} = \begin{bmatrix} 0 \\ 0 \\ 0 \end{bmatrix}. \tag{C.66}$$

First, we investigate the rank of the coefficient matrix:

$$\begin{bmatrix} 1 & 1 & 2 \\ 0 & 1 & 1 \\ 1 & 1 & -1 \end{bmatrix} \sim \begin{bmatrix} 1 & 1 & 2 \\ 0 & 1 & 1 \\ 0 & 0 & -3 \end{bmatrix} \tag{C.67}$$

The rank is 3, and Eq. (C.66) can be written as

$$\begin{bmatrix} 1 & 1 & 2 \\ 0 & 1 & 1 \\ 0 & 0 & -3 \end{bmatrix} \begin{bmatrix} x_1 \\ x_2 \\ x_3 \end{bmatrix} = \begin{bmatrix} 0 \\ 0 \\ 0 \end{bmatrix}. \tag{C.68}$$

(*Note.* This step is valid since we have performed only elementary row operations on the coefficient matrix.) We then have

$$\begin{bmatrix} 1 & 1 & 2 \\ 0 & 1 & 1 \\ 0 & 0 & -3 \end{bmatrix}^{-1} \begin{bmatrix} 1 & 1 & 2 \\ 0 & 1 & 1 \\ 0 & 0 & -3 \end{bmatrix} \begin{bmatrix} x_1 \\ x_2 \\ x_3 \end{bmatrix} = \begin{bmatrix} 0 \\ 0 \\ 0 \end{bmatrix}; \tag{C.69}$$

that is,

$$\begin{bmatrix} x_1 \\ x_2 \\ x_3 \end{bmatrix} = \begin{bmatrix} 0 \\ 0 \\ 0 \end{bmatrix}. \tag{C.70}$$

This result follows directly from the theorem since the rank of the matrix and the number of unknowns are both equal to 3.

EXAMPLE C.15. Examine for nontrivial solutions of the equations

$$\begin{bmatrix} 1 & 1 & 2 \\ 0 & 1 & 1 \\ 2 & 2 & 4 \\ 3 & 3 & 6 \end{bmatrix} \begin{bmatrix} x_1 \\ x_2 \\ x_3 \end{bmatrix} = \begin{bmatrix} 0 \\ 0 \\ 0 \end{bmatrix}. \tag{C.71}$$

Examining for the rank of the coefficient matrix, we have

$$\begin{bmatrix} 1 & 1 & 2 \\ 0 & 1 & 1 \\ 2 & 2 & 4 \\ 3 & 3 & 6 \end{bmatrix} \sim \begin{bmatrix} 1 & 1 & 2 \\ 0 & 1 & 1 \\ 0 & 0 & 0 \\ 0 & 0 & 0 \end{bmatrix}, \tag{C.72}$$

or

$$\begin{bmatrix} 1 & 1 & 2 \\ 0 & 1 & 1 \end{bmatrix} \begin{bmatrix} x_1 \\ x_2 \\ x_3 \end{bmatrix} = \begin{bmatrix} 0 \\ 0 \end{bmatrix}. \tag{C.73}$$

This can be written as

$$\begin{bmatrix} 1 & 1 \\ 0 & 1 \end{bmatrix} \begin{bmatrix} x_1 \\ x_2 \end{bmatrix} = - \begin{bmatrix} 2 \\ 1 \end{bmatrix} x_3, \tag{C.74}$$

or

$$\begin{bmatrix} x_1 \\ x_2 \end{bmatrix} = - \begin{bmatrix} 1 & 1 \\ 0 & 1 \end{bmatrix}^{-1} \begin{bmatrix} 2 \\ 1 \end{bmatrix} x_3 \tag{C.74}$$

$$= - \begin{bmatrix} 1 & -1 \\ 0 & 1 \end{bmatrix} \begin{bmatrix} 2 \\ 1 \end{bmatrix} x_3 = \begin{bmatrix} -1 \\ -1 \end{bmatrix} x_3, \tag{C.75}$$

which is a nontrivial solution.

Note that in this example the rank is 2 and the number of unknowns is 3.

On the basis of these examples, we can state the following properties of systems of homogeneous equations.

Property C.13. A system of n homogeneous equations in n unknowns has nontrivial solutions if and only if the coefficient matrix is singular.

Property C.14. A system of m homogeneous equations in n unknowns ($m < n$) always has nontrivial solutions.

Since a system of nonhomogeneous equations need not always be consistent, we state without proof the following theorem which provides a criterion for determining consistency.

Theorem C.3. A system of m nonhomogeneous equations in n unknowns is consistent if and only if the rank of the coefficient matrix is equal to the rank of the augmented matrix.

One can determine simultaneously the rank of the coefficient matrix and the rank of the augmented matrix by means of elementary row operations on the augmented matrix.

EXAMPLE C.16. Determine the consistency of the nonhomogeneous equations,

$$
\begin{bmatrix}
2 & 1 & 1 & 1 \\
3 & -1 & 1 & -1 \\
1 & 2 & -1 & 1 \\
6 & 2 & 1 & 1
\end{bmatrix}
\begin{bmatrix}
x_1 \\ x_2 \\ x_3 \\ x_4
\end{bmatrix}
=
\begin{bmatrix}
2 \\ 2 \\ 1 \\ 5
\end{bmatrix}.
\tag{C.76}
$$

We can write them as

$$
\begin{bmatrix}
2 & 1 & 1 & 1 & \vdots & 2 \\
3 & -1 & 1 & -1 & \vdots & 2 \\
1 & 2 & -1 & 1 & \vdots & 1 \\
6 & 2 & 1 & 1 & \vdots & 5
\end{bmatrix}
\begin{bmatrix}
x_1 \\ x_2 \\ x_3 \\ x_4 \\ --- \\ -1
\end{bmatrix}
=
\begin{bmatrix}
0 \\ 0 \\ 0 \\ 0
\end{bmatrix}.
\tag{C.77}
$$

The coefficient matrix of Eq. (C.77) is the augmented matrix of Eq. (C.76). To determine consistency, we perform elementary row operations on the augmented matrix:

$$
\begin{bmatrix}
2 & 1 & 1 & 1 & 2 \\
3 & -1 & 1 & -1 & 2 \\
1 & 2 & -1 & 1 & 1 \\
6 & 2 & 1 & 1 & 5
\end{bmatrix}
\sim
\begin{bmatrix}
1 & 2 & -1 & 1 & 1 \\
3 & -1 & 1 & -1 & 2 \\
2 & 1 & 1 & 1 & 2 \\
6 & 2 & 1 & 1 & 5
\end{bmatrix}
$$

$$
\sim
\begin{bmatrix}
1 & 2 & -1 & 1 & 1 \\
0 & -7 & 4 & -4 & -1 \\
0 & -3 & 3 & -1 & 0 \\
0 & -10 & 7 & -5 & -1
\end{bmatrix}
\sim
\begin{bmatrix}
1 & 2 & -1 & 1 & 1 \\
0 & 1 & -\frac{4}{7} & \frac{4}{7} & \frac{1}{7} \\
0 & -3 & 3 & -1 & 0 \\
0 & -10 & 7 & -5 & -1
\end{bmatrix}
$$

$$
\sim
\begin{bmatrix}
1 & 2 & -1 & 1 & 1 \\
0 & 1 & -\frac{4}{7} & \frac{4}{7} & \frac{1}{7} \\
0 & 0 & \frac{9}{7} & \frac{5}{7} & \frac{3}{7} \\
0 & 0 & \frac{9}{7} & \frac{5}{7} & \frac{3}{7}
\end{bmatrix}
\sim
\begin{bmatrix}
1 & 2 & -1 & 1 & 1 \\
0 & 1 & -\frac{4}{7} & \frac{4}{7} & \frac{1}{7} \\
0 & 0 & 1 & \frac{5}{9} & \frac{1}{3} \\
0 & 0 & 1 & \frac{5}{9} & \frac{1}{3}
\end{bmatrix}
$$

$$
\sim
\begin{bmatrix}
1 & 2 & -1 & \vdots & 1 & 1 \\
0 & 1 & -\frac{4}{7} & \vdots & \frac{4}{7} & \frac{1}{7} \\
0 & 0 & 1 & \vdots & \frac{5}{9} & \frac{1}{3} \\
0 & 0 & 0 & \vdots & 0 & 0
\end{bmatrix}.
\tag{C.78}
$$

From the last matrix it is evident that the rank of the coefficient matrix is equal to 3, which is also the rank of the augmented matrix; hence, the equations are consistent. (*Note.* If there were a nonzero element in the last row of the last column, the rank of the augmented matrix would be 4 and the equations would be inconsistent).

The solution can now be determined by considering the "equivalent" system of equations (systems of equations are equivalent if they have the same solution):

$$\begin{bmatrix} 1 & 2 & -1 & \vdots & 1 & 1 \\ 0 & 1 & -\frac{4}{7} & \vdots & \frac{4}{7} & \frac{1}{7} \\ 0 & 0 & 1 & \vdots & \frac{5}{9} & \frac{1}{3} \end{bmatrix} \begin{bmatrix} x_1 \\ x_2 \\ x_3 \\ \text{---} \\ x_4 \\ -1 \end{bmatrix} = \begin{bmatrix} 0 \\ 0 \\ 0 \end{bmatrix} \tag{C.79}$$

or

$$\begin{bmatrix} 1 & 2 & -1 \\ 0 & 1 & -\frac{4}{7} \\ 0 & 0 & 1 \end{bmatrix} \begin{bmatrix} x_1 \\ x_2 \\ x_3 \end{bmatrix} = - \begin{bmatrix} 1 & 1 \\ \frac{4}{7} & \frac{1}{7} \\ \frac{5}{9} & \frac{1}{3} \end{bmatrix} \begin{bmatrix} x_4 \\ -1 \end{bmatrix}. \tag{C.80}$$

Thus,

$$\begin{bmatrix} x_1 \\ x_2 \\ x_3 \end{bmatrix} = - \begin{bmatrix} 1 & 2 & -1 \\ 0 & 1 & -\frac{4}{7} \\ 0 & 0 & 1 \end{bmatrix}^{-1} \begin{bmatrix} 1 & 1 \\ \frac{4}{7} & \frac{1}{7} \\ \frac{5}{9} & \frac{1}{3} \end{bmatrix} \begin{bmatrix} x_4 \\ -1 \end{bmatrix} = - \begin{bmatrix} 1 & -2 & -\frac{1}{7} \\ 0 & 1 & \frac{4}{7} \\ 0 & 0 & 1 \end{bmatrix} \begin{bmatrix} 1 & 1 \\ \frac{4}{7} & \frac{1}{7} \\ \frac{5}{9} & \frac{1}{3} \end{bmatrix} \begin{bmatrix} x_4 \\ -1 \end{bmatrix}$$

$$= - \begin{bmatrix} -\frac{14}{63} & \frac{2}{3} \\ \frac{56}{63} & \frac{1}{3} \\ \frac{5}{9} & \frac{1}{3} \end{bmatrix} \begin{bmatrix} x_4 \\ -1 \end{bmatrix}, \tag{C.81}$$

which is a *general solution*.

A *particular* solution can be obtained by assigning a value for x_4. Let $x_4 = 0$; then,

$$\begin{bmatrix} x_1 \\ x_2 \\ x_3 \end{bmatrix} = \begin{bmatrix} \frac{2}{3} \\ \frac{1}{3} \\ \frac{1}{3} \end{bmatrix}. \tag{C.82}$$

Verification

$$\begin{bmatrix} 2 & 1 & 1 & 1 \\ 3 & -1 & 1 & -1 \\ 1 & 2 & -1 & 1 \\ 6 & 2 & 1 & 1 \end{bmatrix} \begin{bmatrix} \frac{2}{3} \\ \frac{1}{3} \\ \frac{1}{3} \\ 0 \end{bmatrix} = \begin{bmatrix} 2 \\ 2 \\ 1 \\ 5 \end{bmatrix}. \tag{C.83}$$

C.10. EIGENVALUES AND EIGENVECTORS

Consider the equation

$$[A][X] = \lambda[X], \tag{C.84}$$

where $[A]$ is a square matrix of order n, $[X]$ is a column vector, and λ is a scalar. In many applications it is necessary to find nonzero $[X]$ and λ which satisfy (C.84) for a given $[A]$. Equation (C.84) may be written as

$$([A] - \lambda[U])[X] = [0], \tag{C.85}$$

and nonzero solutions exist only if the determinant of the coefficient matrix is zero. That is,

$$\det\left([A] - \lambda[U]\right) = \begin{vmatrix} a_{11} - \lambda & a_{12} & \cdots & a_{1n} \\ a_{21} & a_{22} - \lambda & \cdots & a_{2n} \\ \vdots & \vdots & & \vdots \\ a_{n1} & a_{n2} & \cdots & a_{nn} - \lambda \end{vmatrix} = 0. \qquad \text{(C.86)}$$

The expansion of the determinant in (C.86) is a polynomial in λ, called the *characteristic polynomial* of the matrix $[A]$. If this polynomial is denoted by $\phi(\lambda)$, then the equation

$$\phi(\lambda) = 0 \qquad\qquad \text{(C.87)}$$

is called the characteristic equation of $[A]$. Its roots are the *characteristic values* or *eigenvalues* of $[A]$. The magnitude of the largest eigenvalue of a matrix is called its *spectral radius*. Equations (C.84) have nontrivial solutions for $[X]$ if and only if λ is one of the eigenvalues of $[A]$. The corresponding vector $[X]$ is called an eigenvector of $[A]$.

EXAMPLE C.17. Consider the matrix

$$[A] = \begin{bmatrix} 1 & 1 \\ 4 & 1 \end{bmatrix}.$$

Here,

$$\phi(\lambda) = \begin{vmatrix} 1 - \lambda & 1 \\ 4 & 1 - \lambda \end{vmatrix} = \lambda^2 - 2\lambda - 3,$$

so that the eigenvalues are $\lambda_1 = 3$, $\lambda_2 = -1$. It is easily verified that the corresponding eigenvectors are

$$C_1 = \begin{bmatrix} 1 \\ 2 \end{bmatrix} \quad \text{and} \quad C_2 = \begin{bmatrix} -1 \\ 2 \end{bmatrix}.$$

The following properties are stated without proof.

Property C.15. Nonzero eigenvectors associated with distinct eigenvalues are linearly independent.

Property C.16. A matrix has a zero eigenvalue if and only if it is singular.

Property C.17. The eigenvalues of a triangular matrix are the diagonal entries of the matrix.

Property C.18. The constant term in the characteristic polynomial is the determinant of the matrix.

Property C.19. If $\phi(\lambda)$ is the characteristic polynomial of an nth-order matrix, the coefficient of λ^{n-1} is $(-1)^{n-1}$ times the sum of the diagonal entries of the matrix (called the *trace* or *spur* of the matrix).

Property C.20. (*The Cayley-Hamilton theorem*). A matrix satisfies its own characteristic equation.

REFERENCES AND BIBLIOGRAPHY

In the following list, the first eleven titles refer to works which have direct reference to the concepts and techniques discussed in the text. The remainder constitutes a selected bibliography containing a wider range of related material.

1. BODE, H. W., *Network Analysis and Feedback Amplifier Design*. Princeton, N. J.: Van Nostrand, 1945.
2. CHURCHILL, R. V., *Fourier Series and Boundary Value Problems*. New York: McGraw-Hill, 1963.
3. CHURCHILL, R. V., *Operational Mathematics*. New York: McGraw-Hill, 1958.
4. HOHN, F. E., *Elementary Matrix Algebra*. New York: Macmillan, 1958.
5. KOENIG, H. E., Y. TOKAD, and H. K. KESAVAN, *Analysis of Discrete Physical Systems*. New York: McGraw-Hill (in press).
6. KOENIG, H. E., and W. A. BLACKWELL, *Electro-Mechanical System Theory*. New York: McGraw-Hill, 1960.
7. REED, M. B., *Foundation for Network Theory*. Englewood Cliffs, N. J.: Prentice Hall, 1961.
8. ROE, P. H. O'N., "State Equations for Dynamic Systems," Ph.D. Thesis, University of Waterloo, Waterloo, Ontario, 1962.
9. SESHU, S., and M. B. REED, *Linear Graphs and Electric Networks*. Reading, Mass.: Addison-Wesley, 1961.
10. STANTON, R. G., *Numerical Methods for Science and Engineering*. Englewood Cliffs, N. J.: Prentice Hall, 1961.
11. WIRTH, J. L., "Time Domain Models of Physical Systems and Existence of Solutions," Ph.D. Thesis, Michigan State University, East Lansing, Michigan, 1962.
12. ARSOVE, M. G., "Note on Network Postulates," *J. of Math. and Phys.*, **32**, 203 (1953).
13. BASHKOW, T. R., "The *A* Matrix, New Network Description," *IRE Trans. on Circuit Theory*, **CT-4**, 117–119 (1957).
14. BLACKWELL, W. A., and H. K. KESAVAN, "The Analysis of Large Systems Using Subsystems as Components," *Proc. Fourth Midwest Symposium on Circuit Theory*, Marquette University, Milwaukee, Wisconsin, 1959.
15. BLACKWELL, W. A., "The Linear Graph in System Analysis," Ph.D. Thesis, Michigan State University, 1958.

16. BLACKWELL, W. A., and H. E. KOENIG, "On the General Properties of Terminal Equations, for Polyphase Machines," *The Matrix and Tensor Quarterly,* **1,** IX, No. 1, 2–12 (September 1958).

17. BRYANT, P. R., "The Explicit Form of Bashkow's *A* Matrix," *IRE Trans. on Circuit Theory,* **CT-9,** 303–306 (1962).

18. BRYANT, P. R., "A further note on The Degrees of Freedom in *RLC* Networks," *IRE Trans. on Circuit Theory,* **CT-7,** 357 (1960).

19. BRYANT, P. R., "Order of Complexity of Electrical Networks," *Monograph 335E,* Inst. of Electrical Engineers (June 1959).

20. EULER, L., "Solutio Problematis ad Geometriam Situs Pertinentis," *Ann. Physik,* **9,** 1304–1329 (1902).

21. FIRESTONE, F. A., "A New Analogy Between Mechanical and Electrical Systems," *J. Acoust. Soc. Am.,* **4,** 249–267 (1933).

22. FOSTER, R. M., "Geometric Circuits on Electrical Networks," *Trans. A.I.E.E.,* **51,** 309–317 (1932).

23. FULLER, A. T., "Phase Space in the Theory of Optimum Control," *Journal of Electronics and Control,* **8,** 381–400 (1960).

24. GLINSKI, G. S., "State Space," *Summer Seminar on Modern Automatic Control Theory,* McGill University, Montreal (September 1962).

25. GUILLEMIN, E. A., *Introductory Circuit Theory.* New York: Wiley, 1953.

26. KESAVAN, H. K., and B. R. MYERS, "System Theory in a Unified Curriculum," *IRE Trans. on Education,* **E-4,** 102–110 (1961).

27. KINARIWALA, B. K., "Analysis of Time-Varying Networks," *IRE Convention Record,* **9,** part 4, 268–276 (1961).

28. KIRCHHOFF, G., "Über den Durchgang eines elektrischen Stromes durch eine Ebene, insbesondere durch eine kreisförmige," *Poggendorf Ann. der Phys.,* **64,** 497–514 (1845).

29. KIRCHHOFF, G., "Über die Aufloesung der Gleichungen, auf welche man bei den Untersuchung der linearen Verteilung galvanischer Stroeme geführt wird," *Poggendorf Ann. der Phys.,* **72,** 497–508 (1847).

30. KÖNIG, D., *Theorie der endlichen und unendlichen Graphen.* Leipzig: Akademie Verlag, 1936 (also New York: Chelsea, 1950).

31. KOENIG, H. E., and W. A. BLACKWELL, "On the Codification of Lagrangian Formulation," *Proc. IRE,* **46,** 1428–29 (1958).

32. KOENIG, H. E., and W. A. BLACKWELL, "Topological Graphs of Electromechanical Systems," *Proc. Second Midwest Symposium on Circuit Theory* (September, 1956).

33. KOENIG, H. E., and W. A. BLACKWELL, "Lagrangian Versus Linear Graph Techniques," *Proc. Third Midwest Symposium on Circuit Theory* (May 1958).

34. KOENIG, H. E., and H. K. KESAVAN, "Multi-terminal Representations in Electronic Circuits," *Proc. Fourth Midwest Symposium on Circuit Theory* (December 1959).

35. KOENIG, H. E., and M. B. REED, "Linear Graph Representation of Multi-terminal Elements," *Proc. Nat. Elec. Conf.,* **14,** 661–674 (1958).

36. LAWSON, J. D., "Some One-step Methods for the Numerical Solution of Systems of Ordinary Differential Equations," Ph.D. Thesis, University of Waterloo, Waterloo, Ontario.

37. MAYEDA, W., and S. SESHU, "Topological Formulas for Network Functions," *Bulletin No. 446*, Eng. Expt. Station, University of Illinois (1957).

38. PERCIVAL, W. S., "Solution of Passive Electrical Networks by Means of Mathematical Trees," *J.I.E.E.*, **100**, Part II, 143–150 (1953).

39. REED, M. B., and S. SESHU, "On Topology and Network Theory", *Proc. University of Illinois Symposium on Circuit Analysis*, 2.1–2.16 (May 1955).

40. ROE, P. H. O'N., "Formulation of the State Equations of Electric and Electronic Circuits," *Proc. Sixth Midwest Symposium on Circuit Theory*, Madison, Wisconsin (May 1963).

41. SESHU, S., and M. B. REED, "On Cut Sets of Electrical Networks," *Proc. Second Midwest Symposium on Circuit Theory*, Michigan State University, 1.1–1.13 (1956).

42. SESHU, S., "Topological Considerations in the Design of Driving Point Functions," *IRE Trans. on Circuit Theory*, **CT-2,** 356–367 (1955).

43. SYNGE, J. L., "The Fundamental Theory of Electrical Networks," *Quart. App. Math.*, **9**, 113–127 (1951).

44. TALBOT, A., "Some Fundamental Properties of Networks Without Mutual Inductance," *Proc. IEE*, **102,** 168–175 (1955).

45. TRENT, H. M., "Isomorphisms between Oriented Linear Graphs and Lumped Physical Systems," *J. Acoust. Soc. Amer.*, **27**, 500–527 (1955).

46. TUTTE, W. T., "Matroids and Graphs," *Trans. Amer. Math. Soc.*, **90**, 527–552 (1959).

47. VEBLEN, O., "Analysis Situs," *Amer. Math. Soc. Colloq. Lectures*, **5**, part 2 (1918–1922).

48. WANG, C. L., and Y. TOKAD, "Polygon to Star Transformations," *IRE Trans. on Circuit Theory*, **CT-8,** 489–491 (December 1961).

49. WHITNEY, H., "Non-Separable and Planar Graphs," *Trans. Amer. Math. Soc.*, **34,** 339–362 (1932).

50. WHITNEY, H., "Congruent Graphs and Connectivity of Graphs," *Am. Journal of Math.*, **54**, 150–168 (1932).

51. WHITNEY, H., "On the Classification of Graphs," *Am. J. Math.*, **55**, 236–244 (1933).

52. WHITNEY, H., "Planar Graphs," *Fund. Math.*, **21**, 73 (1933).

53. WHITNEY, H., "Two-Isomorphic Graphs," *Am. J. Math.*, **55**, 245–254 (1933).

54. WHITNEY, H., "On the Abstract Properties of Linear Dependence," *Am. J. Math.*, **57**, 509–533 (1935).

55. WIENBERG, L., "Kirchhoff's Third and Fourth Laws," *IRE Trans. on Circuit Theory*, **CT-5,** 8–30 (March 1958).

56. ZADEH, L. A., "From Circuit Theory to System Theory," *Proc. IRE*, **50**, 856–865 (1962).

57. ZADEH, L. A., "Multipole Analysis of Active Networks," *IRE Trans. on Circuit Theory*, **CT-4,** 97–105 (1957).

58. ZADEH, L. A., and C. DESOER, *Linear System Theory: The State Space Approach.* New York: McGraw-Hill, 1963.

INDEX